THE PURSUIT OF HAPPINESS

GOVERNMENT AND POLITICS IN AMERICA

FOURTH EDITION

John A. Moore, Jr.
California State Polytechnic University, Pomona

Myron Roberts
Professor Emeritus, Chaffey College

MACMILLAN PUBLISHING COMPANY

New York

Copyright © 1989 by Macmillan Publishing Company,
a division of Macmillan, Inc.

Printed in the United States of America

Earlier editions copyright © 1978, 1981, 1985
by Macmillan Publishing Company.

Macmillan Publishing Company
866 Third Avenue, New York, New York 10022

Library of Congress Cataloging-in-Publication Data

Moore, John Allphin, 1940–
    The pursuit of happiness: government and politics in America/
John A. Moore, Jr., Myron Roberts.—4th ed.
      p. cm.
    Bibliography: p.
    Includes index.
    ISBN 0-02-383160-X
    1. United States—Politics and government. 1. Roberts, Myron.
II. Title.
JK274.M67 1989   88-28669
320.973—dc 19   CIP

Printing: 1 2 3 4 5 6 7   Year: 9 0 1 2 3 4 5

Preface

Recent years have seen an effort by many of the world's governments and by political leaders to make the practice of politics less rigidly bureaucratic in the hopes of bringing both their pronouncements and policies closer to the daily lives and concerns of ordinary people.

Whether the study, as opposed to the practice, of politics has become less rigid and formalistic is a different matter. The academic community, its critics notwithstanding, may vigorously advocate change and reform for the larger society but tends to be rather defensive about its own established practices and revealed wisdom.

Our first edition, written over a decade ago, began with the hope that this book would prove helpful to those instructors and students who wished to "place the study of American government and politics within a human perspective." This remains our objective. The United States is not a dull society. There is no good reason why the study of how this society governs itself should not reflect the drama and excitement of an exuberant democracy or the ambiguities inherent in the efforts of 250 million people trying to live together while coexisting with four billion other persons who occupy this planet.

This new edition contains two new chapters dealing with civil rights and the bureaucracy, in addition to updating and revising all appropriate material to include the major political events of the past four years. As in previous editions, we have tried to present a view of government that encompasses content as well as structure, ideas as well as facts, and past as well as present events and issues. We have also attempted to integrate history, economics, literature, science, both popular and classical culture, and journalism into this work in keeping with our belief that government is not simply the business of going to the polls periodically to elect officials or the day-to-day functioning of government bodies, but rather the sum and substance of the ideas, ideals, passions, and actions that engage and define our nation. We have attempted to do these things in a style not bound by conventional academic prose while meeting the strictest standards of accurate scholarship.

We have taken seriously many suggestions for improvement offered by critics, colleagues, and students of earlier editions. In some cases, we have happily made changes; in others we persist in our folly. We wish to express our appreciation to all those who have assisted us in this work. Among these are Professors Susan Roberts (Winthrop College, Rock Hill, South Carolina), Don Dugi (Transylvania College, Lexington, Kentucky), Karen Hult

(Pomona College, Claremont, California), Carl E. Lutrin (California Polytechnic State University, San Luis Obispo, California), R.A. Perchlik (University of Northern Colorado, Greeley, Colorado), Ronald W. Melugin (Cooke County College, Gainesville, Texas), John A. Peeler (Bucknell University, Lewisburg, Pennsylvania), Ed Sidlow (Miami University, Oxford, Ohio), and Larry Elowitz (Georgia College, Milledgeville, Georgia). Colleagues Walter P. Coombs, Richard Hyslop, Richard Johnson, Sheila McCoy, and John Korey—all at California State Polytechnic University, Pomona—have been generous with their suggestions for improving this edition. John Murphy has been an inspiration. Macmillan editors Eben Ludlow, Linda Greenberg and Edward Cone have expertly guided this edition through to completion. We would once again like to thank our wives, Linda and Estelle, for their advice, patience, and assistance. Finally, our gratitude goes to JoAnne Noyes for her patient and diligent help in securing and organizing the illustrative material, and to Laura Jane Moore for her early help and encouragement.

As we noted in the preface to earlier editions of this book, our aim has not been to press upon students a particular view of politics, although even a casual reading will reveal that the authors do indeed have a point of view and do not try to conceal it. Our objective, rather, is to provoke the student to think, to examine his or her life and ideas in relation to the values and institutions of society, with the hope that this may lead to a broader view of both the problems and possibilities of civil life.

J. A. M.
M. R.

Contents

9

Who Rules America? The Elite, the Interests, and the Voter   225

10

The Bureaucrats: Attendant Lords   249

11

Media, the Shadow Government: Power and the Press   265

12

Economics: The Prevailing Smell of Money   299

13

Trumpets and Flourishes: America in the World   333

14

Politics and the Pursuit of Happiness   369

Appendixes   377

Index   430

Introduction

> Thus, we presume to write, as it were, upon things that exist not, and travel by maps yet unmade.
>
> **Walt Whitman**
> *Democratic Vistas*

While the whole world watched, President Ronald Reagan and Soviet leader Mikhail Gorbachev strolled through Red Square in Moscow exchanging pleasantries in the spring of 1988. What, if any, meaning did this event have for the ordinary American college student?

Without attempting to engage in prophecy over the always uncertain future of superpower relationships, we think it is reasonable to anticipate that if the mood of Moscow, 1988 becomes the foundation for construction of a new and less hostile relationship between the United States and the Soviet Union then certain consequences can be anticipated.

For one, it makes less likely the possibility that today's generation of college students will be called on to fight and perhaps die in some remote jungle or desert war nourished by superpower rivalry. For another, at least it creates the possibility that the United States will have to spend less money on arms and may therefore have more funds available for domestic needs, such as student loans. Still another possibility is that the future may see a substantial shift in employment from the "death industry" (i.e., arms) to life-enhancing professions, such as education, medicine, and civil engineering.

We could go on, but the point is that political events, whether they occur thousands of miles away or here at home, shape our lives whether or not we choose to concern ourselves with these matters. In a democratic society, we have some opportunity to influence these events, not only by voting but also by the extent to which we participate in the dialogue of daily life.

Ultimately, that dialogue comes down to choosing the men and women who will lead this nation. If these men and women govern wisely and well, the chances that we the people will enjoy peace, the blessings of liberty, prosperity, and domestic tranquility are greatly enchanced. If they blunder into war or depression or civil unrest, ordinary Americans will pay the price for their mistakes.

In a letter to John Adams, his political foe but personal friend, Thomas Jefferson defended the American government that both men had helped create on the grounds that it provided the best means of elevating what he called the "natural aristocracy" into the offices of government.[1] Jefferson

---

[1]The question of natural versus a hereditary aristocracy is the subject of a letter from Jefferson to John Adams, written from Monticello on October 28, 1813. The Jefferson-Adams correspondence, comprising more than 150 letters between the two old political foes, began in 1812 and continued until both men died on the same day, July 4, 1826.

defined the natural aristocracy as one based on virtue and talent rather than wealth and birth.

In a world in which *talent* is associated with the arts or show business rather than with politics and in which the word *virtue* takes on a somewhat quaint, priggish, and old-fashioned connotation, Jefferson's definition may require some additional explanation. By talent he meant, simply, the ability to govern well and effectively, "to manage the concerns of society," as he put it. What Jefferson meant by virtue is not so easily understood. It had to do with certain qualities that today we might associate with statecraft, qualities such as wisdom, self-control, vision, commitment to the common good, and, perhaps most important, the ability to provide moral leadership to one's follow citizens. Statecraft does not require that a person live as a saint. Certainly Jefferson was not a saint. He owned slaves, although he himself often denounced the moral horror of slavery. There is evidence that he may even have had children conceived outside wedlock, and there are other charges that could be and have been leveled at Jefferson the private individual. But it is quite another matter to fault Jefferson the statesman, who, with the power of his imagination, his words, and his deeds, helped create "a new man and a new earth." In the Jeffersonian sense, the statesman enlightens and ennobles, as compared with a leader who merely administers.

If today there is "no virtue in the Republic," as *Harper's* editor, Lewis H. Lapham, suggested,[2] Jefferson would grieve to know it. He relied on the common people because he believed that such people would demand "virtue" from their leaders. He knew, of course, that there were ambitious individuals, then as now, who might lead the country into defeat, disgrace, and failure. But he believed that the people, aided by education, would find the wisdom to reject the blandishments of the "pseudo-aristoi" and to select leaders who belonged to the "natural aristocracy."

Thus a republic of virtue and talent requires much from its citizens as well as from its leaders. For citizens to participate in the important political events of their time, at the local through the national level, is not simply a right. The relationship between leaders and led may be crucial to a democracy such as ours; that is, to whatever extent the United States is a great and advancing nation or to whatever extent it is in decline is, in part, as much the responsibility of those of us who choose and respond to leaders as it is the responsibility of the leaders themselves.

By 1988, economic issues, high crime and drug addiction rates, and a widely perceived loss of relative power and influence abroad dominated the campaign to select a successor to President Reagan. In that year Japan's gross national product (GNP)—the total amount of wealth produced—actually surpassed that of the United States on a per capita basis. Japan's GNP reached $19,200 per person, versus $18,200 in the United States. In

[2]"The Easy Chair," *Harper's*, August 1976, pp. 10–12.

addition, the United States moved during the Reagan years from the world's leading creditor to the world's largest debtor nation. A massive albeit improving foreign trade deficit and huge federal deficits brought economics to the forefront of the presidential campaign despite years of generally high prosperity.

In foreign affairs there was also ambiguity. Greatly improved U.S.–U.S.S.R. relationships won high praise from all but a handful of super-hawks. (Ironically, these had been among President Reagan's most devout supporters in his "evil empire" era.) At the same time U.S. inability to impose its will on Central America or in the Middle East, and continuing outrages by terrorists around the world, often working closely with foreign governments such as that of Iran, provoked continuing controversy and concern. Finally, revelations that conspirators at the highest levels of the Reagan administration were conducting secret, "off-the-shelf" maneuvers, which included shipping arms to Iran, lying to the U.S. Congress and the American people, and apparently usurping the power of the president without his knowledge, led to widespread discussion, both here and abroad, as to whether the United States was destined to follow ancient Greece, Rome, and the gilded aristocracies of nineteenth-century Europe into inevitable decline.

Has the United States seen the "moment of its glory flicker"? This question seemed to underlie much of the 1988 presidential campaign. Vice President George Bush proclaimed his intention of becoming an "education president" and pointed to his own vast experience in foreign affairs. Michael Dukakis stressed the need for competence in government and the need to rebuild the nation's infrastructure (schools, roads, jobs for the unemployed, etc.), along with a corresponding deemphasis on exotic, expensive military projects such as "Star Wars." Candidate Jesse Jackson generated a substantial and enthusiastic following by calling for what amounted to a new New Deal for the poor and the excluded, a far more energetic war on drugs, and a foreign policy much closer to the hearts of the Third World. Several polls suggested that Americans, worried about the nation's and their own future, were paying close attention.

Moreover, each of the candidates attempted to sound a note that had helped carry such disparate candidates as John Kennedy and Ronald Reagan to the presidency, perhaps best expressed by Lincoln's vision of the United States as "The last, best hope of mankind."

This idealistic vision of ourselves is a recurrent theme in American life and history, from the Puritans to the abolitionists, from Walt Whitman to Woodrow Wilson. Through much of our history, we believed that we should serve as a kind of beacon for an errant humankind. But by the 1980s this leadership role was severely challenged. Many Americans perceived deep crises, reflected in economic problems, in foreign relations and perhaps even in a spiritual malaise in the country.

Whether the American political system as it exists today can meet the

(Drawing by Joseph Mugnaini.)

demands placed on it by Jefferson is one core question that underlies the following pages. One of the most interesting of Jefferson's contributions to American ideas on politics was his decision to inject the curious phrase "the pursuit of happiness" into our most famous document, the Declaration of Independence. Like most memorable phrases ("to be or not to be," "do unto others"), the words glitter but remain somewhat ambiguous. Yet they seem to reflect the essence of American life. Moreover, Jefferson indicated that this pursuit was an inherent *right*, not just a desire, of the American people—a remarkable notion then and now. Does the pursuit of happiness relate to a government and a people committed to virtue and talent? If so, how? Jefferson seemed to suggest that this right could be realized only within the framework of a civilized society—indeed a republic—in which virtue and talent prevailed.

With this in mind we have undertaken to write still another book about American government and politics. Believing, as we do, that the ideas that our government structures reflect are as important as the structures themselves and that politics encompasses a struggle for ends pursued by rational means while at the same time reflecting the complexities, passions, and ecstasies of the human mind and spirit, we have tried to create a book that mirrors the realities of American political life as we encounter and deal with them in the streets, in the media, in the government, and in the voting booth, as well as in the classroom.

If it is the burden of the politician to act and of the voter to decide in the face of ambiguity, the student, we believe, has an additional task: to understand. How does the American government work? What is the American political system? How is the system supposed to work? Who decides, and how and why? Are we "free"? Is there a "power elite"? How did our government get to be the way it is? What could it be like in the future? And if we can help shape that future, how shall we do so and to what ends?

The problems of politics, we believe, are the problems of civil life. From a certain perspective, human beings are not very impressive creatures. They are not as strong as apes or as quick as cats. They are not particularly well endowed to withstand extremes of heat or cold or to survive without food, water, and rest. "The weakest and frailest of all creatures is man," said Montaigne, "and withal the proudest." Yet through politics, human beings live and work together and sustain civilized life. Politics, then, aids us in the organization and direction of human thought and energy for the achievement of certain social goals. At the same time, we see much of the world's population continuing to endure poverty, ignorance, and injustice. In the entire history of the world, there have rarely been times when a part of the human race was not intent upon destroying another part through war. Even today the most "advanced" and "civilized" societies continue to devote much of their wealth and many of their finest minds to building, improving, and using instruments of mass destruction. That, too, is politics.

The study of government is the study of humanity. Focusing as we do on one nation, America, means that we are studying ourselves, our past, our present, and perhaps our future—what we have been and what we hope to be, not just as individuals but also as members of a society that nourishes and shapes us all.

1

Shine, Perishing Republic

• **The American Success Story: Is It Over?** •
• **The Negative Argument** •
• **The Positive Argument** •

> Epochs sometimes occur in the life of a nation when the old customs of a people are changed, public morality is destroyed, religious belief shaken, and the spell of tradition broken, when the diffusion of knowledge is yet imperfect and the civil rights of the community are ill secured . . . the country then assumes a dim and dubious shape in the eyes of its citizens; they no longer behold it in the soil they inhabit . . . nor in the usages of their forefathers; nor in religion, which they doubt, nor in the laws, which do not originate in their own authority; nor in the legislator, whom they fear and despise. . . . The country is lost to their senses . . . and they retire into a narrow and unenlightened selfishness.
>
> **Alexis de Tocqueville**
> *Democracy in America*
>
> While this America settles in the mould of its vulgarity; heavily thickening to empire,
> And protest, only a bubble in the molten mass, pops and sighs out, and the mass hardens.
>
> I sadly smiling remember that the flower fades to make fruit, the fruit rots to make earth.
> Out of the mother; and through the spring exultances, ripeness and decadence; and home to the mother.
>
> **Robinson Jeffers**
> *Shine, Perishing Republic**

The American Success Story: Is It Over?

John F. Kennedy often made the point that the United States, although a relatively young nation, was the world's oldest democracy, with an unbroken tradition of two centuries of representative government. The young president reflected a pride in the past and a confidence in the immediate future shared by most Americans in the early 1960s. The United States was unquestionably, it seemed, the strongest, the wealthiest, and the most stable democracy on earth. Although some Americans may have remained abjectly poor, the great majority (about 80 percent) were enjoying the benefits of the most affluent society in history.[1] Automobiles, television sets, pack-

*Reprinted by permission of Random House, Inc., from *The Selected Poetry of Robinson Jeffers*, Copyright 1925 and renewed 1953 by Robinson Jeffers.

[1]Michael Harrington, *The Other America* (New York: Macmillan, 1962), challenged the widespread assumption that affluence in America was universal and is said to have influenced President Kennedy (and later President Lyndon Johnson) in the formulation of the War on Poverty programs.

A modern skyscraper captures the image of an older style of architecture near Lafayette Park in Los Angeles. "First we shape our buildings," Winston Churchill said, "then our buildings shape us." *(Photographed by Dean Immenschuh, Upland, California.)*

aged foods, and stylish clothing poured out of the seemingly bottomless cornucopia. Our military forces, scattered throughout the world, defended not only our own borders but also much of the noncommunist world. After eight years of leadership by President Dwight Eisenhower, domestic political strife had muted to the point at which scholars were writing about the "end of ideology" in America.[2] Said sociologist C. Wright Mills:

[2]Daniel Bell, *The End of Ideology* (New York: Free Press, 1960).

Underneath this style of observation and comment there is the assumption that in the West there are no more real issues or even problems of great seriousness. The mixed economy plus the welfare state—that is the formula.

White Collar

In the midst of this unprecedented material abundance, the ordinary U.S. citizen enjoyed personal freedom, high mobility, and easy access to education and information. Thus a case could be and often was made that the United States was the most successful society in history, at least in accordance with British political philosopher Jeremy Bentham's classic statement on the proper aim of government: "the greatest good of the greatest number" (published, incidentally, in 1776, the year of the Declaration of Independence). It was widely held that at the core of the "American success story" was the political system created by the unsurpassed wisdom of the Founding Fathers, who had created the framework that made possible the freedom and stability that President Kennedy celebrated. Three decades later we should be hard pressed indeed to find a national leader who could summon up the soaring confidence that characterized President Kennedy's inaugural address.

No question has intrigued historians and political pundits more than the phenomenon of certain societies that rise to great power and wealth and then decline into mediocrity or worse. From Herotodus to Gibbon to Paul Kennedy,[3] scholars have speculated on the rise and fall of empires. Although it is clear that there is a natural cycle of birth, growth, decline, and death for all living things, why should this be true of nations, which are always producing new generations? And even if we accept decline as a law of history, why do some nations flourish for relatively few years, whereas others grow in power and prestige for hundreds of years?

The glory that was Greece and the grandeur that was Rome flourished and faded, as did the once mighty empires of Spain, Britain, and France— to name but a few of the civilizations that have dominated the history of the Western world. The East too has had its Egyptian, Persian, and Chinese eras of glory. Although historians like to point to a single event, often a losing battle, as marking the turning point in a nation's fall from greatness (the sacking of Rome, the defeat of the Spanish Armada, Waterloo), it seems more likely that the process of decline is gradual, taking place over many years, even decades. The citizens of Rome probably did not awaken one day in A.D. 476 and say, "Well now, the Empire has fallen and I will have to lower my expectations." Instead life probably become gradually meaner, harder, poorer as Rome declined from a city of over a million proud inhabitants to an impoverished village of a few thousand souls,

Is the mighty United States of America destined to follow this pattern? Are we already showing the advanced symptoms of decline?

[3]Paul Kennedy, *The Rise and Fall of the Great Powers* (New York: Random House, 1988).

The Negative Argument

A succession of bitter and largely unprecedented blows has shaken American confidence and forced us to question ideas and institutions that seemed faultless only a few years ago. The presidency, the armed forces, public schools, colleges and universities, the mass media, the CIA, the Congress, and even the postal service, all of which seemed so serenely benevolent, have come under unprecedented attack and have suffered a clear decline in public confidence. The mere listing of some of the more traumatic events of the recent past leaves little doubt as to why this has come about:

1. President Kennedy was assassinated in 1963. His murder was followed by the assassination of his brother, Senator Robert Kennedy, in the midst of his campaign for the presidency in 1968 and, in the same year, by the murder of Dr. Martin Luther King, Jr., the nation's most eminent civil rights leader. In 1972 another leading presidential candidate, Governor George C. Wallace, was left crippled by an attempt on his life. President Gerald Ford twice escaped assassination attempts, and President Reagan was seriously wounded by a would-be assassin's bullet. These assaults on the nation's leaders were, in effect and probably intent, also assaults on the stability and confidence of the nation itself and the political system under which we live.

2. The United States fought a long, bloody, and losing war in Southeast Asia. More recently, at least three relatively weak nations that were once totally dependent on American power and direction—Nicaragua, Iran, and tiny Panama—have successfully defied the will of America's leaders and become implacable foes instead of firm friends. President Reagan dispatched American troops to Lebanon to show the flag. After the shocking death of 240 Marines, we simply retreated, reducing American influence in that small state to near zero. Those who plotted and managed the attack remain unpunished. Terrorists too often murder and kidnap American officials and ordinary citizens with relative impunity.

3. Apart from more or less routine political scandals, two major debacles, unprecedented in our history, have shaken the American government. As the result of the Watergate scandal, President Richard Nixon was forced to resign in the face of certain impeachment by Congress. Earlier Vice President Spiro Agnew resigned in a separate, unrelated scandal. Several top officials of the Nixon administration went to prison. In 1986–1987 the nation was rocked by another major scandal, the Iran-Contra affair. This time the president and vice president were spared, in part because they acknowledged negligence and faulty memories, but other government officials were indicted. In separate and unrelated matters, many of President Reagan's closest advisers were indicted and convicted of criminal activity. Was the United States emulating so many other nations where the highest officials of government routinely broke the law?

4. In recent years, the United States has gone from the world's richest creditor to the world's greatest debtor, as our government has borrowed

money around the world to finance astronomical budget deficits and maintain an artificial prosperity. The government's debt was no less staggering than that of private citizens who indulged in their own version of a credit-card economy. One result of this spending binge was that foreigners were using a glut of deflated dollars to buy up American industries, department store chains, and real estate from Bloomingdale's to Firestone to much of downtown Los Angeles. In the words of the conservative British magazine, *The Economist*, "President Reagan's economic policy has, in effect, put the American economy up for sale." At bargain prices.

5. Crime and drug addiction, inseparable in most instances, were turning many of the nation's inner-cities into war zones, statistically more dangerous for the ordinary citizen than Beirut or Saigon in the midst of civil wars. Young hoodlums fighting for control of the streets had become the virtual lords of large areas of the cities, with far more reason to fear one another than the all but helpless police. In several states the drug "business" and its attendant money laundering had become a major industry, penetrating the highest levels of politics, banking, and law enforcement. Several Latin American nations had developed economies that had become dependent on satisfying the insatiable American craving for drugs. America had established a reputation as the most violent and criminal society in the developed world.

6. Hundreds of thousands, perhaps millions, of homeless persons added a new and unsightly dimension to the American landscape—street people. Their very existence seemed to mock a once high and mighty civilization. Ironically, they continued to proliferate at a time when the visible scars of extreme poverty such as beggars and slums were disappearing from many of the world's developed nations.

7. The family, the foundation of society, was in deep trouble. Divorce was commonplace. The traditional two-parent home had become a statistical rarity as Americans embraced a variety of "alternative life-styles."

8. Decades of unbridled affluence and power produced a level of environmental pollution that may well be irreversible. Critics complained of filthy air, rivers so polluted as to constitute a fire hazard, and foodstuffs so adulterated by potentially poisonous chemicals as to threaten the health of every American.

9. By the late 1980s there were alarming reports from both private and public sources that America's educational system was collapsing. Students' scores on all kinds of tests had fallen precipitously over the preceding generation, confirming the widely held view that the basic skills necessary in an advanced society were in severe decline across the country.

10. Some argued that all these problems were but the surface symptoms of a deeper malaise in American society. Despite the best efforts of reformers and liberals, the domestic problems of racism and poverty persisted. Many pointed to signs that the middle class, traditionally the bulwark of American society, was being gradually denuded of both its material

and spiritual strength. There were signs that millions of Americans were being alienated by and from their government, including a gradual and alarming decline in the percentage of adult Americans who bothered to vote in local and national elections. It was as though the nation was fulfilling de Tocqueville's vision of a people who have lost their faith in one another and hence "retire into a narrow and unenlightened selfishness."

The Positive Argument

On the other hand, there were those who continued to take a positive view of the future. They argued that

1. Despite all our problems, it remains true that the American people continue to enjoy one of the highest living standards in the world's history. Personal income has increased steadily for a generation; by the late 1980s infant mortality had dropped to a record low; and life expectancy for the average American is constantly going up.

2. Education and opportunities for cultural and intellectual advance remain abundant, and the percentage of young people who go on to some form of higher education continues to increase as a percentage of the total population. Moreover, there are few governmental restrictions on Americans' rights to travel anywhere on earth; indeed we are the most mobile people in the world. There is, likewise, no people who enjoy a greater degree of personal freedom.

3. The threat of nuclear war, although still very real, seemed to be receding. Implacable hostility and outright combat with China had yielded to what seemed to be a firm friendship that had continued to grow since President Nixon's historic trip to that country. A new leadership in the Soviet Union and a sharply changed attitude on the part of President Reagan had led to much improved relations between the United States and the Soviet Union. If that new relationship could be sustained and improved there was the likelihood that it would lead to a far less dangerous arms race and a realistic possibility of solving many of the problems that have tormented the world for decades. Finally there was at least the hope that East-West trade might open the door to a whole new era of economic growth for both sides.

4. Although many serious problems, such as poverty, energy shortages, and racial conflict, have not been eliminated, these problems have their counterparts in one form or another in every industrial society on earth. Instead of racial problems, Western Europe still struggles with the vestiges of class conflict. Communist countries may not experience much inflation or unemployment, but they tremble at the utterance of an unauthorized thought or the writing of a critical book (although this may be changing).

5. The United States led the Western world out of the recession of the

early 1980s. Although our economic problems persist, and competition from foreign countries continues, the U.S. economy remains, by far, the largest and most productive in the history of the world, a fact that is underscored by the eagerness with which wealthy individuals and corporations around the world invest in American business and property.

6. Although there has been a decline in American military, economic, and diplomatic power relative to that of the rest of the world, this may be a positive rather than a negative development for the United States and the rest of the world. There is no clear evidence that most Americans have any wish to dominate and determine events in Southeast Asia or Iran or Latin America, even if we had the power to do so. Perhaps the world of the 1950s and 1960s, when the Central Intelligence Agency (CIA) was busy scheming to create or destroy governments, eliminate leaders, and shape the social system of foreign nations, when American forces were in distant lands facing death for uncertain aims, was not a healthy or sane world. Also, if other nations are now more inclined to tell us bluntly to stop meddling in their affairs, maybe both they and we are better off for it.

7. Despite the numerous traumas of the past two decades, only a few Americans have abandoned their traditional preference for political leaders who at least appear to be moderate middle-of-the-roaders. Fringe movements, such as the Black Panther party, the Ku Klux Klan, and the American Nazi party, have microscopic support at the farthest fringes of American society. Polls show that despite public concern over crime and political instability, about 80 percent of the people remain adamantly opposed to the introduction of totalitarian techniques for maintaining order, such as wiretapping, mail monitoring, or search and seizure without a warrant.

8. Although "justice for all" remains more an ideal than a reality of daily life, minority groups, such as blacks, Hispanics, and Native Americans, and victims of traditional prejudices, such as women, have become more militant, more visible, and to some degree more powerful than ever before. At least, the problems once swept under the rug of American life have been brought out into the open, a necessary first step to eventual resolution.

9. Culturally and intellectually, the United States remains the most dynamic society on earth. Whether in the arts, in science, or in advanced technical achievements, such as landing a man on the moon, the United States is still the world's leader. Americans continue to win more than their fair share of Nobel Prizes, a sign of the society's continuing creativity and scientific preeminence.

10. Finally, abuses that have undeniably crept into the American system during four decades of unparalleled power and affluence are being recognized and dealt with. Congress has moved to reassert its constitutional balance with the executive branch. Serious corruption of the political process, revealed as the result of recent scandals, has led to a host of reform

measures. The tone of skepticism, particularly toward politics and politi-cians, that has come to dominate public affairs in recent years is probably far healthier in an avowedly democratic society than was the tone of rever-ence for any and all things American that characterized the 1950s.

We have seen that it is possible to argue either that (1) America has entered a period of decline and faces an immediate future of lower living standards at home and decreasing influence abroad or that (2) America remains the world's most dynamic and creative society and, despite surface stresses and strains (themselves caused by our efforts to change and adapt to a new kind of world), shows signs of becoming an even greater and better country in the years ahead.

Some recent polls suggest that many Americans, paradoxically, share both of these attitudes. In August 1988, a survey by the Gallup Organiza-tion showed that 80 pecent of Americans were satisfied with the way things were going for them personally. But only 41 percent were satisfied with the way things were going for the Nation. (See *Los Angeles Times*, August 18, 1988, Sec. 5, p. 3.) These polls indicate that although most Americans feel hopeful and positive about their own futures, they are less sanguine about the nations's prospects. (One would expect Americans to perceive a link between their personal pursuit of happiness and their ability as a people to make wise collective decisions that foster the well-being of the entire nation, but often this is not the case.) What is required is not a blind acceptance of a list of either pros or cons regarding America but, rather, a systematic assessment of the nature of this society and of the government and politics by which it is maintained.

Some historians, like Arnold Toynbee, have argued that the decline of a given society can be attributed to a collapse of religious faith. Others, like Edward Gibbon, take precisely the opposite view. Gibbon argued that Rome fell because Christianity subverted its traditional love of martial power and secular glory. British essayist Thomas Carlyle believed that a society achieved greatness because of the emergence of heroic leaders who carried the whole nation forward, and fell when these heroes failed to emerge or were no longer followed by the masses. Karl Marx insisted that he had discovered a "natural law" governing the growth and decay of nations through dialectical materialism, a theory similar to Darwin's theory of natural selection in the realm of biological survival.

Whatever one may believe or disbelieve about these theories, we would argue that there is little or no evidence to support the notion of inevitable decline for this or any other nation. The future is always a mystery wrapped in an enigma (to paraphrase Winston Churchill). We do not presume upon it. However, this book is written in the hope that its readers will be persuaded to examine their country and their world critically, and use their uncommon intelligence to improve, preserve, and protect it. For the ultimate answer to the question posed in this chapter must lie not with any particular politician or administration but in the capacity of each generation of Americans to respond to the burdens and opportunities that their history has created.

2

The Pursuit of Happiness

- What Is an American? •
- The Puritan Thesis •
- The Frontier Thesis •
- The Melting-Pot Thesis •
- Popular Culture and the American Character •
- Violence and Organized Crime •
- Materialism •
- Racism •
- The American Woman •
- Mobility •
- The Cult of Youth •
- Education in America •
- American Values •

> This is what you shall do; Love the earth and sun and the animals, despise riches, give alms to everyone that asks, stand up for the stupid and crazy, devote your income and labor to others, hate tyrants, argue not concerning God . . . take off your hat to nothing known or unknown . . . re-examine all you have been told at school or church or in any book, dismiss whatever insults your soul, and your very flesh shall be a great poem.
>
> Walt Whitman
> *Preface to Leaves of Grass*
>
> Happiness is the only sanction of life; where happiness fails, existence remains a mad and lamentable experiment.
>
> George Santayana
> *Little Essays*

Although the U.S. Constitution defines the legal framework of American government, and documents such as the Declaration of Independence set forth the principles of the American political system, another factor also influences the practice of politics in this nation: American culture.

Culture is a given group's common ideas, values, attitudes, beliefs, and behavior, including its material and technological state. Culture is normally passed on from generation to generation, although it is sometimes subject to rapid change. The language we speak is part of our culture, as are the clothes we wear, the machines we use, and the ideas we believe to be eternally true. Few people worry about explaining culture, and those who do tend to be academics who are themselves products of a particular culture.[1]

Government does not consist just of passing laws and making speeches. Inevitably it shapes, and is shaped by, the culture of its society. The Declaration of Independence may proclaim that "all men are created equal," and Congress may legislate and judges issue edicts designed to enforce this principle, but if the people do not in fact believe in the equality of races, racism will persist.

[1]In this chapter we frequently use the word *culture*. As is true with a great many words used to summarize abstract but nontheless important forces on human behavior, the word *culture* has many meanings. In one sense it still is used to describe a particular kind of behavior and a set of values usually associated with the upper class. That is, one is or is not a "cultured" person to the extent that one uses one's language fluently or is knowledgeable about such things as classical music, serious literature, and etiquette. Then again, people speak of "pop" culture, "mass" culture, and the culture associated with various ethnic or local groups—sometimes called *subcultures*. Finally, there is the prevailing anthropological usage of the term, which implies that a culture is the way of life of a given group of people. In this chapter this latter definition is meant.

There are problems in clearly defining an American culture because of the diversity of peoples in our country. Although we should think of the term *culture* in its broadest meaning, we should also remember that there may be *subcultures* (Afro-American and Italian American cultures, for example) with different characteristics. This raises interesting questions about what it means to be an "American."

What Is an American?

People speak, imprecisely, of the "thoroughness of the Germans" or the "devotion to family of the Italians" or the "sense of fair play of the English." Such phrases assume, despite obvious exceptions, that it is possible to generalize about the values and the behavior of a given people or nation. But is it possible to speak sensibly about an "American culture"? America is a relatively new nation made up of people from virtually every race and culture on earth. Germans, generally, are fair-skinned, and Italians, generally, are dark. What is the American complexion? Was Jack Armstrong the "All-American Boy"? If so, what about those Americans whose names are Morales or Epstein? What about women? Who, in fact, are the "All-Americans"?

Mark Twain, like most great American writers, attempted to record and illuminate the American experience. In the course of his worldwide travels, Twain once set himself the task of finding something uniquely American, that is, something that had no parallel on earth. What it finally came down to, he concluded, was the American passion for cold drinks. This is not much to build a civilization around, but the fact is that most of what is American, from our language to our political institutions, has been borrowed from foreign countries and then modified to suit American tastes. Even apple pie was borrowed from English fruit tarts, which first became popular in the fourteenth century.

It may be impossible to define the American character, but we nevertheless seem to find it necessary to try. Or so, at least, it has seemed to innumerable writers, sages, politicians, newspaper editorial writers, and sponsors of high school essay contests that begin with the phrase "I am an American because. . . ." The phrase the "American way of life" has become a cliché of our political, commercial, and ceremonial rhetoric. What does it mean? One is tempted to conclude that one way to define an American is that he or she is forever trying to define America.

Historical studies of American character have tended to focus on one of three epochs: the Puritan period, the conquest of the frontier, and the mass migration of Europeans that occurred in the late nineteenth and early twentieth centuries and that is symbolized by the Statue of Liberty. Those who write or speak about America tend to concentrate on one of these three eras and then argue that this was the crucial element that defined the American experience. Such arguments can be labeled as the Puritan thesis, the frontier thesis, and the melting-pot thesis. The Puritan thesis emphasizes American history from the landing at Plymouth Rock (1620) until the Revolutionary War era. It stresses the religious and idealistic motivations of the early settlers of New England, the notion of America as the "New Jerusalem," and John Winthrop's belief that America would be like a "city on a hill" to become a model for older, more sinful Europe.[2] From this standpoint, America can be seen as a newer and perhaps better extension of an old idea, the idea of a distinct Western civilization that used to be called Christendom. The frontier thesis stresses the "winning of the West," roughly from the time of the Louisiana Purchase (1803) to the closing of the western frontier, which occurred at about the end of the nineteenth century. The melting-pot thesis dwells on late-nineteenth- and early-twentieth-century America and the millions who came here seeking refuge from poverty and oppression in Europe, hoping to find a "land of promise."

Although each of these ideas expresses a certain truth about our national development, none of them is, by itself, adequate to explain the full range and complexity of American life. It should also be noted that the historical divisions implied by each of these theses are somewhat arbitrary. People were moving out into the frontier before the Louisiana Purchase and are still doing so today—in Alaska, for example. At the same time that the Puritans were developing a theocratic society in New England, other very different kinds of civilizations were emerging in places like New York and Virginia. Many critics of the melting-pot thesis still argue that it never really melted the various races and ethnic groups coming to America into "one nation indivisible, with liberty and justice for all."

The Puritan Thesis

Many nations have a creation myth that suggests that their beginnings were accomplished with the active assistance of the Almighty.[3] That the Pilgrims—and their later descendants, the Puritans—came here seeking to escape religious persecution and to found the "New Jerusalem" probably helped make this particular group of European immigrants a more popular and likely choice for the role of America's "forefathers" than did other groups that were settling in other parts of America at about the same period. The mundane fact that many Europeans came to America seeking free real

---

[2]"A Model of Christian Charity," in Perry Miller, ed., *The American Puritans* (New York: Anchor Books, 1965), p. 83.

[3]An example is the story of Moses leading the Hebrews across the desert to establish the nation of Israel, which is the subject of the Book of Exodus in the Old Testament. Another example is the story of Romulus and Remus and the founding of Rome.

estate or to avoid military service or to escape imprisonment for crimes or debts is not the stuff of which national myths are made.

Implicit in the Puritan thesis is the belief that Puritan values, ideas, and customs explain much of the historical development of America. The Puritans are usually credited with having given us the Protestant work ethic, which laid the moral basis for America's economic growth. It is often argued that the city of Boston and Harvard College were the intellectual and cultural leaders of the nation, for Harvard was both the nation's first university and has remained the most eminent. Such New Englanders as William Bradford created the nation's first literature, and later others— Nathaniel Hawthorne, Ralph Waldo Emerson, Henry David Thoreau, Henry Wadsworth Longfellow, and Oliver Wendell Holmes—lifted that literature to a place from which it could seriously rival the work of Europe's finest writers. New England's "Boston Brahmins" later became the nation's cultivated, educated, and wealthy elite[4] (although the heirs of Jefferson and Washington, living farther south, would surely have disputed the point). From John Adams to Calvin Coolidge, the Calvinist belief in hard work, self-reliance, and stern morality heavily influenced the familiar image of the "hardworking, hard-driving American" in hot pursuit of what Henry James (a graduate of Harvard) once called the "Bitch Goddess of America, Success."

At the core of Puritanism was the notion of individual responsibility for the well-being of society. As the "elect of God," the Puritans bore a heavy sense of duty (which Wordsworth labeled the "Stern Daughter of the Voice of God") to improve both themselves and their community. This sense of duty can be seen in the dilemma of John Winthrop, who had serious misgivings about leaving England for the New World in 1630, even though Puritans were being persecuted in England by Archbishop William Laud. Winthrop finally convinced himself that in going to the New World he would ultimately be helping reform English society rather than abandoning it. When he landed in Massachusetts Bay, he is reputed to have said, "men shall say of succeeding plantations: 'The Lord make it like that of New England' "[5] That is, Puritan New England would be an example for the rest of the world (including England) to follow.

In a sense, Winthrop's prophecy may be said to have been fulfilled when Winston Churchill, leading an embattled Great Britain against Nazi Germany in the darkest days of World War II, called on "the new world to come to the rescue of the old." Moreover, Winthrop's theme is reiterated throughout our history: in George Washington's Farewell Address, in Abra-

---

[4]Oliver Wendell Holmes, Sr. argues in the novel *Elsie Venner* that "there is, however, in New England, an aristocracy, if you choose to call it so . . . it has grown to be a caste—not in any odious sense . . . which not to recognize is mere stupidity." Holmes goes on to argue that the Boston Brahmin is the natural intellectual and cultural leader of the American race.

[5]See Edmund S. Morgan, *The Puritan Dilemma* (Boston: Little, Brown, 1958), p. 83.

ham Lincoln's Gettysburg Address, in John F. Kennedy's inaugural address, and in Ronald Reagan's acceptance speech at the 1980 Republican National Convention.

The Puritan notion that it was America's duty to serve as an ideal for all humankind was at once noble and audacious. It gave America a sense of historic mission, but it would inevitably cause disappointment, for no matter how much of an example we wanted to be for the rest of the world, we could never be perfect either in our own eyes or in the world's, and several countries (Iran and Vietnam, for example) simply did not want an American way of life imposed on them. Moreover, along with the Puritan commitment to a better world came a certain smug self-righteousness implicit in those who, on the assumption that they were somehow better, presumed to improve other people's morals and behavior. Thus a contemporary (and incomplete) view of the Puritan is of a prudish person bent on controlling our morality.

Even today, in an America where sexual explicitness is commonplace in films and is continually being promoted through advertising, books, and other forms of mass media, and where crime and drug addiction are rampant, the Puritan past retains a powerful hold on millions of Americans. Jerry Falwell's Moral Majority is, at bottom, an effort to restore the country to its Puritan heritage, as has been true of a number of televised evangelists from Billy Graham to Pat Robertson. Robertson sought the Republican nomination for the presidency in 1988 in the belief that he could rally the nation around a moral crusade to restore the "old time religion" at home and in the nation's schools, and do battle with the anti-Christ (i.e., international communism) abroad. Unhappily, the purity of the most conspicuous latter-day Puritans became the subject of considerable national amusement and prurient gossip when some of the nation's most powerful TV preachers were themselves caught in behavior that would have earned them super Scarlet Letters in John Winthrop's New England. One of these, Jim Bakker, confessed to having had carnal knowledge of a young follower, Jessica Hahn, whom he had bribed to keep silent. As a consequence of this scandal, revelations about Jim and Tammy Bakker's lavish life-style received widespread publicity. Bakker lost his ministry and Hahn wound up in residence with *Playboy* publisher Hugh Hefner. Shortly thereafter, another famous TV evangelist, Jimmy Swaggart, who had led the charge to expose Bakker, tearfully confessed that he too had been guilty of various unspecified sins with a New Orleans prostitute. These two incidents tended to confirm an enduring suspicion that much of the posturing in America about moral superiority was simply hypocrisy.

Yet the Puritan tradition accounts for much that is positive in American history; the early agitation against slavery, for example, was centered in New England, as was the movement for free public education. Today a good many environmentalists urge Americans to learn that "small is beautiful," "less is more"—in short, to turn back from the excesses of affluence and relearn the older, and Puritan, values of simplicity, thrift, hard work, and economy.

The Frontier Thesis

As the United States passed from the Revolutionary War period to continental expansion and conquest, it was clear that the ideas and doctrines of New England no longer described the actual experience of the American people, particularly that portion of our people who engaged in building railroads across a continent, who took California and Texas from Mexico by force and steadily pushed their way west, leaving a trail of murdered Native Americans and slaughtered buffalo.

As they created new farms, towns, and territories, the people of the West were also creating new heroes, new values, a new literature, and a new culture. Andrew Jackson and Abraham Lincoln redefined American democracy in terms of homespun rather than broadcloth. Davy Crockett became the first great popular hero of the new "coonskin democracy," to be followed later by a gaudy and colorful procession of western guides, gunslingers, and bad men such as Buffalo Bill, Wild Bill Hickok, and Jesse James. Mark Twain, hailed by the eminent New England critic William Dean Howells as the "Lincoln of Our Literature," became the definitive voice of this new America.

Twain's most memorable literary creations, Huck Finn and Tom Sawyer, came somehow to embody certain American characteristics: youth, simplicity, native shrewdness, scorn for theory and mere bookishness, self-reliance, and, above all, the perennial quest for a new and better life, symbolized by Huck's search for happiness on the breast of the "Brown River God" (the Mississippi) or their desire to "light out for the territory."[6]

The frontier thesis found its most coherent and articulate spokesman in historian Frederick Jackson Turner,[7] who argued that

> the existence of an area of free land, its continuous recession and the advance of American settlement westward, explain American development. . . . [It is] to the frontier that the American intellect owes its striking characteristics. That coarseness and strength combined with acuteness and inquisitiveness; that practical, inventive turn of mind, quick to find expedients; that masterful grasp of material things, lacking in the artistic but powerful to effect great ends; that restless, nervous energy; that dominant individualism, working for good and for evil, and withal that buoyancy and exuberance which comes with freedom—these are traits of the frontier.

[6]See Harry V. Jaffa, "Tom Sawyer, Hero of Middle America," *Interpretation 2* (Spring 1972): 194–226.

[7]Frederick Jackson Turner, "The Significance of the Frontier in American History," American Historical Association *Annual Reports* (Washington, D.C., 1893), pp. 199–227.

But if the frontier left us with a heritage of individualism, equality, and respect for the "common person" (and scorn for "the Elect of God"), it also helped accentuate certain other, less attractive traits. Waste, crime, and a monumental contempt for the natural beauty and harmony of the physical environment, as well as the artistic deficiency noted by Turner, were also characteristic of frontier civilization. Van Wyck Brooks called the West "a gigantic, overturned garbage can." Vernon Louis Parrington noted that between 1871 and 1875, a million head of buffalo a year were slain, "their skins ripped off and the carcasses left for coyotes and buzzards. . . ." "Freedom," Parrington observed, "had become the inalienable right to preempt, to exploit, to squander." The freedom of the frontier, he noted, was the freedom of buccaneers. The new America was "an anarchistic world of strong, capable men, selfish, unenlightened, amoral."[8]

Actually, many of the traits that Turner and others associated with the westward expansion of the United States had been noted by a French nobleman a century earlier when the eastern seaboard was still being settled. Jean de Crèvecoeur was enchanted by the dominant characteristics of the new American civilization. Like Turner, Crèvecoeur noted that the availability of cheap or free land inevitably meant a more fluid class structure and a more open society: "[The] land, descended from its great Creator, holds not its precarious tenure either from a supercilious prince or a proud lord . . . [the laws] are simple and natural. Tis all as free as the air."[9]

Impressed by American prosperity and freedom, Crèvecoeur nevertheless noted that Americans were not truly civilized in the sense that they rarely understood the limits of individualism, as opposed to the needs of society. Although there was no caste system as in Europe, neither was there much concern for the poor and the unfortunate: "This [American] devoid of society learns more than ever to center every idea within his own welfare. . . . How should he be charitable? He has scarcely seen a poor man in his life."

Wealth, not family name or social position, brought power and prestige in this New World.

Implicit in the frontier thesis were many of the ideas and values most often cited by those, even today, who wish either to attack or to defend America. When former Vice President Spiro Agnew attacked his critics in the press and on television, he labeled them part of the "effete eastern establishment," suggesting that it was the old story of the sissified East versus the manly West (although Agnew himself was from Maryland, about

---

[8]Vernon L. Parrington, *The Beginnings of Critical Realism in America: 1860–1920*, vol. 3: *Main Currents in American Thought* (New York: Harcourt Brace Jovanovich, 1958), pp. 16–17.

[9]J. Hector St. John de Crèvecoeur, *Letters from an American Farmer* (New York: Dutton, 1957), chap. 3.

(Drawing by Joseph Mugnaini.)

as far east as you can get in this country). Alabama Governor and frequent presidential candidate George Wallace was also fond of assaulting "pseudo-intellectual snobs."

The frontier spirit continues to be reflected in American films like the Rambo series, in Ronald Reagan's penchant for being photographed on horseback, in the National Rifle Association's insistence on the individual's right to bear arms, in the rash of random shootings on southern California freeways, and in the dismal fact that the United States has the highest illiteracy rate of the world's industrialized nations. Two hundred years ago, Crèvecoeur found the frontiersman lacking respect for intelligence, learning, and wisdom. "Who," asked the Frenchman, "can be wiser than himself in this half-cultivated country?"

Yet the frontier spirit is also seen in the independence and openness of Americans and America, in our insistence that character and performance, not pedigree and "station in life," shall be the measure of human worth, and, in Lincoln's eloquent phrase, "Government of the people, by the people, for the people."

The debate continues over whether the frontier brought us individualism, self-reliance, and democracy or crime, waste, and intolerance. The answer seems to be that it did both.

The Pursuit of Happiness

The Melting-Pot Thesis

In the late nineteenth century, Andrew Carnegie, having built one of the world's mightiest industrial and corporate empires and having acquired an immense personal fortune, turned to writing books. He set forth in plain English the philosophy that had made him rich and America great. "Fortunately for the American people, they are essentially British," he began one essay.[10] By watching and emulating their Anglo-Saxon superiors, argued Carnegie, the flood of Irish people, Italians, and eastern Europeans pouring into the country (many of them to work in Carnegie's mills and factories) could learn to become true Americans and thus share in the nation's material abundance and spiritual grandeur. In this way, Carnegie affirmed, the immigrant's children would be as good as—even indistinguishable from—the *real* Americans.

This was an early and somewhat crude expression of the underlying idea that would eventually find expression in the melting-pot thesis. Anglo-Saxons seemed to embody certain traits and values that contained the genius of Americanism. People of various other races, nationalities, and cultures were welcome to come because their labor was needed for America's burgeoning farms and industries, and through education and assimilation they should be transformed from whatever they had been into true Americans.

The symbol of this idea was the Statue of Liberty, with its premise that the European migrants were "poor" and "wretched," and New York City was the "Golden Door." For millions of Europeans, this undoubtedly turned out to be the reality. For them, America became a "land of opportunity," offering education, personal and religious freedom, and a chance to work hard and thus earn a share of the world's greatest success story. For others, however, America meant sweatshops, bigotry, and new, if more subtle, forms of exploitation.

The melting-pot thesis underscored a certain definition of American character. The "typical" Americans were middle class and middle minded, hardworking and democratic, practical and well intentioned, and optimistic about their own and their country's future. They were clear-eyed and clear-headed. They were the stuff that presidents and popular heroes were made of, in fiction as well as in fact. They were the Lone Ranger (but not Tonto), Huck Finn (but not Jim), Horatio Alger, Frank Merriwell, and, of course, Jack Armstrong, the "All-American Boy." On the screen they were Tom Mix and Gary Cooper and John Wayne. They were invariably white, male, and of Christian, Anglo-Saxon heritage.

Only within the last few decades have we begun to take seriously all the other Americans and Americas—the Tontos and Jims and Giovannis and Nathans—hitherto obliged to ride in the back of the cultural bus. With this

---

[10]Andrew Carnegie, *Triumphant Democracy* (New York: Scribners, 1888).

new awareness, the popularity of the melting-pot thesis has declined. Today American scholars are more likely to use the salad as a metaphor for the variety of American cultures. Preserving rather than destroying the ancestral heritage of the migrants is an increasingly recognized social and national goal. Black Africans, brought to the country unwillingly, experienced a most brutal form of "assimilation." In order to ensure that black people would accept first slavery and later segregation, blacks were legally denied access to education. (In the nineteenth century, many Southern states outlawed the teaching of reading and writing to slaves.) Black families were disbanded and scattered. Even after the Civil War, blacks were systematically denied the right to participate in rewarding or prestigious occupations. (As late as World War II, when blacks for the first time were hired to work in a Detroit auto assembly line, as the result of wartime labor shortages and the insistence of the federal government, riots ensued.) Yet, despite this long and bitter repression, black Americans have endured, and some have even prospered, adding new dimensions to American culture.

Similar, if not quite so systematic and deliberate, examples of repression and exploitation can be cited by virtually every other minority group coming to America. Children of migrants were taunted and condemned, even by their teachers, for "not speaking English" or for dressing, eating, or behaving in an unfamiliar way. For a period in the nation's history, "un-Americanism" was considered a virtual crime, and special committees of the House and the Senate and many state legislatures set out to investigate those whose patriotism was suspect.

Perhaps the failure of the melting pot can be measured best by the fact that politics in America, particularly at the local level, is still very much concerned with voter blocs of various ethnic, religious, racial, and national origins. Even those who decry "bloc voting" often tend to practice it in reverse by appealing to the "middle American" and the "Silent Majority." Even our foreign policy bears a heavy imprint of America's ethnic diversity. No president or secretary of state can ignore the substantial influence of Jewish Americans when dealing with questions regarding Israel's security. Our policy with respect to undocumented workers is obviously influenced by the political impact of Hispanic voters in Southwestern states such as California. And our policy toward Africa must be sensitive to the concerns of American blacks.

Within a generation after Carnegie's essay was published, Randolph Bourne was calling America a "transnational" nation, with "a color richer and more exciting than our ideal has hitherto encompassed."[11] Bourne envisioned the United States as the first truly "international nation" in a world dreaming of internationalism. More recently, a number of critics and scholars have tended to see virtue in the fact that we have *not* become a single homogeneous people. The richness, diversity, and complexity of

[11]Randolph S. Bourne, "Trans-National American," *Atlantic Monthly* (July 1916): 86–97.

American life may pose some of our greatest problems, but they are also sources of much of our strength and vitality as a nation. "I hear America singing," wrote poet Walt Whitman in *Leaves of Grass*, "its *varied* carols I hear" (italics added). "America," he wrote, "is not a nation but a teeming nation of nations. The United States themselves are essentially the greatest poem. It would be a poor sort of America where all sang the same songs."

Thus an important political challenge for the nation is not unlike the major challenge for the world: how to recognize and encourage diversity while at the same time maintaining social and political harmony among a great variety of peoples.

Jesse Jackson's Rainbow Coalition, the cornerstone of his 1988 presidential campaign, demonstrated the enduring appeal of the melting-pot thesis under a different name. Jackson's powerful rhetoric reached out to most of the groups that typically were at the bottom of American social and economic life—blacks, Hispanics, Native Americans, and the poor. Another group that responded strongly to Jackson's appeal were affluent, well-educated liberals—often the descendants of immigrants—who saw in him a leader who might return the nation to the glory days of the New Deal. Michael Dukakis, with his Greek heritage and Jewish wife, although different in style from Jackson, likewise sought to portray himself as an example of the validity of the American Dream of an immigrant ethnic family that within two generations rose from poverty to the pinnacle of success. On the other hand, George Bush, with his "preppie," New England background (his claim to being an adopted Texan notwithstanding), his lifelong association with such bastions of establishment power as the CIA and big business, seemed the embodiment of an evolving Puritan elite.

Thus the principal actors in the 1988 presidential campaign continued to reflect the ideas of long-dead historians and philosophers, without ever mentioning their names or perhaps even being aware of their existence.

Popular Culture and the American Character

In popular mythology, at least, America is the country "where the common man is king." The tradition that "any boy can grow up to be president" clearly has some validity when one considers the obscure origins of the most recent American chief executives, such as Richard Nixon, Harry Truman, Dwight Eisenhower, Gerald Ford, Jimmy Carter, and Ronald Reagan. Following World War I, America created history's first consumer society, built around high wages for ordinary working men and women, mass production of goods, and high levels of consumption. At about the same time, Henry Ford was shocking the industrial world by paying his assembly-line auto workers the then unheard of wage of $5 per day (on the shrewd premise that these workers would buy Ford's cars). What was then the world's tallest skyscraper, the F. W. Woolworth Building, was erected as a symbol of

America's new "five-and-ten-cent store" culture. Ordinary people could go into Woolworth's, or any of the five-and-dime chain stores proliferating across the nation, and for the expenditure of a few dollars, come out with a bag full of the wondrous new products of American industry: hairpins, dolls for the girls and tin soldiers for the boys, cheap perfume, fake jewelry, bubble bath, and photos of favorite film stars. The new movie business was discovering the tricks and themes guaranteed to draw huge new audiences all across the nation; these included stories about gangsters or cowboys and about "flappers" (usually society or college women who wore short skirts, smoked cigarettes, and "petted" in the rumble seats of Ford roadsters and hence were called *fast*). William Randolph Hearst, Joseph Patterson, and Colonel Robert Rutherford McCormick had created a new kind of literature for the masses: tabloid newspapers that sold for a penny or two and were designed to be read on the subway, featuring enticing headlines, copious photos of crime and sex, gossip about celebrities and the rich, advice to the lovelorn, the "funnies," and sports. The 1920s were a sports and show business Golden Age. Jack Dempsey drew the first million-dollar gate for a single fight. Sports heroes Babe Ruth, Red Grange, and Bobby Jones became national idols, along with actresses Clara Bow and Theda Bara. America, in short, was creating a new way of life, and Europeans began to grumble about the danger of becoming "Americanized." It was the first society in history in which leading politicians, business tycoons, publishers, film producers, and radio executives found themselves diligently studying the tastes and wants of the common person.

In the process, Americans either created or brought to a new level of accuracy and refinement the arts of measuring and manipulating mass taste and mass opinion. The Hearst empire spread from newspapers to magazines to the movies. Denied the opportunity to become president himself because of personal idiosyncrasies, Hearst instead made and unmade presidents. (His last-minute support was critical in securing the Democratic nomination for Franklin Delano Roosevelt in 1932. In 1898 he had boasted that he could start a war between the United States and Spain over Cuba, and the war came.)

With the invention and the proliferation of inexpensive radio sets, a new pop music, mostly the product of Broadway's Tin Pan Alley, filled the air. Madison Avenue became the worldwide headquarters for a new and strange industry, advertising. Intellectuals such as H. L. Mencken sneered at the new mass culture and claimed that the United States had created a new species of human, the "boobus Americanus" (the American boob), a new religion ("110 percent Americanism"), and a new class (the "boobocracy") made up of insurance salesmen, movie fans, chiropractors, "sob sisters," Bible-thumping clergymen, cow-college professors, stock swindlers, and politicians so ignorant, venal, and crooked that Mencken claimed to have trained himself to pull the lever on a voting machine with one hand while holding his nose with the other. Novelist Sinclair Lewis took up the theme and won a Nobel prize for his satires of America's Main Street and the businessmen Babbitts who presided over its affairs. (Others, like Ernest Hemingway and poet T. S. Eliot, simply left the country.) Asked why he did not follow the "expatriate" American artists and intellectuals who were flocking to Europe, Mencken insisted that he remained so that he could laugh himself to sleep every night watching the spectacle of American public life.[12]

Depending on one's attitude or tastes, America's mass society and "pop" culture have reached new heights of organization and technique and are still viewed as either a fulfillment or a travesty of the American Dream.

Violence and Organized Crime

We have noted that the media of the 1920s were quick to discover and seek to capitalize on the public's interest in two types that were soon to become mythical heroes of the mass society: the western cowboy and the eastern gangster. What these two characters had in common was a predilection for violence as the natural means of settling life's problems and the willingness to kill on the slightest pretext—in short, the gun. By the early twentieth century, the real cowboys and the frontiersmen had all but vanished from America, to be replaced by a new breed of actors in the movies, the circus, and the rodeo. Like his forerunner, the medieval knight, the authentic cowboy was lost in the fanciful image of a hard-hitting straight-shooting hero of the plains. The gangsters, on the other hand, were just beginning to come into their own. In Chicago, the prototype of the hoodlum-hero, Al Capone, ruled a very tangible empire. At the height of his power, Capone liked to appear at massive public gatherings, such as a Chicago Cubs baseball game. He would usually arrive late, surrounded by an entourage of hoodlums, and head for the box seat reserved for him. Upon Capone's appearance the action stopped, and the crowd would usually rise and applaud their appreciation of the honor bestowed on them by this "great" man's presence.

Capone was credited with being a sort of Henry Ford of the underworld. He organized it and transformed random lawlessness into a major industry. *Organized* crime became a peculiarly American institution, mirroring a certain paradox that permeated much of American life. Order and organization, technique and technology, all somehow managed to go hand in hand with the most extreme forms of "rugged individualism."

The evolution of organized crime into a major industry as well as an influence on politics, entertainment, and business can be explained through a unique set of historical circumstances and cultural proclivities. The Mafia

[12]See Frederick Lewis Allen, *Only Yesterday* (New York: Harper & Row, 1931), chap. 9.

first emerged in Sicily as a sort of underground resistance movement that flourished during periods when that island, temptingly situated in the heart of the Mediterranean Sea, was overrun by a series of foreign invaders. At various times the island was ruled by Greeks, Turks, French, Arabs, and even Americans. It is often the case that an occupying power, to facilitate control over a subject people, will work with selected leaders of the native population, leaders who can either cause trouble or ensure compliance by the majority. The Mafia played this role throughout much of Sicily's history, alternately organizing warfare against the foreign overlords or cooperating with them. Thus, in the later years of World War II, once Sicily had been liberated from the Germans, American officers sometimes turned to the Mafia for assistance in governing the native population. This cooperation was granted at a price. The local village Mafioso frequently became the person who controlled access to American food, jobs, and favors. In short, the Mafia was a kind of shadow government, unofficial and illegal, and therefore ruling largely by terror.

Among the large numbers of Italians migrating to America in the early part of this century, many came from the poorest villages of southern Italy and Sicily—precisely the region dominated by the Mafia. Like other groups, they brought their culture and tradition with them. Although the majority of Italian immigrants were honest, hardworking men and women who struggled to earn a living in their adopted country (and generally succeeded), a few prospered by adapting the old code—cunning, silence, violence—to the new world. They found in America certain elements that stimulated the growth of a criminal culture. One was the American propensity to wink at certain classes of crime and even to make heroes out of outlaws. Another was the existence in American cities of corrupt urban political machines that could be induced to cooperate with the new American Mafiosi in precisely the same way and for the same reasons that foreign conquerers had cooperated in Sicily.

What distinguished the Mafia from other American criminals was their predilection for combining crime with business, that is, for seeking out some enterprise or service that was illegal but still widely in demand and applying to it certain entrepreneurial techniques. Prostitution was one obvious example. With the passage of the Eighteenth Amendment (Prohibition) in 1919, banning the sale of liquor, the Mafia was presented with an opportunity to expand from small-time activities into racketeering on a national scale. Wars were fought for control of the liquor industry; families merged; and the Mafia became big business. By the time Prohibition was repealed, the Mafia had become an established American institution, and legalizing the liquor business simply moved it from illegal to legal enterprises. Then, for the same reasons, organized crime moved into the illegal drug business.

The growth and power of organized crime in the postwar years may have been aided by the fact that the only organization strong enough to control it on a national scale, the Federal Bureau of Investigation (FBI), was under the directorship of J. Edgar Hoover, who concentrated the agency's efforts on ferreting out communists and political radicals. There is even evidence that in the 1960s the CIA sought Mafia cooperation in efforts to assassinate Cuba's premier, Fidel Castro.

By the 1980s, organized crime in America was celebrated unofficially in books and films such as *The Godfather*, which sympathetically portrayed, as a kind of American success story, the rise of a gangster family through several generations.

The success of the Mafia created a pattern that would be followed by the drug lords of Latin America and Asia in the 1970s and 1980s. By the late 1980s, millions of Americans were habitual users of illegal drugs, creating an industry that generated perhaps $100 billion a year in revenues to be parceled out among the drug lords and the street gangs that had become the de facto rulers of large sections of most American cities.

Jesse Jackson was the first presidential candidate to make drugs a major issue in the 1988 presidential campaign. He insisted that drugs, not international communism, was the major threat to the security of the people of the United States. Polls taken in that year indicated that the majority of Americans agreed with him. Drugs—not poverty, illiteracy, unemployment, inflation, or the threat of nuclear war—had become the major threat to the peace and happiness of ordinary Americans. Critics of American society, at home and abroad, invariably pointed to it as the clearest symptom of a society that had become rotten and decadent and that was already in the advanced stages of historic decline.

Apart from the havoc wrought by drug use on the individuals and their families who became addicted to drugs, the most compelling by-product of the drug culture was the rise of street gangs. In Los Angeles, street gangs murdered one another and—often—innocent bystanders with such reckless abandon that normal life for the people who lived in the proliferating gang-dominated areas was far more dangerous than in nations at war or those experiencing revolutionary uprisings. In fact, the drug lords were well on the way to becoming a revolutionary army, armed with sophisticated weapons and fortified by billions of tax-free dollars that could be used to buy or intimidate government officials throughout the world, including the United States. While politicians debated the fine points of international treaties and the rise and fall of the GNP, there was more than a remote possibility that they might awaken one day in the not too distant future to discover that the country they thought they were governing had in fact been enslaved by its own passion for a quick fix.

Superficially, America is a very orderly and certainly a highly organized society. Traffic flows with efficiency and smoothness. The great industries, supermarkets, and department stores of America have set a standard for the entire world. At the same time, lawlessness has been and is one of the most distinctive of American traits. More murders are committed each year in many American cities than occur in whole countries. Our presidents have become popular targets for random assassins. Murder as a cause of death is so rare in much of Europe that it is statistically negligible. In the United States, it is the second-highest cause of death among young men, exceeded only by auto accidents.

Certain features of popular culture in America clearly feed on and perhaps nourish this penchant for murderous assault. It has been estimated that the average American child has witnessed at least twelve thousand television murders by the time he or she reaches maturity.[13] Crime shows, usually containing a murder or an aggravated assault every few minutes, are the staple of prime-time television. The movies have become steadily more bloody, so that mindless brutality has become a universal trademark of the American film. Author Tom Wolfe pointed out that the growing popularity of such "sports" as the demolition derby reflects the destructive impulses of the people. The symbolic meaning of the demolition derby, says Wolfe, is the violent annihilation of the extension of our person: the automobile.[14]

A recent poll claims that 90 million guns are in private hands in America. Crime has become a major issue in the nation. By the late 1970s many American cities were being abandoned, particularly at night, by middle-class families, often out of simple fear. Certainly, at least one cause of the financial crisis afflicting many large American cities could be found in ordinary street crime. New York City alone had a reputed 200,000 heroin addicts, most of them presumably sustaining their habit through crime.

Just as street crime was afflicting the nation's cities, so assassination attempts and threats seemed to be transforming the nature of American politics. A factor in Senator Edward Kennedy's decision not to run for the presidency in 1972 or 1976 was a steady stream of murder threats received in the mail. By late 1975, President Gerald Ford reportedly was receiving an average of 30 death threats a month; he was the victim of two assassination attempts and at least one other assassination plot that was aborted because the plotters were jailed on an unrelated charge. Kennedy and Ford both said, in effect, "You just learn to live with it." But can democracy live with it? Or will the mindless, murderous few finally succeed in forcing the peaceably inclined majority to transform America into a police state?

A final word on this topic. The United States is not simply a victim of violence. The United States is a leading seller of arms to nations around the world.

In fairness, most Americans are not addicted to the cult of violence. Moreover, pacifism and nonviolence have a long, distinguished history in the United States, from the colonial Quakers to Martin Luther King's leadership of the civil rights struggle in the 1960s. It should also be noted

[13]This estimate was made by Nicholas Johnson, former chairman of the Federal Communications Commission, based on FCC studies of televised violence.

[14]Tom Wolfe, *The Kandy-Kolored Tangerine-Flake Streamline Baby* (New York: Farrar, Straus & Giroux, 1965), chap. 2.

that many of the ideas that inspired Mahatma Gandhi to lead India to freedom through nonviolent resistance came from the Indian leader's study of the works of Henry David Thoreau, a nineteenth-century American writer and philosopher. Public opinion polls also have repeatedly indicated that most Americans disapprove of excessive violence on television and favor some restrictions on gun ownership.

Materialism

A commonplace criticism of American culture is its excessive preoccupation with material goods and corresponding neglect of the human spirit. Americans, it is alleged, worship only "the almighty dollar." We scramble to "keep up with the Joneses." The love affair between Americans and their automobiles has been a continuing subject of derisive commentary by both foreign and domestic critics. Americans are said to live by a quantitative ethic. Bigger is better, whether in bombs or bosoms. The classical virtues of grace, harmony, and economy of both means and ends are lost on most Americans. As a result, we are said to be swallowing up the world's supply of natural resources, which are irreplaceable. Americans constitute 6 per-

Main Street, U.S.A. *(Photograph by Dean Immenschuh, Upland, California.)*

cent of the world's population but consume over a third of the world's energy. These are now familiar complaints. Indeed, in some respects Americans may believe the "pursuit of happiness" to mean the pursuit of material things.

However, it should also be noted that although Americans do consume on a lavish scale, they also produce a disproportionate share of the world's goods, particularly with respect to food—the most basic of all commodities. And if it is true that Americans are consuming too much of the world's dwindling supply of oil, it is also true that American technology, industry, and capital discovered and developed much of that oil in the first place—and in the process made rich many once-impoverished lands.

By the late 1980s, however, it was clear that Americans were consuming on a level far in excess of the wealth they created. As a result, our government was forced to borrow heavily from foreign investors to maintain the forced prosperity of the Reagan-era boom at home and massive military expenditures abroad. These debts, accumulating in the hands of Japanese corporations, British bankers, German industrialists, and Latin-American drug dealers, returned to America in the form of investment in American land, buildings, and businesses. Not a bad trade-off, some economists argued, but disturbing to others who believed we were simply selling off the nation's future economic independence to sustain an extravagant life-style that, in fact, we could not afford.

Racism

Evidence of American racism is overwhelming. It reaches from the constitutional provision that counted black slaves as three-fifths of a person to the inescapable fact that virtually every statistical measure, such as income, health, longevity, education, and housing, shows that blacks, Hispanics, and Native Americans (but not Jews or Asians) are at the bottom of American society). This dilemma has plagued our society from its beginning.[15] The issue was dodged by the Constitutional Convention (lest it split the nation before it became a nation) but emerged again during the Civil War and Reconstruction. Slavery was abolished at the price of a great national trauma, only to be replaced by a system of segregation called *Jim Crow*. Most of the nation's great cities are caught in the race-related grip of unemployment, crime, and poverty. Riots flared in virtually every major city in the nation in the late 1960s (and in Miami in 1980) but seemed to change little or nothing. Every fall, Americans brace themselves to watch embattled adults attacking children and police on television newscasts as the result of efforts to integrate schools somewhere in the country. Racism

[15]See Paul Jacobs and Paul Landau, *To Serve the Devil* (New York: Random House, 1971).

unquestionably has been and remains one of our fundamental domestic problems.[16]

It often happens that revolutions occur during periods when oppression is being relaxed, rather than the reverse. This appears to be so because a revolution stems not from despair and defeat but from rising expectations. The riots that swept American cities in the 1960s occurred shortly after Congress passed a whole series of civil rights acts that destroyed the legal basis for segregation, particularly in the South, and created the framework for positive efforts to integrate society in the 1970s.

Such efforts achieved substantial success. By the 1980s many American cities had black mayors. Black political figures have taken on national prominence and black voters now are courted by all serious national politicians. The number of blacks in college, about 11 percent of all college students, just about equaled their proportion in the total population; and there was marked economic improvement among middle-class black Americans by the end of the 1970s. In 1983 both houses of Congress overwhelmingly passed, and the president signed, a law making the birthday of the late civil rights leader Martin Luther King, Jr., a national holiday. This was done, in part, according to one white senator, to symbolize America's commitment to completing the promise of equality announced in the Declaration of Independence. Still, black income lags behind that of whites, and the traditional ills associated with segregation—poverty, illness, high crime rates, and undereducation—continue to plague black communities more than they do white ones.

Similar problems afflict another, potentially larger minority group—Hispanic Americans. Other migrants (Irish, Jews, Italians, and Asians) who poured into this country at an earlier stage of our history seem to have flowed into the mainstream of American life, and optimists believe that the American system will find a way to absorb the new "migrants"—who of course are not migrants at all, as most black Americans are descended from families that have been here for hundreds of years, and Hispanics lived in what is now southwest America before it became part of the United States.

Finally, there are the American Indians, first to be affected by the coming of white Europeans to the North American continent and, in economic, social, and political terms, the most deprived.[17]

Americans did not invent racism. Racist feelings and attitudes toward other ethnic groups have been and are common throughout much of the world. Also, as we have noted, the United States has moved dramatically within the last two decades to outlaw or restrain legal and institutional racism and to equalize opportunity for various disadvantaged groups. Moreover, recent public opinion surveys show a growing tolerance among

---

[16]See the discussion of "New Racism" in Eleanor Randolph, "Blacks Focus on Complex New Issues," *Los Angeles Times*, December 18, 1979, pp. 1ff.

[17]See Peter Collier, "The Red Man's Burden," *Ramparts 8* (February 1970): 27–38.

Black for President (%)			
	Yes, Would	No, Would Not	No Opinion
1987	79	13	8
1983	77	16	7
1971	70	23	7
1969	67	23	10
1967	54	40	6
1965	59	34	7
1963	47	45	8
1958	38	53	9
Source: The Gallup Report, July 1987.			

whites for racially different people (see, for example, the accompanying Gallup Poll). Although there have been setbacks and there remains much to be done, there is a conscious public policy in this country to combat racism, and important strides have been made.

The American Woman

The position of women in America has always been different from that of their counterparts in other parts of the world. During the colonial period, the scarcity of women, the need for labor, and the demands of the frontier resulted in certain advantages uncommon elsewhere. For example, in contrast with the situation in England, the married woman in the colonies had property rights, could enter contracts, and had the right to testify against her husband in a court of law. This is not to say that women were at all equal to men. They were excluded from most professions and crafts; they did not vote; and they were expected to take care of the home.[18]

In early American history, women were frequently expected to be the "guardians of morality." There was an assumption that women were innately more delicate, sensitive, and compassionate than were men and that sexual passion was a far greater force in masculine behavior. The ideal Victorian woman was expected to be self-sacrificing and devoted to family, church, and community life. Nonetheless some women began the long struggle to gain equal rights for their sex.

By the early nineteenth century, an active women's movement was well under way. Focusing on opposition to slavery as well as the promotion of women's rights (including the right to vote), the movement culminated in 1848 in a well-attended convention at Seneca Falls, New York, where delegates called for the "independence" of women (to correspond to the

[18]Carl Degler, *Out of Our Past* (New York: Harper & Row, 1970), pp. 54–58.

independence demanded by men in 1776). But the movement suffered, as the issue of slavery absorbed the energies of the reformers and the Civil War occupied the attention of the nation. By the end of the nineteenth century, women were still denied the vote, were discouraged from pursuing higher education, and were restricted from certain jobs. A momentous breakthrough came in 1920 with the passage of the Nineteenth Amendment to the Constitution, granting women the right to vote. Nonetheless, their position remained a subordinate one for many years thereafter.

Some students of "women's liberation" believe that the contemporary feminist movement began with the publication in 1963 of Betty Friedan's *The Feminine Mystique.* Friedan's widely read book suggested that as women became more educated and more aware, they found less attractive the traditional role of housewife and the prospect of isolation in a suburban home. Since the first edition of this book, the women's movement has stressed equality of opportunity and the raising of consciousness of both men and women to create an awareness of the artificial stereotypes to which both sexes have been accustomed. The results are spectacular. Today about half the work force is female, and at least 50 percent of all adult women are now working outside the home. According to a 1983 report of the U.S. Census Bureau, this represents a 173 percent increase since 1947 in the number of women in the work force, reflecting almost revolutionary changes in the demographic, social, and economic character of this society.

Meanwhile a dramatic change has taken place in higher education. One-half of the enrollment in colleges and universities is now female (it was 29 percent in 1948), and college women now outnumber college men in the eighteen- to nineteen-year-old population group.[19] Moreover, women are moving into professions such as law, business, and medicine that were traditionally the bailiwick of men, and recent evidence has shown a sharp increase in recent decades in the percentage of women who regard a full-time job outside the home as necessary to the ideal life.[20] Of course, inflation has proved a powerful economic incentive to women's entering the work force, regardless of political or social philosophy. (For tens of millions of American families, it has become necessary to have two incomes to enjoy the traditional middle-class life-style.)

There are other evidences of the activity of women in the mainstream of our national life. In recent years Jeane Kirkpatrick, U.S. ambassador to the United Nations; Elizabeth Dole, secretary of transportation; Margaret Heckler, secretary of health and human services; and Katherine Ortega, U.S. treasurer, became examples of prominent women serving in the national administration. Sandra Day O'Connor became the first woman appointed to the U.S. Supreme Court, and in 1984 Geraldine Ferraro became the nation's first woman nominee for vice president.

[19]*The Chronicle of Higher Education,* January 9, 1978, pp. 1ff.
[20]Gallup Report, August 1982.

Woman for President (%)			
	Yes	**No**	**No Opinion**
1987	82	12	6
1984	78	17	5
1983	80	16	4
1978	76	19	5
1971	66	29	5
1969	54	39	7
1967	57	39	4
1958	52	44	4
1949	48	48	4
1937	31	65	4

Source: The Gallup Report, July 1987.

These events have effected alterations in our life-styles and in the American family. Although critics of the feminist movement cite alarming divorce statistics as an alleged consequence, others note the improving opportunities for women to have fulfilling and professional lives. Married couples are increasingly sharing a wider range of activities and duties, including housework and child-rearing responsibilities. Some even argue that such sharing enhances rather than diminishes the well-being of all members of the family, and a 1983 study conducted by the federal government showed that despite the acceleration in the changes in the sexual roles, the number of divorces in the United States was beginning to decline.

Although many feminists are disturbed at the defeat of the equal rights amendment to the Constitution and although equality of opportunity has as yet not been achieved (for example, women still earn less than men in the labor market[21]), the attitudes of both sexes regarding the roles of men and women have undergone substantial alteration. Most Americans recognize the breakdown of traditional and stereotypical sex roles, believe that the roles played by women are changing a great deal, and favor efforts to strengthen and change women's status.[22]

Mobility

The history of America is a history of migration. From the Pilgrims' landing in New England to the suburbanites' carrying their television sets into new tract houses, Americans have always been among the most mobile of the earth's people, in both a physical and a sociological sense. Europeans grow

[21]See Labor Department report in the *Los Angeles Times*, September 13, 1978, p. 5.
[22]See *Current Opinion*, May 1977, p. 51.

up in their grandparents' houses. Americans move on the average of once every four or five years. Americans regard a neighborhood less as a community than as a place to move away, and preferably up, from.

For most Americans, mobility is an important part of the American Dream, because *social* mobility implies the right of ordinary Americans to strive for a better life than their parents knew and to move from a lower to a higher social class. Many of our historical heroes, from Abraham Lincoln to Thomas Edison, rose from simple family backgrounds to positions of great eminence by taking advantage of the openness and freedom of America. Although sociologists question widespread social mobility in our country, it continues to be a part of our system of beliefs.

Mobility in America has, of course, been intensified by technology. The railroad, the automobile, and the airplane have offered Americans more opportunity to travel than almost any other people in history have had. Our freeways and expressways are filled with the crush of traffic every morning and afternoon as commuters go to and from work. But we do not stop there. We travel widely throughout the world, and the numbers of American travelers overseas are expected to grow in coming years. The consequences of such mobility are mixed. On the one hand, Americans on the move seem to reflect a dynamic, progressive society. Certainly, wide-ranging travel enhances the tolerance and cosmopolitanism of our people, and the travel and automobile businesses represent important stimulants to a healthy economy. But there are problems. The automobile, the most characteristic mode of transportation for the individual, uses up a precious, expensive energy source and pollutes the air. Additionally, some critics have found in the movement of Americans a symptom of "rootlessness."

Both academic sociologists like David Riesman (*The Lonely Crowd*) and popular journalists such as William Whyte (*The Organization Man*) have studied the paradox of American individualism and conformity seeming to exist side by side, often within the same individual. The prevailing image of American college students, for example, passed from the "mindless conformity" of the "silent generation" of the 1950s to the wild radicalism that many believed characterized the student generation of the 1960s and back to a kind of numbing passivity in the 1970s. None of these images may be wholly accurate—average students probably do not really change very much from year to year or generation to generation except perhaps for such things as hair styles and skirt lengths—but they do reflect the most active and visible students at the most important and prestigious universities.

Another frequently noted paradox in America is that although ours is a mobile, urbanized, and industrialized society, most of our national myths and values are rooted in the rural past. We are a people who work in cities, live in suburbs, and dream of the countryside. From Jefferson's warnings to Americans to avoid the corrupting city, to Huck Finn's "lighting out for the territory" lest Aunt Sally "civilize" him, to former President Ford's fulminations against the wicked ways of New York, a historic antipathy to the urban life and all its works seems to permeate the American people, who, nevertheless, are among the most urban peoples on earth.

Our myths are of wagon trains pushing west, sturdy farmers conquering the plains, presidents who were born in log cabins, lonesome cowboys and plantation belles, and "good ol' boys." Until recently, when a number of black and Jewish American writers such as James Baldwin and Norman Mailer began writing about the urban experience, our literature was usually set in the country or in small towns, and the themes of such writers as William Faulkner, Ernest Hemingway, and John Steinbeck were largely a celebration of the pastoral virtues, as opposed to urban vices. Many of the political leaders of both parties play shrewdly to the American penchant for equating the countryside with honesty, simplicity, and "common sense." Jimmy Carter, from the small town of Plains, Georgia, is an example. So too is Ronald Reagan, born and raised in a small community in Iowa and even as president preferring life on his California ranch to life in the city.

The future of the ever-more-mobile, on-the-go American is cloudy, in part because of the rising costs of energy and the potential depletion of petroleum resources. Moreover, the jobs and action are in urban areas. Already there is mounting evidence of people's moving back to the cities from the outer suburbs. Perhaps in the long run an important effect of the periodic oil crises may be their impact on the American worship of cheap and easy mobility. For Americans to learn to abandon their large automobiles and spacious suburbs in favor of clinging together in energy-efficient cities would be a revolution indeed.

The Cult of Youth

Another important characteristic of American culture that is an unfailing source of both admiration and concern to foreign observers of the American scene is its extraordinary emphasis on youth. Traditionally in European and Asian societies, there have been only two kinds of people: children and adults. America invented the idea of adolescence and coined the term *teenager* to describe a status unique to American life. In Europe and Asia, the young typically leave school early and go to work, usually at menial and low-paying jobs. The young remain subject to parental control and discipline until they leave home, marry, and/or become self-supporting.

Perhaps because our affluence permits youth to enjoy a longer period relatively free from adult responsibilities, perhaps because we have always considered ourselves a young country, perhaps because Americans tend to look forward rather than backward, or perhaps because of all three—the young in America are the envy of their counterparts throughout much of the Western world. They have cars, money, and personal freedom to an extent unheard of in most cultures. When the French or the Italians complain that their country is being "Americanized," they usually mean that their own young people are beginning to take on "airs" like those of the American young.

The young in America have become an important element in the nation's economy. The pop-recording industry, for example, caters largely to young girls between the ages of 12 and 16, who buy most of the records sold in this country. Advertisers quickly learned that the mature tend to follow the young, rather than the reverse, in matters of taste and style, particularly in such industries as clothing, automobiles, and personal items (for example, hair sprays). As a result, most Americans are bombarded with propaganda showing young, attractive people looking clean, radiant, and happy, whereas older people worry about things like stopped-up drains and iron-deficiency anemia.

Traditionally, the American young have not been a very potent political force. This changed, however, in the 1960s, when young people protested the war in Vietnam and racism. Young people joined the "children's crusade" that helped Senator Eugene McCarthy become a major candidate for the Democratic nomination for the presidency in 1968. In 1972 Senator George McGovern, relying largely on a staff of people in their twenties, won the Democratic nomination. However, in the ensuing campaign against Richard Nixon, the young seemed to become disenchanted with McGovern and politics in general. Only about 20 percent of the newly enfranchised voters (under age 21) bothered to go to the polls, and these tended to follow the rest of the population in giving most of their votes to Nixon.

In the late 1960s and early 1970s, a rash of books appeared (Charles Reich's *The Greening of America*, Theodore Roszak's *The Making of a Counter Culture*) prophesying that American life was about to be transformed by a new, youthful "counterculture." But by the 1980s most of this talk seemed foolish. Although the American young, particularly students, were an important political force in the 1960s, by the 1970s they had reverted to their more traditional political apathy. The 1980s may well see another reversal. At the height of the anti-Iranian feeling in late 1979, many were astonished to discover pro-American demonstrations at several American campuses, perhaps a harbinger of things to come.

Finally, the median age of Americans, which for the three decades after World War II was in the mid-twenties, went over thirty years of age in 1983 and is expected to move higher as we approach the twenty-first century. With birthrates declining and life expectancy increasing, Americans, however symbolically young, are actually growing older, and the consequences may be significant. The problems of aging are demanding more attention from scholars and public policymakers. Already more television commercials are addressed to an older clientele than they were a few years ago. Books and new magazines appeal to the middle-aged, and there are active "gray panther" pressure groups springing up in various communities. Some sociologists predict that as the average age rises, there will be a decline in crime and a rebirth of the cities.[23] For the foreseeable future Americans may seek to retain the image of a youthful nation while actually maturing.

Education in America

In his old age, James Madison, a Founding Father of this republic and a former president, wrote in a private letter: "Knowledge will forever govern ignorance: and a people who mean to be their own governors, must arm themselves with the power which knowledge gives."[24]

Had Madison been alive in the spring of 1983 he, along with many Americans, would have responded with concern as a presidential commission on excellence in education, using language that was unusual—even shocking—for such a group, concluded that American public schools were being engulfed by mediocrity, or worse. The dean of the University of California at Los Angeles's school of education warned that the public schools faced possible total collapse.[25] Objective test scores, such as the national SATs (Scholastic Aptitude Tests), given to applicants to colleges have shown a constant decline for two decades. A University of Michigan professor, Joseph Adelson, pointed out that in 19 tests in which American students competed against students from other developed nations, the United States never ranked first or second and was at the very bottom in seven categories. Moreover, other data showed that in an average month, 7 percent of all *junior* high school students were assaulted, slightly more robbed, and 10 percent of the teachers were victims of theft.[26]

These objective studies confirmed the subjective arguments of American teachers, parents, and the students themselves. Literacy and competence at calculation were in sharp decline[27]; the dropout rate was increasing (in 1983 it was about 30 percent for all public school students, higher for minorities); and crime and hoodlumism were rampant.

In 1987, a book about the state of American higher education, written by a Chicago University philosophy professor, Allan Bloom, astonishingly led the nation's best-seller lists. Titled *The Closing of the American Mind*, Bloom's book argued that most American universities had surrendered their academic integrity during the student uprisings of the 1960s and had gone steadily downhill ever since. H. G. Wells once wrote: "Civilization is a race

[23]"The Graying of America," *Newsweek*, February 28, 1977, pp. 50–65.

[24]James Madison to W. T. Barry, August 4, 1822; inscription on entrance to the Madison building of the Library of Congress.

[25]John J. Goodlad, *A Place Called School* (New York: McGraw-Hill, 1983).

[26] Joseph Adelson, "How the Schools Were Ruined," *Commentary*, July 1983.

[27]One study found about 23 million illiterate Americans (10 percent of the population). Among seventeen-year-olds the rate was 13 percent. *Los Angeles Times*, August 11, 1983, Sec. 1B, p. 4.

between education and disaster." Continued deterioration of the public school system seemed a sure recipe for long-term disaster.

For a nation that has been committed for 150 years to equal educational opportunity for its citizens, believing that mass education was imperative in a democracy, these were sobering facts. What was to blame? Television, which attracted youngsters away from homework, reading for pleasure, and conversation? Movies, attended mostly by teenagers? The automobile, providing the young with easy transport away from school, library, and home? Excessive demands on our schools—babysitting for children, integration of the society, equality of station, and much more—thus depriving them of the ability to concentrate on learning? The sharp decline in public financing and public support of education, initiated by the Howard Jarvis–inspired tax-cutting program for public services in California?

By the 1980s, the debate on the function and future of education and the role government should play in educating our children had moved beyond PTA gatherings and school board meetings, spilling over into a larger nationwide debate. President Reagan began to appear before various educational groups, including a normally hostile convention of the American Federation of Teachers, and all serious presidential candidates began to craft political positions on the issues of education. Also, by the middle of the 1980s, various polls and surveys showed that public concern for education was beginning to result in a growing approval for more financing and support for our public schools. And some test scores began to edge up after decades of decline.

In the 1988 presidential campaign both major candidates cited educational reform as a priority issue. If Madison was right, this heightened awareness and desire for improvement are crucial to the future of our republic.

American Values

One can see running through American society a mixture of both utopianism and pragmatism, the same traits that have been characteristic of our most quintessentially American political leaders: Benjamin Franklin, Thomas Jefferson, Franklin D. Roosevelt, John F. Kennedy, and, perhaps most important, Abraham Lincoln. These men had in common a shrewd and practical approach to politics as well as a certain idealism. They all were attacked for being both dreamers and hypocrites, and in a certain sense, their detractors were right on both counts.

As we have noted, it is possible to dispute almost any claim made about "American culture" simply because the nation is so large and so varied. Yet few other nations are quite so preoccupied with efforts to achieve self-identity. The phrase the "American way of life" appears constantly in political and ceremonial speeches. One does not hear or read about the "French way of life," the "German way of life," or the "Italian way of life" nearly so frequently, perhaps because in these older societies people know what their way of life is and hence have little need to discuss it.

It may be possible, however, to cite a few basic ideas and values that do underlie most political rhetoric in America and that are usually affirmed, at least verbally, by almost all Americans.

We believe these are

1. *Democracy*. Democracy is a vague term, but most Americans say they believe in it. It means rule by the people. Our democratic system requires that political power be vested in people chosen by a majority of those registered voters who use the franchise and that we have alternatives from which to choose when we vote. There have been no military coups in America, and there is unlikely to be one so long as most people continue to believe in the electoral process, rather than force, as a means of resolving political and social differences. Groups such as the American Nazi party, which are frankly antidemocratic, get little support from the American people. Radical left-wing groups, which sometimes begin by preaching the necessity of armed revolution, often turn to electoral politics as they mature. (An example is the Black Panther party.) The fundamental problem of almost all totalitarian movements in America for the past century, left or right, has been the lack of anything remotely resembling popular support. The immense majority of the American people remain committed to ballots rather than to bullets as a means of achieving social and political programs.

2. *Justice*. Justice is a more complicated idea than democracy. Justice is an ideal, like true love or perfect happiness, that is rarely ever achieved but that nevertheless powerfully animates human behavior. The Ten Commandments, for example, are one expression of this ideal. Leon Jaworski, special prosecutor in the government's prosecution of the various high governmental officials involved in the Watergate scandal, said that he came away from this experience convinced that the American people still strongly believe in the concept of equal justice. (Thus, when President Ford pardoned Richard Nixon for his part in the affair, the polls reflected strong public disapproval.)

In America, justice has usually been associated with the belief in equal opportunity under the law, rather than equality of incomes, status, or power. The Supreme Court's "one person, one vote" decision was clearly a manifestation of our belief that the law should give no added advantage to some persons over others.[28] On the other hand, most people see nothing

---

[28]This was the landmark Supreme Court decision in *Baker v. Carr* (1962) that ruled that in apportioning state legislatures, each legislative district is to represent an equal number of voters; thus each voter in a state is equal to every other voter.

wrong or inherently unjust about some people's amassing fortunes and others' living in poverty. Nor are there many objections to the fact that popular athletes may earn hundreds of thousands of dollars a year, whereas others—presumably doing work, such as teaching school, that is at least as useful socially—make a small fraction of that sum. In short, we believe in the equal right to become unequal.

On the other hand, it must be noted that even this concept of justice is difficult to achieve in practice. How could one argue, for example, that a child born to a black sharecropper in Alabama at the turn of the century was endowed with opportunity equal to a Rockefeller's?

3. *Freedom and individualism.* Most Americans appear to believe that personal freedom is the most important value of American life, the foundation on which our society rests. Of course, we disagree as to what freedom means. For example, there was vigorous opposition to those who demonstrated against the war in Vietnam in the late 1960s and early 1970s, including documented efforts by the government to suppress and/or disorganize such demonstrations. At the same time, a good many of the antiwar protesters were themselves none too scrupulous about the rights of others. Still, most Americans appear to believe that people should be free to speak their minds, that the press should be free to criticize the government, and that individuals should be free to live their lives according to their own lights within the limits imposed by the law. Also, the evidence is strong that most Americans believe in the private ownership of property.

As senator and former ambassador to the United Nations Daniel Patrick Moynihan has pointed out, these are rights respected by a small, perhaps dwindling minority of the world's governments. Whether under a king, a dictator, or an all-powerful "party," much of the world throughout history has regarded public order and "national unity" as more important than personal freedom. Even in America, maintaining the rights guaranteed to all Americans by the first ten amendments to the Constitution has been a continuing struggle. In the late 1960s, the editors of great newspapers, such as the *New York Times*, found themselves faced with the possibility of going to prison for defying a government order not to publish the Pentagon Papers. (The Supreme Court validated the paper's right to publish.) More recently, Americans were shocked by disclosures that organizations such as the FBI and the CIA were engaged in opening the mail and tapping the phones of law-abiding citizens. However, it is significant that such activities were usually conducted in clear violation of existing laws designed to protect individual privacy. Efforts to curb violence in America by restricting the sale of guns, for example, have usually foundered in the face of the belief that such a curb would represent a significant assault on personal freedom. So too have many attempts at protecting the environment failed because the price of cleaner air, for example, involves some limitation on the right to drive private automobiles.

Related to our belief in freedom is a belief that the individual has certain "inalienable rights."[29] Statist political philosophies assume that the individual is subordinate to the state. Few Americans would agree. The state, we insist, exists to serve the people. Moreover, the individual should be free from the arbitrary power of the state. This is why we have the Bill of Rights (see the discussion in Chapter 3). Again we do not always live by the ideals of freedom and individual dignity, but most of us believe in them, and this belief has important consequences in daily life as well as in the practice of politics.

4. *Reason.* From eighteenth-century thinkers such as Jefferson we have come to believe in the primacy of reason. Intellectuals in the eighteenth century (also called the Age of Enlightenment) believed that humankind was capable of understanding the world and that humans could, in consequence, control that world to their advantage. Use of reason by the individual thus replaced the authority of religion or of a ruling family as the means by which public policy was to be made (see the discussion of the "Enlightenment" in Chapter 3 for an elaboration of this theme). Thus, today students are educated in courses like American history and government because it is believed that they can reason and that if they become more knowledgeable about their society and government, they will, hence, be able to render more reasoned individual judgments as citizens.

5. *Accommodation.* Because politics in America must reflect a variety of interests, we have evolved both a system of government and life-style founded on compromise and conciliation rather than on force or brute strength. We believe that most differences of opinion, most conflicts of interest, can be reconciled through reasoned discussion. Sometimes compromise fails us. (The Civil War is an example—there compromise seemed pitted against the principle of antislavery, a principle that could not be compromised.) More often it does not. Most schools and other public institutions function through a committee system based on the idea that if responsible people meet and reason together, they will be able to solve their problems. Clearly, great legislative bodies such as the U.S. Senate or House of Representatives could not function without carefully constructed compromises, and our greatest legislative leaders have understood this.

6. *Progress?* Had this book been written three decades ago, we probably would have felt constrained to include the idea of "progress" in this brief outline of basic American beliefs. Today the necessity of its inclusion is not so clear. Continuing exposure to the realities and dangers of pollution resulting from unbridled economic development, a series of rude shocks to Americans' self-image as "winners" (outlined in Chapter 1), including the "loss" of Vietnam, Watergate, frequent assassinations and assassination attempts, inflation, unemployment, recession, and energy crises, all have

[29]Americans' dedication to individual rights seems to be growing. A 1973 study by the National Opinion Research Center, University of Chicago, indicated a greater tolerance for individual rights among Americans than in the past.

played a part in causing some to wonder whether bigger is really better and to question whether more might really mean less. Until fairly recently, most Americans believed that progress was built into the American system—that each new year must necessarily bring a somewhat higher level of abundance, an increase in American power and prestige, and more opportunity for a better life for more people. Today, many believe that such notions need to be seriously reexamined.

America has celebrated its two-hundredth birthday. No other major Western nation observes a "birthday."[30] Even if they should wish to do so, most countries would not know which day to celebrate because most nations have evolved over hundreds, even thousands, of years of wars, famine, migration of peoples, and many other factors only dimly known and even less well understood. The United States, on the other hand, was *willed* into existence. It was deliberately created by specific individuals at a specific time and place. Moreover it arrived, so to speak, with a silver spoon—the culture of Europe—in its mouth. Finally, it was free to take what it wished from the accumulated experience of other peoples while being largely protected, as the result of sheer geographic luck, from some of the less attractive aspects of the older civilizations, such as a rigid class system.

Given the task of writing the Declaration of Independence, thirty-two-year-old Thomas Jefferson, with the help of John Adams and aging Benjamin Franklin, undertook to begin this document with a statement about the young nation's reason for being. He decided to borrow English philosopher John Locke's phrase "life, liberty, and property" as best describing the purpose of the new nation, but then he dropped the word *property* in favor of "pursuit of happiness." Two hundred years later, it may not be possible or even necessary to try to improve upon Jefferson's intuition. He obviously intended this admittedly vague phrase to include the activities of New England Puritans, Pennsylvania businessmen, and Virginia farmers.

Happiness may have different meanings to different people. Few are against happiness, but at least before the eighteenth century, happiness was not often regarded as among the most important of human pursuits (certainly not as important as salvation). Glory, grandeur, greatness, and power are the stuff of history. Thus we speak of Alexander the Great, not Alexander the Happy. And, of course, we, like others in the past, want our country to be great and powerful and glorious.

But Jefferson's notion that the individual's right to pursue happiness is the purpose of government is a legacy for us to ponder. Perhaps we have too easily translated "happiness" into material gain. We would suggest that materialism is not to be omitted from the quest for a happy life. Certainly, material things—food, housing, clothing, medicine, and the other artifacts

[30]See Henry Fairlie, "Anti-Americanism at Home and Abroad," *Commentary*, December 1975, pp. 29–39.

of daily life—are indispensable to a happy existence. Likewise, however, good health, an opportunity to exercise talents and abilities, and the chance to participate in the important events and institutions of one's lifetime—including government—should be components of the happy life. In regimes before Jefferson's, these activities tended to be the perquisites of the few; Jefferson intended them to be available to the many.

Thus happiness is a prime concern of a democracy, and in its pursuit, Americans have created the world's first and richest consumer economy; have undertaken to mass produce education, entertainment, and goods on an unprecedented scale; and have sought to build a society in which most people would be free to follow the star of their own destiny in their own fashion. And if in the process, we have become a restless, troubled, and sometimes divided people, that is a price that had to be paid for having shifted the focus of politics from the grandeur of the few to the well-being of the many.

3

The Constitutional Framework

• Origins •
• Principles •
• Federalism •

> **Of all men that distinguish themselves by memorable achievements, the first place of honor seems due to Legislators and founders of states, who transmit a system of laws and institutions to secure the peace, happiness, and liberty of future generations.**
>
> **David Hume**

In the summer of 1787, 55 men gathered in the city of Philadelphia to draw up the Constitution of the United States of America.

The document they created begins with a memorable phrase: "We the people of the United States." The convention thus undertook to create a nation rooted in the supreme authority of "the people." But of course, the 55 delegates were being somewhat presumptuous. Although they assumed the right to speak for the people, they in fact were representative of only a small, elite group within the total population. They all were, for example, male, white, and from the upper-middle or upper class. Half of them were college graduates. Many, like Alexander Hamilton, James Madison, and Benjamin Franklin, were intellectuals. Could they really speak for black slaves, for women, for the illiterate poor—let alone the Native Americans, who, of course, had every right to affirm that *they* were really "the people"? The so-called three-fifths compromise, concluded on July 16, 1787, illustrates the point. Despite proclaiming a social contract among all the people (and having all read the Declaration of Independence, which proclaimed "All men are created equal"), the founders faced a particularly sticky issue. Were slaves equal? Did they have "inalienable rights"? Representation in the House of Representatives was to be apportioned to each state according to population. So, too, were taxes.[1] Clearly, those states in which slavery was practiced (in the South) wished to count slaves as persons when calculations were made to determine how large their House delegations would be. Conversely, when taxes were levied (again according to population), those same states preferred to consider slaves property rather than people. Nonslave states (in the North) would, of course, have an opposite point of view. The dilemma was solved by the curious technique of counting a slave as three-fifths of a person in both instances! In this fashion, the Constitution indirectly sanctioned slavery.[2]

In short, from the moment of its birth, America represented a paradox between the stated ideals and principles according to which the nation was to be organized and the practical realities of daily life. Had the Founding Fathers chosen to include blacks, women, and Native Americans in their

[1] The Sixteenth Amendment, providing for an income tax, modified this provision.

[2] The word *slavery* was not used, but the distinction among "free persons," "Indians," and "three fifths of all other persons" made the intention clear. See Article 1. Section 2 of the Constitution.

definition of the people by extending to them the full rights of citizenship, including the vote, the Constitution might never have been ratified and the United States would not have been created. There were potentially serious North-South divisions that compromises such as that just described attempted to smooth out for the sake of union. Yet anyone tempted to deify the Founding Fathers has only to contemplate this unusual compromise to recognize that they were, after all, mortals, attempting to deal with political reality.

Indeed, this conflict between ideals and practical reality remains with us today. Perhaps it will continue to trouble us as long as the United States exists as a political entity. For although the framers of the Constitution could claim to speak for the people, Americans were not then and probably are not now *a people* in quite the same sense that the French, the Italians, the English, or the Germans are a people.

In 1787 there were only 13 states and 3.9 million people (according to the first census of 1790) who made up the United States. Today, 50 states and over 240 million people make the United States one of the largest and most heterogeneous nations in the world. From an agricultural, rural country, we have matured into a highly technological, industrial, urbanized society. Modes of communication were slow in the eighteenth century, and other places in the world were remote. Today we have virtually instant communication around the globe and military commitments in most geographic areas of the world, and Americans have walked on the moon. These developments, together with the mounting problems and concerns mentioned in Chapter 1, force on us the question of whether or not our Constitution, the oldest written constitution in the world, is any longer viable.

Yet despite whatever lack of prophetic power characterized those now sanctified Founding Fathers of 1787, they were concerned with certain fundamental issues of political society that still confound us today: How does a large, complex society maintain order and yet uphold individual freedom? How much individual freedom should be allowed? How much direct rule should be accorded to the people (whoever they are)? How much—and what kind of—power should be allotted to a central government? How can a constitution ensure that excessive, or even arbitrary, power not converge in a single individual (like the president) or a single group (like the oil companies)? What is excessive power? And so on. These are issues as familiar to American students of the late twentieth century as they were to the American statesmen of the late eighteenth century.

Origins

The Constitutional Convention capped a period in American history that can be described as revolutionary. In breaking from the British Empire, the United States became the first colonial possession to achieve independence from the mother country.[3] Separation from England created a technical problem with which later revolutionaries would have to deal. Once the break was made, what was to be the legal basis for government? By what right would government govern? Before the Revolution, the source of political authority had rested in allegiance to the monarch in England. What now? This juridical dilemma was solved by the first large-scale use of what we call *constitutionalism*. The former colonies—in some instances simply revising their colonial charters slightly, in other instances making substantial changes—created written documents describing the functions and limitations of state governments. Such a practice had historical sanction in earlier "compacts" such as the Mayflower Compact and the Fundamental Orders of Connecticut, in which the members of a community gathered together to agree on the rules that would govern them.

The first nationwide constitution was the Articles of Confederation, proclaimed in force on March 1, 1781. Designed to provide a loose political union of the 13 independent states, the articles described the U.S. "confederation" as a "league of friendship." The central government had limited authority, and there was only one national branch: the Congress. Among the most debilitating restrictions on the Congress were the inability to levy taxes (which could be requested only from the states) and the lack of authority to coin money and regulate commerce. Although some scholars have argued that under the articles the new country was doing quite well,[4] there were problems. For example, Alexander Hamilton and others believed that the new nation needed a sounder and more sufficient currency, which could best be provided by a central government. Some people feared the consequences of trade wars among states that could establish tariffs against one another. Substantial citizens in the East became alarmed in September 1786 when Daniel Shays led a rowdy group of western Massachusetts farmers to the capital at Springfield to protest various government policies. Although the militia crushed Shays's Rebellion, the event convinced an increasing number of people that a stronger central government might be needed to restrain civil disorder. Finally, the confederate nature of the United States caused serious difficulty in the conduct of foreign affairs. For example, was John Adams, the American minister to London, to negotiate a trade agreement between England and the United States or between England and 13 separate states?

In September 1786, five states sent delegates to the Annapolis Convention to discuss problems of commerce. On the initiative of Alexander Hamilton, this convention extended an invitation to all the states to convene

---

[3]It might be argued that the Dutch revolt against the Hapsburgs in the sixteenth and early seventeenth centuries represented such a struggle, but in the context of our remarks, we may consider it an internal European political and religious struggle.

[4]Merrill Jensen, *The Articles of Confederation* (Madison: University of Wisconsin Press, 1940).

the next year for the purpose of devising ways to make the Articles of Confederation "adequate to the exigencies of the Union." Congress, petitioned by the Annapolis delegates to call such a convention, sensed the danger to itself if such a meeting took place. After considerable debate, it recommended that the states appoint delegates to meet in Philadelphia the following spring, but only for the "sole and express purpose of revising the Articles of Confederation." This injunction was ignored, for between May 25 and September 17, 1787, in a convention closed to public view, the delegates produced a brand-new document of government: the Constitution of the United States.

It would be a mistake to assume that the Philadelphia delegates met only in an atmosphere of fear of social unrest, trade wars, and deficient diplomacy. These men, relatively young, well educated, and prosperous, represented, in the best sense, professional politicians. None among them believed that a perfect government was possible or that there could ever be unanimous agreement on any particular provision of the Constitution. Yet for such men this was an extraordinary opportunity to wipe clean the slate of history and draw up as fine an instrument of government as their instincts, wisdom, and experience could create.

Various influences conditioned their thoughts. For one thing, these were men of property and wealth. George Washington, chairman of the convention and owner of a large estate in Virginia, was reputed to be the richest man in America. This kind of information has led some scholars to contend that the framers were not the virtuous patriots we learned of in grade school but were instead rich, elitist conservatives whose chief aim was to protect their economic interests and solidify their political power. Led by historian Charles Beard, who published his influential *An Economic Interpretation of the Constitution* in 1913,[5] this school of thought emphasizes that the founders opposed democracy. According to Beard, they held large amounts of Continental securities—pieces of debt paper circulated by the Continental government to pay soldiers and provide a circulating currency. These securities had depreciated in value, and the holders reasoned that a strong central government (with, presumably, a central bank) would redeem the securities at face value. Together with other conservatives who wanted a strong national government to check radicalism among poor farmers who owed them money, these men sought to establish a government designed to protect their elite status as well as their pocketbooks. Because local, popular rule was, by this theory, the chief culprit, it was best to create a strong central government, to guarantee the rights of property, and to gain for the propertied class a dominant position in the new government. This antidemocratic elitism, scholars like Beard have maintained, meant that the Constitution of 1787 actually represented a counterrevolutionary conspir-

[5]Charles Beard, *An Economic Interpretation of the Constitution* (New York: Macmillan, 1935, first published in 1913).

acy against the Declaration of Independence and the Revolution. In an age when wealthy and powerful oil companies, conglomerates, and enormously wealthy and influential people often play a dominant role in government, such a thesis has a certain attraction. But we must be cautious in imposing our present-day impressions (and/or prejudices) on the events of 1787. For one thing, the Industrial Revolution, which fundamentally altered American society and created some very rich and powerful people, was barely on the historical horizon in 1787. Additionally, if the founders had really wished to protect their propertied interests, why had they not included in the Constitution a property qualification for voting or even for holding public office? One might argue that they knew full well that the states would devise stiff property qualifications for political participation. But it was those states, the conspiracy theorists suggest, that were too radical for the Philadelphia "conservatives." Moreover, as historian Robert Brown showed in his severe criticism of Beard,[6] most men of the eighteenth century held enough property to meet any state's qualifications for voting. We should also note that by the 1820s most states had removed any property qualification at all. It is not legitimate to place a twentieth-century power-elite thesis on the events of 1787. Clearly, as we have noted, many people were left out of politics in those days. But sometimes quickly, sometimes too gradually, the framework created by the Constitution absorbed more and different kinds of people into the political process.

There were more important influences on the founders than the economic interests emphasized by Beard. First, these were men who had participated in a revolution. In this sense, certainly, they were not eighteenth-century conservatives.[7] They were literate, informed men, familiar with political thought dating from the ancient philosophers. Finally, they were men of the Enlightenment, a term that refers to the development of philosophical, political, and social thought in the eighteenth century. Impressed by English physicist Isaac Newton, who had postulated a law of gravitation, thinkers in the eighteenth century believed that there were cosmic "natural" laws governing human society as well as the physical universe. Newton's theory implied that the universe was in rational order. Many political thinkers believed that by the use of reason, a rational order could be discovered in politics as well. Enlightened human beings, they believed, could design a more perfect state, and the result would be human progress, just as an engineer might design a machine to make human labor more efficient.

The leadership of the Enlightenment was centered in France. Here the so-called *philosophes*, led by, among others, the satirist Voltaire and the

---

[6]Robert Brown, *Charles Beard and the Constitution* (Princeton, N.J.: Princeton University Press, 1956).

[7]An excellent short essay assessing the Founding Fathers is Stanley Elkins and Eric McKitrick, *The Founding Fathers, Young Men of the Revolution* (Washington, D.C.: Service Center for Teachers of History, 1962).

political theorist Montesquieu, began to apply the test of reason and observation to existing social, political, and economic institutions, often finding these institutions (like schools, churches, and governments) in need of serious reform, if not wholesale change.[8] The framers of the Constitution were well aware of the advanced thought of the Enlightenment, being intellectuals as well as practical businessmen, politicians, and lawyers.

Other influences were also present at the convention. Delegates considered the features of state constitutions, the practices established over a century and a half of colonial development, and, finally, the influence of the English political tradition of which they had recently been a part, which included the ideas of representative government, supremacy of law, and liberty of the subject.[9]

Thus the Constitution they ultimately drew up was rooted in at least three major sources: the abstract ideas of the Enlightenment, the practical experience of the colonies and the states, and the traditions of English law and government.

With these forces at work, the delegates arrived at Philadelphia. Edmund Randolph, governor of Virginia, introduced the first plan. Influenced by James Madison, this "Virginia" or "large-state" plan represented sweeping changes, and it became the basis of discussion for most of the convention. It provided for a central government with three branches: a legislature of two houses, a national executive (the position that ultimately became the presidency), and a national judiciary. The legislature would choose the executive (or executives) and the members of the judiciary, and representation from the states in the legislature would be according to population. The smaller states sponsored an alternative plan, the "New Jersey" or "small-state" plan, introduced by William Paterson. Much closer in spirit to the Articles of Confederation, its key difference with Randolph's scheme was the assumption that all states were equal in the union and that sovereignty rested in the states individually rather than in the people as a whole. Consequently, Paterson recommended that each state have equal representation in the Congress.

A compromise on July 16 resolved these conflicting views. The states gained an equal vote in the Senate, and representation in the House of Representatives was to be accorded by population. With this and some other disagreements settled, the delegates signed the Constitution and sent it to the states for ratification in special conventions.

Serious and long debates characterized many of these state meetings before the requisite nine states ratified the document to place it in effect. The *Federalist Papers*, written anonymously by Alexander Hamilton, James

---

[8]See Carl L. Becker, *The Heavenly City of the Eighteenth-Century Philosophers* (New Haven, Conn.: Yale University Press, 1932).

[9]Clinton Rossiter, *The First American Revolution* (New York: Harcourt Brace Jovanovich, 1956), pp. 7–10.

Madison, and John Jay, propagandized in favor of the new document. Circulated throughout the country and widely read by state convention delegates, the *Federalist Papers* not only aided the passage of the Constitution but also represented an important and scholarly discussion of constitutionalism. The new government commenced in early 1789, and by May 1790 all 13 states had ratified the Constitution.

The document thus approved had seven articles. The first three provided for and explained the branches of the national government: the legislature, the presidency, and the courts. Article 4 dealt with relations among states and between the states and the national government. Article 5 described how the Constitution could be amended, whereas Article 6 spoke to the nature of the union and the Constitution, which is described as "the supreme law of the land." Finally, Article 7 provided for the establishment of the Constitution upon the ratification of nine states.

Many Americans feared that the concentrated power of the national government would be manipulated to undermine individual rights. To prevent this from occurring, they insisted that a specific statement of the rights of individual Americans be included in the Constitution. In 1791 James Madison, distilling several reservations and recommendations from various states, drew up the first ten amendments, which the states quickly adopted. Called the Bill of Rights, these amendments are usually considered part of the original document.

Principles

It is important to remember that the Constitution created a *republic*. This word, which derives from ancient political theory and political practice, refers to a government in the common interest rather than a government of or for a person (a monarch or tyrant) or of or for a family or certain group of people. Thus the word *commonwealth* had a similar meaning in the eighteenth century. Republic has also come to mean a representative government.[10] Likewise, a constitution is frequently deemed necessary for a viable republic.

A constitution, by a definition deriving from 1787, is a written document that grants powers to and limits the authority of government (thus the notion of "limited government"), that defines the organs of government, and that explains the relationship between the government and the governed. One should read the U.S. Constitution. It is mercifully short and worthy of careful perusal. The essential principles contained in it are the following:

---

[10]The debate over whether the United States is a republic or a democracy can best be resolved by calling it a democratic republic. See Martin Diamond, *The Founding of the Democratic Republic* (Itasca, Ill.: F.E. Peacock, 1981).

The Pursuit of Happiness

1. Rule by law.
2. Popular sovereignty.
3. Separation of powers.
4. Checks and balances.
5. Judicial review.
6. Civilian supremacy in military matters.
7. Protection of individual rights.
8. Possibility of change.
9. Federalism.

Let us examine these with some care.

1. The principle of *rule by law* is an obvious extension of the definition of constitutionalism. Rather than have governmental actions take place at the whim and caprice of an individual or a special interest group, we expect rule by law and proper procedure. In this way the government is significantly limited. For example, if we are arrested for committing a crime, we expect to have a trial, to have access to legal help, and not to be incarcerated until and unless we have been clearly proved guilty. Also, a law cannot be proclaimed in effect by a president, a member of Congress, or an oil company. Rather, to become effective, it must pass both houses of Congress and be approved by the president. It must then be obeyed by all, unless the courts, following litigation, proclaim it unconstitutional.

A controversial example of this principle has to do with the so-called exclusionary rule. The Supreme Court has ruled that evidence illegally obtained by the police cannot be introduced in a trial (that is, it must be *excluded*). Thus the police, the upholders of the law, must also obey the law. Then, too, in the course of the Senate Watergate investigations, which were televised nationally in 1973, Senator Sam Ervin, widely reputed to be among the foremost constitutional scholars in Congress, rose at one point to challenge a claim by presidential assistant John Ehrlichman that he believed that the president had the power to order a secret break-in into the office of a Beverly Hills psychiatrist in the interests of "national security." Quoting an old English maxim, Ervin argued that even in the humblest dwelling of the poor, "The sun may enter, the wind may enter, but the King may not enter" without specific legal authority, that is, a warrant. Thus even a president is not above the law.

2. The principle of *popular sovereignty* is an integral part of the Constitution; yet it raises perplexing questions. The Constitution rests sovereignty in the "people," which is fundamental to the concept of democracy. Sovereignty means the greatest authority and power to command all others. Sovereignty resides somewhere in every stable national state. It may reside in a king (the "sovereign") or in a parliament. Under fascism, it rests in the state. Under the Articles of Confederation, it rested in 13 states. But the Preamble to the Constitution declares, "We the people of the United States of America . . . do ordain and establish this Constitution for the United

In response to the fears voiced by many that the federal government would prove oppressive, Congress passed on September 25, 1789, twelve articles of amendment to the Constitution. Except for the first two, the articles were ratified by the required number of states by December 15, 1791. The remaining ten amendments have subsequently been known as the Bill of Rights. The original is on display at the National Archives, Washington, D.C. *(Photograph by Steven Ross.)*

States of America.'' Perhaps this language was fortuitous; no one knew in what order the states would ratify, and so the Preamble could hardly say ''We the states of Georgia, New York, Pennsylvania . . .'' More important, the Founding Fathers had every intention of using this language. The notion of a compact among the people of a community had developed historically in the American colonies. (The Mayflower Compact is one of the best-known examples of this.) Moreover, the idea of a ''social contract'' among the members of a political society was a widespread and popular political theory in the eighteenth century. The most important social contract theorist for Americans was the seventeenth-century Englishman John Locke. In his *Second Treatise on Government* (1690), Locke explained that on balance, human beings were decent and good and that in an ideal state of nature they could live fairly happily. However, because virtually all people have certain needs that can be met only by an organized society, some

The Pursuit of Happiness

method must exist to bring about such a congregation. Earlier theorists, such as Englishman Thomas Hobbes, had argued that for the sake of order, individuals should convene themselves under the control of a single monarch who would be the ultimate sovereign. Locke's social contract was considerably different. Reasoning that human beings were, by nature, free, equal, independent, and reasonable, he believed that they came together by consent, retaining as much freedom as possible. Moreover, once this "contract" had established a society and a government, the latter could always be changed, preferably by majority rule but, if necessary, by revolution. The Founding Fathers, like Hobbes, certainly had grave doubts about the goodness of human beings, but, in the aftermath of a war against a "sovereign" king, they found altogether practical the Lockean notion of resting sovereignty in the people.[11]

Still, who are these "people" in whom sovereignty rests? Are they the people who can vote? If so, what about those who are not registered? And what about those who are registered but do not vote? Do the people include youths under 18? Women before their voting rights were obtained in 1920? Black Americans before the voting rights acts of the 1960s? Are some people more sovereign than others? In simple words, *popular sovereignty* is an important but difficult term. At its best, we can hope that it means an ever-improving democracy that seeks to draw more and more of the citizenry into the bloodstream of political decision making.

3. The doctrine of *separation of powers* derived from political theory as old as the classical Greeks and gained further credence in Montesquieu's study *The Spirit of the Laws* (1748). The founders, as we have seen, wanted to establish a government of energy and effectiveness, yet they also wanted to avoid concentrated power, for they feared power as much as they disliked governmental ineffectiveness. James Madison in *Federalist* 37 argued, "Energy in government is essential to that security against external and internal danger. . . ." Yet, at the same time, he worried about a majority faction gaining so much power that it would repress a minority or individuals. "A dependence on the people is, no doubt, the primary control on the government," Madison conceded in *Federalist* 51; but what if the people became a majority faction? Madison went on to say, "Experience has taught mankind the necessity of auxiliary precautions." Federalism, as we will see, was one mechanism to effect a dispersal of power. So too was the separation of functions at the national level among a Congress, a president, and a court system. This *separation of powers* was intended to deny "the accumulation of all powers, legislative, executive, and judiciary, in the same hands," which, according to Madison, "may justly be pronounced the very definition of tyranny" (*Federalist* 47).

[11]Richard Hofstadter, *The American Political Tradition* (New York: Random House, 1948), chap. 1. Locke suggested that the legislature would be the sovereign, whereas Hobbes implied that the executive would fill this role.

But what if different public officials in the different branches got together to consolidate their power? Or what if an overwhelming majority of voters brought such pressure on all three branches that the national government began to act in a tyrannical way against minorities or individuals? Separation of powers was certainly essential, but perhaps not enough.

4. A partial answer offered by the founders was the system of *checks and balances*, a significant codicil to separation of powers. The idea here was to create constitutional means to enable each branch to withstand the power of the others. Although none of the three branches would be fully dependent on any other, there would always be some restraining interdependence (for example, the president appoints Supreme Court justices with the consent of the Senate; the Congress can pass laws but the president can veto them; the Supreme Court can declare laws unconstitutional even if the president approves). Furthermore, to ensure checks and balances and to deprive any one class, interest, or faction of undue domination of the government, the personnel of each branch were to be chosen in different ways: the president by an independent electoral college, the judges by the president, the members of the Senate by state legislatures, and the members of the House of Representatives by popular vote. There have been some changes in these three branches, particularly in the methods by which their members are chosen. The president, though officially chosen by the electoral college, is actually elected by popular vote. In effect, this means that we vote for electors pledged to a presidential candidate rather than having a separate set of electors mull over and finally choose a president as the framers may have intended. Senators too are now chosen by popular vote rather than by state legislators.[12] Moreover, the rise of national political parties has, to some extent, modified the fragmentation of political power. This is because the president, senators, and House members of the same party often work together for common programs.

Despite these changes, the concern with curtailing excessive and concentrated power has continued to the present time. In recent history, this concern has focused on the presidency. For example, when President Nixon impounded funds appropriated by Congress (that is, neither signing nor vetoing legislation but refusing to spend monies authorized in bills duly passed by the House and the Senate), critics insisted that he had violated the separation of powers by unilaterally acting as the legislature. When President Carter in 1978 terminated a defense treaty with Taiwan, several senators argued that he could not do so without the concurrence of the U.S. Senate.[13]

Finally, one of the most contentious controversies regarding checks and balances occurred with the so-called *Iran-Contra* scandal. A few presidential aides, working out of the White House National Security Council, from

[12]See the Seventeenth Amendment, ratified in 1913.
[13]Federal courts ultimately upheld the president on this issue.

1985 to 1986 planned to sell U.S. arms to Iran and use the profits to fund the American-backed Contra rebels in Nicaragua. Some of this money apparently found its way to the Contras during a period when such aid was precluded by congressional act; that is, a foreign policy involving the selling of weapons to a nation hostile to the United States and the providing of funds to a guerrilla group in Central America was carried out without congressional approval or even knowledge. When revelations regarding this affair surfaced in the media, congressional critics were quick to assert that the activity may well have violated the principle of checks and balances.

5. The Constitution does not directly mention but does imply *judicial review*. Judicial review means the right of the federal courts to determine whether or not a piece of law, whether state or national, is consonant with the Constitution. The power to review state laws is implied in Article 6, Section 2: "This Constitution . . . shall be the supreme law of the land; and the Judges in every State shall be bound thereby, anything in the Constitution or laws of any State to the contrary notwithstanding." Thus, from the beginning, federal courts could determine the legitimacy of state laws and constitutions. The right to review national laws was established in the landmark case *Marbury v. Madison* (1803), when the Supreme Court unanimously struck down a section of the Judiciary Act of 1789, finding that it violated a provision of the Constitution. Although the right of the court to judge the constitutionality of federal law was thus established, it has continued to cause discord. Controversy reached a high point during the 1930s. Responding to the crisis of the Depression, the Congress passed several pieces of New Deal legislation some of which were declared unconstitutional by the Supreme Court during the court session of 1935. A tremendous uproar ensued, and President Franklin D. Roosevelt even introduced legislation to force the resignation of older justices and to expand the number of the Court so that he could appoint more liberal members. The Court survived this presidential onslaught and so did judicial review, which, ironically, was used in the 1950s and 1960s in rulings that many old New Dealers applauded.

In the landmark case of *Brown v. Board of Education* (1954), the Supreme Court, led by Chief Justice Earl Warren, in effect ruled that state laws providing for segregated education on the basis of race were unconstitutional. This action provided the legal basis for numerous challenges to the prevailing practice of racial segregation throughout the United States and helped launch a civil rights revolution (that is, efforts by American blacks and other minorities finally to achieve that equality implicitly proclaimed by the Declaration of Independence).

In our discussion of the system of justice (Chapter 6) we shall once again look at this principle of judicial review.

6. Deeply embedded in the Constitution is the principle of *civilian authority*, which means that military forces are subordinate to and separate from civilian administration. Military policy is to be directed by constitu-

tionally chosen officials, not by the military establishment. Article 2, Section 2 grants the president broad authority. The president (normally not a military person) is the commander in chief of the armed forces. The most celebrated controversy regarding this principle arose in 1951, when President Harry Truman, citing insubordination, dismissed General Douglas MacArthur when the latter openly demanded that the president's war policy in Korea be changed.

Of course, Congress as well as the president has constitutional responsibilities in the conduct of military policy. According to Article 1, Section 8, not only must appropriations for military activity come from Congress, but also only Congress can declare war. This provision has led a number of critics, in and out of the legislature, to argue that American participation in the war in Indochina was unconstitutional.

Finally, the Constitution makers decided to limit the appropriation of funds for a standing army to a two-year period, thereby mitigating the danger posed by the growth of a professional military class, which many believed to be a menace to republican government. Some critics warn that the dangers the Founding Fathers feared have become a permanent part of our society, because of enormous governmental expenditures for the military. Because even though Congress is responsible for overseeing military spending, it is simply unable to keep track of the hundreds of weapons programs and thousands of weapons contractors. Moreover, because it is in the interest of many members of Congress to obtain defense contracts for their districts, they may be less inclined to seek restraints on military spending and influence than what would be in the best interest of the nation.[14]

7. Perhaps the most audacious and certainly one of the most important principles of the Constitution is the *protection of individual rights*. Based on the concept of the dignity of the individual, this principle reverses the common notion that the individual is subordinate to the state and declares the most important characteristic of a just society to be the recognition of individual worth.

The original Constitution (Article 1, Section 9) forbade bills of attainder (the conviction of a person of a crime by formal congressional declaration) and *ex post facto* laws (a criminal law whose effective date precedes its passage). But the Bill of Rights contains the most sweeping and substantive protections. Included, among other liberties, are the well-known rights to freedom of speech and of the press, the right to a recognizable procedure in criminal law, and the freedom of religion. Each of the rights outlined in the Constitution is worthy of a lengthy dissertation, but noting just one, the

---

[14]See the discussion of the military-industrial complex in Chapter 9, "Who Rules America?" Also see the special report in the *Los Angeles Times*, "Servants or Masters? Revisiting the Military Industrial Complex," July 10, 1983, pt. 6.

freedom of religion, accents how advanced the framers were. Until 1787, no major Western state had ever had the courage or the inclination to separate the institution of government from the practice of religion. By forbidding all religious tests for officeholding and by separating church and state, the Constitution represented a significant milestone in the history of individual liberty.

Two relatively recent and hotly controversial applications of the principle of the protection of individual rights involved the career of the late Senator Joseph P. McCarthy and the publication of the Pentagon Papers by the *New York Times*.

In the case of Senator McCarthy, the Wisconsin legislator used his power as chairman of a powerful Senate subcommittee to issue subpoenas to dozens of Americans, many of them prominent in the arts, in government, and even in the military. Riding the crest of a wave of popular fear and hostility toward communism and all those who might have had some association with communists, the senator made himself a feared and controversial figure in Washington during the late 1940s and early 1950s. He used the power of investigation, exposure to maximum publicity, and inquisitorial "hearings" to drive prominent persons from public life. Many of McCarthy's victims sought refuge in various provisions of the Bill of Rights. For a while the term *Fifth-Amendment Communist* was widely used in the press to describe many of McCarthy's "witnesses," that is, victims who sought refuge in the constitutional prohibition against being forced to testify against themselves.

Only after McCarthy's investigations reached into the highest levels of the military command did President Dwight D. Eisenhower decide to challenge the senator's power. The Army-McCarthy hearings, broadcast live on television, were widely understood to be a test of power between the executive branch and the senator. They resulted in an erosion of the senator's popular support around the nation and a consequent move shortly thereafter to censure him in the U.S. Senate. Only belatedly did the nation come to realize that the weapons that McCarthy used to defame ordinary citizens could be and indeed were turned against the highest levels of authority, and if the rights of citizens could be violated with impunity, sooner or later so too could the rights of senators, generals, diplomats, and perhaps ultimately the president.

Another test of this principle (in this case, freedom of the press) came when Dr. Daniel Ellsberg, an employee of the Rand Corporation engaged in preparing a secret report on the origins of the U.S. government's decision to intervene militarily in the war in Vietnam, took copies of this secret document to the *New York Times* for publication. The *Times* announced its intention to publish these papers despite the official label of government secrecy. The Nixon administration sought to prevent publication. In a historic decision, the Supreme Court decided that the federal government had no right to "prior restraint" under the terms of the constitutional amendment guaranteeing freedom of the press; that is, the government could not legally censor such publication but could only wait until the offending material had been published and then take action against the newspaper, Ellsberg, or both. The *Times* published, and the government proceeded to prosecute Ellsberg. However, the constitutional merits of the case were never finally resolved, as the presiding judge dismissed all charges against Ellsberg because of various governmental improprieties.

8. As we have seen, sovereignty in our system theoretically rests in the people. It would follow that the people have a *right to change the Constitution*. Article 5 provides the mechanism to do just that. Still, changes have not come often. Indeed, following the approval of the first ten amendments, only 16 others have become part of the Constitution.[15] The normal procedure is for Congress, by a margin of two-thirds of those voting in each house, to approve an amendment. It is then submitted to the state legislatures, three-fourths of which must approve it (a majority vote being required in each legislature). It then becomes effective.

The Constitution provides two other methods for change. Congress may submit a proposal to special state conventions instead of legislatures (as was done in the case of the Constitution and the Twenty-first Amendment), or Congress, on the demand of two-thirds of the states, must call a convention to draw up amendments that would then be ratified by the states. The latter method has never been used.

Federalism

Federalism is a principle invented by the framers. Because in 1787 it was a unique form of government and because it affects almost all the other principles, it requires more lengthy discussion. *Federalism* is a dual form of government in which there is a functional and territorial division of authority. We can understand federalism by contrasting it with other forms of political organization.

The most common form of political grouping we term *unitary*. Such a government has no autonomous units: the ultimate governmental authority rests in a central government. In such a situation, policies can be applied uniformly to the whole country. Most nations today are unitary. In fact, each state in the United States is, in theory, a unitary government. Unitary government in no way denies popular sovereignty but merely means that there is *one level* of ultimate governmental authority: the central government.

[15]The Twenty-first Amendment revoked the Eighteenth—Prohibition. Thus there have been only 14 permanent amendatory changes since 1791.

An alternative form of political grouping is a *confederation* such as existed under the Articles of Confederation. The common central agency in a confederation may discuss policy and advise separate members, but it has no meaningful power. Each member unit (state, province, or whatever) retains ultimate governmental authority.

Federalism is a compromise between unitary and confederate political organization. In the United States, this means several things. First, there is a division of political authority (for example, the central government is responsible for coining money—the states cannot—whereas the states establish laws regulating marriage and divorce). Second, there are certain powers that both levels have, for example, the power to tax. Finally, the two levels can cooperate. The usual method by which this is done is through grants-in-aid, which are monies provided by the national government to the states to help finance a state program.

Although the Tenth Amendment leaves to the states "reserved" powers, these have never been adequately defined. Indeed, in explicit terms, the Constitution only limits state authority while granting no specific powers.

The Constitution would never have been adopted had not provision for state sovereignty been retained. One could argue that the framers sought a compromise and came up with federalism out of necessity. However, there is also evidence that the framers, particularly James Madison, had thought carefully about how to unify a large and possibly expanding area with outlying territories and a variety of interests. The key problem, as political thinkers of the eighteenth century saw it, was that a single faction or interest would almost certainly control the government. Consequently, as the widely read French political philosopher Montesquieu had suggested, a republic (a nonhereditary government reflecting the various interests in the state) could exist only in a city or a small territory. This reservation was based on the common assumption that nation states would be unitary. To solve this problem, Madison and the framers invented federalism, which dispersed political sovereignty geographically as well as functionally.[16]

But which of the levels of government—state or national—has *ultimate* sovereignty? Article 6 of the Constitution strongly implies that it is the national level. Most citizens, if asked, would probably agree. Many, in fact, might insist (perhaps unhappily) that the national government has over the years gained power at the expense of the states, some even contending that the states have lost power. Such is simply not the case. Since World War II, the fundamental trend has been for both levels of government to increase their activity. Indeed, in terms of expenditures, state governments have

[16]Several of the *Federalist Papers* explain the meaning and benefits of federalism. Also see Garry Wills, *Explaining America* (Garden City, N.Y.: Doubleday, 1982), and Douglass Adair, " 'That Politics May Be Reduced to a Science': David Hume, James Madison, and the Tenth Federalist," *Huntington Library Quarterly* 20 (August 1957): 343–360.

actually increased their activities more rapidly than has the national government since the end of the war.[17]

There is no doubt, however, that the national government has grown in power since 1787, in some instances at the expense of the states. There are many reasons for this. For one, the victory of the North in the Civil War determined clearly that the nation was one of the people more than it was one of sovereign states. Thus no state, at its own whim, could leave the union (as, presumably, a member of the United Nations could leave that organization). Second, the doctrine of *implied powers* has given the national government authority not expressly stated in the Constitution. The Supreme Court's decision in *McCulloch v. Maryland* (1819) established this doctrine. In 1816 the Second Bank of the United States received a federal charter. It opened a branch office in Baltimore under the cashiership of one James W. McCulloch. The state of Maryland (along with other states) looked unfavorably on the bank because the state wished to charter its own bank. The issue was complicated by the unsavory (though profitable) activities of McCulloch and certain directors of the branch office, whose practices one scholar has described as systematic "looting" of the bank.[18] Furthermore, there is evidence that opposition within the state of Maryland came chiefly from envious bankers there who wished to indulge in similar financially rewarding enterprises with state-chartered banks. In response to these latter interests, the state of Maryland enacted a law taxing the branch bank's bank notes—an attempt to drive it out of business. The imperturbable McCulloch simply refused to pay the tax and was in turn sued by the state, and the case went into the federal courts, arriving in 1819 before the Supreme Court. Now, Article 1, Section 8 of the Constitution accords no specific power to Congress to charter a bank. Chief Justice John Marshall ruled, however, that because the U.S. government had a right to exist and a right to collect money (the Constitution does specify the authority to tax), it should have a place to put that money; that is, the Congress could reasonably determine that the establishment of a national bank was "necessary and proper" for carrying out its constitutional functions. Such a power was not specified in the Constitution but was *implied*. Moreover, the Court's unanimous decision went on to declare Maryland's tax on the bank notes unconstitutional because in a federal system a state (though, of course, having the right to tax) could not cripple the national government in carrying out its legitimate powers. Thus the national government, by implication, had more power than those specified in the Constitution and the states could not interfere with those powers.

"The government of the union, then," concluded Chief Justice Mar-

[17]Walter W. Heller, "Balanced Budget Fallacies," *Wall Street Journal*, March 16, 1979, p. 22. Also see U.S. Department of Commerce, *Statistical Abstract of the United States*, 1978 (Washington, D.C.: U.S. Government Printing Office, 1978), pp. 256–257, 286–287.

[18]Bray Hammond, "The Bank Cases," in John A. Garraty, ed., *Quarrels That Have Shaped the Constitution* (New York: Harper & Row, 1964).

shall, "is emphatically and truly a government of the people. In form and substance it emanates from them, its powers are granted by them, and are to be exercised directly on them, and for their benefit."[19] Of course, the Civil War physically confirmed this principle.

A third reason for the expansion of national governmental authority is the *interpretation* of express constitutional powers. For example, Congress can tax and thus supposedly spend money, even for reasons as vague as "to promote the general welfare." Congress can "regulate commerce among the several states." In *Gibbons v. Ogden* (1824), the Supreme Court ruled that such "commerce" included all forms of commercial intercourse.[20] Thus the national government has enacted laws fixing minimum wages and maximum hours and regulating child labor in any business involved in interstate "intercourse."

Finally, the national government's powers have expanded because of constitutional amendments. For example, the Sixteenth Amendment, ratified in 1913, gives the national government the immense and specific authority to collect income taxes, and the Fifteenth, Nineteenth, and Twenty-sixth Amendments establish national guidelines for voting requirements (a function initially accorded to the states) by giving the right to blacks, women, and those 18 years of age and older. Each of these amendments gives Congress (that is, the national government) power of enforcement "by appropriate legislation."

Federalism seems to imply that each state will act independently of the other states as well as independently of the national government. In fact, cooperation and coordination among the various levels have become characteristic of the system. The *interstate compact* has come to be used to effect such cooperation. These compacts are designed to handle problems affecting two or more states. The Port of New York Authority is perhaps the best example of such a compact. It operates the harbor and coordinates the operation of airports in Greater New York for the states of the area.

Cooperation between the states and the national government is achieved mainly through grants-in-aid. First used in the nineteenth century, a grant-in-aid is a grant of money to a state to help finance some state activity, such as building a highway or providing welfare payments. The normal practice has been for Washington to place conditions on these grants: the money must be spent for a specific purpose; the state must meet certain federal standards (for example, money for education cannot be given to districts with segregated schools); and the state must match federal funds (for example, for every $9 the national government contributes to building a highway, the state must contribute $1). In recent years, both conservative and liberal critics have advocated an end to aid from the national government with strings attached, substituting instead direct grants with no federal

[19] 4 Wheaton 316 (1819).
[20] 9 Wheaton 1 (1824).

government requirements at all. This scheme has been called *revenue sharing*. Federal legislation now provides for some revenue-sharing funds, resulting in the flow of large sums of money into states, to be used however those states wish. Although revenue sharing has grown increasingly popular, there are criticisms, some of which have resulted in the retention of certain federal guidelines. Critics point to the grants to states of money that the federal government has collected, thus separating the taxing and spending agents, which might lead to less responsible expenditure. Others say that the system rewards inefficient states, such as those that refuse to enact a state income tax, knowing that they will receive large sums from Washington. Some city officials worry that state governments might not funnel enough of the money to urban areas. In response, Congress has legislated that two-thirds of the money must go to counties, cities, and towns. Civil rights groups raised fears that the money might be used to support segregated facilities, and Congress responded by making adherence to the civil rights laws a requirement of revenue sharing. Finally, some critics have suggested that the system is basically inefficient, that for every $3 the federal government collects for revenue sharing, only $2 makes its way back to the state. The remaining $1 goes to the bureaucracy collecting and then distributing the money. Despite these criticisms, revenue sharing remains popular. The federal government, mainly because of the income tax, can collect money from all citizens more easily than can individual states. Because the national government is the major source of money and because the states are in need of funds (and some cities are going broke), revenue sharing may be, proponents say, the most reasonable way to make federalism viable.

But does, or can, federalism really work as we approach the twenty-first century? Is tiny Rhode Island in any way similar or equal to Texas? Or is Alaska really comparable in any way to California, with its 25 million inhabitants? What kind of allegiance can we reasonably be expected to have to one state over any other? The major social aggregate with which most of us are familiar is the city (or megalopolis), not the state. People live, work, and identify with Greater New York or Greater Los Angeles. In fact, some have said that New York City is so different from the rest of New York that it should be a separate state. The city and its surrounding suburbs also pose such large and complex problems for America that they may perhaps be too complex for traditional states to handle. And what sense does it make to allow every state to have different laws regulating marriage, divorce, and a host of other things? Is it fair that a rich person can fly to Reno for a "quickie" divorce, whereas a poorer person must wade through a lengthy litigation or simply give up and live unhappily ever after? Or is it fair for a person who lives in New Jersey to commute to work in New York, yet pay no taxes there?

Of course, such criticisms will be leveled at federalism as long as it exists. However, there may be advantages that we do not wish to give up. Federalism offers a certain flexibility and possibility for experimentation not readily available in a unitary system. Most political and social reforms have begun in states and have later come to the national government. The direct, democratic election of U.S. senators is an example. Several states set the precedent long before the Seventeenth Amendment was added to the Constitution, and Wyoming instituted women's suffrage many years before the passage of the Nineteenth Amendment. Furthermore, an individual state may provide valuable examples for other states. California's creation in the early 1960s of a master plan of higher education established a model that many other states followed.

Finally, in a large and complex society, the principle of there being a government (however complex) that is closer to the citizen than Washington, D.C., is still quite attractive. This, after all, is something that Madison and the Founding Fathers knew, and that is why they invented federalism.

These, then, are the core principles of the U.S. Constitution. Noting them, however, does not explain everything about the Constitution. The document is short and frequently ambiguous, and scholars and politicians easily disagree over its meaning. Many recent questions highlight this disagreement. What, for example, under our Constitution, constitutes an impeachable offense by a president? Is busing a constitutional way to achieve racial integration in the schools? To these and many other questions, the Constitution may not offer a universally agreed-upon answer but rather only a guide to action for our institutions of government.

Four final points should be made regarding the Constitution.

First, it is a genuinely national document. In the dispute between "states' rights" and national power, the latter takes precedence. (Disagreement over this issue, of course, was a factor in precipitating the Civil War.) The history of the origins of the Constitution, briefly outlined here, underscores this point. So does Article 6, Section 2, which proclaims the Constitution and the laws made under it "the supreme law of the land."

Second, the Constitution was not completely satisfactory to anyone. In fact, Edmund Randolph, the sponsor of the Virginia plan, did not even sign the final draft. It was a compromise document, designed by well-informed, practical politicians who knew that much remained to be done to make the new government workable.

Third, the Constitution was revolutionary, both in technique and by its very nature. Its adoption was technically illegal because Congress had charged the convention only with amending the Articles of Confederation and because this latter document required unanimous approval among the states for any changes (recall that the Constitution provided that nine states' approval would put it into effect). Also, as the first major written constitution, proclaiming the principles of the most advanced and in some cases the most radical thinkers of the age, it can reasonably be called a major document of what one scholar has called the "Age of the Democratic Revolution."[21]

Fourth, the Philadelphia delegates and the members of the first governments formed under the Constitution had a freedom of action unmatched in present-day revolutionary situations. Since World War II, any colonial possession that has successfully separated from a mother country, no matter what the nature of its constitution, almost automatically had to look forward to some amount of "aid" or hindrance from other nations of the world. A striking example is the Congo (now Zaire), which, although gaining independence in 1960, experienced pressures and influence from Belgium (the former colonial possessor), the United States, the Soviet Union, and finally the United Nations, which stationed an international armed force there. Because of the long lines of communication and because Europe was soon (1789) to become absorbed in the French Revolution and subsequent wars, America was spared this kind of interference. Although a new state, born in revolution, America was able to develop independently. We can only speculate as to the positive effect this independence had on the system of government outlined in the Constitution.

Whatever its weaknesses (and we shall discuss some of these in ensuing chapters), the Constitution has accomplished its primary objective remarkably well. The country has held together for two hundred years under a single document. (France, in contrast, has had 14 different constitutions in the intervening years.)

Social critic Edmund Wilson noted that the United States is more a "society" than a "nation." (Alexis de Tocqueville made the same point.) By this Wilson meant that the United States, unlike most of the world's countries, is made up of different races and nationalities and that it lacks many of the institutions that characterize most nations. There are no established religions, no hereditary aristocracies, and few ancient traditions that are universally understood and honored. The Italian people, although achieving political unity relatively recently (1860), have a civilization that dates back twenty-five hundred years. Thus the Italians are often said to be indifferent to their government because they are bound together by religion, language, culture, and traditions that go far deeper than politics.

The United States in a sense is in the opposite condition. Divided by race, creed, and national origin, as well as by sheer physical size, Americans are dependent on organized government to maintain national unity and social cohesion. This suggests the importance in a Constitutional republic such as ours of promoting what Thomas Jefferson called virtue.[22] Also the Consti-

[21]R. R. Palmer, *The Age of the Democratic Revolution*, 2 vols. (Princeton, N.J.: Princeton University Press, 1959).

[22]See the Introduction. In the words of conservative columnist George Will: "By virtue I mean good citizenship whose principal components are moderation, social sympathy and a willingness to sacrifice private desires for public ends." From "In Defense of the Welfare State," *New Republic*, May 9, 1983, p. 25.

tution was designed to create a framework that would permit Americans to remain united while preventing any single faction, group, or class from seizing absolute control. Whether or not it has done so remains a question of moment. However, that we can continue to seek a just society with a people so diverse is in no small measure due to the gift of the Founding Fathers.

Thus the Constitution has evolved over two centuries to become a secular version of "holy writ" for Americans. For as Mosaic law provided the cement that bound together the ancient Hebrews and as the New Testament defines and unites Christianity, so the Constitution has become the definitive statement of American life and government.

4

The President: Shadow and Substance

- Leadership •
- Presidential Styles •
- The Nixon–Ford Presidency •
- The Carter Presidency •
- The Reagan Presidency •
- What Is the Presidency? •
- Precedents •
- Roles, Power, and the President •
- Checks: Real or Imagined? •
- The Milieu of the President •
- What's Wrong? •
- Democracy and the President •

> On some great and glorious day the plain folks of the land will reach their heart's desire at last, and the White House will be adorned by a downright moron.
>
> H. L. Mencken
> *On Politics*
>
> The President is a steward of the people, bound actively and affirmatively to do all he can for the people.
>
> Theodore Roosevelt

In 1983, the Gallup Organization interviewed 1,032 American adults, selected to represent a cross section of the American people, as to which of all American presidents of the past they wished were president at that time. The people's choice, by far, was John F. Kennedy, who was named three times as often as his closest competitor, Franklin D. Roosevelt. Well back in the pack were Lincoln and Washington, and Jefferson and Adams were not even mentioned.[1]

The poll, which generally confirms similar findings by other polling organizations, is richly suggestive of how Americans view the presidency and the role of the person who occupies the White House. The poor showing of eighteenth- and nineteenth-century presidents, mainly known to the people through history books, suggests that the great men of this era are now regarded as almost mythical figures whose virtues are largely irrelevant to the modern world. On the other hand, all those presidents who are known to the people through frequent appearances on television news or documentaries about recent history somehow seem more real and relevant.

The continuing and growing affection and esteem with which Kennedy is held by Americans is also instructive. Historians, political scientists, and scholars generally agree that Kennedy's career in the House and the Senate was mediocre, dedicated mainly to preparing himself for his successful bid for the presidency. As president, Kennedy's domestic record was modest, resulting in no great reforms or changes in American law or social programs. His foreign policy record was more controversial; his detractors blame him still for his cold war rhetoric, and his sympathizers give him credit for beginning to break away from the sterile clichés of the 1950s and starting the process of peacemaking through such achievements as negotiation of the first treaty with the Soviets banning the testing of nuclear weapons in the atmosphere. Certainly Kennedy's domestic achievements were not as remarkable as President Lyndon B. Johnson's Great Society;

---

[1]*Newsweek*, November 28, 1983, contains the poll and a cover story on the twentieth anniversary of President Kennedy's death.

The Pursuit of Happiness

nor did his foreign policy achieve the concrete results brought about by President Richard Nixon. And yet the people continue to cling to their belief that Kennedy was a greater man and a better president. For some reason, millions of Americans, and indeed more millions throughout the world, seem to feel that Kennedy touched their lives in a personal and meaningful way. All this suggests that Americans look to their president for something more than the ability to preside over a prosperous economy and a successful foreign policy. The president is the personification of the whole nation and that persona is known to Americans and to the world primarily through television. If, as in the case of Kennedy, that image is one of intelligence, compassion, commitment, and vitality and if, to paraphrase Rudyard Kipling, he can demonstrate the elegance, style, and "cool" of the aristocrat with an authentic concern for the well-being of the common people—in a word, what most people call "class"—then the nation sees itself as a bit larger than life, as better, perhaps, than it is.

History demonstrates that politicians, particularly if they are invested with the enormous power inherent in the American presidency, and even more if they happen to have the gift of moving people with words, can bring out the best and the worst in people. Adolf Hitler, Gandhi, Franklin Roosevelt, and Winston Churchill all lived in the same tumultuous times, and all had enormous gifts for moving masses of people—but for different ends.

The myth that has grown up around the life and death of John F. Kennedy, like that which grew up around Abraham Lincoln in the nineteenth century, was nourished by the capacity each man had for touching some deep idealism in the American people, suggesting that as individuals and as a nation we wish our lives and our work to contribute to some loftier and grander goal than personal comfort and well-being.

The president's real powers and policies may often appear less important than how well he plays the role of leader.

The paradox of President Reagan's relatively high ratings in the polls at the same time that a majority of Americans were registering specific differences with his tax and economic programs (which many labeled *unfair*), his expanded military budgets and his stationing of American marines in Lebanon and advisers in Central America (which most Americans regarded as unwise) illustrates this point.

Perhaps the answer to this seeming contradiction may be that the average American knows little about economic or foreign policy and knows that he or she does not know. Will the economy prosper more if business is taxed very lightly and social welfare programs are reduced, or will the reverse be true? Do high budget deficits cause inflation, as President Reagan argued vehemently before becoming president; or are they relatively unimportant, as his actions suggested after becoming president? Learned, Nobel prize-winning economists do not agree on these matters, and so how is the average citizen to decide? Is the B-1 bomber outmoded and simply a disguised form

President Reagan (at podium) with former presidents Ford, Nixon, and Carter as they set out to attend the funeral of assassinated Egyptian leader Anwar Sadat. (Los Angeles Times *Photo*.)

of welfare for the military-industrial complex or an essential element in modernizing America's defenses? Will deploying new and more deadly missiles make war more or less likely? Was President Reagan's "Star Wars" proposal simply another escalation of the arms race, or did it offer a great hope for peace and security? Scientists, military leaders, and diplomats disagree. How does one begin to judge?

Leadership

The question of leadership, therefore, is a critical questions of politics.[2] The leader normally makes decisions for the group. Should he or she fail to do so, he or she ceases to be the leader in fact, if not always in form. (There is a familiar joke among students of politics about the leader during the French Revolution who, from inside his apartment window, saw a mob marching through the streets, grabbed his coat, and rushed out the door. "Where are you going?" his wife asked. "To find out where the people are going so that I can lead them," replied the politician.)

What gives one person the right to make a decision that may shape the

[2]See James MacGregor Burns, *Leadership* (New York: Harper & Row, 1978).

lives of hundreds of millions of his or her fellow citizens? Some people—anarchists, libertarians, even proponents of direct democracy—affirm that no one should have such a right. But in history many groups have preferred or at least accepted an institution that—in one form or another—conferred the power to decide on a single individual. Attempts to rationalize the exercise of such power have revolved around what political scientists refer to as *legitimacy*. Among many political groups, as well as among most modern states, the authority that created and supported the power of the ruler was often thought to be divine. Moses was chosen by God to lead the people of Israel. Napoleon liked to tell his troops that he had extraordinary power to read their thoughts. He made it a point to expose himself to enemy fire in battle and had at least five horses shot out from under him but was never wounded. He did not discourage the soldiers' belief that this was because he was under some form of divine protection.

In the final analysis, leadership may be less important than *statesmanship*. There are a number of examples of leadership in history: Hitler led the Germans and Mahatma Gandhi led the Indians. But whereas Hitler led his nation to ultimate defeat and humiliation, Gandhi (using nonviolent means) led his people to independence from the British. A statesman may be a person whose leadership ultimately promotes the public good. Thus one dilemma of political society is how to form and maintain a governmental structure that will encourage statesmanlike leadership. This dilemma was certainly on the minds of the Founding Fathers.

Despite their unhappy experience with George III, the creators of the American political system perceived the need for a single person to serve as both the symbol and the leader of the new nation, and so they created the presidency. But because they feared that the president might assume kingly airs and powers, they limited his power. The right to declare war was reserved for Congress, along with the right to levy taxes and authorize expenditures and the right to override a presidential veto. Congress could impeach the president for "high crimes and misdemeanors." Later, more constraints on the exercise of presidential power were added, such as the two-term limit for any president, and more recently, Congress restricted the right of the president to sustain troop involvement in foreign lands without its sanction. The Supreme Court gradually acquired the right to strike down both presidential and congressional acts in the name of the Constitution and the law. The Constitution, not the president's will, is the supreme law of the land.

Yet, despite the clear intent of the Founding Fathers and the formidable barriers erected by Congress, the courts, and the Constitution, we have gradually developed what one scholar has called the "imperial presidency,"[3] that is, an office with such power and authority, such abilities to

[3]See Arthur M. Schlesinger, Jr., *The Imperial Presidency* (Boston: Houghton Mifflin, 1973).

act without restraint (especially in foreign relations), and such trappings of deference (the secret service, the White House press corps, instant television exposure, a large staff to command), that it resembles the emperor's position in ancient Rome. Indeed, the presidency of the United States is often described as the "most powerful office on earth."

This power seems to have accrued to presidents naturally and almost inevitably throughout the two centuries of the republic. Although most U.S. presidents, and almost all candidates for the presidency, have affirmed their personal and philosophical opposition to the concentration of power in the hands of one person, the office has grown in strength. A striking paradox was the presidency of Richard Milhous Nixon, who campaigned on the basis of limiting government power. But it was during Nixon's administration that the debate among Americans as to the proper limits of presidential power reached its climax. (The issue had been discussed at least as far back as Franklin D. Roosevelt's time.) Whether this debate and its fatal consequences for President Nixon's administration were simply a passing thing, an ephemeral response to a president who happened to rub too many people the wrong way, or whether they signified a profound and permanent change in American politics remains to be seen. The question is not merely academic, for how it is answered will surely affect the fate of the nation.

Presidential Styles

Styles in presidential leadership, like those in music or the length of women's skirts, seem to run in cycles. During the 1920s, for example, no one complained about an imperial presidency. During his three years in office President Warren Harding was criticized only for devoting too much of his time and attention to playing poker, drinking bootleg whiskey, and flirting with the White House chambermaids while some of his cronies, later dubbed the "Ohio Gang," looted the nation.

His successor, "Silent Cal" Coolidge, was honest and sober and a model of sexual continence, but perhaps overly fond of sleeping, to the point that he was given to taking little catnaps in the midst of cabinet meetings or other presidential business.

Herbert Hoover followed Coolidge and was widely perceived as doing too little too late to meet the challenge of the Great Depression.

After Franklin Roosevelt's four terms in office, most American presidents—with the exception of Dwight Eisenhower—took an activist role in both foreign and domestic policy. Harry Truman, John Kennedy, Lyndon Johnson, and Richard Nixon were very unlike one another as human beings, but they obviously shared a taste for politics and power, and each sought to reshape the nation and the world according to his own vision.

There are times, then, when the nation seems to need and want a strong leader, hence an FDR or a Kennedy. But there are other times when a cool, honest, and capable administrator suits the nation's temper, hence a Coolidge or an Eisenhower.

The Nixon–Ford Presidency

August 8, 1974, was a remarkable day in our history: for the first time a president of the United States resigned. Richard Nixon, who fewer than two years earlier had won reelection to the presidency by a remarkable landslide, left the office that he had craved, planned for, and fought to possess for almost two decades. (Nixon first won election to the vice presidency in 1952 and appeared on his party's presidential ticket no fewer than five times, making him the most durable politician in our history, with the single exception of FDR, who was also a five-time candidate for the presidency or vice presidency.)

As Nixon began his second term of office in the winter of 1973, his power seemed virtually unassailable. On his own authority he had authorized an invasion ("incursion") of Cambodia and the massive bombing of Laos. He had issued orders to the FBI, the CIA, and the Internal Revenue Service to use their police powers legally and illegally to harass his enemies. He impounded funds for various projects authorized by law and not vetoed. When Congress sought to investigate his actions, he cited "executive privilege" and issued orders to high officials in his administration not to cooperate with congressional committees seeking the information they needed to determine whether or not the president was acting properly and within the Constitution.

The president's disregard of the traditional American concept of a balance of power and his refusal to consult with, and in many cases even talk to, members of Congress (even one of Nixon's strongest supporters, Senator Barry Goldwater, complained that he could not reach the president on the telephone) or to members of his own cabinet, many of whom were effectively sealed off from the president by presidential aide H. R. "Bob" Haldeman's "zero-defect" system, confirmed for many critics that the presidency had in fact become imperial. But the imperial presidency was not always unpopular with the people. One month after he unilaterally ordered the carpet bombing of Vietnam, in December 1972, public opinion polls showed Mr. Nixon's popularity at an all-time high.

Both the march of events and the American constitutional system, however, soon undid this apparent omnipotence. In 1973 and 1974, the country began to feel the effects of both an unprecedented inflation and a sharp business downturn, which tended to erode Nixon's popularity. The second critical factor that began to undermine the Nixon presidency was the continuing Watergate scandal. Beginning as a simple investigation of what the Nixon administration had dismissed as a "fifth-rate burglary"—the break-in in June 1972 at the Democratic National Committee Headquarters at the Watergate Hotel in Washington, D.C.—the developing scandal soon went far beyond this, and *Watergate* became synonymous with a growing perception of the Nixon administration as lawless, arrogant, and arbitrary. Neither the Constitution nor the people called for a weak presidency. On the contrary, both seemed to require a strong chief executive who, together with his family, would serve as a symbol of the nation and whose voice would be decisive in national affairs. But neither the Constitution nor the people envisioned a president who, acting without consultation or formal authorization, would launch wars, order illegal acts, and seek to suppress public criticism of his actions.

By the summer of 1974, actions by both the Congress and the courts had severely checked the president. On July 24, the Supreme Court (containing four justices appointed by Mr. Nixon) unanimously rejected the president's contention that he could withhold 64 tapes subpoenaed by special prosecutor Leon Jaworski. Then, by the end of July, after the Judiciary Committee of the House of Representatives had agreed on three articles of impeachment, it became certain that the president would be impeached by the House and convicted by the Senate. Under the gathering storm, Mr. Nixon had little choice but to leave. Even under these extreme circumstances, with little or no important support left, there were fears that Mr. Nixon might resort to an unconstitutional seizure of power to maintain his presidency. A Nixon-appointed cabinet member, Defense Secretary James Schlesinger, sent secret orders to the armed forces designed to prevent a possible presidential coup.[4]

The end of the Nixon presidency highlighted a perplexing set of questions that had developed over the preceding decades: Henceforth, what should be the nature of presidential leadership? Should Congress now take a larger role in initiating policy? Did the president really have too much power? Or, paradoxically, did he have too little, particularly in domestic affairs? Had the imperial presidency finally come to an end?

In trying to answer these questions, the country turned to the new president, Gerald Ford. In style, President Ford was unlike his predecessor. He was a friendly, outgoing man, willing to listen. Much was made of his personal humility: the president was shown picking up his own newspaper in the morning and cooking his own breakfast. Mr. Ford had not even been elected vice president but had been appointed to the office by the now deposed Mr. Nixon less than a year earlier to replace Spiro T. Agnew, who had been forced to resign when evidence emerged that he had taken illegal payoffs while vice president! A more dramatic change in the presidency could hardly be invented by the most imaginative mind.

Overnight we had deposed a famous leader known for his toughness, his passion for privacy, and his record as a bruising political in-fighter, in favor

[4]See the Staff of the *New York Times, The End of a Presidency* (New York: Bantam, 1974).

The Pursuit of Happiness

of a man largely unknown to the American people but with a reputation among his colleagues and Washington commentators for being "a nice guy" in a profession in which "nice guys finish last."

So here was Gerald Ford, president by choice of Mr. Nixon, with no election and certainly no mandate, no normally understood sanction for action—in short, no "legitimacy" aside from a series of bizarre historical accidents. Was the presidency at its nadir? Were we to repeat the history of the late nineteenth century, when, following the assassination of a very strong president (Lincoln), the Congress became the leading branch of the national government? Was the imperial presidency dead? Certainly, with the collapse of the Nixon administration the tide seemed to have turned. Gerald Ford was, in certain ways, a throwback to the succession of Republican presidents in the late nineteenth century as well as in the 1920s.

In addition to the political problems facing unelected President Ford, he inherited a serious economic recession that, together with Watergate, resulted in sweeping victories by the Democrats in the 1974 congressional elections. Despite these problems and widespread disapproval of his decision to pardon President Nixon for any crimes he *may* have committed, Ford's calm, reasonable, and honest conduct of the presidency helped guide the nation through what might have been a terrible era, capped by our disastrous retreat from Vietnam.

In 1976 Ford defeated a challenge for the Republican presidential nomination from Ronald Reagan and was narrowly defeated by Jimmy Carter in a surprisingly close race. Like Harry Truman before him, Ford demonstrated that ordinary people, with few of the dramatic qualities that are normally associated with leadership at the highest level, can and often do serve the nation well.

The Carter Presidency

Jimmy Carter too, took a rather quiet, low-key—critics would even say "soft"—approach to the exercise of presidential power. He did not polarize friends and enemies, as Kennedy and Lyndon Johnson did. He did not reveal a grand, global strategy, as Nixon and Kissinger did. Rather, he attempted to deal with the nation's problems as they emerged—inflation, energy, the Panama Canal, the Middle East, the Soviet invasion of Afghanistan, the hostage crisis in Iran. Each of these problems was treated as a more or less discrete event. Characteristically, the president responded to these problems by gathering groups of experts together in the White House or at Camp David. After several days of listening, Carter then decided on a course of action that was prudent, moderate, and somewhere in the middle of the various extremes of opinion about what ought to be done or not done. (The most striking exception to the normal style of Jimmy

Carter's presidential leadership occurred when he brought the leaders of Israel and Egypt together at Camp David in 1978. It may have been his most glittering success.)

It is important to remember that Jimmy Carter came to the highest office in the land in the aftermath of Watergate, Vietnam, and the activist presidencies of Nixon, Johnson, and Kennedy. In many respects his election represented a backlash against a strong presidency. As he entered the White House, he had to confront a Congress less pliant than in the recent past and more determined to chart an independent course (see Chapter 5). Thus there was a certain irony in Carter's presidency that shortly became a liability: He was elected in part because he was an "outsider," one who was separated from the perceived venality of Washington, who could restore decency and modesty to the White House in place of the wheeler-dealer, too often corrupt, and excessively strong leadership of his predecessors; yet, because he was an outsider and because Congress was stronger, he seemed unable (and perhaps unwilling) to exert the kind of leadership necessary to carry out his campaign promises. In the spring of 1977 he announced an ambitious energy proposal (the focus of his legislative program), but it took 18 frustrating months before finally emerging from the Congress, a considerably different document from that he first envisioned. Meanwhile his young White House aides (Hamilton Jordan, Jody Powell, and others), only recently arrived in the capital, irritated veteran politicians with their lack of understanding of the ways of Washington. The president's position was made even more difficult when one of his closest advisers, Bert Lance, was forced to resign from the Office of Management and Budget in the face of alleged misconduct in his banking business. Meantime, proponents of a strong military criticized his decision to abandon the B-1 bomber, and those opposed to the arms race disapproved of the increased defense spending and the president's support of the M-X missile. Others simply found the president unable to make up his mind on major issues, such as defense, détente, or confrontation with the Soviet Union, and accused him of an inability to develop coherent policies. Politically more omnious still was the steady and alarming increase in the inflation rate, which by early 1980 had approached an annual rate of 20 percent. During the summer of 1979 Carter attempted to reenergize his faltering administration by means of a wholesale change in his cabinet, but still inflation soared while the president's popularity plunged.

All this notwithstanding, by 1980 the Carter administration could cite some significant accomplishments: Unemployment had been significantly reduced; a comprehensive energy bill *had* passed (the first in history); and later additions to the energy program began to make their way through the Congress; by early 1980 the Congress finally approved the president's plan to deregulate petroleum and impose a massive windfall profits tax on the oil companies; two new departments—energy and education—were created, fulfilling campaign promises; Congress passed the president's civil service

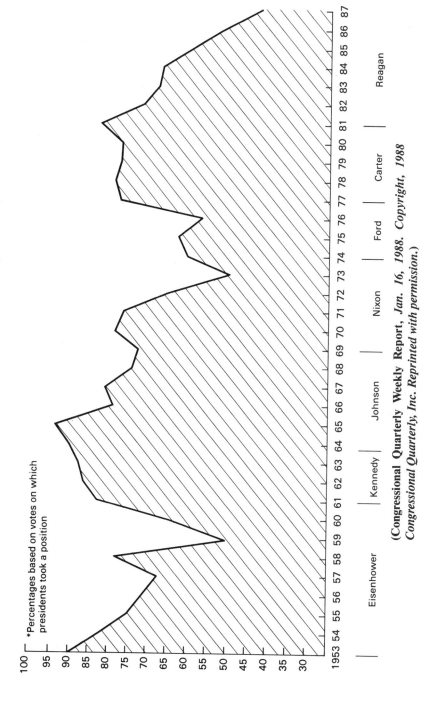

PRESIDENTIAL SUCCESS ON VOTES, 1953-1987*

*Percentages based on votes on which presidents took a position

(Congressional Quarterly Weekly Report, Jan. 16, 1988. Copyright, 1988 Congressional Quarterly, Inc. Reprinted with permission.)

The President: Shadow and Substance

reform bill; and the president moved diligently toward a balanced budget. Indeed, the relations of President Carter with Congress were, given the resurgence of congressional independence, reasonably good.

In foreign policy, too, the Carter record was mixed. His most notable achievement may be that in the four years he was president, America did not become embroiled in foreign wars or "police actions" (as in Korea, Vietnam, and, more recently, Lebanon). As one result, fewer Americans died at the hands of an enemy during the Carter era than in the administration of any other modern president. This was not an accident; it happened because Carter and his principal foreign policy advisers avoided military confrontation whenever possible. The negative side of this policy is that it permitted many of Carter's critics, such as Ronald Reagan, to claim that America had become weak and impotent in the face of a growing threat from the Soviet Union and its friends.

In his role as peacemaker, Jimmy Carter guided Israel and Egypt to sign the landmark Camp David peace accords in 1978, perhaps the most significant move thus far toward peace in the explosive Middle East. Carter also managed to win Senate approval of a revised Panama Canal treaty, probably avoiding years of conflict and possible warfare over that sensitive issue; and in 1979 he announced the historic recognition of the once-feared People's Republic of China.[5]

Peaceful achievements are, almost by definition, less exciting, and hence less memorable, than is conflict. Carter's greatest defeat, and likely the wound that was to prove mortal in his bid for reelection, was, to an extent, self-inflicted.

On November 4, 1979, radicals in Teheran, Iran, occupied the American embassy and took the Americans in it hostage. The government of Iran, which had promised the United States it would protect its embassy personnel, instead endorsed the act and issued a series of ransom demands, the most important of which was that the United States hand over its former ally, the deposed shah of Iran, for trial and inevitable death at the hands of the vengeful Iranians. At the time, President Carter was engaged in a primary battle for his party's nomination with Senator Edward Kennedy. The polls showed Carter far behind. Carter thereupon chose to make the Iranian hostage problem the overriding issue of that election year. He announced that he would not campaign but instead closed himself in the White House to deal personally with the "emergency" on a virtual round-the-clock basis. American and allied diplomats were sent scurrying all over the world seeking to make a deal that would release the Americans. News bulletins and "leaks" were fed to the press on a daily—sometimes hourly—basis. The network television companies were encouraged to go to Iran for

---

[5]But the SALT (Strategic Arms Limitation Talks) agreement with the Soviet Union, which Carter considered a priority item, was not ratified by the Senate, and the president removed the treaty from consideration following the Soviet invasion of Afghanistan.

　　　　　　　　　　　　　　　　　　The Pursuit of Happiness

on-the-spot interviews with the captives, under the watchful eyes of the Iranians. Nothing, of course, could have delighted the Iranians more, as their primary object was to show their contempt for the "Great Satan"— America—and to demonstrate America's impotence.

At first the barrage of publicity had the predictable effect. Americans traditionally rally around the president in times of crisis, and the imprisonment of the 50 or so Americans had been deliberately escalated into the most important issue in the world. Carter's standing in the polls improved, and that spring he won several primary victories over Senator Kennedy. But in the end, as so often happens with foreign policy crises that are exploited for short-term gains, the president's inability to win release of the prisoners probably played a critical role in his defeat by Ronald Reagan.

None of this, of course, was necessary. Americans have been taken hostage by unfriendly foreign forces at other times in our history without these incidents' becoming matters of overwhelming national or international crisis. For example, when the crew of the *Pueblo*, a U.S. naval ship, was captured and imprisoned by the North Koreans during the Vietnam War, President Lyndon Johnson sought to cool rather than inflame public reaction. Eventually the sailors were released through quiet diplomacy. Few regarded the affair as a gross stain on American honor. Diplomats, military personnel, and even private business people who venture into countries clearly hostile to the United States are always at some risk. Indeed, some are killed, and some are taken prisoner. This is regrettable but unavoidable, as the only alternatives are to have no contact whatsoever with unfriendly countries or go to war every time someone is brutal to an American, which would mean that we would be at war more or less permanently.

Thus it is ironic that one of the most peaceably inclined of all the men who have occupied the presidency was, to paraphrase Shakespeare, stabbed by his own sword.

A fair assessment of the Carter presidency should not omit what may become his most important contribution to American foreign policy: his dedication to human rights. Throughout his administration, Carter insisted on making known his displeasure with governments that repressed, murdered, tortured, and imprisoned their opponents, muzzled the press, and gave their people little or nothing to say about the conduct of affairs. This policy helped restore some of the moral authority lost to America during the Vietnam War, and it properly highlighted an essential difference between the democratic West and the totalitarian East. But it also angered the Soviet Union, probably making progress on arms reduction and other aspects of the policy of détente more difficult. It encouraged radicals to overthrow despotic but pro-American regimes in Iran and Nicaragua. Early in his administration, President Reagan, a frequent critic of Carter's human rights policies, indicated that the policy was being abandoned. Reagan's UN ambassador, Jeane Kirkpatrick, distinguished between "authoritarian regimes" that were favorable to our side, like Argentina, which may have systematically murdered thousands of opponents but could not be considered to be all bad because they permitted freedom of religion, and totalitarian regimes, like the Soviet Union, which suppressed both political dissent and religious practice. The distinction was not much appreciated by a world tired of murderous tyrants, whether they wore the hat of commissar or colonel, and gradually President Reagan seemed to become more receptive to a policy that did not simply divide the world into our side and theirs, with the implication that ours were the good guys. Carter's commitment to the idea of human rights as a fixed value of American foreign policy, therefore, seemed likely to endure.

The Reagan Presidency

Ronald Reagan assumed the office of president proposing to make the most sweeping changes since the administration of Franklin D. Roosevelt. However, the economic and political realities facing the country in 1981 were much different from those of 1933. Roosevelt had taken command of a stricken nation in which millions were unemployed, thousands of banks had collapsed and more were going under each day, hunger—even starvation—was commonplace, and the stock market was a wreck and business demoralized. Roosevelt was swept into office along with a party that had overwhelming control of both houses of Congress. The press and the public were largely united behind the new administration.

President Reagan was elected by a substantial but hardly overwhelming number of voters. He actually received only half of all the votes cast, and almost half of those who could have voted chose not to. The Democrats remained the majority party, controlling the House by a wide margin and narrowly losing control of the Senate. The press was, on the whole, skeptical of the former movie actor turned politician. The country faced serious economic problems, specifically high interest and inflation rates, but nothing remotely comparable to those of the 1930s.

Despite these and other formidable obstacles, the president succeeded in getting most of his domestic program through Congress. In essence, the president's program lowered taxes for business and wealthy people, reduced government programs of aid for the poor, and sharply raised spending on military programs.

In financial terms the net effect of all this was to make some Americans a great deal richer. (Senator Edward Kennedy, for example, asserted that Reagan's tax cuts, which he had opposed, had increased his income by $250,000 per year.) This was the logical and deliberate consequence of the philosophy of "supply-side economics" (see Chapter 12 on economics), which held that by increasing rewards and reducing restraints on the "suppliers" of economic goods, everyone would be better-off.

The benefits of supply-side economics, however, did not become immediately apparent to ordinary Americans. Although both inflation and interest rates did come down, the most immediate effect of "Reaganomics" was to plunge the nation into the worst recession since the 1930s, with soaring unemployment, a record number of business bankruptcies, and widespread suffering, particularly by the poor, who saw their jobs disappear at the same time that governmental "safety net" programs became more porous and, in many cases, nonexistent.

By 1983, however, either the medicine began to work or the natural health of the economy reasserted itself despite the doctors. The economy turned up, business profits soared, and Wall Street rushed to new records of optimism. Unemployment dropped, although it remained significantly above the level of the Carter years until late in 1984. The Reagan administration claimed, with some credibility, that its program had set America on the road to recovery after years of decline caused by the excesses of the welfare state. The major flaw in an otherwise bright economic picture for the administration were the staggeringly high budget deficits, which came about inevitably as the result of combining major tax cuts with substantial increases in military spending, just as Jimmy Carter had said they would. Whether these budget deficits portended some future disaster or were simply a matter of bookkeeping, with no real importance for the future health of the economy, remained for economists to dispute and the future to judge.

The Reagan years also brought about some significant changes in the power relationships of various segments of the American population. In the early months of his first year in office, Reagan was faced with an illegal strike by the nation's aircraft controllers' union. Reagan told the union members, all of them government employees, that they could either go back to work or be fired. They did not, and the union was broken. This was, deliberately or not, a signal to major corporations all over the nation. Henceforth the government would not look with disfavor on efforts by corporate management to reduce the power of unions. Through the recession years of 1981 and 1982, many unions found themselves negotiating not for the accustomed annual raises and increases in fringe benefits but for actual reductions in pay and benefits.

Reagan's foreign policy began with the premise that the Carter years, and to some extent those of Nixon and Ford as well, were a time of growing American weakness and Soviet strength. Therefore Reagan's first priority as president was to increase sharply the size and scope of America's military forces. Accompanying and, to a certain degree, complementing the military buildup was an escalation of anti-Soviet rhetoric. Describing the Soviets as the masters of "an empire of evil," Reagan made his foreign policy seem simple and clear: most of the world's troubles, from terrorism in the Middle East to revolution in El Salvador, could be traced to the Soviet Union. Therefore America's policy would be anti-Soviet virtually everywhere and on virtually every issue, while building up our armed forces to the point that the Soviets would be forced either to spend themselves into bankruptcy trying to stay in the race or to change their wicked ways.

A rapid buildup of American military forces, accompanied by a far greater willingness to use force, characterized Reagan's first years in office. American aircraft bombed Libya, U.S. forces invaded Grenada, a "peace-keeping" force of U.S. Marines sustained hundreds of deaths as the result of a terrorist bombing in Lebanon, and there was a steady escalation, both covert and overt, of American involvement in Central American civil wars. These acts, along with Reagan's fiery anticommunist rhetoric, dominated the nation's foreign policy during an era that could be called Reagan I.

In 1984 former Vice President Walter Mondale challenged Reagan's bid for reelection. Mondale offered the nation a less truculent foreign policy, higher taxes for the wealthy, and more generous treatment of the poor. He particularly criticized Reagan's failure even to meet with his Soviet counter-part—the first American president since FDR not to have done so.

Running on a program that stressed that Reaganomics was working and that he helped the nation regain its self-respect and "stand tall" after the humiliating Vietnam War and Iranian captive episodes, Reagan was swept into office again by winning 49 of 50 states.

Reagan II was another matter, in some ways almost a mirror opposite of Reagan I. The overall economy continued strong through Reagan's second term, but there was a growing number of homeless and the booming econ-omy did little or nothing for the poor. Budget deficits soared almost beyond belief while Reagan adamantly refused to consider tax increases, par-ticularly for those who could most afford them. A massive trade deficit developed that, combined with the need to borrow money from foreigners, principally the Japanese, to finance the budget deficits, led to many of America's most valuable property and powerful corporations being sold to overseas investors.

In October 1987 the stock market crashed and there were widespread fears of another 1930s-style depression (fears that did not materialize, in part, because of lessons learned from the crash of 1929).

Reagan's second term was rocked by the Iran-Contra scandal, which led to disclosures of a curiously "laid back" style of Reagan White House management. The president insisted he simply did not know about, or could not remember important events, while National Security Adviser Admiral John Poindexter and Lt. Colonel Oliver North were engaged in subverting the law of the land and his own often repeated vows never to pay ransom to terrorists for the release of American hostages.

There was a good deal of skepticism about Reagan's avowal of lack of knowledge until the publication of a whole series of "kiss and tell" books by former high administration officials in the following year. Among the authors of these books were former chief of staff Donald Regan, former presidential aide Michael Deaver, and former press secretary Larry Speakes.

A common theme ran through all these books, reinforcing the findings of the Tower Commission, which had investigated the Iran-Contra affair, and earlier books by former secretary of state Alexander Haig and former budget director David Stockman. In sum they presented a nearly unanimous picture of a president who was a wonderful person, much admired by all who knew him, but who seemed wonderfully ignorant of and/or indifferent to the day-to-day business of running the government.

Regan, to cite but one example, complained that in his years as secretary of the treasury—perhaps one of the two or three most important jobs in the government—he had never once met alone with President Reagan to discuss the nation's economic policies. The president carried the theory of nondirective management to hitherto unimagined length.[6]

Offsetting these "negatives" was what one Reagan administration official described as "the capstone" of the Reagan presidency—his series of meetings with Soviet leader Mikhail Gorbachev. Reagan, who in two decades of public life had opposed every arms-limitation treaty negotiated by both Republican and Democratic presidents, signed a treaty eliminating medium-range missiles in Europe and began negotiations for a sweeping 50 percent reduction in all nuclear weapons. Perhaps more important, he and Gorbachev seemed to set the stage for an entirely new and better US–USSR relationship in the years ahead. These moves were widely applauded in the United States and around the world. Europeans, accustomed to thinking of Reagan as a gun-slinging embodiment of John Wayne westerns, now saw him as man of peace, goodwill, and wry humor. On the other hand, many of those who had most ardently championed Reagan I were bitterly disappointed. Conservative columnist George Will suggested that in the future it might be better for confirmed cold warriors to vote Democratic, because a Democratic president could never win Republican support for more arms reduction treaties with the Soviets.

Reagan's two terms in office were characterized by a spectacular lack of tenure on the part of his closest and most important appointees. In eight years Reagan was served by four different chiefs of staff and no fewer than six national security advisers.

Summing up the Reagan years may well prove more taxing to future historians than the administration has been to its wealthy admirers. They have been years of prosperity and poverty, of peace and war, lofty rhetoric and low standards.

[6]The major "kiss and tell" books, a phenomenon unique to the Reagan administration, were: Terrel H. Bell, *The Thirteenth Man: A Reagan Cabinet Memoir* (New York: Free Press, 1987); Alexander M. Haig, Jr., *Caveat: Realism, Reagan and Foreign Policy* (New York: Macmillan, 1984); David A. Stockman, *The Triumph of Politics: The Inside Story of the Reagan Revolution* (New York: Avon, 1987); Michael Deaver, *Behind the Scenes* (New York: William Morrow, 1988); Larry Speakes, *Speaking Out* (New York: Scribners, 1988); Donald T. Regan, *For the Record: From Wall Street to Washington* (New York: Harcourt Brace Jovanovich, 1988).

What Is the Presidency?

The modern presidency has three basic components. First, it is defined in and has developed from Article 2 of the Constitution. Second, it is a product of historical forces. Finally, it is a reflection of the people who have held the office and the precedents that they have established.

The Constitution defines the presidency in the following manner.

The presidency exists as a separate branch of government, unlike the parliamentary system currently favored in most European democracies. A prime minister is, in a sense, the leader of his or her party in parliament, the "first among equals." Presidents, on the other hand, have no formal, binding relationship to their party. In this sense, they are free to act with greater autonomy.

Thus the president can be only one person (as Lyndon Johnson was fond of reminding his opponents, "I'm the only President we have"), and his election is not tied to the election of the legislature. The president serves for a fixed term, four years, and could have been, until adoption of the Twenty-second Amendment, reelected indefinitely. The president's powers are specifically detailed by the Constitution, and these are different from those given to Congress. Some authorities claim that the phrase "the Executive power shall be vested in the President of the United States of America" is much broader than the specific powers allocated to the president (see the section entitled "Roles, Power, and the President" in this chapter). Furthermore, there is no "council of revision" with the power to overrule the president, although this was a common feature of state government at the time of the Constitutional Convention, and some members advocated that it be included. Finally, the president or any member of his administration is precluded from serving simultaneously in either house of Congress. This again tends to reinforce the "separateness" of the presidency.[7]

Clearly, these decisions, embedded in the Constitution, create a presidency of considerable strength, and certain historical forces have added to that strength.

First, the economic developments that changed the United States from an agrarian, rural society into a highly industrial, technological, and urban society have influenced the presidency. Independent farmers have less need for strong leaders than do urban populations. Also, particularly in the twentieth century, there have been increasing demands on government to control and/or ameliorate the problems associated with industrialization and urbanization. This growing reliance on government has resulted in legislation that has hastened the expanding power of the federal government, particularly that of the presidency. Think, for example, of the growing bureaucracy designed to deal with such problems: the departments of

[7]Clinton Rossiter, *The American Presidency* (New York: Mentor Books, 1956), pp. 56–59.

The Pursuit of Happiness

The Presidents	
George Washington	1789–1797
John Adams (Federalist)	1797–1801
Thomas Jefferson (Democratic-Republican)	1801–1809
James Madison (Democratic-Republican)	1809–1817
James Monroe (Democratic-Republican)	1817–1825
John Quincy Adams (Democratic-Republican)	1825–1829
Andrew Jackson (Democrat)	1829–1837
Martin Van Buren (Democrat)	1837–1841
William Henry Harrison (Whig)	1841
John Tyler (Whig)	1841–1845
James K. Polk (Democrat)	1845–1849
Zachary Taylor (Whig)	1849–1850
Millard Fillmore (Whig)	1850–1853
Franklin Pierce (Democrat)	1853–1857
James Buchanan (Democrat)	1857–1861
Abraham Lincoln (Republican)	1861–1865
Andrew Johnson (Union-Republican)	1865–1869
Ulysses S. Grant (Republican)	1869–1877
Rutherford B. Hayes (Republican)	1877–1881
James A. Garfield (Republican)	1881
Chester A. Arthur (Republican)	1881–1885
Grover Cleveland (Democrat)	1885–1889
Benjamin Harrison (Republican)	1889–1893
Grover Cleveland (Democrat)	1893–1897
William McKinley (Republican)	1897–1901
Theodore Roosevelt (Republican)	1901–1909
William Howard Taft (Republican)	1909–1913
Woodrow Wilson (Democrat)	1913–1921
Warren G. Harding (Republican)	1921–1923
Calvin Coolidge (Republican)	1923–1929
Herbert Hoover (Republican)	1929–1933
Franklin Delano Roosevelt (Democrat)	1933–1945
Harry S Truman (Democrat)	1945–1953
Dwight D. Eisenhower (Republican)	1953–1961
John F. Kennedy (Democrat)	1961–1963
Lyndon B. Johnson (Democrat)	1963–1969
Richard M. Nixon (Republican)	1969–1974
Gerald R. Ford (Republican)	1974–1977
Jimmy E. Carter (Democrat)	1977–1981
Ronald Reagan (Republican)	1981–1989
George Bush (Republican)	1989–

Labor, Agriculture, Health and Human Services, Education, and Housing and Urban Development; the Federal Energy Office; and more. This elaborate bureaucracy is under the direction and command of the president. (For a discussion of *bureaucracy*, see Chapter 10.)

A second historical force affecting the president has been the growing involvement of the United States in international affairs and foreign wars. As late as 1938, America belonged to no military alliance, had no troops stationed in any foreign country, and had an army of fewer than 200,000 with a budget of less than $500 million. At the peak of the Vietnam War, on the other hand, the United States had 1.5 million soldiers and sailors stationed in over one hundred countries, military alliances with 48 nations, and a defense budget of about $80 billion.[8] This whole diplomatic and military operation is presided over by the president, in some instances directed solely by him.

A third historical factor affecting the presidency has been the rapid growth of the country in both its geography and its population, and it has devolved upon the president to be the national representative of this large area. There are members of Congress, mayors, governors, and state legislators; but the personage around which controversy swirls is the president. We all can focus on him. Harry Truman's famous remark that "the buck stops here" is a simple explanation of the truism that when the most important and fundamental decisions are made, they are made by the president. That fact suggests enormous responsibility and enormous power.

Also, the presidency is a highly democratic office. That is, the president is the only person chosen from the electorate of the entire nation. The extension of the suffrage to women, minority groups, and eighteen-year-olds has created the largest and perhaps the most unwieldy political constituency in history. It is, nevertheless, solely the president's.

Precedents

Certain leaders who have held the office have, by initiative and innovation, created an image of what the office is. Recent presidents have been more inclined to justify their actions by pointing to the precedents of their predecessors than they have by pointing to the Constitution.

Important individuals who have influenced the office are George Washington because he was first and because his precedents (such as the origin of the cabinet and the traditional two-term limit) have the most sanctity; Thomas Jefferson because he was Thomas Jefferson and also because he was the first president to become the political leader of a political party; Andrew Jackson, who ostensibly proved that a commoner could be president, because he considered himself the "voice of the people" and showed what could be done with the veto (he used it more times than did all previous presidents combined); and Abraham Lincoln because he led the country

---

[8]Stephen E. Ambrose, *Rise to Globalism* (Baltimore: Penguin Books, 1983), p. 13. The 1988 defense budget was about $300 billion.

through its most trying crisis (and because he is the closest thing to a religious/mythical figure we have).

By the end of the nineteenth century, certain patterns of behavior had been established for the president. He was expected to run for two terms only (Washington, Jefferson, Madison, Monroe, Jackson, Grant, and Cleveland all served eight years, and McKinley was elected to a second term but was assassinated). The president was the leader of his party but was not expected to be the chief initiator of legislation, as is the case today. Several early presidents had first served as secretary of state, a post that seemed to be a stepping-stone to the presidency (Jefferson, Madison, Monroe, John Quincy Adams, and Van Buren), but by the end of the century this practice no longer obtained. Only three early presidents (John Adams, Jefferson, and Van Buren) were elected after serving as vice presidents (several, of course, have assumed the higher office following the death of the incumbent), and it has not been until recent times that the vice presidency has been considered an appropriate training ground for the presidency. High-ranking military figures were frequently elected to the office (Washington, Jackson, W. H. Harrison, Taylor, and Grant, and Civil War veterans Hayes, Garfield, B. Harrison, and McKinley). In the twentieth century this tradition has applied only to Theodore Roosevelt and Dwight Eisenhower, both war heroes with high military rank.[9]

Following Lincoln's death in 1865, the presidency declined in authority. Andrew Johnson, who assumed the office after Lincoln's assassination, was impeached by the House of Representatives and barely avoided being removed from office by the Senate. Congress took over unilateral direction of Reconstruction (policies to end the Civil War, bring the South back into the union, and establish legal rights for black citizens) and became the dominant branch in the national government. Johnson was succeeded by several presidents who could not be characterized as strong executives.

Theodore Roosevelt's ascendancy to the White House, as a result of the assassination of McKinley in 1901 (Roosevelt was vice president) began the modern, twentieth-century presidency. Roosevelt, a vigorous and popular leader, believed that the president should be the steward of the people and that the office was a platform from which to teach and lead. He became the national leader of the so-called Progressive Movement (a reform movement to democratize politics and increase the role of the government in economic affairs), an active diplomat (he won the Nobel peace prize for negotiating peace between Japan and Russia in 1905), an imperialist (his government "took" Panama from Colombia in 1903 and began construction of the canal there), and the first celebrity president (his picture appeared regularly on the front pages of the newspapers, and his activities continued to be major news even after he left the White House).

Two other twentieth-century presidents have influenced the office most

[9]Several presidents served in the military, but those listed were either generals or colonels.

spectacularly. Woodrow Wilson was very influential. Using his expertise as a Ph.D. in history and political science and with a Democratic-controlled Congress, he effected a greater body of domestic legislation than had any president before him. More important, Wilson led us into our first European war *with allies* and then told us and the world that we were morally superior to those allies and sought a different and better peace settlement. His vision of international order, with a world government on the lines of American democracy and led by the United States, has affected America's perception of its place in the world from that time forward. Wilson was a strong, religious, charismatic, and sometimes unbending man. His notions of international affairs were at first rebuffed in the United States, but by the end of World War II, they had become sacrosanct principles of our foreign policy. The strong image that he imprinted on the executive office should not be underestimated.

Even more important than Wilson was Franklin Delano Roosevelt, who led the country through the Great Depression and World War II, in the process breaking the two-term tradition and serving as president longer than anyone. A master of politics, he also proved himself adroit with the new technological device of radio. The enormous bureaucracy that is our government today began under FDR to fight the Depression and Germany. (For a fuller discussion of the bureaucracy, see the discussion in Chapter 10.) Some people during and even after his lengthy incumbency associated interchangeably the presidency and Roosevelt. Some political scientists have even argued that in the aftermath of Roosevelt, the notion of a "textbook President" developed, overemphasizing the beneficence, competence, and near omnipotence of the office.[10]

Thus, to recapitulate, the modern presidency is a combination of Article 2 of the Constitution, historical forces, and precedents established by individual presidents. All these have led to a certain general perception of the president's role in American life.

Roles, Power, and the President

Each of us assumes certain roles at different times in our lives, sometimes at different times in the same day. At times we are a son or a daughter, at times a student, a teacher, a wife or a husband, a boss, a lover, a best friend, and many more. These roles carry with them expected behavior. For example, someone's expected actions as a student in a classroom differ from the same person's expected actions as a lover. The combination of all roles a person plays is his or her total behavior.

---

[10]Thomas E. Cronin, "Making the Presidency Safe for Democracy," *Center Magazine*, September-October 1973, pp. 25–31.

Any individual who becomes president assumes unique roles that make up the total behavior of the presidency as an institution. Many of these roles are mandated by constitutional law and by historical precedent. Moreover, in virtually every instance, these roles represent power—rarely if ever a position of subservience.[11]

The constitutional roles of the president are the following:

He is the *head of state*, that is, he is the ceremonial head of the government, just as a king or a queen would be. He grants pardons, receives ambassadors, and holds state dinners. Presidents Reagan and Kennedy, for example, performed this function with great success. Presidents have frequently complained about the amount of time that such ceremonial functions take away from other duties. And yet, as has been noted in *Newsweek*, "ceremony is essential to the magisterial awe that surrounds the nation's highest public office, and a powerful weapon in any Chief Executive's political arsenal."[12]

Second, the president is charged by the Constitution to be the *chief executive* of the United States. According to the first line of Article 2, the executive power is vested in the president. He is responsible for taking care "that the laws be faithfully executed." As a consequence, the president, explicitly or implicitly, has the powers of appointment and removal, and as the administrative head of government, he directs the federal bureaucracy.

The president is the *chief diplomat*. Authority over the State Department, negotiation of treaties and executive agreements, recognition of governments, and appointment of diplomatic personnel are some of the responsibilities of the president as the chief minister of foreign affairs. Presidential power has increased enormously during the twentieth century as a consequence of this authority.[13] Moreover, despite considerable controversy regarding the conduct of foreign policy during the last months of Nixon's tenure and despite large Democratic majorities in both houses of Congress, the White House with a Republican president still evinced great power in the field of diplomacy. The conclusion of an important Egyptian-Israeli agreement in 1975 under the guidance of Secretary of State Henry Kissinger was indicative of this. A more dramatic example was the indefatigable personal diplomacy of President Carter in bringing about the Camp David peace accords between Israel and Egypt. Clearly, the president is still expected to be the chief diplomat.

The Constitution designates the president as the *commander in chief of the armed forces*. During wartime, as was the case in the Civil War, this power expands tremendously. Today the president, as commander in chief, has at his command the Defense Department, the Joint Chiefs of Staff, the

[11]See Thomas E. Cronin, *The State of the Presidency*, 2nd ed. (Boston: Little, Brown, 1980).

[12]"King or Country," *Newsweek*, September 8, 1975, p. 65.

[13]Aaron Wildavsky, "The Two Presidents," *Trans-Action*, December 1966, pp. 7–14.

National Security Council, the Central Intelligence Agency, an enormous army, the most powerful navy and air force in history, commitments all over the globe, vast nuclear power, and a little red box containing a telephone ready to alert the whole defense establishment to a nuclear war. Simply in technological terms, this is enormous power. (It should be noted that in the War Powers Act of 1973 Congress limited presidential initiative by setting a 60-day limit on the president's power to wage undeclared war. This was in response to American involvement in Indochina, where the United States participated in a decade-long war conducted by Presidents Johnson and Nixon with no formal congressional declaration of war. In 1983, Congress, with the concurrence of the president, invoked the War Powers Act for the first time, limiting the stay of U.S. marines in Lebanon to 18 months. The president subsequently removed these forces before the time limit was up.)

The president holds the position of *chief legislator*.[14] From the constitutional mandate to "from time to time give to the Congress information of the state of the union, and recommend to their consideration such measures as he shall judge necessary and expedient" (Article 2, Section 3), the president has become the chief lawmaker. He is responsible for presenting the annual budget to Congress, and he is expected to introduce and seek the passage of a legislative program. Of course, Congress can (and perhaps sometimes should) successfully restrain the president. For several years presidents periodically refused to spend funds appropriated by Congress and not vetoed by the executive. The legislature became particularly irritated in the early 1970s, charging President Nixon with abusing this practice. In 1974 the House and Senate passed the Congressional Budget and Impoundment Control Act that provided mechanisms for congressional disapproval of such impoundments and also improved congressional procedures for handling budget and tax legislation.

One of the president's prerogatives as chief legislator is his authority to *veto* legislation (veto derives from a Latin term meaning "I forbid"). Every bill or resolution passed by Congress must be approved or disapproved (vetoed) by the president. Congress can override the veto only by a two-thirds vote of both houses, and fewer than 6 percent of all vetoes have been overridden. The president can also use the "pocket veto." This takes place if within ten days before adjournment Congress passes a bill and the president merely ignores it, neither approving nor disapproving it. In this case the bill does not become law. It should be emphasized that the president is expected to initiate a great deal of legislation. President Reagan, for example, supported major tax bills in 1981 and 1982. He then worked diligently with Congress and saw his tax program passed relatively quickly by both houses.

There are other roles, not precisely mandated by the Constitution, that the president has assumed. He is, for example, the *head of his political*

[14]See Stephen J. Wayne, *The Legislative Presidency* (New York: Harper & Row, 1978).

Reagan delivers the State of the Union Message to Congress. *(Bill Fitz-Patrick, The White House.)*

party. He is nominated by a party and elected largely on the efforts of that party. He chooses his own vice president, he selects the chairperson of his political party, he campaigns for members of his party, and (especially when his party is a majority in Congress) he works with the party to pass his legislative program. During his first years in the White House, President Reagan worked well with Republican members of the House and Senate, and Republican candidates for office frequently sought the president's open support and hoped he would campaign with them. Such popularity among the president's own party had not been so evident with Carter or Ford.

Some observers have called the president the *tribune of the people*, or the spokesman for the country. In a society of such political diversity as ours, this is a difficult task, but certainly no one else can speak for the whole nation. When the country found itself all but prostrated by the Great Depression, newly elected President Franklin D. Roosevelt seemed to accept personal responsibility for leading the people back to prosperity. His efforts were not altogether successful or always wise, but the people responded to his evident concern for their welfare by electing him to an unprecedented four terms. John F. Kennedy, an attractive and charming figure, used television as FDR had used radio—to establish a personal rapport with millions of Americans who admired the leader, whether or not they agreed with his policies. President Dwight D. Eisenhower likewise seemed to enjoy an abiding sense of the people's faith in his good judgment throughout his administration, so that even when his opponents opposed his policies or programs, they were careful to avoid criticizing him personally.

Other responsibilities of the president might include *maintaining domestic order*. Lincoln's suppression of the Southern rebellion and Eisenhower's sending of troops to Little Rock, Arkansas, in 1957 to enforce court-ordered integration are examples of this.

The president, especially since the 1930s, has been held *responsible for the economic health of the country*. The Employment Act of 1946, which virtually makes it illegal to have another depression, established the Council of Economic Advisers to be used by the president to preserve the economic well-being of the country, and the Humphrey-Hawkins Act of 1977 (calling for a reduction of unemployment to 4 percent and a cut in inflation) further underscored this responsibility. Whether a person is an economic conservative or an economic liberal, he or she tends to praise or blame the *president* for price stability or inflation, high or low employment, and the general health of the economy.

Emerging concerns in the area of the environment and energy have given the president other responsibilities. President Carter apparently accepted the new roles of *protector of the environment and administrator of energy*. Carter's support of a cabinet-level energy department and his comprehensive energy proposals are examples of this.

These roles represent a vast reservoir of power. In fact, given the economic, technological, and war-making strength of the United States, it is clear that today's president is the most powerful person in the history of the world. Alexander the Great, Napoleon, and Hitler would surely have envied such power.

Does this vast array of power represent a form of despotism that would frighten our Founding Fathers? Or are the restraints on presidential authority adequate?

Checks: Real or Imagined?

There are both constitutional and institutional checks on the president. Constitutional limitations include the four-year term, qualifications on the power of the veto, and the ban on the third term.

There are also institutional checks, of which Congress is the most important. Intended as a coequal branch with the executive, Congress has the important power of appropriating or not appropriating whatever money the national government needs or whatever the president wants. Congress must approve all new agencies of the bureaucracy; Congress, after all, makes the laws that the president will carry out. Congress can investigate presidential actions and can impeach and remove the president from office. Congress can override a presidential veto by a two-thirds vote of both houses. The Senate must approve appointments by the president and all treaties (by a two-thirds vote). And theoretically, only Congress has the right to declare war. Of course, presidents can circumvent these checks. Nixon, for example, authorized the invasion of Cambodia in 1970 without congressional sanction, and he impounded funds duly authorized by Congress. On the other hand, Congress was on the verge of impeaching the president at the time of his resignation.

President Reagan's policy of supplying military aid to the Nicaraguan rebels, called Contras, was a continuing source of conflict during his two terms in office. Congressional Democrats, who controlled the House during all of Reagan's presidency and the Senate in his last two years in office, rejected the president's policy of trying to topple the Sandinista government by force, using the Contras as a kind of proxy army, supported and controlled by the United States.

Congress, always hesitant to confront a popular president on a matter of national security, vacillated, now voting funds to support the Contras, then banning such aid through passage of the Boland amendment, attached to a continuing resolution, which directly outlawed direct or indirect aid to the Contras. (This act played a major role in the Iran-Contra scandal.) Responding to a peace proposal by President Oscar Arias of Costa Rica and under the leadership of House Speaker Jim Wright, Congress agreed to nonmilitary assistance to the Contras while the warring sides discussed a possible peace early in 1988.

On this and other issues Congress and Reagan supporters repeatedly clashed over matters of defense spending and foreign policy. Reagan's spokesmen argued that the Constitution clearly makes the president the nation's chief architect and implementor of foreign policy. Congress insisted that it too had a constitutional role to play. The president is the commander in chief of the armed forces. But only Congress has the right to declare war, appropriate funds, and, in the case of the Senate, approve treaties. The issue, therefore, is moot because in this as in so many other questions, the authors of the Constitution seem to have had in mind a system of shared power.

Another institutional check is the judicial branch. However, the courts rarely hamper presidential power. Exceptions to this rule are the steel seizure case in 1952 (*Youngstown Sheet and Tube Company v. Sawyer*), which denied President Truman the power to take control of a steel plant during the Korean conflict, and *U.S. v. Richard M. Nixon* (1974), which denied Mr. Nixon's claim of executive privilege in withholding tapes.

Other potential checks include periodic elections, which, however, might increase a president's power by giving him an apparent mandate (as in the presidential elections in 1964 and 1972) as well as check him by increasing the strength of the opposition party (as in the 1986 elections).

The federal bureaucracy represents a restraint of sorts simply because of its enormous size and occasional inertia. This is particularly true for active presidents, such as John Kennedy, who found himself frustrated by the executive bureaucracy.

The political system itself may represent a check. The opposition political party keeps up a fairly constant criticism of the administration, and even in his own party the president sometimes must make concessions to achieve harmony.

The press represents another, very important check on the power of the presidency. As the war in Vietnam dragged on, one version of that war was presented to the American people by the Johnson and Nixon administrations, and quite another was presented by newspaper and television reporters who were covering the day-by-day events. The government's story was that we were successfully helping a gallant ally defend itself against a cruel foreign invader. Certain sections of the press told the people more and more that we had involved ourselves in a civil war between factions and that the side we were supporting was weak, corrupt, and often unwilling to fight. More important, they told us that the war was simply not being won. Ultimately, the people had to choose between believing the "official" presidential view of the war or the picture presented by the press. In this struggle, the press—not Presidents Johnson or Nixon—ultimately proved to be correct.

Even more dramatic was the confrontation between the press and President Nixon. Nixon, never a favorite of the media (although ironically, he was invariably supported by the great majority of newspapers in all his bids for public office), developed an intense dislike for the press and clashed openly with reporters on television. Later, the press certainly played an instrumental role in forcing the nation to deal with Watergate and Iran-Contra as serious national scandals (see Chapter 11).

Finally, public opinion may represent a check, but the nature and depth of this restraint are difficult to analyze. The president has enormous manipulative powers over public opinion. He is always front-page news. He can call a presidential press conference or make a public speech whenever he

EXECUTIVE OFFICE OF THE PRESIDENT

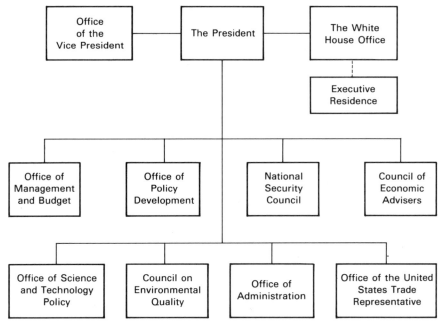

Source: U.S. Government Manual, *1987–1988.*

wishes and command a large audience. Yet even the most active president cannot lead the people outside the realm of common expectation.[15] This may explain why FDR was unable to pack the Supreme Court in 1937, why Richard Nixon encountered so much hostility in the last year of his presidency, and why Iran-Contra shocked so many Americans.

The Milieu of the President

Powers and restraints are not the whole story. There are important conditions that make up the milieu of the modern president and that influence the effectiveness of presidential leadership. Think, for example, of the awesome structure of the presidency. It includes 14 cabinet departments; the White House staff, including special assistants, aides, and the press secretary; the National Security Council; the Council of Economic Advisers; the Office of Management and Budget; and many more.

It is estimated that the president is personally involved in the selection of

[15]Harold J. Laski, *The American Presidency* (New York: Grosset & Dunlap, 1940), Chap. 1.

The President's Cabinet	
Department	**Year Established**
State	1789
Treasury	1789
Interior	1849
Agriculture	1862
Justice	1870
Commerce	1903
Labor	1913
Defense (replaced War Department)	1947
Health and Human Services	1953
Housing and Urban Development	1965
Transportation	1966
Energy	1977
Education	1979
Veterans Affairs	1989

perhaps the top two hundred officials in the executive branch. These are "the president's men," sometimes shadowy figures, little known to the public but nevertheless wielding considerable power (such as Reagan aides James Baker, Edwin Meese, and Michael Deaver). Others are better known, such as President Nixon's national security adviser, Henry Kissinger. Because the nature of the presidency tends to isolate the president from access to the kind of easy give-and-take of opinion that many Americans are exposed to in the course of their work, school, or social lives, members of the president's "inner circle" often have enormous power simply because they can and do control the flow of information and the people that go into the Oval Office. Some observers have noted that as a consequence of this inner circle, presidents are becoming increasingly remote from the real world. How can a president accurately assess a problem and reach a solution when he is surrounded by sycophants and when those who disagree with him are excluded from his councils?[16]

A second condition in the environment of the modern president has to do with the technological advances in communications. The age of radio, television, and instant news means that the president's image can be projected instantaneously before millions of people. This may give him great manipulative power. It also means that his image may become more important than the substance of his acts. It is essential that he appear resolute, firm, dominant, and responsible, never soft or uncertain. President Reagan has performed within this environment expertly and with relish.

The world is much more complex today than ever before. Nuclear weap-

---

[16]George E. Reedy, *The Twilight of the Presidency* (New York: World, 1970).

onry, rising nationalism, economic interdependence, and energy problems around the globe all affect America. The president's environment, unlike that of the rest of us, is the whole world, and he must live in it and be aware of it every day.

At the same time, American society has grown more, not less, complex. The president's constituencies are many and vociferous, as can be seen in the rising demands of women, minorities, youth, labor, environmentalists, and others. All this, too, surrounds the president.

It is understandable that dealing with this environment would be difficult, and it has been made more difficult by certain excesses and secretive actions during the war in Vietnam and the cover-up of the Watergate activities that created in the public mind a cynicism regarding any statement emanating from the White House. President Ford, obviously aware of public suspicions of presidential deception and overstatement, removed the normal hyperbole from the 1975 State of the Union Address. "I must say," he told Congress, "that the state of the union is not good." He had bad news, he said, "and I don't expect much if any applause." Such humility helped gradually restore faith and credibility to the White House during Ford's two years in office. President Carter was plagued less with suspicions of his credibility than with a lack of confidence that he could do anything about serious problems. For example, although polls showed that most Americans believed him to be honest and hardworking, it mattered not what he *said* the government would do about inflation; the price level still continued at a very high rate well into 1980. Thus, to a certain extent, cynicism regarding the honesty of the White House had turned into frustration that the presidency was unable to handle major challenges to the nation.

The problem reemerged in almost comical proportions during the Reagan administration. Throughout his administration the president was fond of delivering off-the-cuff remarks to the press or making formal statements in public speeches that turned out to be factually wrong or in flat contradiction to the stated policies of his own administration. It was commonplace for the White House to issue "clarifications" of presidential remarks that, in effect, said the president had not meant what he plainly said. The problem was compounded by revelations in various books published by resigned presidential aides and advisers to the effect that the president had little information and less interest in a variety of national and international issues, including a statement by Reagan's former press secretary Larry Speakes that noted that trying to brief Reagan for a press conference was "like reinventing the wheel." The Tower Commission made the same point.[17]

The question of how well informed a president or vice-president need be

[17]See *The Tower Commission Report* (New York: Bantam, 1987), especially pp. 79–83.

emerged again with the nomination of Senator Dan Quayle as Vice-President Bush's running mate in the 1988 campaign. The day of Quayle's nomination by the GOP convention in New Orleans, the *Los Angeles Times* noted that he had received a "D" in Political Science as a college student. The article also quoted a former professor as noting that Quayle was the perfect embodiment of an old educational cliché, "C students run the country."

Clearly intellectual achievement and wide knowledge about current problems and affairs are not major criteria for choosing potential American presidents. But should they be?

Another condition that has come to be part of the president's daily life is the threat of assassination. President Ford's brushes with death in California in September 1975 and President Reagan's encounter in 1981 only highlight the striking fact that in fewer than one hundred years four presidents were assassinated (Lincoln, Garfield, McKinley, and Kennedy), many others were shot at, and candidates for the office are in constant danger. Within the political consciousness of readers of this book are the political assassinations of John F. Kennedy, Robert F. Kennedy, and Martin Luther King, Jr., and the attempts on the lives of George Wallace and Presidents Ford and Reagan. Moreover, Gerald M. Kaplan, director of the National Institute of Law Enforcement and Criminal Justice, says that the number of potential presidential assassins is on the increase.[18]

The issue of assassination raises the further question of stability in the presidency. In fact, stability and order may be mythical, and the real condition may be impermanence. Consider, for example, the presidents of the twentieth century. Only *two*, Dwight Eisenhower and Ronald Reagan, served an actual, normal two terms. Theodore Roosevelt assumed the presidency on the assassination of McKinley, and although he won his own election in 1904, he retired in 1908 and then was unsuccessful in a try for reelection in 1912. William Howard Taft served one term and was defeated in 1912. Wilson was elected twice but was totally disabled by a stroke midway through his second term. Harding died in office. Coolidge, who succeeded him, won election in 1924 but was snubbed by his party in 1928. Hoover was defeated for reelection in 1932. Franklin D. Roosevelt broke all precedents by winning four terms but then died in office. Truman, who succeeded him in 1945, won election in 1948 but was very unpopular in 1952. John F. Kennedy was assassinated. Lyndon Johnson carried the country with a landslide in 1964 but was almost politically impotent by 1968 and unable to run for reelection. Nixon resigned during his second term. Ford was defeated. Carter lost his bid for a second term. Thus, contrary to popular conception, there is no stable, normal tradition for the presidency.

---

[18]Robert J. Donovan, "Alone in the Crowd . . . with a Gun and a Goal," *Los Angeles Times*, September 11, 1975, Sec. 2, p. 7.

What's Wrong?

Given all that has been said, what, specifically, is wrong with the presidency, and what, if anything, can be done about it? Is the structure of the office acceptable, does it need to be changed, or do we simply need to find the right person for it?

The process of nominating and electing a president has often been cited as a problem. What makes a successful candidate in modern American politics may not always make a good president. More and more of the process of "selling" a presidential candidate to tens of millions of Americans has become a matter of "sell the sizzle instead of the steak"; that is, sell the "image" of the person that you think most people will approve of rather than the real human being with both virtues and shortcomings. Many Americans were shocked to discover the disparity between the real President Nixon, as revealed by the publication of the contents of taped presidential conversations (even after the more colorful epithets were deleted), and his carefully contrived public image. President Lyndon B. Johnson, according to the testimony of those who served him, was a vain, crude, domineering, colorful, and earthy man who, among other things, loved to collect and tell stories about the sexual improprieties of famous politicians. The public image he sought to project was of a wise, tolerant, experienced, and selfless leader. The real Lyndon B. Johnson may have been a more interesting and a greater person than the public LBJ was, but most of us never really knew much about him until after his death.

In all probability, the sort of person that the public seems to want its president to be—a sort of super Boy Scout leader, YMCA secretary, and pillar of rectitude—would not dream of running for the presidency in the first place and could probably not be elected if he did. Presidents are not supposed to be human. It is not permissible for them to have an eye for pretty women, as JFK and FDR certainly did, or like to swear, as LBJ and Nixon did. Harry Truman was a skilled pianist who liked classical music, but in public he had to keep playing "The Missouri Waltz," which he privately disliked. And even Eleanor Roosevelt objected when her husband showed a strong interest in good food, as she thought that a president should have more important things to think about.

The practice of manufacturing presidential images is not new and certainly was not invented by Madison Avenue, but it has apparently become more important in recent years than the candidate's prior public service. Whereas past presidents usually served in the national legislature or were elected directly from their governorship of a large state, many recent candidates hold no public office and spend all their time campaigning. Examples include Jimmy Carter in 1976 and Ronald Reagan and George Bush in 1980. This phenomenon led Howard Baker, an unsuccessful candidate for president in 1980 (later President Reagan's chief of staff), to comment wryly that a person needs to be unemployed in order to be successful in presidential campaigning. An additional concern, given the nature of modern elections, is that being a good *candidate* for president is not the same as being a good president. Yet to get to the office one must be successful only at the former (see Chapter 8 for further discussion of elections in America).

Certain critics find that a major defect in the presidency rests in the president's relations with Congress. Earlier discussions underscored this problem. The built-in constitutional hostility between the two branches often precludes any significant governmental action, particularly when Congress is of one party and the White House is of another. Some scholars have suggested a constitutional amendment to allow the president to choose part of his cabinet from leading members of Congress.[19] Others have simply said that the president ought to pay more attention to Congress.

Some suggestions pertain to making the presidency more efficient. One member of Congress, Henry Reuss, for example, proposed an amendment to the Constitution that would create a separate office of "chief of staff," thus leaving more time to the president to carry out other functions.[20] There are motives other than efficiency in Representative Reuss's proposal: he wishes also to remove some of the trappings of majesty that so enhance presidential power.

Thus we return to a fundamental question. Does the president have too much power? Various contemporary critics answer yes. Others believe that the president actually has too little power. Still others, although conceding that the president has overgrown his bounds in foreign affairs, believe that he is too weak in domestic affairs.[21]

The common argument for a stronger president has been that in an age of rapid change and constant crisis, we need someone who can act instantaneously and before it is too late. This would be particularly true in matters of foreign affairs and defense policy in which hesitation and the normal deliberative process of gaining congressional sanction might well prove dangerous, if not fatal, for the nation. Thus presidents, elected, after all, by the whole body of voters and with as much information as possible, are really in the best position to make judgments regarding war and diplomacy.

But is this assumption correct? In light of recent history, have we been better served since presidents have bypassed Congress and unilaterally decided on diplomatic and war-making actions? Several examples would suggest that the answer is no. Think of all the ill-advised and at times disastrous interventions just since 1960: the Bay of Pigs (1961); the Dominican Republic (1965); Vietnam, Cambodia, and Laos (1960s and 1970s); and

[19]Edward S. Corwin, *The President* (New York: New York University Press, 1957), p. 297.

[20]"A Federal Master of Ceremonies," *Newsweek*, September 8, 1975, p. 65.

[21]Robert Sherrill, *Why They Call It Politics*, 3rd ed. (New York: Harcourt Brace Jovanovich, 1979), chaps. 1 and 3.

many would add, Central America in the 1980s. It is conceivable that in each of these instances the long-run interests of the nation would have been better served by the normal constitutional processes of debate, discussion, and consultation.[22]

Yet the question penetrates deeper than does the issue of power or no power. On the one hand, we must distinguish between power misused or abused and power used constitutionally, and on the other hand, we must consider the nature and the necessity of "leadership" in the modern world. It is unlikely that we will divest the presidency of the power that it has. But how can it be controlled so that we retain a constitutional government and avoid despotism? The Greek philosophers thought that that was almost impossible, and imperial Rome proved them accurate. How can we use that power to attack the problems that confront contemporary society? In an age of environmental decay, erosion of energy sources, urban blight and financial uncertainty, and the danger of nuclear war, we can ill afford a succession of weak presidents.

There is a distinction between acting and leading. The former requires competence to be successful, and the latter requires charisma (at least in a democratic society). Of course we need and want competence in our public officials, and in our presidents we seek leadership, and especially in difficult times we seek what we earlier called statesmanship. Does the unique American institution of the presidency provide us with the possibility of finding a competent, charismatic, statesmanlike, and yet constitutional figure to assume the most important, interesting, and powerful position in the world?

Democracy and the President

Shortly after the second unsuccessful attempt on the life of President Gerald Ford, a woman anonymously called a local radio talk show in Los Angeles to observe: "President Ford cannot walk the streets safely, and neither can I." This comment highlights a curious notion: Somehow the fate of 240 million Americans and the fate of the president of the United States are inextricably bound together. In the minds of most people, the tragedy of the Civil War and the fate of President Lincoln can never be separated. On the other hand, the triumph of America in World War II and the leadership of Franklin Roosevelt are no less a unity.

The American people grow up idealizing presidents as naturally and inevitably as a Roman Catholic grows up idealizing the popes. Most elementary school classrooms contain pictures of presidents, and most of us learn our history largely in terms of presidential personalities. George Wash-

[22]This argument is made by Henry Steele Commager, "The Misuse of Power," *New Republic*, April 17, 1971, pp. 17–21.

Evaluations of Presidential Performance		
Newsweek Poll—1983 (Public Opinion)	**Murray Poll—1983** (The Opinion of Professional Historians)	

Of all the presidents we have ever had, who do you wish were president today?		*Great*	*Average*
Kennedy	30%	Lincoln	McKinley
F. Roosevelt	10	F. Roosevelt	Taft
Truman	9	Washington	Van Buren
Reagan	8	Jefferson	Hoover
Carter	5	*Near Great*	Hayes
Lincoln	5	T. Roosevelt	Arthur
Eisenhower	4	Wilson	Ford
Nixon	3	Jackson	Carter
T. Roosevelt	2	Truman	B. Harrison
Ford	1	*Above*	*Below Average*
L. Johnson	1	*Average*	Taylor
Washington	1	J. Adams	Tyler
Other	2	L. Johnson	Fillmore
Don't know	19	Eisenhower	Coolidge
		Polk	Pierce
		Kennedy	*Failures*
		Madison	A. Johnson
		Monroe	Buchanan
		J. Q. Adams	Nixon
		Cleveland	Grant
			Harding
			Not Rated
			Reagan
			W. H. Harrison
			Garfield

Sources: Gallup Poll for *Newsweek* (11/28/83). Copyright 1983, by Newsweek, Inc. All Rights Reserved. Reprinted by permission; Murray, Robert K. and Tim H. Blessing, "The Presidential Performance Study: A Progress Report," *Journal of American History*, 70 (Dec. 1983), 533–35 (table, pp. 540–541).

ington embodied the Revolutionary War as Lincoln embodied the Civil War, as FDR has come to embody America during the Great Depression, and as Eisenhower seemed to personify the 1950s and JFK the early 1960s.

A kind of fear, similar to that which might afflict us if someone had tried to kill a member of our immediate family, grips the whole nation when an attempt is made on the life of the president. Except for a tiny and irrational minority, it matters not whether we approve or disapprove of a given president's policies or person; we react with horror to a threat of violence against him. President Nixon, despite his evident abuses of power, had, and still has, a substantial following among the people who felt that regardless of what he may have done or not done, driving a president from office represented an almost unthinkable indignity, not for one man but for the country. Yet as Lyndon Johnson used to point out, there are "president haters," people who take an unreasoning, automatically negative view of anything a president does. He did not add that there are also president lovers, people for whom the president can do virtually no wrong.

Both the Constitution and common sense tell us that the president is a mere mortal. But in a secular and democratic society, there is clearly a need for spiritual as well as political leadership, and the president is virtually the only person in the nation who is in a position to provide that leadership to the great majority of the people. It is not enough that he be an efficient administrator and an honest servant of the people. If there is to be some sense of national direction or purpose, only the president can provide it. The nation may exist to serve the well-being and support the freedom of the individual. But the individual is unlikely to find either freedom or well-being except within the context of a sound and healthy nation. The president's task is to keep the nation sound and healthy, not, of course, all by himself, but in cooperation with the Congress, the courts, and the people. As Harry Truman once said, "My job is to get people to do what they ought to do anyway." That is why the quadrennial selection of a president is the nation's most important business.

5

Congress and Its Critics

- What's Wrong with Congress? •
- Representation •
- The Achievements of Congress •
- The Functions of Congress •
- Congressional Committees •
- Making Law •
- The Lawmaker •

> **There is no distinctly native American criminal class except Congress.**
> **Mark Twain**
> *Pudd'nhead Wilson*
>
> **Congress is the great commanding theatre of this nation.**
> **Thomas Jefferson**
> *Letter to William Wirt, 1808*

It is almost impossible to imagine a democracy without a popularly elected legislature. Certainly none has ever existed, for democracy implies a system under which, in one form or another, people choose other people to represent them, and these representatives come together to make the laws that will govern society. (The only conceivable alternative to this might be a system of direct democracy, in which the people themselves voted on every item of legislation, obviously a practical impossibility in a nation of 250 million persons.)

Other democracies have chosen their chief executives by means other than by the vote of the people and have given those executives different kinds of power and responsibility; other democracies have no institution quite like our Supreme Court; but all democracies have a popularly elected lawmaking body. Hence one might assume that the most universal and indispensable element of a democratic government is the legislative branch. Yet polls taken over the years have found the following:

1. The public does not think very highly of members of Congress, ranking them toward the bottom of all groups of American leaders but slightly ahead of business executives and labor leaders.
2. At the same time, most Americans think that their own representative in Congress is doing a pretty good job. (Most, however, could not name their congressional representative or senators, and fewer still knew whether those members were Democrats or Republicans.)

To compound the problem, pollster Louis Harris found that members of Congress defined their job in terms much different from those of the general public. Representatives and senators told Harris that they thought their most important job was to legislate, presumably for the whole nation. Voters, on the other hand, felt that the most important responsibility of members of Congress was to act as a sort of bird dog for the people of their district, that is, to secure lucrative contracts that would help the district's economy, to help smooth the way for people who were having problems with the federal bureaucracy, and to perform similar chores.

Thus there appears to be some confusion in most people's minds about both the function and the effectiveness of Congress.

A classic condemnation of legislative bodies (with which few democrats would agree) was the condemnation by Adolf Hitler, who, remembering a visit to the Austrian parliament of his youth, once said

> There is no principle which, objectively considered, is as false as parliamentarianism. A wild gesticulating mass screaming all at once in every different key, presided over by a good natured old uncle. . . . The majority can never replace the man.

> Adolf Hitler
> *Mein Kampf*

Germany's experiences under Hitler's leadership suggest that decisions made by large, inefficient, and sometimes unimpressive groups can be less catastrophic than those made by self-proclaimed heroes. Even our own recent experiences in Vietnam, the Watergate affair and the Iran-Contra scandal underscore the essential validity of having a functioning legislative branch as a counterbalance to the executive.

What's Wrong with Congress?

Nonetheless, commonplace yet exaggerated criticisms of Congress abound. It is said that

1. Congress is dominated by an "old boy" (seniority) system that virtually guarantees that the leaders will be aged mediocrities whose principal interest is political survival and personal power rather than public policy. In the words of the late Speaker of the House Sam Rayburn, "You have to go along to get along."

2. The Congress represents so many diverse interests, regions, and loyalties that it is hopelessly inefficient. President Kennedy once observed that if any private corporation were as inefficient and clumsy as Congress, it would be bankrupt within a year. President Truman made the "do-nothing" Eightieth Congress the target of his successful race for the presidency in 1948. Virtually all presidents since have attacked Congress, usually with little or no fear of arousing public anger.

3. Representatives and senators are often third-rate political hacks whose primary concern is serving the parochial interests of "the folks back home" and whose knowledge of or interest in broader national concerns is sadly limited.

4. Congress is irresponsible. It spends money wantonly. It cannot be trusted to guard vital secrets (as in the furor that surrounded the congressional investigations of the FBI and the CIA).

5. The congressional power to conduct investigations for the purpose of legislation can be abused, so that congressional hearings often turn into headline-grabbing "circuses" intended to gain the national spotlight for ambitious individuals rather than gathering needed information. (Such criticisms were heard from the left during the era of Senator Joseph McCarthy and the House Un-American Activities Committee and from conservatives more recently.)

6. Because Congress, as a body, is clearly incapable of controlling and conducting foreign policy, its efforts to meddle in the process often produce division at home and the appearance of weakness abroad.

7. Members of Congress are more frequently involved in corrupt practices and sex scandals than in making laws. For example, according to press reports in early 1980, seven members of the House of Representatives and one senator allegedly took bribes from undercover FBI agents posing as representatives of a fictitious Arab sheik. This "ABSCAM" (for Arab Scam) operation was but one in a series of headline-grabbing stories that seemed to show a lamentable lack of common sense or ordinary prudence on the part of these men.

8. Finally, the point is often made that Congress is not truly a representative body, as its members are usually older, richer, and better educated than is the average American. Clearly, Congress does not represent women, minority groups, and the young in anything like their proportions of the population.

These criticisms deserve careful attention and assessment. Such assessments often demonstrate that the charges outlined above are more often than not uninformed and exaggerated. A key complaint has been that the rule of seniority gives too much power to older, more conservative representatives from states in which there is little political competition. It is frequently charged, for example, that in the one-party South once Democratic candidates are victorious in a primary, their chances are great of remaining in Washington and moving up the seniority ladder. This process accounts for the disproportionate number of Southerners (normally more conservative) in positions of power in Congress. Interestingly, the rule of seniority was developed in 1911 as a reform tactic designed to take excessive power away from the speaker of the House, who, until then, had appointed the chairmen of committees. This arrangement had created a one-person rule in the House, and younger, reform-minded legislators actually promoted the rule of seniority to modify the authority of the leadership and to give more independence to the committees. More recently, seniority itself has come to represent a problem for many people. During the 1960s, a liberal bloc of reform-minded Democrats, known as the Democratic Study Group, began to agitate for changes in the House of Representatives. When the Ninety-fourth Congress convened in January 1975, these liberals found themselves in control of the Democratic caucus, and they effected some of the most

	87th Congress 1961–1962		95th Congress 1977–1978	
Region	**Percent of Members**	**Percent of Chairships**	**Percent of Members**	**Percent of Chairships**
House				
East	26	25	28	32
Midwest	19	10	23	23
South[a]	42	60	31	27
West	13	5	18	18
Senate				
East	14	0	23	25
Midwest	18	0	21	12
South[a]	37	63	30	38
West	31	37	26	25

Committee Chairships: The Decline of the South in the Democratic Party

[a]The South is defined as the 11 states of the Confederacy plus Kentucky and Oklahoma.
Source: William J. Keefe, Congress and the American People © 1980, p. 76. Reprinted by permission of Prentice-Hall, Inc., Englewood Cliffs, New Jersey.

dramatic changes since 1911. The seniority system was altered to require that chairs of committees be subject to secret ballot approval at each new Congress. The Democrats then dislodged four powerful Southern chairmen from important committees, despite their seniority. These changes, according to Maurice Rosenblatt, founder of the National Committee for an Effective Congress, meant that Congress would "never be the same again, for it will be far more responsive than in the past to majority opinion."[1]

Another, and related, charge against Congress, particularly the House of Representatives, has been that it disproportionately represents rural over urban interests. Journalist and critic Robert Sherrill pointed out that most important chairmen are from small, rural towns and can hardly appreciate the problems and needs of the majority of Americans, who live in urban-suburban clusters.[2] This circumstance is due in part to a combination of the seniority system and the nature of representation characteristic of Congress until recently. We must keep in mind that members of the national House of Representatives are chosen from districts within states. How many districts a state has depends on its population. Every ten years there is a national census, and the 435 seats in the House are awarded to states on the basis of the census findings: some states gain seats, some lose them. After 1980, for example, California received the largest number of seats (45) because it had

[1]"Weakening of the Seniority System Will Strengthen Hand of Congress," *Los Angeles Times*, January 26, 1975, Sec. 5, p. 1.

[2]Robert Sherrill, *Why They Call It Politics*, 3rd ed. (New York: Harcourt Brace Jovanovich, 1979), chap. 4.

the largest population. Traditionally it was the *state* legislature that every ten years was responsible for drawing up these *national* congressional districts within its state. Because state legislatures were usually disproportionately dominated by rural interests (until the 1960s Los Angeles County had the same number of state senators—one—as did counties with much smaller populations), they tended to carve up congressional districts to the advantage of the less populated rural areas. This practice changed with certain dramatic decisions by the Supreme Court. In 1962, in the case of *Baker v. Carr*, the Court ruled that under the equal-protection-of-the-law clause of the Fourteenth Amendment, all citizens of each state should have equal representation in state legislatures. This was the so-called one-person, one-vote rule. By the early 1970s, after considerable haggling and finally court intervention, most state legislatures were thus apportioned. This meant that as state legislatures came to represent more substantial urban interests, so too would the national Congress. To ensure this, the Supreme Court extended the "one-person, one-vote" rule to national congressional districts in the 1964 decision *Wesberry v. Sanders*. Thus the courts have reformed Congress, and we now have a more representative and urban-oriented legislature than in the past.

Other criticisms of the Congress include the charge that it is made up largely of business people, lawyers, men, and old people. Certainly it is made up mainly of business types and lawyers, as these are people that seem to go into politics. Although there have been some important political victories recently for women, the Senate in 1988 had only two women (Nancy Kassebaum, R., Kans., and Barbara Mikulski, D., Md.), and the proportion of women in the House of Representatives in no way approximated the percentage of women in the population. On the other hand, contrary to popular myth, Congress has been getting younger (see the accompanying table).

Critics also charge that Congress is more responsive to "special interests" than to the "people."[3] This, of course, takes us back to the discussion of who the people are. Most of the "people" are at least tangentially associated with one or more interest groups. Large corporations lobby members of Congress, but so do environmentalists. Common Cause, Ralph Nader and friends, welfare rights organizations, labor groups, the National Rifle Association, and others *are* special interests. Congress can hardly ignore these groups, and neither can any other level or branch of government.

The charge of corruption is often leveled at Congress, and in the case of maladroit and even illegal uses of campaign funds, or outright bribery, it is a justified criticism. Yet is is not unfair to consider the relative proportion of corrupt members of Congress as compared with the number of corrupt

[3]See, for example, Mark J. Green, James M. Fallows, and David R. Zwick, *Who Runs Congress?* (New York: Bantam, 1972), pp. 29–52.

The Pursuit of Happiness

Average Age, 100th Congress (Ages as of Nov. 8, 1986)			
	All members	**Senate**	**House**
Both Parties	52.5	54.4	50.7
Democrats	53.1	55.1	51.1
Republicans	51.9	53.6	50.2

(Statistics based on apparent winners as of Nov. 6, 1986)

Average Age, 89th through 99th Congresses*			
	All members	**Senate**	**House**
99th	50.5	54.2	49.7
98th	47.0	53.4	45.5
97th	49.2	52.5	48.4
96th	50.9	55.5	49.8
95th	50.3	54.7	49.3
94th	50.9	55.5	49.8
93rd	52.0	55.3	51.1
92nd	52.7	56.4	51.9
91st	53.0	56.6	52.2
90th	52.1	57.7	50.8
89th	51.9	57.7	50.5

*Average age calculated at or near the beginning of each Congress.
Source: Congressional Quarterly Weekly Report, Nov. 8, 1986.

persons in other walks of life. Moreover, congressional corruption is rarely of the magnitude of the campaign corruption that was revealed regarding the presidency in the early 1970s. Nor can it be claimed that Congress was plagued by more charges of corruption and scandal than was the executive branch of government during the Iran-Contra affair or during the various indictments of former executive officials by special prosecutors during the late 1980s.

A related problem has to do with conflicts of interest. For example, how disinterested can a representative's vote on a tax bill be if that bill contains provisions that might financially affect a company in which the member of Congress owns stock? There has never been a satisfactory answer to this problem. Recently, suggestions for exposure of some or all the assets of members of Congress have gained ground.[4] Of course it should be stressed that we have every right to expect our public servants to be above reproach.

For years Congress has been criticized as being ineffective and obstructive. In the House, the Rules Committee, which must usually issue a rule to bring a bill to the floor, has frequently been cited as a hindrance to progress

[4]Interview with Representative Glenn Anderson (D., Calif.), August 1975.

Characteristics of 100th Congress

Women in Congress

House (23)

California: Sala Burton, D; Barbara Boxer, D.
Colorado: Patricia Schroeder, D.
Connecticut: Barbara B. Kennelly, D; Nancy L. Johnson, R.
Hawaii: Patricia Saiki, R.
Illinois: Cardiss Collins, D; Lynn Martin, R.
Kansas: Jan Meyers, R.
Louisiana: Lindy (Mrs. Hale) Boggs, D.
Maine: Olympia J. Snowe, R.
Maryland: Helen Delich Bentley, R; Beverly B. Byron, D; Constance A. Morella, R.
Nebraska: Virginia Smith, R.
Nevada: Barbara F. Vucanovich, R.
New Jersey: Marge Roukema, R.
New York: Louise M. Slaughter, D.
Ohio: Marcy Kaptur, D; Mary Rose Oakar, D.
Rhode Island: Claudine Schneider, R.
South Carolina: Elizabeth Patterson, D.
Tennessee: Marilyn Lloyd, D.

Senate (2)

Kansas: Nancy Landon Kassebaum, R.
Maryland: Barbara A. Mikulski, D.

Blacks in Congress

House (23)

California: Ronald V. Dellums, D; Julian C. Dixon, D; Mervyn M. Dymally, D; Augustus F. Hawkins, D.
District of Columbia: Walter E. Fauntroy, D.*
Georgia: John Lewis, D.
Illinois: Charles A. Hayes, D; Gus Savage, D; Cardiss Collins, D.
Maryland: Kweisi Mfume, D.
Michigan: John Conyers Jr., D; George W. Crockett Jr., D.
Mississippi: Mike Espy, D.
Missouri: William L. Clay, D; Alan Wheat, D.
New York: Floyd H. Flake, D; Edolphus Towns, D; Major R. Owens, D; Charles B. Rangel, D.
Ohio: Louis Stokes, D.
Pennsylvania: William H. Gray III, D.
Tennessee: Harold E. Ford, D.
Texas: Mickey Leland, D.

Non-voting delegate.

Characteristics of 100th Congress, continued
Hispanics in Congress
House (14)

California: Tony Coelho, D; Edward R. Roybal, D; Matthew G. Martinez, D; Esteban Edward Torres, D.
Guam: Ben Blaz, R.*
New Mexico: Manuel Lujan Jr., R; Bill Richardson, D.
New York: Robert Garcia, D.
Puerto Rico: Jaime B. Fuster, Popular Dem.*
Texas: E. "Kika" de la Garza, D; Henry B. Gonzalez, D; Albert G. Bustamante, D; Solomon P. Ortiz, D.
Virgin Islands: Ron de Lugo, D.*

Non-voting delegate.
(Statistics based on apparent winners as of Nov. 6, 1986)

Members' Occupations						
	House			**Senate**			**Congress**
	D	**R**	**Total**	**D**	**R**	**Total**	**Total**
Actor/Entertainer	0	1	1	0	0	0	1
Aeronautics	0	3	3	1	1	2	5
Agriculture	10	10	20	2	3	5	25
Business or Banking	66	76	142	13	15	28	170
Clergy	2	0	2	0	1	1	3
Education	24	14	38	6	6	12	50
Engineering	2	2	4	0	1	1	5
Journalism	11	9	20	6	2	8	28
Labor Officials	2	0	2	0	0	0	2
Law	122	62	184	35	27	62	246
Law Enforcement	6	1	7	0	0	0	7
Medicine	1	2	3	1	0	1	4
Military	0	0	0	0	1	1	1
Professional Sports	3	2	5	1	0	1	6
Public Service/Politics	59	35	94	13	7	20	114

Because some members have more than one occupation, totals are higher than total membership.

Members' Religious Affiliations						
	House			**Senate**			**Congress**
	D	**R**	**Total**	**D**	**R**	**Total**	**Total**
African Methodist Episcopal Zion	1	0	1	0	0	0	1
Apostolic Christian	0	1	1	0	0	0	1
Baptist	32	9	41	4	7	11	52

Characteristics of 100th Congress, continued							
Members' Religious Affiliations							
	House			Senate			Congress
	D	R	Total	D	R	Total	Total
Christian Church	1	1	2	0	0	0	2
Christian Reformed Church	0	1	1	0	0	0	1
Christian Science	0	2	2	0	0	0	2
Church of Christ	3	1	4	0	0	0	4
Disciple of Christ	1	0	1	0	0	0	1
Episcopal	21	19	40	6	14	20	60
Greek Orthodox	2	4	6	1	0	1	7
Independent Bible Church	0	1	1	0	0	0	1
Jewish	25	4	29	4	4	8	37
Lutheran	9	11	20	2	1	3	23
Methodist	37	25	62	9	4	13	75
Mormon	3	5	8	1	2	3	11
Presbyterian	21	25	46	9	2	11	57
Roman Catholic	82	41	123	13	6	19	142
Seventh-day Adventist	0	1	1	0	0	0	1
Unitarian	5	2	7	1	2	3	10
United Church of Christ and Congregationalist	4	5	9	3	2	5	14
Unspecified Protestant	9	18	27	2	1	3	30
Unspecified	2	1	3	0	0	0	3

Source: *Congressional Quarterly Weekly Report*, Nov. 8, 1986.

in the legislature. In the Senate, the most famous (or infamous) of obstructionist tactics has been the filibuster, the allowing of unlimited debate, which provides opponents of a bill the opportunity to talk continuously until a bill is removed from consideration. Here again, there have been some changes. In 1961, under pressure from President Kennedy, the Rules Committee was enlarged from 12 to 15 members, and it has become more responsive to progressive legislation since then. The most direct way to get a bill by the Rules Committee (or out of any committee that has refused to act on it) is through what is called a *discharge petition*. This is difficult but can be done if after the bill has been in committee for 20 days, such a petition is signed by 218 representatives (one-half the total). In that case, the bill must come to the full House.

To stop a filibuster in the Senate is at least as difficult. Traditionally two methods have been used. First, the majority can keep the Senate in continuous session and hope that the speaker will give up, and second, supporters of the bill can try to gain *cloture*. Until 1975, cloture required that 16 senators sign a petition to discontinue debate. Two days later a vote was taken, and if two-thirds voted to discontinue debate, no senator would be allowed to speak for more than one hour, after which the bill would be brought to a vote. In March 1975, the Senate liberalized the rule to require only a three-fifths vote (60 votes as a minimum) rather than the two-thirds needed to close off debate. The new rule is more effective in curtailing filibusters only if there is a large attendance in the Senate, because under the *old* rule, two-thirds of *those present and voting* could close debate; under the new rule three-fifths of the whole Senate (of 100 members) is required. In 1979 the Senate made more effective its restraint on the filibuster by disallowing the excessive use of obstructive parliamentary tactics like quorum calls and roll call votes that had been used by individual senators to hold up the passage of legislation favored by the majority.

Representation

As noted earlier, one of the complaints leveled at the Congress is that individual members serve the interests of their local constituents to the detriment of broader national needs. Yet most of us usually prefer a member of Congress who will be sensitive to our local concerns. Thus, in one sense of the word, a *representative* should be a reasonable facsimile of those whom he or she represents; in another, a representative acts as an "agent" for others, just as an attorney represents a client.

In Congress representatives may view their role in a number of ways: as *delegates* who reflect the constituents' interests and accept their instructions (thus Southern representatives might vote against civil rights laws because their constituents disapprove of them, whether or not the members believe them right); or as *trustees* who decide on legislative matters on the basis of conscience or the national interest, whatever the views of the constituency; or as *partisans* who tend to vote with their political party; or as *politicos* who play all these roles.[5]

Whichever the case, members of Congress are local products. By constitutional requirement both senators and representatives must be legal inhabitants of the states from which they are elected, and because of custom and political necessity, representatives reside in the districts that they serve. Consequently, of the various roles that legislators may assume, it is not surprising to find them acting most frequently as delegates, catering to the needs of constituents and seeking to advance their interests.

Thus, in theory, as well as in practice, legislative bodies—local, state, and national—are chosen by and are responsible to the people of the districts

[5]See Neal Riemer, ed., *The Representative* (Lexington, Mass.: Heath, 1967).

that they represent. Of course this is not always the case. Election to public office normally requires liberal supplies of money, publicity, and political organization, and such entities as corporations, labor unions, and professional organizations (for example, the National Education Association and the American Medical Association) often find it useful to supply whatever it is that candidates for public office require, on the theory that such candidates, once elected, will not prove ungrateful. Generally speaking, the more vulnerable an organization is to public pressure on its business or activity, the more it will be involved in politics. The liquor and racetrack industries, for example, can usually be counted on to provide generous assistance to candidates favorable to their interests, as they are engaged in businesses that many people view with suspicion, if not open hostility.

A classic example of this sort of "influence peddling" took place in the post-World War II years in California by Arthur Samish, a professional representative of liquor, racetrack, and highway contractor interests, once widely referred to as "the uncrowned king of the California legislature." On one occasion, then California Governor (later chief justice of the Supreme Court) Earl Warren confessed quite candidly to a reporter that "on matters affecting his clients, Arthur unquestionably has more power with the legislature than I do,"[6] a startling admission from a popular and highly respected governor. Samish liked to boast about his power. Once he posed for a picture for *Collier's* magazine with a dummy on his lap. The dummy was labeled *The California legislature.* The California liquor industry levied what in effect was a tax of five cents on its members for every case of beer or bottle of liquor sold in the state. This money was turned over to Samish to be used at his discretion to promote the industry's interests and protect it from competition. An example of how this money was used is cited by Samish himself in his book *The Secret Boss of California.* A member of the state assembly, Clair Woolwine, aroused Samish's anger by voting contrary to Samish's wishes. Samish was determined to defeat Woolwine when he next faced reelection. The district that Woolwine represented included an old section of downtown Los Angeles where derelicts congregated, known as "skid row." Seeking an opponent for Woolwine who lived in the district, Samish visited one of the downtown soup kitchens where free meals were handed out and selected one of the derelicts as his personal candidate. The man was equipped with a hotel room, a new suit, and some spending money and was instructed to have a bath and a shave. Samish did the rest. That November his candidate was elected over the incumbent Woolwine. Unhappily, Samish's man died in office, thereby prematurely ending what might have been a brilliant political career. Samish later defended his actions by pointing out that as many of the people in that district were derelicts, why shouldn't they be represented by one of their own? This is an extreme

[6]See Arthur Samish and Bob Thomas, *The Secret Boss of California* (New York: Crown, 1971).

The Pursuit of Happiness

example of the *mirror theory* of representation: representatives mirror their constituency.

Two current examples of the mirror theory of representation are Representative Jack Kemp of New York and Representative Ronald Dellums of California. Kemp is politically conservative, white, middle class, and a former professional football player—characteristics that are all reflective of the values of his upstate constituents. Dellums is black, liberal, urban, and an articulate representative of his Berkeley/Oakland constituency.

It may be simple enough to list and explain the various roles that a member of Congress could assume. But in practice the matter of representation is more complex. For example, what if a given representative disagrees with the views held by a majority of the district's constituents? Is the representative bound to vote as the constituents wish, or according to his or her own conscience? This dilemma is not an uncommon one for members of Congress. A legislator may believe that strict economy is necessary to control inflation. What then should that legislator do about a controversial but popular defense project (such as the M-X missile) that would cost a great deal but could well mean thousands of jobs for the district's constituents? Or legislators might feel that busing is essential to achieve an integrated society, whereas a majority of their constituents see the matter quite differently. Does Senator Edward Kennedy's view of the Constitution take precedence over his obligation to the voters of Massachusetts? It is for good reason that legislators are sometimes called *solons*, after a very wise man and lawgiver of ancient Greece, for it often requires the wisdom of a Solon to resolve successfully the commonplace problems of a conscientious lawmaker.

In the United States, members of the House of Representatives are elected to represent districts and senators to represent states, so that each is the national spokesperson for a given number of people and a certain geographical area. But collectively Congress acts not only for 435 separate districts and 50 states but also for the whole nation. When local interests and concerns conflict with the national welfare, what is a legislator's duty? Legislators are pledged to act and speak for their people and area. The legislator is also pledged to uphold the Constitution and serve the nation.

A reflection of this dichotomy is found in the fact that a member of Congress must often occupy two homes (in one extreme case, Representative Robert Legett, D., Calif., even had two families), one in or near Washington and another in the home district. The divided residence may symbolize a certain divided loyalty. Let us cite a hypothetical example:

Young Congressman Smith, having just seen the film *Mr. Smith Goes to Washington* on late-night television (a film about a young idealist who successfully battles the corrupt Washington congressional establishment), was recently elected to the House of Representatives. He goes to Washington determined to be honest, faithful, reverent, and true. Let us further postulate that the people in his home district badly need or want some federal assistance, such as defense contracts, a new dam, or help with a proposal to create a rapid-transit system. Naturally Congressman Smith will do his utmost to get one or more of these good things approved by his colleagues. Upon arriving in Washington, Congressman Smith is shocked to discover that several key leaders of Congress are corrupt, alcoholic, or otherwise unsuited to their roles, which they have acquired largely as the result of seniority. Other, like-minded young representatives ask Smith to join them in battling the leadership and exposing its unfitness. The leaders, on the other hand, approach Congressman Smith and give him a bit of helpful advice. If Congressman Smith expects the House leaders to look favorably on his bills to help his district, he had best not associate himself with the "radicals" who want to change a system that has been worked out over the course of two hundred years. Further, if Congressman Smith, who has a certain amount of personal ambition, would like to be appointed to important committees, committees that would help keep him in the public eye and benefit the folks back home, he had better learn to cooperate. Finally, his work as a young congressman will be made less burdensome, and his way smoother, if he happens to be assigned to an attractive office, near the parking lot, and with a nice view.

Our idealistic hero must make a hard decision: to fight the system and consign himself to the outer limits of the congressional club, thus rendering himself ineffective in terms of his ability to serve the people who elected him, or to become part of the very thing that he came to Washington to try to change.

What do the folks back home want and expect him to do? If the question were put as we have put it, most would probably encourage him to choose the harder but apparently more moral course. But in practice the voters frequently make a quite different kind of choice. In most cases, voters seem to believe that a powerful, well-connected member of Congress brings many benefits to constituents. A "well-respected," easily reelected member of Congress is apt to be someone like James Wright of Texas, currently the majority leader of the House of Representatives. Wright is a powerful member of the House and a hardworking legislator who has also been tenacious in seeing that his district is helped financially in federal legislation, and he is virtually unbeatable.

Another aspect of a representative's job is important but not very well understood by the public. It is what might be called customer service or being the district's "ombudsman." An average of a third of a typical representative's time may be spent servicing the personal and private needs of the representative's constituents.[7] Some of this service is providing help to innocent tourists and to visiting constituents, meeting schoolchildren who want an autographed picture, and so on. But the bulk of activity in this

[7]Donald G. Tacheron and Morris K. Udall, *The Job of the Congressman*, 2nd ed. (Indianapolis: Bobbs-Merrill, 1970), pp. 303–304.

Much of a congressperson's work involves servicing the personal and business needs of his or her constituents. Here Congressman Glenn M. Anderson (D., Calif.) chats with representatives of a major employer of the people in his district. *(Reprinted with permission.)*

area goes into trying to meet the demands of various individuals for special favors of one kind or another. People who want their children appointed to a military academy, veterans who think they should be getting a better pension from the Veterans Administration, business executives with tax problems or those seeking a piece of the federal action, corporate officials looking for laws that will inhibit foreign competitors, people accused of crimes who want a letter on their behalf to the judge, and even schoolchildren who ask help from their representative or senator in doing homework—all look to their congressional representative in Washington.

Many members of Congress spend decades in Washington without ever pushing very hard or conspicuously for or against nationally important and well-publicized legislation and still remain popular with voters simply because they are diligent about handling these personal requests. Again, a legislator must often choose between devoting limited time and attention to studying complex legislative matters or "taking care of the folks back home."

But even this is an oversimplification. Most Americans rarely if ever write to their representative in Congress. Fewer still would dream of seeking congressional help for the resolution of a personal problem. Most people would be surprised to discover how far their representative or senators will go to help them if they take the time to visit their office. That is true because only a handful of the half million or so people that a member of Congress represents ever go anywhere near the office.

Thus the mundane and practical realities of a Congress member's job may be somewhat removed from the vision of the "people's champion" and spokesperson inherent in the theory of representative government. The work of the elected representative is important, indeed indispensable, to the maintenance of a free government and hence a free society. But it is sometimes difficult to extrapolate that truth from the daily routine of a working member of Congress. Like the people who bring our homes water or electricity, we tend to think about members of Congress only when they fail.

Thus, despite the all-too-frequent sex and financial scandals surrounding Congress in recent years, and although Congress as an institution normally ranks very near the bottom in polls of public regard for major American institutions, it can be reasonably argued that Congress serves the American people at least as well as, and perhaps a great deal better than, other branches of government.

The Achievements of Congress

For decades the mass media (newspaper cartoons, films, and television comedians) have pictured the representative or senator as a figure of comedy or corruption, whereas the other two branches of government—the presidency and the Supreme Court—are normally treated with respect if not reverence. Yet consider the relative position of Congress, the presidency, and the courts on some of the most important issues to face the United States during the recent past.

1. It was Congress that led official opposition to the war in Vietnam. Whereas presidents insisted on pushing that struggle to its dismal conclusion, such people as Senator J. William Fulbright, chairman of the Senate Foreign Relations Committee, were, for years, critics of the war. Largely as the result of specific laws passed by Congress, American forces were withdrawn from Indochina. And by the War Powers Act of 1973, passed over President Nixon's veto, Congress gained the right to approve the president's stationing of American forces in other countries and the ability to force a president to remove such forces after a set period of time. This act was first used in 1983 when American troops were placed in Lebanon. However, President Reagan, though agreeing to invoke the act, challenged its constitutionality, and as a consequence of a landmark decision of the Supreme Court in 1983 (*Immigration and Naturalization Service v. Chadha*) finding

unconstitutional the so-called legislative veto, that section of the War Powers Act allowing Congress to force a president to remove forces engaged in hostilities is now questionable. (Indeed, the long-term effects of the Supreme Court's decision on executive-legislative relations could be quite dramatic. "Legislative vetoes" have been written into about two hundred statutes during the last half century. As a result of most of these laws, either or both houses could block, by a simple majority, specified actions taken by the president or the bureaucracy to carry out the law. The Supreme Court ruled that this violated the principle of separation of powers—whereby Congress passes laws and only the executive executes them, that is, carries them out. This decision could prove to be a roadblock in the resurgence of Congress's powers in checking the president.)

2. It was Congress, acting with what many observers have described as great skill, prudence, and patience, that brought the Watergate scandal to a decisive and yet peaceful conclusion, culminating in 1974 in the resignation of President Nixon to avoid certain impeachment and conviction.

3. It was Congress, acting in the 1970s through its power to investigate, that brought to light the scandalous and dangerous abuse of power by the CIA in the Nixon era, and the FBI under J. Edgar Hoover, which, unchecked, might well have constituted a threat to the personal freedom of every American citizen.

4. Although presidents like to appear frugal and conservative in fiscal matters and frequently accuse Congress of wasteful expenditures for political purposes, the fact is that the executive, not the congressional, branch has most consistently sought larger and larger appropriations for what is certainly the most expensive and probably the most wasteful single element in the national budget, military expenditures. Furthermore, it was the executive branch that decided to fight the war in Vietnam on credit, which was an important element in undermining world confidence in the dollar and setting off a serious inflation. Also, the Congressional Budget and Impoundment Control Act, passed by Congress in 1974, created House and Senate Budget committees to establish spending and tax goals and the Congressional Budget Office to provide technical information about the economy and the budget. This has allowed Congress to follow more coherent and long-term budget planning. Public response to this congressional reform has been quite positive.[8]

5. In recent years Congress has advanced a number of reforms to make its business more open to public view. So-called sunshine rules, established in the 1970s, require that committee sessions in both houses be open to the public (unless members of the committee vote in public to close them), and the House of Representatives is allowing television coverage of its sessions.

6. In 1977 both the Senate and the House passed codes of ethics by which members are barred from accepting private money for office expenditures

[8]"The Wild Spenders Take a Break," *Los Angeles Times*, July 14, 1976, Section 2, p. 6.

or gifts from lobbyists beyond those of small value. In addition, the code requires all members of Congress to make annual public disclosures of their financial holdings and limits them severely on outside earned income. The intention of this is to make it difficult for special interests to control members of Congress, and it certainly provides ample information to interested voters to determine whether representatives are looking out for the public interest or themselves. (Of course it does nothing to solve problems of covert and illegal acts, such as the alleged bribery posed by the ABSCAM case.)

7. Despite the sound and the fury that seems to emanate from the halls of Congress, in the end constructive and reasonable legislation frequently manages to emerge. An example is the energy program put forth by President Carter. After much travail and modification, a mutually acceptable series of energy proposals did win passage and become law in 1978. Likewise, in 1983 Congress passed the important Social Security Reform Act, praised by both Democrats and Republicans.

Congress is the most representative element in the structure of representative government. Supreme Court judges are appointed for life and are thus shielded against changes in public mood, at least insofar as tenure of office is concerned. The nature of the presidency also creates a certain barrier between the people and the person who occupies the Oval Office. Even the most well-intentioned and democratic of presidents must find it difficult if not downright dangerous to do more than "press the flesh" of the ordinary citizen. Presidents may appear before the people and speak to the people. But they can rarely find a practical means of listening to the average citizen, even if they so desired. Representatives and senators, on the other hand, *must* listen to the people if they are to survive in office.

History indicates that Congress does indeed reflect the national mood far more reliably than does any other branch of government. For example, when the American people were generally supportive of the war in Vietnam, Congress responded with an overwhelming endorsement of the Tonkin Gulf Resolution, which in effect authorized President Johnson to escalate the war. (It is interesting that the only two senators to vote against the resolution, Ernest Gruening of Alaska and Wayne Morse of Oregon, were defeated in their next bid for reelection, evidence of what sometimes happens to legislators who vote according to their conscience rather than the public opinion polls.) By 1975 most Americans had turned against further direct involvement in the war, and in the spring of that year Congress refused President Ford's request for supplemental financial appropriations designed to make it possible to continue the struggle.

In the fall of 1983, despite publicly expressed misgivings from the White House, Congress voted overwhelmingly to establish a national holiday celebrating the birth of the late civil rights leader Martin Luther King, Jr., and President Reagan, sensing the mood of the country, went along with Congress and signed the bill. In 1988, Congress passed the Civil Rights

Restoration Act, reaffirming the principle that any organization receiving federal funds was required to abide by nondiscriminatory federal statutes in all its departments or programs. This was a congressional response to an earlier Supreme Court ruling (the so-called Grove City case) that had held that under existing law an organization had only to apply such rules to the specific department or program receiving the aid (for example, a college awarded federal aid for an English program was not required to apply nondiscriminatory practices in the athletic department). The 1988 act, clarifying Congress's intention in civil rights law, was vetoed by President Reagan, but Congress subsequently overrode the veto. The presidency, clearly, has superior means to shape and lead public opinion, but once that opinion forms and settles on a clearly discernible path, Congress is usually responsive.

Thus the notion that the presidency is the embodiment of our democratic way of life is to some extent misleading. For it is Congress, rather than the presidency, that most nearly embodies the ideal of self-government in a pluralistic society.[9] The president, being one person, is limited on matters of public policy. But Congress, being many men and women, comes far closer to reflecting the scope of American society with all its divergent interests and outlooks.

Yet it is probably inevitable that the image of hundreds of people—arguing, compromising, bargaining, and striving to reach a consensus acceptable to the majority—is less dramatic and less aesthetically satisfying than is the image of a single individual struggling to make a decision on weighty matters—knowing all the while that the lives of millions, perhaps even billions, of people will be affected by what he alone has the power to decide. For although it is not so in practice, it usually appears to the general public that Congress can propose but only the president can dispose. From the standpoint of drama, all presidents are continuously playing Hamlet—the tragic, lonely, soul-searching individual—and Congress plays the crowd. The president is the star. Congress is the supporting cast, whose names flicker quickly by on the screen *after* the drama is over.

What and how we think about Congress is normally a reflection of our estimate of the person who occupies the presidency, because Congress is, in the nature of our constitutional system, a countervailing force to the White House. Even when Congress is dominated by members of the president's own party, it is frequently perceived by the public as an antagonist to the president's role as protagonist. Thus admirers of Franklin Roosevelt and John Kennedy tended to be critical of Congress for not being willing to enact all the legislation that these two liberal presidents proposed. On the other hand, conservatives saw the heavily Democratic Congress elected in the immediate post-Watergate era as a profligate foe of President Ford's efforts to control federal deficits and hence inflation. Democratic President

[9]For a discussion of pluralism, see Chapter 9.

Harry Truman deliberately made the Republican-controlled Eightieth Congress the foil of his campaign to win reelection in 1948, apparently with some success. Liberals chastised Congress for its reluctance to follow Roosevelt's leadership in mobilizing the nation prior to America's entry into World War II, but most of the same people praised Congress for the restraints it imposed on President Nixon during the war in Vietnam.

In recent years it has been increasingly clear that Congress takes seriously its role of countervailing force to the presidency. This was seen when Congress resisted President Reagan's proposals to alter social welfare programs, ranging from Social Security cutbacks to the proposed dismantling of such agencies as the Department of Education, until the president compromised his efforts to restructure the domestic role of the government.

Congress played a major role in investigating the Iran-Contra affair. In 1986 Congress discovered that officials of the president's staff, along with nongovernment personnel, had secretly sold arms to Iran and transferred some of the profits of the sales to the Contras in Central America (the Contras were guerrillas fighting against the Nicaraguan government). Because such sales of arms and diversion of profits were illegal, each of the two houses of the legislature reacted by forming a *select committee* (see discussion of committees below) to investigate these activities and recommend what actions might assure that legal and constitutional procedures would be followed in the future and to underscore the necessity of a congressional role in foreign policy matters.

The nomination of Judge Robert Bork to fill a vacancy on the Supreme Court sparked a historic face-off between the Senate and the president. President Reagan vigorously supported his nominee, but after lengthy, televised hearings before the Senate Judiciary Committee in the fall of 1987, the Senate voted against confirmation of Judge Bork.

Administrative ideologues, whether of the left or the right, usually draw heavy fire from congressional leaders, who tend to be practical and inclined to compromise rather than wage holy wars for this or that scheme that promises to provide instant solutions to deep and complicated problems. Yet in foreign policy, Congress is more reluctant to challenge presidential leadership, partly because the Constitution grants the president prime responsibility for conducting foreign affairs and also because of the fear of appearing disloyal in the face of an international challenge, real or imagined. Thus, most presidential initiatives, ranging from Lyndon Johnson's escalation of the Vietnam War to President Reagan's decision to send American troops to Lebanon, are met with initial support by the overwhelming majority of both houses of Congress. Only later, when the bills and casualties mount, do congressional leaders begin to ask hard questions. When the answers are unsatisfactory, congressional criticism and active opposition build. This may be explained in part because Congress is a deliberative body that seeks a consensus among a majority of diverse members. Rapid decisions, such as the ones described here, are uncharacteristic of this body. Once Congress has had time to deliberate and a consensus is formed, it may fully support presidential actions (as in World War II) or oppose them (as with Vietnam).

Privately, many members of the House and Senate complain that theirs is the least understood and appreciated branch of American government. Lawmakers receive numerous letters of complaint, few of praise. (Again, this is the opposite of the case of the president—most of whose mail is normally laudatory.) Among the large numbers of Americans who rarely or never write letters, Congress is held in low esteem.[10] Only about half the people know who their congressional representative is, and even fewer know which party controls Congress.[11] Members of Congress may try to close the gap that separates them from the public, but usually without much success. A legislator elected from California, for example, may fly home 20 to 30 weekends a year and accept virtually any and all speaking engagements or opportunities to meet the public. Still, at the end of a two-year term, that representative will have had personal contact with only a fraction of the constituents whom he or she represents.

With respect to coverage by the major media, the lawmaker is clearly at a disadvantage. Most Americans now rely on television for daily news, and except in rare instances, a single senator, let alone a representative, is simply not important enough to warrant much attention by television, the important metropolitan newspapers, or the weekly national news magazines. The most notable exceptions occur when the House or Senate is conducting a spectacularly interesting investigation, such as was the case with the Senate Watergate Committee in 1973 or with the televised Iran-Contra hearings conducted in 1987.

On the other hand, representatives and senators with little taste for engaging in large-scale media events, who prefer hard, quiet, but conscientious work on the nation's problems, are rewarded with almost total anonymity. For example, Senator Sam Ervin spent much of his life in Congress and achieved a reputation among his fellow legislators and a handful of knowledgeable observers as a wise and witty man, a serious constitutional scholar, and an able legislator. But he remained unknown to the nation at large until he was named to head a Senate committee to investigate the Watergate scandal, whereupon he became a national idol.

One sure way to national attention for most members of Congress is through scandal. Thus Representative Wilbur Mills became one of the few nationally known members of Congress, not because as chairman of the

[10]The *Gallup Poll*, 1982, p. 175, shows 29 percent of respondents approving of Congress, 54 percent disapproving, and 17 percent with no opinion.
[11]Donald E. Stokes and Warren E. Miller, "Party Government and the Saliency of Congress," *Public Opinion Quarterly* 2 (Winter 1962): 531–546.

powerful House Ways and Means Committee he had played a critical role in making the nation's tax policy—which directly affected the economic well-being of virtually every American—but because his mistress leaped into a shallow creek after the two were stopped by the Washington police following a minor traffic incident. Before this incident, few Americans knew or cared anything about Wilbur Mills, although he was certainly one of the most powerful men in Congress and in the nation.

(The reluctance of the media and/or the public to focus attention on Congress was illustrated, in a negative sense, by the ABSCAM incident. When the charges that eight members of Congress had accepted bribes from FBI agents posing as wealthy Arabs were made public, many believed that the nation was about to endure another major scandal on the order of Watergate. But within a few weeks both the public and the media appeared to lose interest, and developments in the case were relegated to the back pages of newspapers or ignored altogether. Had a similar scandal touched the president or his close associates, the media and the nation would surely have been far more excited.)

Finally, if a member of Congress were to receive "equal time" in the national media with the president—a rarity—how could he or she presume to speak for 535 members?

The Functions of Congress

Whatever we think about Congress, what it does is important and affects all of us, because its essential function, accorded to it by the Constitution, is to make laws. Congress is bicameral, made up of a House of Representatives of 435 members, each representing an approximately equal number of constituents, and a Senate of 100 members, 2 from each state. Representatives and senators earn $89,500 a year, not a paltry sum, but not as much as some could earn in law practice or a business firm. Representatives serve two-year terms, and all 435 run for reelection in every even-numbered year. Senators serve six years, and one-third are elected every two years.

Both houses must agree on the exact wording of a bill before it is passed and sent to the president for signature. Besides its most important function of making laws, Congress has other duties, provided by the Constitution:

1. Congress can, by a two-thirds vote, propose amendments to the Constitution.
2. The House has the power to impeach (by majority vote), and the Senate the power to try, any civil officer of the United States. If the Senate upholds the impeachment charges by a two-thirds vote, the officer will be removed.

3. Congress has powers of investigation. For example, in the mid-1970s the Senate Select Committee on Intelligence, chaired by Senator Frank Church, investigated activities of the CIA and FBI pursuant to recommending legislation. Investigations such as those of the Church committee frequently cause public controversy, with opponents charging that they represent witch hunts and blemish the reputation of civil servants with allegations unproved in court. Supporters of congressional investigations argue that they are necessary at times to help Congress draw up legislation (as on campaign financing, watchdog control over the CIA, and so on) and that they properly expose excessive and at times unconstitutional activities within the executive branch of government.
4. Congress also has the authority to establish its own rules, that is, the procedures that it will follow in all its functions.
5. The Senate has some functions that the House does not. The Senate advises and consents to treaties by a two-thirds vote. In practice this has come to mean approving treaties negotiated by the executive branch. The Senate also confirms most presidential nominations (to the cabinet, the federal courts, and diplomatic posts). Such confirmations require only a majority vote.

There are other differences between the two houses.

The Founding Fathers had intended each house to check the other. They supposed that the democratic House of Representatives, with frequent elections, would check the more aristocratic Senate, and vice versa. Today the key differences are size and constituency. The House is much larger and thus requires a more formal hierarchical organization and more rigid rules by which to conduct its business. Without such strict rules and structure, the confusion of 435 disparate views would make it virtually impossible for the House to function. On the other hand, the rules and procedures of the Senate are more flexible. Additionally, senators, who serve for a longer term and represent a larger constituency, are believed to have more prestige and higher visibility.[12]

Congressional Committees

The group or committee system for making decisions is easily derided ("A camel is a horse designed by committee"). Its decisions usually come as the result of compromise and consensus, neither of which seems very heroic. But the committee system is characteristic of most large institutions, public

[12]Lewis A. Froman, Jr., *The Congressional Process* (Boston: Little, Brown, 1967), p. 7.

or private. We can best understand the nature and necessity of the committee system in the national legislature if we keep in mind that power in Congress is fragmented; that is, power is dispersed among a variety of different, and competing individuals and interests. Just as the country is made up of different interests (business and labor, whites and blacks, old and young, Southerners and Northerners, farmers and city dwellers, environmentalists and developers, conservatives and liberals), so too is Congress. The reason that committees are so important in Congress is because of the need for all these competing interests to come to terms with very complicated issues, deal with an increasingly high volume of bills and resolutions, and somehow moderate their differences to get legislation passed. The Senate or the House, acting as a single chamber, simply could not handle so much business. Moreover, given the large membership in both houses, it is not difficult to understand why Congress has divided itself into smaller, more manageable components to deal with legislation in certain categories.

We should add that the committee structure of Congress clearly illustrates the dispersal of power in the legislature. Committees and subcommittees in both houses are relatively independent, and the content and success of legislation depend much more on decisions made in committee than on decisions made on the floor of either house.[13]

Thus if you were to visit Washington, D.C., and attend a formal session in one of the houses of Congress, you might be astounded at how few members of Congress are on the floor. The reason is that most of the work of legislators is done in committees or in subcommittees. There are four kinds of committees in Congress: standing, special (or select), joint, and conference.

Standing committees are permanent and the best known of the congressional committees. The House has 22 such committees, which include committees of Appropriations, Ways and Means, Rules, and so on. The Senate has 16 standing committees, including Foreign Relations, Judiciary, and others. Standing committees are bipartisan, but the majority of their members are from the majority party. The chairperson of the committee is also from the majority party and is normally chosen by seniority; that is, the majority party member of a committee who has had the longest continuous service on that committee is its chairperson. (As noted earlier, the absolute rule of seniority was significantly challenged by the Ninety-fourth Congress in 1975. Suffice it to say that seniority is the normal manner of determining chairs.)

Committees may hold hearings that are either open or closed. Decisions are made by majority vote. The chair of a committee has considerable

[13]William J. Keefe, *Congress and the American People* (Englewood Cliffs, N.J.: Prentice-Hall, 1980), pp. 2–9.

The Organization of Congress	
Congressional Leadership, 101st Congress	
Senate	*House*
President—J. Danforth Quayle	The Speaker—James Wright (Texas)
President Pro Tempore—Robert Byrd (W. Va.)	Majority Leader—Thomas Foley (Wash.)
Majority Leader—George Mitchell (Maine)	Majority Whip—Tony Cuelho (Calif.)
Majority Whip—Alan Cranston (Calif.)	Minority Leader—Robert Michel (Ill.)
Minority Leader—Robert Dole (Kansas)	Minority Whip—Robert Cheney (Wyoming)
Minority Whip—Alan Simpson (Wyoming)	*House Standing Committees*
	Agriculture
Senate Standing Committees	Appropriations
Agriculture, Nutrition and Forestry	Armed Services
Appropriations	Banking, Finance and Urban Affairs
Armed Services	Budget
Banking, Housing and Urban Affairs	District of Columbia
Budget	Education and Labor
Commerce, Science and Transportation	Energy and Commerce
Energy and Natural Resources	Foreign Affairs
Environment and Public Works	Government Operations
Finance	House of Administration
Foreign Relations	Interior and Insular Affairs
Governmental Affairs	Judiciary
Judiciary	Merchant Marine and Fisheries
Labor and Human Resources	Post Office and Civil Service
Rules and Administration	Public Works and Transportation
Small Business	Rules
Veterans' Affairs	Science and Technology
	Small Business
	Standards of Official Conduct
	Veterans' Affairs
	Ways and Means

power, appointing subcommittees, calling meetings, and determining the agenda.

In the House, Republicans are placed on committees by the Committee on Committees. Democrats are chosen by the Democrats on the Steering and Policy Committee and are elected by the Democratic caucus. In the Senate, the Democratic Steering Committee appoints Democrats to standing committees, and Republicans have a counterpart Committee on Committees.

Special or select committees are temporary committees instituted for specific purposes. Examples of select committees in the Senate have included the Select Committee on Watergate, chaired by Sam Ervin, and the Select Committee on Intelligence, chaired by Frank Church.

Joint committees are usually permanent and are composed of members from both houses. The joint committee on taxation and the joint economic committee are the two current examples.

Conference committees are, technically, special joint committees. They are temporary and contain members from both houses. Their purpose is to discuss and reach agreement on legislation when there are disagreements between the versions passed by the two houses. Thus these committees have great power because they decide what will be in the law.

In 1977 the Senate, for the first time in 30 years, reorganized its committee system by a vote of 89 to 1. The chief sponsor of the reorganization was Adlai Stevenson, III (D., Ill.), who argued that the reorganization would help make the Senate a more democratic body and cut back on multiple and overlapping committees. Stevenson also stressed that the new structure would enable the Senate to work more smoothly with the Carter administration's efforts to reorganize the government. The plan reduced the number of standing Senate committees, and it sought to eliminate overlapping hearings and legislative work. It also created a new Energy and Natural Resources Committee, limited the number of committees on which a senator may serve, and restricted the number of committees that a senator may chair. Also in the 1970s the House of Representatives limited to one the number of standing committees a member could chair, and earlier, in its Legislative Reorganization Act of 1946, Congress reduced the number of standing committees. Thus Congress has taken seriously the urgings to make its workings more efficient and more democratic. Yet among the results of these reforms have been the proliferation of subcommittees and the diffusion of power in both houses. (In fact, some legislators are having second thoughts about the various reforms of recent years. Although designed to make Congress more responsive and more "democratic," by dispersing power they have also often made the legislative process more unwieldy.[14]

In addition to committees, each house has a hierarchy of leadership that, among other things, appoints members to select, joint, and conference committees. Leaders in both houses are elected by their party, which makes such decisions in the *party caucus*, a meeting of all members of the party, that adopts rules, devises strategies, and elects leaders. In the House, the majority party elects the speaker, who is the presiding officer. The minority party elects its leadership as well. In the Senate, the majority party elects the president pro tempore, a position more of honor than of power, and the majority leader.

[14]"Congress: Chaos vs. Consensus," *Christian Science Monitor*, February 6, 1987, pp. 18–20.

Making Law

"To live is to choose," said French existentialist Jean-Paul Sartre. A government, if it is to govern, must decide. There are two ways in which decisions can be made: (1) by a group of people, usually representing various interests and points of view, collectively by voting, and (2) by a single individual. There is no known alternative except to do nothing at all. Thus, as one scholar said, "the choices of Congress are the choices of the nation."[15] And those choices become the law of the land.

It is the whole labyrinthine procedure that a bill must go through that confuses and frustrates many Americans. Briefly, this is the procedure:

1. A bill is introduced. Anyone can draw up a bill—a member of Congress, the president, or a student. Many major bills are either conceived or written elsewhere. Thus members of Congress spend considerable time processing what has been invented outside Congress. However, official introduction of a bill can come only from a representative or a senator. In the House, a member puts the bill into a box called a *hopper* or gives it to a clerk. A senator orally introduces a bill to the floor.

2. The bill is referred to committee by the leadership in that particular house.

3. The committee takes action (or, usually, no action). If the committee approves the bill, it is reported to the full House. In the House of Representatives, the Rules Committee issues a rule of resolution to bring it to the floor.

4. The bill then goes on a calendar, which is a traffic-regulating device. In the House, there are five calendars: the union calendar for revenue and appropriations bills, the House calendar for all other public bills, the consent calendar for items having no opposition, the private calendar dealing with private matters such as a veteran's pension, and the discharge calendar for bills brought out of committee by discharge petition. In the Senate, there are two calendars, one legislative and one "executive," the latter containing treaties and nominations.

5. The bill goes to the floor (usually in its order on the calendar, although the Senate, by majority vote, and the House, by a special rule from the Rules Committee or a two-thirds vote, can bring up a pressing matter out of order). In the House, the bill will probably go to the committee of the whole, which is all the House in informal session, usually under the rules of debate established by the Rules Committee. The House then resolves itself into formal session and votes. The smaller Senate maintains formal sessions, in which, as we have seen, debate is unlimited.

6. After a bill is passed by one house, it goes to the other, in which frequently a similar bill has been considered, although the bill could be ignored or rejected.

[15]Keefe, p. 1.

HOW A BILL BECOMES LAW

This graphic shows the most typical way in which proposed legislation is enacted into law. There are more complicated, as well as simpler, routes, and most bills fall by the wayside and never become law. The process is illustrated with two hypothetical bills, House bill No. 1 (HR 1) and Senate bill No. 2 (S 2).

Each bill must be passed by both houses of Congress in identical form before it can become law. The path of HR 1 is traced by a solid line, that of S 2 by a broken line. However, in practice most legislation begins as similar proposals in both houses.

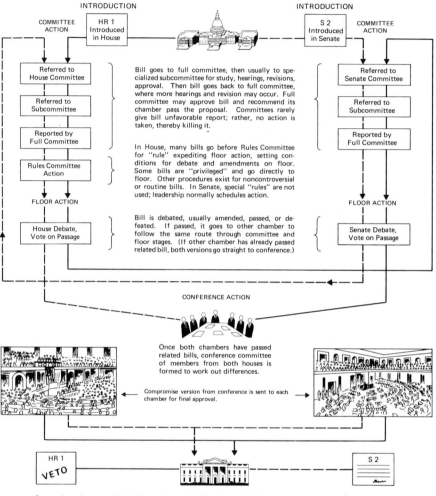

(Redrawn from Congressional Quarterly Inc., Current American Government, Fall 1980, p. 145.)

7. If there are similar bills from both houses, a conference committee will meet to resolve differences.

8. Once the exact wording is agreed upon by both houses, the bill goes to the president for approval or veto.

The Lawmaker

It is instructive to consider the environment that surrounds a member of Congress. To begin with, we might contrast two kinds of legislatures: congresses and parliaments. The word *parliament* derives from the French verb *parler*, meaning "to talk," whereas *congress* comes from the Latin word *congredi*, meaning "to come together." Also, in the British Parliament, members more regularly represent a political party, as contrasted with a locality or constituency. The party elects its candidates, and the majority party organizes the Parliament and chooses its leaders, who in turn form a cabinet and act as the executive of the government. Of course, there is no scarcity of talk in the U.S. Congress, but party loyalty is frequently less important than is loyalty to local interests. Thus, almost as though to confirm the linguistic distinction, one feature of the U.S. Congress is that it is a "coming together" of representatives of many diverse interests.

We must also always keep in mind the relationship of Congress to the executive, about which we have commented earlier. We alternately tend to blame Congress for moving too slowly and ineffectively to create needed policies or blame the president for not being able to move Congress to enact laws. But the Constitution purposely created two competing branches to check the power of both. Whereas the president wants to initiate and carry out policy (for example, in foreign affairs and trade), Congress wants to protect its right to make law, and it usually does so much more deliberately than the president wishes. Moreover, the constituencies of the two branches are different. The president must be concerned with the needs of the entire nation, whereas Congress represents local and particular interests. Typically, the institution that smooths relations between the president and Congress is the political party. But this works only when the president and the majority of Congress are of the same political party, and even then not as well as might be expected.[16] In fact, the occasions are rare in American history when the president and Congress are of such single mind as to work cooperatively and rapidly to create public law (the first 100 days of Franklin Roosevelt's New Deal in 1933 and the period of Lyndon Johnson's Great Society programs in the mid-1960s are among the few examples).

Members of Congress, in order to carry out their duties, rely to a considerable extent on their staff, that is, their administrative assistants, press secretaries, legislative aides, field representatives (who work in the

---

[16]Some students of Congress have pointed out that when floor votes are taken, the traditional two parties are less important in Congress than are ideological coalitions. For example, a conservative coalition of Northern Republicans and Southern Democrats can frequently outvote the remaining Democrats. See *Congressional Quarterly Weekly Report*, June 26, 1980, pp. 193–198.

home district), and several more. Currently there are over eighteen thousand persons employed by Congress, and this represents an enormous growth in professional staffs. The reasons for this growth are not difficult to understand. No representative or senator can be expected to be an expert on all issues that come before the legislature, and the complexity and increasing number of these issues have caused members of Congress to rely more and more on staff expertise. Also, staff are expected to handle the growing communication with constituents, which has increased dramatically in recent years.[17] (Yet, as CBS reporter Dan Rather pointed out in 1988, the staff of the White House has, in recent decades, grown at least as rapidly as that of Congress. Indeed, the staff hired by George Bush when he was vice president, a position with limited responsibilities, was actually larger than that of President Franklin Roosevelt during World War II.)

One current member of the Congress, Glenn M. Anderson (D., Calif.), believes that the low opinion that most polls show people to have of the Congress may be misleading. He points out that although it is true that people generally are critical of Congress, most seem to think their own particular representative is doing a good job. (Only about 5 percent of the members of Congress that seek reelection are defeated in a normal election.) Furthermore, Anderson believes that the poor collective view of Congress may be based on a widespread misunderstanding of the congressional role in our form of government. Congress, he points out, is a legislative body, never intended to be a group that actually runs the nation. Under the Constitution, Congress passes laws and reviews executive actions and proposals. It is not and cannot be an alternative to a strong and popular executive. Typically, Anderson added, it takes at least a year for a congressional proposal to work its way through complex committee hearings and find its way to the point at which it will be approved or repudiated by the members.

Leaders of Congress like Jim Wright and Robert Dole are chosen because they are moderates, respected by their colleagues for their fair-mindedness. They are rarely hard-driving executives chosen because they have provided outstanding leadership on important issues.

Finally, in the facedown between heads of congressional committees and representatives of the executive department, Congress is almost always at a disadvantage. Cabinet officers and other executive department heads are usually well-known, often distinguished authorities in their fields. A member of Congress who happens to head a committee on taxation or foreign affairs or transportation may have been trained and educated in some other, entirely unrelated field. He or she got the job through seniority and by being agreeable to voters and fellow representatives and party leaders. He or she understandably feels a certain insecurity at being asked to cross swords with

[17]Keefe, pp. 95–100; and James L. Sundquist, *The Decline and Resurgence of Congress* (Washington, D.C.: Brookings Institution, 1981), pp. 402–414.

the former head of a giant industry or corporation on matters of economics or with a four-star general on defense policy.

It might be possible for Congress to take a much more aggressive role and to reorganize itself so that it could more effectively compete with the president in providing an alternative national leadership, Anderson acknowledged. But he believes that it could not do so without departing from the clear intent of the Constitution and perhaps becoming a less representative and a more dictatorial body. In short, he argued that Congress is functioning well, along the lines intended by the framers of the Constitution and traditionally approved by the American people.[18]

Still, there is a pervasive sense that Congress does not serve the nation as well as might reasonably be expected. Maurice Rosenblatt, founder of the National Committee for an Effective Congress, acknowledged that "there is an anti-parliamentarian mood in the country." He stated that Congress reflects the "emotional malaise and intellectual indecision" of the nation. He believes that Congress is in a "transitional" phase, with one foot firmly planted in the past while the other foot is groping for a toehold in the 21st Century."[19]

Because Congress is the most representative agency of government, disaffection with it may to some degree reflect underlying uncertainties about the future of self-government itself. We continue to be confronted with problems of inflation, energy depletion, environmental pollution, inadequate public transportation, and much more. Can Congress and the president adequately address these issues?

As we have said, Congress's indispensable function is to enact legislation. But there appears to exist a widespread disbelief in the efficacy and wisdom of passing laws and spending tax dollars to solve specific social ills and achieve certain goals. The government has passed laws and appropriated tremendous sums to eliminate poverty, but the poor are still with us. The government has sought to achieve racial integration, but America remains a largely segregated society. Cynics may believe that Congress will suffer the fate of the Roman senate, which became less and less effective as Rome changed from a republic to an empire. The culmination of the senate's loss of power and prestige came when a Roman emperor appointed his horse a member of that once-august body. References to Congress, both as individuals and as a group, made by the inner circle of the Nixon administration and revealed by publication of the contents of the White House tapes, are hardly less disparaging to the dignity of the U.S. Senate. Such belittling

[18]Some information here and elsewhere in this chapter is based on interviews conducted in summer 1975 and fall 1980 with California Representatives Glenn Anderson and Jim Lloyd and members of their staffs.

[19]Maurice Rosenblatt, "Congress Torn Between Activism and Restraint," *Los Angeles Times*, February 1, 1976, Sec. 8, p. 3.

remarks are not uncharacteristic of other presidential staff or of the general public.

We should, however, keep in mind that recent Congresses have passed a number of important pieces of legislation, including an energy bill and a federal bureaucracy reform law, and the Senate, after considerable debate, approved the historic Panama Canal treaty. Moreover, as we have seen, Congress has made a start toward reversing a historic decline in congressional influence and power, by severely limiting the president's ability to conduct foreign policy unilaterally (and eliminating the power to engage in undeclared wars),[20] by demanding increased accountability from and authority over such powerful agencies as the FBI and the CIA, by creating a joint Senate-House Budget Office designed to give Congress more control over federal expenditures, by adopting more stringent rules regarding the ethical behavior of its members, and by streamlining its committee structure.[21] Such steps may be the harbingers of a stronger and more effective Congress acting in concert with the president to find new solutions to chronic problems.

[20]President Reagan challenged these limitations by ordering U.S. ships into combat zones in the Persian Gulf and conducting a military operation in Grenada without seeking congressional approval before or after the fact.

[21]For a full explanation of these developments, see Sundquist, especially pt. 2.

6

The Courts: The Search for the Just Society

- The Just Society •
- The Supreme Court •
- The National Court Structure •
- The Venerable Court •
- Judicial Review •
- The Warren Court •
- The Burger Court •
- The Rehnquist Court •
- Justice: Where Do We Stand? •

> **Fishes and beasts and the fowls of the air devour one another. But to man, the gods have given justice.**
>
> > Homer
> > *The Iliad*
>
> **It is emphatically the province and duty of the Judicial department to say what the law is.**
>
> > Chief Justice John Marshall
> > *Marbury v. Madison (1803)*

Like love, justice is praised perhaps more than it is practiced. Virtually all governments—dictatorships no less than democracies—claim to be just. Indeed all attempt to *justify* their acts. Hitler's government found just the systematic murder of millions of Jews. Stalin had little quarrel with the mass imprisonment and murder of those who aroused his wrath. At one time the CIA apparently thought that the assassination of unfriendly foreign leaders was justifiable. During 1980 the government of Iran saw nothing unjust in holding hostage American embassy personnel.

Justice is a complex idea. A simple synonym is fairness; within the context of a constitutional political society, justice may mean equal rights before the law (or no favoritism before the law).[1] The word *justice* reflects an ideal that probably predates recorded history. Wealth, power, and brute force have always played important roles in human relationships and in attempts to establish and maintain governments among men and women. But few if any have attempted to govern—that is, to control the behavior of other human beings—without appealing to some notion of justice, however primitive. In one sense, politics may be viewed as a struggle for power. Yet political societies likewise proclaim their desire to achieve justice. Ideally a government, which has power, can also dispense justice.

Some would argue with this statement. An anarchist, for example, presumably believes that all forms of power are inherently unjust, because power, by definition, implies coercion—the right to make others behave as one wishes them to behave through force, actual or implied. Libertarians base much of their political philosophy on the premise that virtually all forms of governmental power carry at least the possibility of abuse, and hence political "bureaucrats" are unjust by definition. (For instance, many believe that compulsory income tax laws represent an unjust theft of one person's property by the government for the purpose of bestowing it on

[1]See John Rawls, *A Theory of Justice* (Cambridge, Mass.: Harvard University Press, 1971); also see the series of review articles of Rawls's theory in the *American Political Science Review* 69 (June 1975): 588–675.

others.) Leftists, on the other hand, approach private wealth (that is, private power) with much the same built-in hostility. "All property is theft," said nineteenth-century socialist Pierre Joseph Proudhon. Thus the private acquisition of wealth is inherently unjust, and the rich are the eternal and inevitable enemies of a just society.

As people clearly do not, and perhaps never will, agree on what justice is, why bother at all about the word or the concept? Yet, there seems to be no way to exclude the idea from human affairs. In every relationship involving two or more persons, there will inevitably be some discussion, from mild disagreement to murderous hostility, about what is "fair" or "right"—that is, what is just. Husbands and wives, parents and children, teachers and students, no less than governments and citizens or governments and other governments will disagree, each insisting that its own point of view is right. Democrats argued that President Reagan's economic policies were unfair. Republicans say the same about Democratic welfare programs. If human beings could live without morals, ethics, or abstract intelligence, they would have no need for a definition of justice.

The Just Society

An ancient and classic study of the relationship between justice and government was written by the Greek philosopher Plato. In *The Republic*, Plato wrote that the search for justice was the foundation of all civil society. *The Republic* began and ended with an attempt to define the nature of the just society. Clearly, Plato did not settle the argument, for statesmen, philosophers, politicians, and citizens have been debating the same questions ever since.

Plato (using his teacher Socrates as the main character or "discussant" in *The Republic*) questioned two notions of justice popular in his own time, as in ours. Justice, he affirmed, cannot simply be a matter of giving people what they want or think they want. Suppose that a friend were to give you a sum of money with instructions to safeguard it for her. A little while later, this friend reappears, obviously drunk and with no self-control, and demands the return of the money. Would it be just to give it back under those circumstances? No, Plato argued, there are times when it is just to do not what is wanted but what is best in the long run. Should a physician treat every patient according to that patient's wishes, even when the physician knows that carrying out the patient's desires will do harm rather than good?

A second common definition of justice was offered by the intellectual character Thrasymachus, who argued simply that "justice is the interest of the strong," or might makes right. Stated this baldly, most people would disapprove of the definition, and yet Thrasymachus attempted to prove that in fact this is what we really mean by justice. For example, the notion might be applied to the power (just power?) that parents have over children. Of course, we may disapprove and call unjust an act of force, such as a robber's stealing money at the point of a gun, when it occurs—so to speak—on the retail level, as the private act of a private person. But when it happens wholesale, as when a ruling class passes laws that ordain that they shall pay little or no taxes, and middle-income people shall bear the cost of government, we accept it, and some even defend it as "just." (For instance, in practice, the very rich in America often pay a much smaller percentage of their total income in taxes than does the middle-class worker.) Or we may accept it as "right" that strong and populous nations like the Soviet Union or the United States should have far more influence in world affairs than do small and weak countries.

Plato has his character Socrates question this argument with the assertion that the purpose of any art, such as medicine or farming or government, should be the well-being of others. A physician should be a healer of the sick, not just "a maker of money." Teachers must impart knowledge to their students. Likewise, a ruler should be guided by "the interest of his subjects." Justice, then, may be an idea emphasizing concern for the well-being of others.

Both the ideal and the system—that is, the machinery of justice—that exist in the United States are the product of centuries of such philosophizing by those wise and unwise. They are also the product of human experience. In an attempt to resolve disputes among human beings peacefully and justly, rather than through sheer force (which would obviously make civil life impossible), we have developed a system of laws and courts. The police and, when needed, the military support and enforce the edicts of the courts. Only the government, except in rare instances, usually involving self-defense, has the right to resort to force to settle a question of right or wrong. If two drivers approach the same intersection on a collision course, it is the law, not who is stronger or braver or who has the bigger car, that is supposed to determine the question of who will stop and wait for the other. There are times when the law itself may be unjust (for example, the segregation laws that existed in most Southern states before the 1960s were thought to be unjust by Dr. Martin Luther King, Jr., who proceeded to organize mass violations of these laws that ultimately succeeded in having them changed or abolished). On the other hand, in most instances the professed aim of the law is to provide equity and justice for all.

The system of laws and courts that exists in the United States today is the product of our Constitution and of history. Article 3 of the Constitution provides for the court system. We have also borrowed from the ancient Greeks and Romans, from English common law, and from the Old and the New Testaments in creating our judicial system. Both the system and the laws are subject to continual change and evolution. At one point in our history, the system of segregation under the doctrine of "separate but equal" was upheld by our courts. At a later time, this doctrine was ruled unconstitutional—that is, illegal—because "separate was and is inherently unequal."[2] In the 1950s the people of Little Rock, Arkansas, physically sought to prevent the enforcement of a court order integrating their high schools. They felt that such an order was unjust and a violation of their rights. A conservative president, Dwight Eisenhower, who may have shared their distaste for compulsory integration, nevertheless felt constrained to enforce the court's order with the use of federal troops. Even Ronald Reagan, the nation's most conservative president in years, acknowledged that he would feel constrained to enforce the protection of civil rights law "at the point of a bayonet if necessary." More recently, the citizens of Boston and Los Angeles, who probably approved the integration of Little Rock's high schools in the 1950s, have gone into the streets protesting court-ordered busing for the purpose of achieving integration. Still, the courts have maintained the necessity of integration.

People who favor capital punishment sometimes cite the Bible as an authority for the death penalty for certain crimes. The Bible proves, they argue, that the death penalty is in accord with God's will and hence is just. Biblical scholars opposed to the death penalty believe that, on the contrary, specific punishments for specific crimes were included in the Bible because the death penalty was then a popular form of punishment for virtually *all* crimes, including some that we today would consider trivial or nonexistent (such as witchcraft). Hence the effect of the prescribed death penalty for certain offenses and not others was to bring a more humane and enlightened concept of crime and punishment to the people of that era. We should live, it is felt, by the spirit, not the letter of the law. For the letter killeth, quite literally.

In the same way, many persons have stated that because "swift and sure punishment" is the best, if not the only, deterrent to crime, legislatures should prescribe fixed and severe punishments for crimes of violence, thus removing from judges the discretionary powers to grant probation, to accept plea bargaining, and to use other devices that some believe have made the administration of justice more humane and flexible but that opponents believe have resulted in "coddling criminals" and thus encouraging crime.

Most Americans were shocked when President Ford granted Richard Nixon a full pardon for any and all criminal acts in which he may have been involved in regard to the Watergate scandal. Several of Nixon's subordinates went to prison, whereas Nixon was granted a pardon. Many Americans believed that the pardon violated the concept of "equal justice under the law." It seemed unjust that the president's men should go to prison for carrying out his instructions while he lived in a palatial home in San Clemente, California, enjoying a substantial government pension and other privileges associated with his role as a former president. Moreover, because the pardon was issued before any conviction, it precluded the possibility of

[2]This was the landmark case *Brown v. Board of Education, Topeka* (1954).

the nation's learning all the details of Watergate during a trial of the former president.

A difference in opinion about the nature of justice distinguished the Reagan administration from others since the end of World War II. Through both Republican and Democratic administrations, Americans who earned high incomes were taxed so that at least a portion of the revenues so received might be redistributed through various federal government programs, such as food stamps, entitlement programs of one sort or another, housing subsidies to poor people, and school funding. In a prosperous, modern society, it was deemed just that the winners should allocate at least a portion of their wealth to the losers and that one important function of government was to see that this was done fairly. Although President Reagan was not politically able to do away with these programs, he did manage to cut them substantially as a percentage of total government spending. The basis for this was not the president's indifference to human suffering but his often expressed belief that "the taxing power of government must not be used to regulate the economy or bring social change." In other words, he tended to believe that taxing the well-to-do for the purpose of ameliorating the welfare of the poor was unjust and an abuse of political power. Liberal opponents expressed the opposite view of what was proper in a just society.[3]

The struggle over civil rights, the conflict between labor and management over who gets what, the complaints of students about the fairness of grades, disputes between buyer and seller—all are predicated on varying definitions of what is just. Because what we deem to be "right" and "fair" is to a large extent determined by what we have become accustomed to in our upbringing, nations such as the United States, with a large and varied population and many different kinds of cultures, are likely to experience more and deeper disagreements than are relatively homogeneous populations.

The Supreme Court

For this reason, Alistair Cooke, author and narrator of a popular television series on the history of America, concluded, as have some other observers, that the true strength of American society lies in a uniquely American invention: the Supreme Court.[4] Given the divisions among our people, there is need for a body that has the power to decide, once and for all, what is or is not constitutional.[5] In the one instance in which the Court failed to find a

[3]For a discussion of this question, see George F. Will, "In Defense of the Welfare State," *New Republic*, May 9, 1983.

[4]Alistair Cooke, *America* (New York: Knopf, 1974), pp. 144–147.

[5]What is constitutional—that is, what is "the supreme law of the land"—is not necessarily synonymous with what is "just."

The Supreme Court. From left to right (front row): Thurgood Marshall, William J. Brennan, Jr., William H. Rehnquist, Byron R. White, Harry A. Blackmun; (back row): Antonin Scalia, John Paul Stevens, Sandra Day O'Connor, Anthony M. Kennedy. *(Copyright © 1988 Supreme Court Historical Society. Reproduced with permission.)*

solution to a great national issue acceptable to the entire nation, the result was civil war, Cooke stated. Thus when the Court fails, the only alternative, he suggests, may lie in armed conflict. "Liberty and justice for all" may be more of an ideal than a reality in the United States, even today. But the Court exists to sustain the ideal and the society that rests on this premise. Yet, although the Court's responsibilities are as important as Cooke suggested, its power, at least on the surface, is very limited. As *Federalist* 78 noted,

> The judiciary . . . has no influence over either the sword or the purse; no direction either of the strength or of the wealth of the society; and can take no active resolution whatever. It may truly be said to have neither force nor will, but merely judgment . . . the judiciary is beyond comparison the weakest of the three departments of power.

Nevertheless, the U.S. Supreme Court commands a measure of reverence and dignity not frequently accorded to the two other branches. "In a nation with no monarchy and no established church," according to *Newsweek* magazine, "the Supreme Court of the United States approaches the level of a sacred institution."[6]

[6]*Newsweek*, November 1, 1971, p. 16.

In 1980, however, the dignified aura surrounding the Court was brought under scrutiny by the publication of the controversial book, *The Brethren*.[7] The authors used two years of interviews with law clerks to penetrate the private lives of the justices. Done in the Watergate style of investigative reporting, the book was an unflattering group portrait of the Court, in which readers learned of the justices' making deals and nursing enmities against one another. Critics maintained that this book was muckraking at its worst and that it could well erode the respect and dignity necessary for the Court to do its work. The authors argued that the book merely demonstrated that the justices were human beings and that in the end the Court would be capable of executing its legitimate constitutional functions. What seemed clear was that the book was an in-depth study, with a point of view, of the inner workings of the Court. The book may be useful if considered within the larger context of the Supreme Court's constitutionally required deliberations and the effects of those deliberations on the nation.

Justices of the Supreme Court are appointed for life by the president, with the approval of the Senate. By giving the justices a lifetime tenure of office, the authors of the Constitution hoped to create a body of learned judges who would be insulated from personal ambition and political pressure, thus providing the republic with a certain stability. By and large, the Court probably has been a more stable element in the American system of government than have either of its two counterparts, the presidency and Congress. At the same time, the Court has played from time to time an innovative and sometimes even a revolutionary role in American life.

Because the justices appointed by a given president normally outlast the tenure of that president and the Congress that appointed them, the Supreme Court may reflect a political philosophy somewhat different from that of the existing president or Congress. In the heyday of the New Deal, the Court acted as a brake on Franklin D. Roosevelt. During the conservative Eisenhower era, the Warren Court became an instrument of great social change.

When the United States was in the grip of anticommunist hysteria during the Truman and Eisenhower eras, it was the Supreme Court that ultimately upheld and proved the surest defender of the right of political dissent. It was the Warren Court, that opened the path to the civil rights movement with the *Brown v. Board of Education* decision. The Court that helped bring the Watergate crisis to a peaceful resolution, by insisting unanimously that President Nixon must cooperate with the prosecution, included several jurists and a chief justice who were Nixon appointees, thus vindicating the wisdom of the Constitution in insulating the justices from politics. On the other hand, the Court has sometimes failed to meet its responsibility to act as a counterbalancing force to the passions of the moment. For example, it failed to take exception to the enforced and blatantly unconstitutional

[7] By Bob Woodward and Scott Armstrong (New York: Simon & Schuster, 1980).

internment of Japanese Americans during World War II following the attack on Pearl Harbor. Ironically, it was Earl Warren, then attorney general of California, who was a leader in the clearly unconstitutional detention of thousands of American citizens of Japanese ancestry. That Warren later became the chief justice of perhaps the most liberal and civil rights–oriented Court in the nation's history may suggest that the Court, like the presidency, often seems to improve the character and extend the range of the people who join it. Another example of this process was the tenure of Justice Hugo Black, a member of the Ku Klux Klan in his youth, who later became one of the most distinguished defenders of equality and civil liberty in the Court's history.

The Supreme Court has not avoided controversy: our history is strewn with frequently vitriolic attacks on it.[8] Although Chief Justice John Marshall, who served from 1801 to 1836, presided over some of the most important decisions in our history, he also feuded openly with two of our most powerful presidents: Jefferson on matters of presidential appointments and Andrew Jackson on the issue of the national bank. One can hardly imagine a more explosive court decision than the case of Dred Scott in 1857, in which the Court of Chief Justice Roger Taney declared slavery to be legally binding on all states and maintained that even free blacks could not expect to be treated as citizens under the Constitution. The Dred Scott controversy helped to create the Republican party, and Illinois lawyer Abraham Lincoln established a national reputation by criticizing it. In the 1930s, the "nine old men" of the Court angered another powerful president, FDR, by striking down New Deal legislation. Roosevelt attempted to push through Congress legislation that would set up a mandatory retirement age for judges and expand the number on the Supreme Court to allow him to install justices more favorable to his views. Roosevelt failed in this attempt.

Finally, there were a number of proponents of the impeachment of Earl Warren, who has been gone from the bench since 1969 and died in 1974. The popular hostility against the Warren Court (1953–1969) has been a recent reflection of how controversial the Court has become.

But the Court has held up against assault, and any liberals who believe the Warren Court's decisions to have been prudent and protective of fundamental rights probably are pleased that FDR was unsuccessful in attempting to establish a precedent for popularly elected officials' meddling with the judicial branch.

This discussion, of course, raises the interesting point of the nature of judicial appointments. Earl Warren was a three-term Republican governor of California and thus represented a partisan political appointment. Nixon's appointments were less representative of political partisanship than of ideological "conservatism." During the third presidential debate of

<hr>

[8]See Robert G. McCloskey, *The American Supreme Court* (Chicago: University of Chicago Press, 1960).

Chief Justices of the United States		
Chief Justice	Appointed by President	Years of Service
John Jay	Washington	1789–1795
Oliver Ellsworth	Washington	1796–1800
John Marshall	Adams	1801–1835
Roger B. Taney	Jackson	1836–1864
Salmon P. Chase	Lincoln	1864–1874
Morrison R. Waite	Grant	1874–1888
Melville W. Fuller	Cleveland	1888–1910
Edward D. White	Taft	1910–1921
William Howard Taft	Harding	1921–1930
Charles Evans Hughes	Hoover	1930–1941
Harlan Fiske Stone	Roosevelt	1941–1946
Fred M. Vinson	Truman	1946–1953
Earl Warren	Eisenhower	1953–1969
Warren E. Burger	Nixon	1969–1986
William H. Rehnquist	Reagan	1986–present

Note: Omitted is John Rutledge, who served only for a few months in 1795 and who was not confirmed by the Senate.

1976, Jimmy Carter maintained that he would base his court appointments on a careful screening process to find the most competent jurists. Yet, when pressed further, Carter conceded that if several potential appointees were of the same level of competence, he would pick the one most compatible with his own views. During the 1980 election campaign, Ronald Reagan, under fire for his opposition to the equal rights amendment, promised to appoint a woman to the Supreme Court, a promise he fulfilled with the choice of Sandra Day O'Connor.

Many Supreme Court justices have proved surprisingly independent of the views of the presidents who appointed them. For example, Earl Warren, appointed by President Eisenhower, became a liberal and activist, which surprised most observers, including Eisenhower.

The National Court Structure

Article 3 of the Constitution only vaguely defines the organization of a court system, calling simply for a Supreme Court, with inferior courts to be created by Congress. In the Judiciary Act of 1789, the First Congress divided the nation into districts, an essential principle of division that continues today. The current structure, from bottom to top, includes district courts, courts of appeals, and one Supreme Court.

There are currently 94 *district courts*. Each state has at least one district court, and there is one in the District of Columbia and one in Puerto Rico. Larger states have more than one. This is the level at which most national court work is done. There may be one or more judges at each district court. District judgeships are filled by the president with the consent of the Senate. All district judges hold office for life (unless they are impeached). District courts are courts of original jurisdiction, so, if you violate a federal law, you will be charged in and go to court before a district court. These are the only national courts that use *grand juries* (indicting juries) and *petit juries* (trial juries).

If a case is successfully appealed, it will normally go to a *U.S. court of appeals* in one of 11 judicial circuits in the country (including one in the District of Columbia). These courts have only appellate jurisdiction. They do not use juries, and they have from one to nine judges, all appointed for life by the president with the consent of the Senate.

Next, and at the top of the hierarchy, is the *Supreme Court*, whose jurisdiction is both original (this original jurisdiction is severely limited in Article 3, Section 2 of the Constitution) and appellate. The Court spends most of its time on cases on appeal. It is the Court of last resort, with the last word on matters falling within the jurisdiction of the Constitution.

Now, two cautionary notes must be emphasized: (1) the national court structure outlined here is different from but related to the *state* court systems, and (2) the *prosecution* of law violators is different from but related to the court system.

Most states also have a hierarchical system, ranging from lower courts to a state supreme court. These courts try civil (such as divorce) and criminal (such as murder) cases in which state laws are violated (there are some areas of concurrent jurisdiction). As a general rule, the only national court that can review a state court decision is the Supreme Court—and this only after all appeals at the state level have been exhausted (that is, the case has gone all the way through the state supreme court).

Judges, whether in national or state courts, decide cases; they do not prosecute people. At the national level, government prosecution is the responsibility of the Justice Department, part of the president's cabinet. The Justice Department is directed by the attorney general and aided by the solicitor general (who argues cases for the government before the Supreme Court). The department uses U.S. attorneys throughout the country, who are appointed for four-year terms to the district courts by the president with the consent of the Senate. Assisted by the FBI, which is housed within the Justice Department, these attorneys commence criminal and civil proceedings in district courts for the government.

When members of the executive branch were being investigated during the Watergate matter, serious confusion arose. In effect, members of the Nixon administration (in the Justice Department) were investigating (preliminary to prosecution) their own administration (two former attorneys general—John Mitchell and Richard Kleindienst—were directly or tangentially touched by the scandal). This is why Congress maintained the right to create a "special" prosecutor, distinct from but active in the Justice Department. When Archibald Cox, the first special prosecutor, threatened Nixon's tenure, the president fired him in October 1973 (as he would fire any member of his cabinet). Neither the attorney general at the time, Elliott Richardson, nor the deputy attorney general, William Ruckelshaus, was willing to carry out the firing because they believed it was an action of bad faith vis-à-vis Congress. Solicitor General Robert Bork was thus temporarily elevated to attorney general, whereupon he officially fired Cox. The ensuing public outcry became so intense, however, that Nixon had to agree to another special prosecutor, Leon Jaworski, who ultimately unraveled so much of the scandal that the president had to leave office.

In an effort to avoid such an event in the future, Congress in 1978 enacted the Ethics in Government Act, establishing a procedure to appoint an "independent counsel" to investigate wrongdoing in the executive branch of the government. As amended in 1982, the act requires the attorney general, whenever he receives specific, clear evidence of a possible crime by an official of the executive branch, to launch a preliminary investigation. If the charges are substantial, the attorney general then is to ask a specially convened panel of three federal appellate judges to appoint a special prosecutor to investigate, and if appropriate, prosecute wrongdoers. In addition, the Ethics in Government Act restricts lobbying by former high-level government officials for a set period of time after they have left government service. This law had an unfortunate impact on the Reagan administration. By 1988, two of President Reagan's closest longtime aides, Michael Deaver and Lyn Nofziger, had been convicted on criminal charges brought by special prosecutors. A third, Attorney General Edwin Meese III, resigned after an investigation by a special prosecutor, and yet another special prosecutor had brought indictments against John Poindexter, Reagan's former national security adviser, and Oliver North, formerly of the president's National Security Council, for illegal actions in the Iran-Contra affair. In April 1988, one of these appeals arrived before the Supreme Court. The Reagan administration argued before the Court that the special prosecutor law was unconstitutional because it violated the Constitution's doctrine of "separation of powers," by which the executive branch is responsible for executing the law, including the prosecution of lawbreakers. Supporters of the law argued that it was necessary to assure a remedy against conflicts of interest that would face any administration if political associates and administration colleagues (including even the attorney general) were implicated in possible crimes. In June, 1988, the Supreme Court, in a 7-1 decision (*Morrison v. Olson*) upheld the independent council law. The opinion, written by Chief Justice William H. Rehnquist, was a setback for the Reagan White House. The court ruled that the independent council law did not "impermissibly undermine the power of the executive branch" nor did it "disrupt the proper balance of power between congress and the president."

The Venerable Court

Ultimately it is the Supreme Court that makes history, but it does so selectively, for although it takes cases on appeal from both state courts and lower national courts, it takes only a few, and these few are usually of national importance.

For a case to come before the Supreme Court from a *state* court, a national question must be involved (for example, a constitutional question or a question involving a national law or treaty), and litigants must have exhausted their appeals at the state level. Even then, the odds are against the case's being presented to the Supreme Court. The Court also uses extreme discretion in deciding which appealed cases from lower national courts it will review. In either case, a disappointed litigant must petition the Court. If at least four justices find the case worthy, the Court will issue a *writ of certiorari* (Latin for "make more certain") to the lower court, ordering it to send up all records of the case.

Thus the Court essentially performs two functions. First, it determines what cases it will hear (a small minority of the total appealed to it); second, it hears and issues judgments on those cases. The court is in session from October through June in the palatial and dignified Supreme Court building

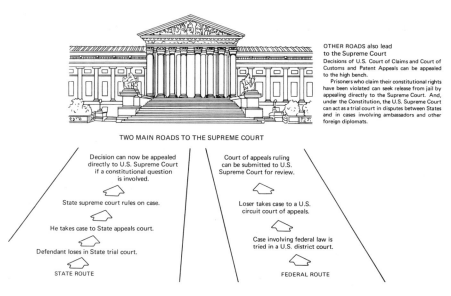

OTHER ROADS also lead to the Supreme Court
Decisions of U.S. Court of Claims and Court of Customs and Patent Appeals can be appealed to the high bench.
Prisoners who claim their constitutional rights have been violated can seek release from jail by appealing directly to the Supreme Court. And, under the Constitution, the U.S. Supreme Court can act as a trial court in disputes between States and in cases involving ambassadors and other foreign diplomats.

TWO MAIN ROADS TO THE SUPREME COURT

Decision can now be appealed directly to U.S. Supreme Court if a constitutional question is involved.

State supreme court rules on case.

He takes case to State appeals court.

Defendant loses in State trial court.

STATE ROUTE

Court of appeals ruling can be submitted to U.S. Supreme Court for review.

Loser takes case to a U.S. circuit court of appeals.

Case involving federal law is tried in a U.S. district court.

FEDERAL ROUTE

How cases get to the Supreme Court. *(Based on a copyrighted chart in* **U.S. News & World Report,** *May 9, 1977, p. 52.)*

in Washington, D.C. The justices hear cases in the courtroom there and discuss them among themselves in a private chamber. Decisions are made by a majority vote, and the Court almost always announces its reasons for each decision. These can come in an *opinion for the Court*, which is the majority opinion, written by one of the majority; a *concurring opinion*, again written by a member of the majority, but one who wishes to emphasize different views; and, of course, *dissenting opinions*, written by those who voted in the minority, explaining their reasoning.

Judicial Review

The Supreme Court has maintained an awesome authority, in part because of the right of *judicial review*. Although the Constitution does not explicitly grant the judiciary the right to rule on constitutional issues, Alexander Hamilton, writing in the *Federalist Papers*, maintained that the framers intended the courts to have the duty "to declare all acts contrary to the manifest tenor of the Constitution void."[9] The term *judicial review* needs careful clarification. It refers first to the national court's power to decide whether a *state* law or provision of a *state* constitution is consonant with the U.S. Constitution. This authority is based on the statement in Article 6 of the Constitution that the Constitution is "the supreme law of the land . . . anything in the Constitution or laws of any state to the contrary notwithstanding." The Judiciary Act passed by Congress in 1789 confirmed this power of the courts.

Judicial review refers second to the national court's right to declare whether or not a piece of statutory legislation passed by the *national* congress or a presidential action is consonant with the Constitution. The precedent for this latter authority was established in the landmark case *Marbury v. Madison* (1803). In the election of 1800, Thomas Jefferson defeated incumbent John Adams for the presidency. Followers of Jefferson also won control of Congress from Adams's Federalist party. However, as the newly elected administration was not scheduled to assume office until March 4, 1801, lame duck President Adams, with his lame duck Federalist Congress, had the opportunity to place Federalists in the national court system. Congress accordingly created several new judicial posts, and Adams hastened to fill them. In the late rush, not all the commissions were delivered. Interestingly, Adams's secretary of state, who was responsible for delivering the commissions, was a Virginia Federalist, John Marshall, whom Adams had appointed chief justice of the Supreme Court. William Marbury had been appointed to a judgeship in the District of Columbia but had not received his commission, and after March 4, 1801, the new secretary

[9]*Federalist* 78.

of state, James Madison, under orders from Jefferson, refused to deliver it. Marbury then appealed to the Supreme Court for a *writ of mandamus* (an order to a public official to perform a specified duty). According to Section 3 of the Judiciary Act of 1789, the Supreme Court was authorized to issue such writs to persons holding U.S. office.

Chief Justice Marshall spoke for the unanimous Court. He said first that Marbury was entitled to his commission, but second and surprisingly, he said that the Supreme Court could not issue such a writ of mandamus, because Article 13 of the Judiciary Act of 1789 was contrary to Article 3, Section 2, of the constitution, which accorded the Supreme Court *original* jurisdiction *only* in cases affecting ambassadors or foreign ministers or in cases in which a state was a party. Marbury fit none of these definitions! Thus Article 13 of the Judiciary Act of 1789 was invalid. Although in this particular case Marshall limited the power of the Court, by effecting judicial review of national legislation, he provided the Court with immense power.[10]

Such power has led some critics to complain that the judicial branch too often *makes policy* rather than simply interpreting the Constitution. In fact, it could be argued that the courts make policy whenever they interpret or reinterpret the law in significant ways. For example, the Supreme Court, by interpreting the Constitution, has established guidelines for affirmative action programs (see the following discussion of the Bakke case), and by a reinterpretation of the Constitution, the Court has decreed that public schools must be integrated. These are policies made by the Court rather than by the legislature.

A key question concerning the Court is just how activist the judiciary should be in making policy. The Supreme Court under Earl Warren was considered activist because it frequently took on new kinds of cases and made significant judgments on them that changed public policies (see the following discussion of the Warren Court). Advocates of an activist Court usually cite the view of Charles Evans Hughes, chief justice during the 1920s and 1930s, who once said that "the Constitution is what the judges say it is." Other eminent justices, such as the late Felix Frankfurter, insisted that judges should avoid "private notions of policy" and interpret the Constitution strictly, thus leaving policymaking, as far as possible, to legislators and executives.

Despite the authority of judicial review, there are certain checks on judicial power. Congress can determine the size, salaries, and jurisdiction of the judicial branch, and judges are selected by the president, with the concurrence of the Senate (of 143 presidential appointments to the Supreme Court, 27 nominees of 15 presidents have failed to win Senate confirma-

---

[10]An excellent essay regarding this case is by John A. Garraty, "The Case of the Missing Commissions," in John A. Garraty, ed., *Quarrels That Have Shaped the Constitution* (New York: Harper & Row, 1964), pp. 1–14.

tion). Moreover, Congress can impeach and remove judges from office. Only once has this been tried at the Supreme Court level, when the House impeached Samuel Chase in 1804, though he was not removed, as the Senate failed to vote conviction.

Also, Congress and the states can react to a Supreme Court decision by amending the Constitution. The Sixteenth Amendment is an example. This amendment provided for an income tax that earlier had been declared by the Supreme Court to be unconstitutional.

In the two centuries of the republic only a few more than one hundred acts or parts of acts have been declared unconstitutional, and many of these were unimportant. Of those of more substance (such as the New Deal legislation of the 1930s—the Court struck down 11 New Deal statutes), most were replaced by new legislation so revised as to meet the Court's requirements.

The Warren Court

Since World War II, the Supreme Court review of state laws and actions has created the most public controversy. One reason for the increased activity of the Court during Warren's term was the Court's insistence that the provisions of the Bill of Rights protecting individual rights against the national government also apply to state governments. This position is based on the Court's reading of the Fourteenth Amendment, passed during the Reconstruction period after the Civil War.[11] Let us look at Section 1 of this amendment, which contains four important ingredients. First is a definition of U.S. citizenship: "All persons born or naturalized in the United States, and subject to the jurisdiction thereof, are citizens of the United States and of the State wherein they reside." Second is a restriction on states, protecting individual rights: "No State shall make or enforce any law which shall abridge the privileges or immunities of citizens of the United States." Third is a statement restricting states with respect to *just* procedure: "nor shall any state deprive any person of life, liberty, or property, without due process of law" (due process of law means, basically, that justice demands a knowable procedure for someone accused of a crime; thus there must be a law before there can be a violation, and there must be a formal accusation, a show of cause for detention, a right to counsel, a formal plea, and a trial). A final restriction on states is that they may not "deny to any person within [their] jurisdiction the equal protection of the laws."

---

[11]Many of the landmark decisions of the Warren Court, outlined here, were based on the extension of rights in the First, Fifth, and Sixth Amendments to states as well as the federal government. See Charles H. Sheldon, *The Supreme Court: Politicians in Robes* (Beverly Hills, Calif.: Glencoe, 1970).

This short paragraph of the Constitution has provided the fodder from which a judicial revolution of sorts developed during the 1950s and 1960s. For it was during these years that the Warren Court came to be concerned about and active in supporting substantive individual rights. It was in this regard that the Court was both condemned and praised for its "judicial activism." When Nixon ran for election in 1968, one of his main promises was to bring the Court into line by appointing "strict constructionists" to replace the "loose constructionists" then on the Court. Gerald Ford, while he was in Congress, led a movement to impeach one of the most liberal judges—William O. Douglas.

Why was the Warren Court so controversial? Did the Burger Court substantially reverse the impact of its predecessor?

As to the first of these questions, the Court was probably controversial because of the subject matter of the cases and the people involved. The Court was concerned with civil rights and individual rights for ethnic minorities, the economically underprivileged, and the politically unpopular (atheists and communists, for example). In each instance, however, the Court firmly contended that it was upholding the Constitution, particularly the First, Fourth, Fifth, Sixth, and Fourteenth Amendments. Indeed, Hugo Black, who joined the majority in most of the controversial issues, argued persuasively that he was in fact a "strict constructionist."

Let us look at the most important cases of the Warren Court:

1. First, we must consider the category of *racial integration* of public schools. In 1954, the Court issued its famous decision in *Brown v. Board of Education, Topeka, Kansas*. For 58 years the Court had consistently held that separate public facilities could be considered equal and therefore constitutional. The question before the Court was whether segregation deprived black children of equal educational opportunities and thus of the equal protection of the law (see the Fourteenth Amendment). The Court, in a unanimous decision, answered yes, holding that separation was inherently unequal, thus reversing the separate-but-equal doctrine of *Plessy v. Ferguson* (1896). As we have seen, there was considerable resistance to this decision.

2. In the category of *freedom of political expression*, the Court in *Yates v. United States* (1957) overturned the conviction of some second-string communists on the basis of free speech, no matter how unpopular the issue. In other cases the Court upheld the right of freedom of expression.[12]

3. *Separation of church and state.* In *Engel v. Vitale* (1962), the Court dealt with a New York State Board of Regents' requirement of an opening-day prayer at all schools. Ten parents had brought suit against the requirement. The Court ruled that this state-mandated prayer violated the First Amendment as applied to the states by the Fourteenth Amendment. Thus

[12]See Robert L. Cord, *Protest, Dissent and the Supreme Court* (Cambridge, Mass.: Winthrop, 1971).

New York law violated the constitutional wall of separation of church and state. As Jefferson would have certainly agreed, the government, according to the Court, should neither deprive religious freedom nor further particular religious beliefs. Unpopular among many Americans, this decision underscored the secular nature of our political society, which had been a unique contribution of our revolutionary era.

4. *Equal voting rights.* We discussed equal voting rights in our chapter on Congress. To recapitulate, in *Baker v. Carr* (1962), the Court ruled that under the equal-protection-of-the-law requirement of the Fourteenth Amendment, state legislative districts must represent people equally on a one-person, one-vote basis. The principle was extended to national congressional districts in *Wesberry v. Sanders* (1964). Thus today, all members of the House of Representatives represent the same number of constituents, and each of us, then, is equal to all other voters in being represented in the House. One implication of this ruling is that more representatives now come from the more heavily populated urban and suburban areas.

5. *Rights of the accused.* The key decision in the category of rights of the accused was *Miranda v. Arizona* (1966). The Court said that when individuals are deprived of their freedom (in this case by state officials), they have certain rights consonant with the principle of due process (see the earlier discussion of the Fourteenth Amendment). In reviewing this case, the Court discovered that certain police interrogation methods violated the right against involuntary self-incrimination. The essence of the ruling was that the arresting and investigative unit (the police) must inform individuals of their rights the moment that they have been detained. Under the *Miranda* formula, you would (a) be told that you may remain silent, (b) be told that anything you say can be held against you, (c) have a right to counsel prior to and during questioning, and (d) if indigent, have a right to have counsel appointed for you. The decision clarified the rights of an accused person (not a convicted criminal).

The Burger Court

These are the important areas in which the Warren Court made controversial decisions. A comparison of these decisions with judgments by the Burger Court should reveal how dramatically the later Court reversed (or did not reverse) its predecessor's actions. In making this comparison, we should keep in mind how difficult it is to describe a coherent political philosophy of a particular Court. Because the justices on the Supreme Court are appointed for life, less regular changes in the Court's philosophy would be expected than in other branches of the government. Yet it is inadequate to characterize a particular Court as "liberal" or "conservative" (although most observers called the Warren Court "activist"). The

Burger Court seemed to lack a dominant, consistent philosophical majority, and it also at times was activist and at other times passive. One critic complained of "an unpredictable pattern" in the Burger Court, "with the Justices confounding preconceptions founded even on their own past conduct."[13] Nevertheless it is instructive to look at certain important decisions of this Court.

First, under the category of *school integration*, the Burger Court actually implemented earlier decisions, even going so far as to condone busing to achieve racial balance. Nixon's first appointee, Chief Justice Burger, wrote that "all things are not equal in a system that has been deliberately constricted and maintained to enforce racial segregation . . . Desegregation plans cannot be limited to the walk-in school"; bus transportation, he said, is "one tool" for desegregation. The court stuck by this judgment.[14] In 1983 the Court upheld the power of the Internal Revenue Service to deny tax-exempt status to private schools that discriminate on the basis of race.[15]

In terms of *freedom of political expression*, the Court maintained the Warren tradition.[16] In one of the most dramatic expressions, the Court let stand California court rulings that it was unconstitutional for black activist Angela Davis to be fired from the UCLA faculty because she was a member of the Communist party.

For the most part, the Court also maintained support of the doctrine of *separation of church and state*, most particularly by holding unconstitutional any state laws that directly or indirectly represented government sponsorship of religious activity. Thus, despite the support of both Presidents Nixon and Ford for government aid to private and parochial schools, the Court denied or struck down any laws that would provide such aid. However, in later decisions the Court altered this position somewhat by condoning public aid to church-related private colleges. The majority of the Court still opposed such aid to elementary and secondary schools but decided that institutions of higher learning spend little time on religious teaching and are rarely influenced by church authorities.[17]

The Court likewise maintained the "one-person, one-vote" principle in reapportionment cases.

The Burger Court even entered some controversial areas never, or only slightly, touched by the Warren Court. For example, the new Court ruled

[13]Robert Shrum, "The Supreme Court and the Idea of Retrogress," *Politics Today*, September–October 1979, pp. 16–20.

[14]*Los Angeles Times*, February 27, 1972, sec. G, p. 2; October 25, 1972, sec. 1, p. 3.

[15]*Bob Jones v. U.S.* (1983). This eight-to-one vote represented a defeat for the Reagan administration, which had tried to gain tax-exempt status for such schools.

[16]For an interesting discussion of the history and importance of First Amendment decisions, see Alexander M. Bickel, "The 'Uninhibited, Robust, and Wide-open' First Amendment," *Commentary*, November 1972, pp. 60–67.

[17]This was the 1976 case *Roemer v. Maryland Public Works Board*. The decision was by the barest of margins, five to four.

that women had a constitutional right to an abortion in the first three months of pregnancy. This 1973 decision struck down antiabortion laws across the country.[18]

In the apparent conflict between freedom of expression and freedom from "obscenity," the Court took some action, but the results remained ambiguous. Within the past few years Americans have witnessed considerable change in standards of public morality. The result has been more open acceptance of sex in literature, art, and motion pictures. Thus there is today an increasing number of profit-making "skin" magazines, underground sex newspapers, and explicit, X-rated movies. Some private individuals and government officials have tried to suppress such material, only to be opposed by those who say that the First Amendment prohibits actions against freedom of expression. The Warren Court attempted to define and limit "obscenity" by ruling that material "utterly without redeeming social importance" was not protected by the Constitution.[19] But application of the principle proved ineffective in checking the increase in alleged obscene material that contained even the slightest "social value." In 1973 the Burger court ruled that local communities in effect could set their own standards as to what was or was not tolerable in works dealing with sexual conduct.[20] Thus, although state legislatures can apparently pass laws giving local communities more control over such matters, the money-making explosion in pornography continues. (Where such businesses exist is usually determined by zoning ordinances.)

The one category in which the later Court substantially altered precedents established by the Warren Court was in the area of due process and the rights of the accused. For example, the Court made more flexible the rules requiring police to obtain court warrants for search and seizure, even deciding that many persons detained on minor charges (such as traffic violations) may be searched for evidence of more serious but unrelated offenses. Moreover, the Court (1) permitted prosecutors to introduce into Court statements made by defendants before being told their right to counsel, (2) allowed testimony by witnesses whose identity was determined during illegal interrogations, (3) authorized the introduction in court of a confession after a subject had asked for an attorney, and (4) allowed police to proceed with an interrogation even after a suspect has invoked the right to silence. Three cases in the summer of 1984 considerably modified *Miranda*. In the first of these (*Nix v. Williams*), the Court adopted new limits on the controversial exclusionary "rule" (whereby evidence illegally obtained by police officials was *excluded* in criminal trials). The court ruled that improperly obtained evidence may be used in trials if its eventual

[18]The 1973 case was *Roe v. Wade*. In 1983 the court reaffirmed this position in *Akron v. Akron Center*.
[19]*Roth v. United States* (1957).
[20]*Miller v. California* (1973).

discovery by legal means was "inevitable." In the second case (*New York v. Quarles*), the court held that police do not need to advise suspects of their constitutional rights when public safety is at stake. Finally, in the so-called "good faith" case of *U.S. v. Leon*, the court allowed judges to admit illegally seized evidence in court if police officers believed the search warrants they were using were valid.

A highly publicized Burger Court decision was the Bakke case,[21] which pointed up the difficulty of finding a single, absolute definition of justice. In the years following the civil rights movement in the South, there was a general consensus in the nation that black Americans had far too long been denied their rightful "equal justice under the law." Laws passed at both the federal and state levels tried to eliminate past inequities inflicted on black people. Likewise, "affirmative action" programs were instituted to compensate for past inequities forced on Native Americans, Hispanics, and women. Thus the medical school at the University of California at Davis set aside in each year's entering class 16 of 100 places for such disadvantaged candidates. Eighty-four places were determined through open competition among all candidates, and 16 places were reserved for minorities only, with admission to these places determined by a separate committee using lower academic standards. There were many arguments in favor of this "quota" system: minorities needed to be encouraged to enter the professions like medicine to establish better role models for youngsters and to provide professional service to minority communities; the program was necessary to make up for past injustices to minorities; and many more doctors, including minority doctors, were desperately needed.

A well-qualified white student, Alan Bakke, denied admission to one of the 84 places, sued on the grounds that under the university's special admission program, less qualified minority applicants had been given priority over him, thus denying him the benefit of equal protection of the law. After a lengthy hearing, the Supreme Court handed down a hair-splitting decision that though ruling in Bakke's favor, nevertheless carefully avoided striking down all special admission programs. By two separate five-to-four votes, the Court held that "quotas" were unacceptable but that race might be considered as one factor in a university's admissions policy. Thus the Court ruled for Bakke while at the same time approving the principle of affirmative action.

A potentially far-reaching action by the Burger Court struck down the so-called legislative veto.[22] (The possible impact of this decision was discussed in the chapter on Congress.) The Court swept aside the 50-year-old practice used by Congress to grant authority to the president and then block his actions under the law when it disagreed. Speaking for the majority of the Court, Chief Justice Burger argued that the legislative veto violated the

[21]*Regents of the University of California v. Bakke* (1978).
[22]*Immigration and Naturalization Service v. Chadha* (1983).

constitutional requirement of separation of powers. Henceforth Congress may restrain executive action only if a bill to that effect passes both houses and receives the president's signature or if the legislature simply refuses to pass statutes granting presidential authority.

The Rehnquist Court

By 1988 the Supreme Court had a clearly conservative personality. Not since Lyndon Johnson had a Democratic chief executive appointed a Supreme Court justice, and seven of the nine members of the court had been chosen by Republicans. When President Reagan promoted William H. Rehnquist from associate to chief justice in 1986 (Burger retired to chair the presidential commission on the celebration of the bicentennial of the U.S. Constitution), the Court seemed certain to move in a much more conservative direction. As though to assure this, Reagan picked Robert Bork, an appellate judge, noted for his intellectual conservatism, to replace Lewis Powell upon the latter's retirement. But for a number of reasons Bork was not confirmed by the Senate. Serving as solicitor general for President Nixon in 1973, Bork had been responsible for firing special prosecutor Archibald Cox. In his long career as a lawyer, professor, and judge he had penned some controversial opinions and written some articles that struck a number of Senators as at least out of the mainstream of American jurisprudence. The long hearings before the Senate Judiciary Committee, chaired by Senator Joseph Biden of Delaware, provided television viewers with a remarkable seminar in constitutional law. In the end the committee and the full Senate rejected the nomination. Eventually, Appellate Judge Anthony M. Kennedy

The Supreme Court in 1989		
	Appointed by	**Date**
Chief Justice		
William H. Rehnquist	Reagan	1986
	(appointed associate justice by Nixon, 1972)	
Associate Justices		
William J. Brennan, Jr.	Eisenhower	1956
Byron R. White	Kennedy	1962
Thurgood Marshall	Johnson	1967
Harry A. Blackmun	Nixon	1970
John Paul Stevens	Ford	1975
Sandra Day O'Connor	Reagan	1982
Antonin Scalia	Reagan	1986
Anthony M. Kennedy	Reagan	1987

was picked for the vacant spot on the court and was approved quickly by the Senate. For the moment, liberals believed that they had thwarted the Court's rapid move to the political right. Yet Rehnquist himself had developed a reputation as the most conservative member of the Court, and he was now chief justice. Whether or not the Court would begin to alter precedents set since the end of World War II remained a matter of speculation as Kennedy moved into his new job. What was certain was that President Reagan, a strong conservative himself, had, with his nominations, dramatically influenced the court for some years to come.

Two recent issues before the Court gave some evidence of future directions. In *Falwell v. Hustler Magazine* (1988) the Court ruled unanimously that the First Amendment protects the most outrageous kinds of free speech. The Court overturned a jury's award of $200,000 to the Reverend Jerry Falwell, head of Moral Majority, for "emotional distress" over an unflattering and clearly offensive parody published in *Hustler* magazine. At the same time, the Court, by a 5-to-4 vote in April 1988, agreed to reconsider whether existing civil rights laws prohibit private racial discrimination. The specific case to be reviewed was a 1976 ruling (*Runyon v. McCrary*) that interpreted a nineteenth-century congressional statute as outlawing racist white academies. But because the 1976 decision was based on *statutory*, not *constitutional*, law, should the Court reverse its earlier ruling, the Congress theoretically could remedy the situation by passing a new act clearly outlawing private racist practices. Nonetheless, some civil rights activists worried that a new majority on the Court had signaled a willingness to roll back well-established Court precedents regarding racial practices.

Justice: Where Do We Stand?

Implicit in the idea and the practice of judicial review is the notion that government rests on a "social contract." The individual must obey the law, but in return the law must not trample on the rights of the individual. Judicial review suggests that there are some things that even the most popular president or the most powerful Congress cannot and must not do.

If the judicial system has been concerned, at least in part, with maintaining public order and political stability while sustaining the freedom of individuals, it has had some success in achieving both objectives. The Constitution has remained alive for two hundred years, and despite monumental problems, the U.S. government remains among the most stable on earth. Our elections are settled with ballots, not guns. There has never even been a serious attempt at a military coup in our entire history—something of which very few nations can boast. Additionally, Americans continue to enjoy a degree of personal freedom that can be matched by only a handful of the world's population.

When Nikita Khrushchev prepared to make his bid for power in the Soviet Union, he found it prudent to carry a pistol with him into the meeting of the men who ruled the country. He had to be prepared to arrest or, if necessary, shoot the head of the Soviet secret police before the secret police arrested or shot him. This is not an ideal way to select the leader of one of the most powerful and technologically advanced nations on earth. The constitutional system has succeeded in preventing anyone from taking power in America except by lawful means. This balanced system is in part a legacy from the framers of our Constitution, and certainly the judiciary has been a crucial component of the system.

In many nations today, men and women who openly attack and defy the policies of their government, particularly in time of war or national crisis, face deportation, prison, or execution. Large numbers of Americans did attack and defy the policy of their government during the war in Vietnam. When the government attempted to jail some of the more prominent dissident leaders, as in the trial of the Chicago Seven, the effort failed. Most of the antiwar leaders are free today; many hold prominent positions, including positions in the government; and at least one, Tom Hayden, is an influential political force in California. Although there unquestionably was some repression of the right of antiwar leaders, such as illegal opening of their mail, wire taps, and other forms of harassment, on the whole the government was prevented by the judicial system from crushing resistance to the war in Vietnam.[23]

When novelist Aleksandr Solzhenitsyn wrote books critical of the Soviet Union's political leaders, his works were suppressed in the Soviet Union, and he was deported. This would be more or less the normal response of many governments to criticism from a popular artist or a leading intellectual. But American writers can and do write the most defamatory things about our political leaders and customarily can expect to receive nothing but substantial royalty checks by way of reprisal. They are protected by the law.

When the *New York Times* decided to publish the classified Pentagon Papers, which revealed some embarrassing truths about the nature of our gradual involvement in Vietnam, in direct defiance of a government order not to do so, the Supreme Court defended the *Times*'s right to publish without submitting to government censorship. Later, when the man who brought the Pentagon Papers to the *Times*, Daniel Ellsberg, was tried for stealing these documents, the judge threw the case out of court because the government had acted improperly. This action prevented a clear-cut decision on the substance of the case itself. But a subsequent poll of the jurors indicated that most were prepared to acquit Ellsberg.

Most Americans do not live in fear of sudden and mysterious arrest should they happen to criticize the authorities or back the losing side in an

[23]For a variety of views on the extent to which political protest should be allowed, see Marvin Summers, *Free Speech and Political Protest* (Lexington, Mass.: Heath, 1967).

election. Freedom in the United States is far from perfect. But on the whole it need not fear comparison with any other nation.

On the other hand, the judicial system has failed to extend "equal justice under the law" in a number of important respects.

Although few Americans fear arbitrary and unreasonable arrest, many do fear to walk the streets of their communities, particularly after dark. And although they do not live in dread of a midnight raid by secret police, many do fear that the sanctity of their homes will be invaded by armed hoodlums. Older people, many of whom are forced by limited incomes to live in high-crime areas of major cities, are too often virtual prisoners in their own shabby apartments. Old people living alone are frequently the prime targets of cruel young hoodlums, not only at home but also when walking the streets or even when riding steetcars or subways. It is cold comfort not to be repressed by the police if one's fellow citizens behave like predatory animals.

When the United States complains that the Soviet Union is a repressive police state, and the Soviets reply that America is a nation wallowing in crime, both are substantially correct. As we have previously noted, the United States is probably the most crime-ridden society in the Western world. Efforts by conservatives to curb crime by "getting tough" and "law-and-order" campaigns have not helped very much. Neither have efforts to apply humanitarian principles—counseling services and greater welfare benefits and educational opportunities. A few decades ago most enlightened people believed that crime was an unnatural course of behavior usually brought about by poverty, lack of educational opportunity, and family or societal neglect. But increased educational opportunity and greatly increased efforts on the part of society to deal with criminals, particularly young criminals, with understanding and compassion have not lowered crime rates. Perhaps there would be less crime if the "do-gooders" would abandon the field to the police. Perhaps what we have been doing is totally irrelevant, like some of the "cures" for certain deadly epidemics that swept the world in past ages. No one can say for sure, because we simply do not know what causes some people to prey on others.

But the fact remains that "equal justice under the law" depends on people's being willing to respect one another's rights, as much as it does on official actions. Many Americans feel that the government, particularly the courts, has failed them in this respect.

A second serious concern with America's legal system was dramatized by the Watergate case. Many of the principal culprits in this tawdry series of events, including the president and the attorney general, were lawyers, presumably individuals trained to respect and enforce law, who used their special knowledge and training to break the law. (It is, of course, true that most of those who prosecuted the Watergate defendants were also lawyers.) As a result of Watergate, more and more Americans began to wonder if there were not some serious flaw in the very nature of the legal system or in the training and education of lawyers. The national attention focused on the legal profession by Watergate simply highlighted a widespread popular impression that the special skills of lawyers are too often used to obstruct justice and cheat individuals of their rights.

In this respect, the legal profession is unique among the learned professions in the degree to which the benefits of its knowledge are disproportionately commanded by the rich and the powerful and denied to the ordinary citizen. Many American families are able to secure at least a reasonable degree of medical care through either government or private health insurance programs. Access to education, including higher education, although not ideal, is widely available, and although the rich can still afford the most exclusive private colleges and the middle class cannot, in many areas of the nation the best schools and universities are public, tax-supported institutions open to all at relatively modest fees.

Only the legal profession appears to remain largely what it has always been—primarily a tool of the affluent or the wealthy corporation or the labor union or the governmental bureaucracy. The very poor can get free legal services, but no one believes that such services are in any way comparable to the kind of legal power that a great corporation can muster or that wealthy individuals have at their disposal. Litigation is expensive, often too expensive for the ordinary family to contemplate except under the most extreme circumstances.

Additionally, according to a growing number of critics, the court system simply has become too overcrowded. Between 1970 and 1975 the average number of cases pending before a federal district judge increased from 285 to 355, and in state courts the crowding is even worse.[24] For those in jail awaiting trial but without sufficient funds to afford bail, the system seems hardly just. Part of the reason for the important role of lawyers and the increase in cases is that the United States tends to be an adversary culture, based in large part on an emphasis on individual rights, as contrasted with the authority of the government. Additionally, we consider ours a nation ruled by laws rather than by people. Consequently, we tend to seek resolution of problems and conflicts in courts of law rather than through a church (as in the Middle Ages) or by the neighborhood (as in China). Conflicting interests create cases and seek out lawyers. In 1973 there was 1 lawyer for every 475 Americans, as compared with 1 for 1,800 English, and 500 French (yet, interestingly, in 1900 there was a higher proportion of lawyers in the population than today).[25]

If "equal justice" is to become more than rhetoric, clearly some fundamental reforms are needed. Legal services must be made more widely and

---

[24]"Too Much Law," *Newsweek*, January 10, 1977, pp. 42–47. Also see "Interview with Warren E. Burger," *U.S. News & World Report*, February 22, 1982, pp. 36–40.

[25]See Joel B. Grossman and Austin Sarat, "Litigation in the Federal Courts: A Comparative Perspective," *Law and Society Review 9* (Winter 1975): 321–340.

cheaply available, or the laws must be simplified so that the average person can go into court without an attorney, and/or lawyers must be made responsible to human rights rather than legal hairsplitting.

An investigation of the Federal Bureau of Investigation in 1975 by a congressional subcommittee headed by Representative Otis G. Pike (D., N.Y.) revealed that during the administration of the late director J. Edgar Hoover, the agency was used to harass people such as civil rights leader Martin Luther King, Jr., on no other grounds than that Hoover happened to dislike and disapprove of King's politics. It was also revealed that for decades Hoover had run the agency like a feudal lord, rewarding and punishing agents largely on the basis of loyalty to the director, using its vast police power to spy on and harass reporters and politicians who were critical of the director, and gathering secret dossiers on the private lives of prominent persons, specifically on their sexual activities, so that many congressional representatives, senators, and perhaps even presidents of the United States feared exposure by the director and were thus hesitant to curb his power. That such power could be concentrated in the hands of one man, despite the aforementioned constitutional guarantees and Supreme Court decisions intended to protect the rights of Americans, is evidence that the formal, legal structure, however liberal, is never adequate in and of itself to preserve personal freedom from powerful and ruthless bureaucrats. The finest system in the world can be subverted by determined and ambitious individuals who choose to ignore the law, particularly if they happen to be the very people responsible for enforcing those laws.

What happened to the FBI under Hoover suggests that the Constitution and the court system cannot by themselves secure the liberties of the American people if and when the people grow careless about their freedom and loath to exercise the rights guaranteed to them by the law. But on balance, the judicial system of the United States has served the nation and the people well—perhaps better than most systems yet devised by mortals. But the ideal of the just republic remains less a fact than a goal.

7

Free at Last:
Civil and Uncivil Liberty

- Civil Liberties: The Individual and the State -
- First Amendment Rights -
- Equal Protection of the Law -
- Life, Liberty, and Property -
- Process and Rights -

> **Freedom is the right to obey a policeman.**
>
> **German Proverb**
>
> **Free at last! Free at last! Thank God Almighty, Free at last!**
> **Dr. Martin Luther King, Jr.**

The early Christian martyrs died for the right to practice the religion of their choice, but when they became the dominant church in Europe, they persecuted heretics, atheists, and Jews and made war on Muslims. America's seventeenth-century New England founders are said to have come to this country seeking religious freedom. But they proceeded to establish rules to impose theological conformity, particularly in matters affecting religion and morals, to punish those who would not practice their faith according to their prescriptions, and to slaughter pagan Native Americans with the righteous certitude that they were obeying God's laws.

Most people who affirm that they believe in "freedom" really mean to assert freedom for themselves and those who happen to agree with their ideas. Those who disagree are not for freedom—they are rebels, malcontents, heretics, subversives, agitators, or just plain troublemakers.

Nevertheless, the twentieth century has seen an enormous increase in the number of people who are relatively, but never absolutely, free, particularly in the Western world. People who, a few decades ago, were routinely denied such fundamental freedoms as the right to vote, equality before the law, the right to buy a home, even the right to marry the person of their choice, are now protected by a network of laws. More important, perhaps, they have gained a measure of public acceptance that was unthinkable not long ago. Racial and ethnic minorities, women, homosexuals, atheists, and political and social radicals are now far freer to live their lives according to their own lights than ever before.

Through most of the world's history, and even today in all but a handful of democratic societies, political, social, or religious dissent from the views of the prevailing majority was considered wicked, dangerous, and a threat to the established order, and was therefore punished unmercifully by both the authorities and ordinary people. The notion that personal freedom is a positive factor in society is a relatively new idea that began to take hold in the eighteenth century. Prior to that time, loyalty, obedience to the king or the established church and to the values and practices of one's forefathers were considered essential to a well-ordered society and a morally praiseworthy life. For many, even in the most modern democracies, these traits are still considered far more important than freedom.

The curious "acrobatic" idea (to use Ortega y Gasset's term) that freedom is a positive and fundamental element in human happiness and a value to society arose with the growth of capitalism. Free market economics and political and personal freedom are not synonymous, but they seem linked in history. They appeared first in England and spread to France and America. They were institutionalized by the American and French revolutions and the emergence of the liberal Whig party in England. They were popularized by writers and philosophers like John Locke of England, Adam Smith from Scotland, French philosopher Voltaire, and Thomas Paine and Thomas Jefferson in America. Through succeeding years, the relative success of "free" societies both as economic and military powers, and the failures of more traditional, autocratic societies like Russia and Prussia, seemed to affirm the practical superiority of liberty as a means of increasing not only the happiness but the wealth and power of those states that permitted it. The worst fears of the philosophers and theologians who had argued that liberty would lead to license, which would lead to social chaos and national weakness, seemed to be proved wrong. Free England became the center of a worldwide empire unmatched in its wealth and power. Free France was the envy of the world for its cultural achievements. Free America enjoyed one of the world's highest living standards and was destined to become the world's leading nation. The ancient autocracies wallowed in decline, plagued by defeat in war and revolution at home.

The practical achievements and triumphs of free societies continued into the modern age. Japan and Germany, turning from dictatorship to democracy after World War II, have become economic superpowers. More recently, the two communist giants, China and the Soviet Union, have tacitly acknowledged that they must encourage more individual freedom to compete effectively with the dynamic economies of the West. A number of Latin American and Asian nations, like Argentina and South Korea, appear to be moving in the same direction.

But freedom is not an unmixed blessing. In the United States, for example, millions of people have freely chosen to become drug addicts, criminals, and child abusers, or to live only for themselves and the gratification of their own wishes, polluting the environment, preying on others, and generally behaving as if they owed nothing to the society that created the wealth they plunder and the pleasures they abuse. As a result, millions of Americans live in daily fear not that the police will arrest them for criticizing the government or the clergy will denounce them from the pulpit, but that their predatory neighbors may mug, murder, cheat or otherwise violate them. It is a fine question as to which is the more important: freedom to criticize your political leaders or freedom to walk the streets of your own community without fear of assault.

Civil Liberties: The Individual and the State

The Declaration of Independence rings with an announcement of the meaning of government: "We hold these truths to be self-evident, that all men are created equal, that they are endowed by their Creator with certain unalienable Rights, that among these are Life, Liberty and the pursuit of happiness. That to secure these rights, Governments are instituted among Men, deriving their just powers from the consent of the governed."

We have seen elsewhere in these pages that the promise contained in the Declaration was, and remains, one to be fulfilled. Be that as it may, we have here the assertion of abstract rights, which, according to Jefferson, are self-evident (they do not need to be proved) and are ours by our "nature." Of course, the Constitution sets up the rules that must be followed to make these abstract rights concrete.

Jefferson's Declaration derives in large part from English political philosopher John Locke, who in 1690 had published his *Second Treatise on Government*. We have discussed Locke earlier, but because his views were important to the founders and represent a fundamental theoretical underpinning of our current ideas regarding civil liberties, it is important that we accord him an extended look. In the *Second Treatise*, Locke portrays human beings existing in a state of nature that precedes political organization. Within this state of nature, human beings live, on the whole, a fairly good life. All are equal, property is held in common, and each person has "rights." This is Locke's way of describing what he believed to be human "nature." We can actually think of a situation something like a "state of nature," that is, a condition in which there is no organized institution. Say we got a class of our student friends to gather late one night in a city park. Let us further assume that there are no police around to protect us, no parents to provide for us, and no teachers to guide us. We are perfectly free, there are no institutional restraints at all. On the whole, we might find it a pleasant enough situation. Our friends, we would think, are friendly, pleasant, and willing to share any food or drink we have brought along. All property is held in common. Yet there are some gnawing problems despite the basic decency of all these people. What if there are some less than pleasant people lurking in the shadows on the periphery of the park? Of course, there may not be many of these types, but there may be some, and the group needs some kind of protection, just in case. And what if a modest disagreement arises among some of the friends? Who decides who is right? What if some basic rules had to be established? Who would do that? Or how would rules be determined? Who would make sure the rules were carried out? When there were disagreements, who would decide the meaning of the rules? At this point Locke would say that all the people involved would agree to come out of the state of nature into a state of society to address these very questions. *But*, they all come into the state of society in order to better maintain the rights they enjoyed in the state of nature. Therefore, Locke argues, the organization of society is not for the purpose of glorifying the group, or worshiping a particular god, or achieving national greatness. The purpose of congregating is to protect rights that individuals each had *prior* to the "social contract" among them. The people now will form a government, by consent, to carry out the basic functions of legislating,

The Pursuit of Happiness

executing, and judging laws. But again, the fundamental purpose of government, as seen in the Declaration's reassertion of Lockean principles, is "to secure these rights." Thus, the individual has preeminence over the state in this particular political theory.

But this proposition raises some difficult questions, because to protect individual rights, a government must first protect itself. If a government is weak or defeated by foreign powers, it is in no position to protect anyone. And under some circumstances it is conceivable that a government might have to curtail rights in order to withstand serious challenge to its existence. When President Lincoln suspended *habeas corpus* (see page 186 for a discussion of this right) during the Civil War, he was acting in this way. Indeed, though the first aim of government, according to Locke, is to preserve and protect individual freedoms, the primary aim of any state is to preserve itself. Thus, there is frequently a difficulty in balancing individual rights and national strength.

Note, too, that the Declaration, conforming again to Lockean theory, announces that governments "derive their just powers from the consent of the governed." This means we are to be a democracy, or at least a representative democracy. But we can easily understand the potential contradiction between democracy and individual freedom. What if a majority votes to curtail individual liberty? Or what if a majority determines to suppress a minority? What, for example, happens if an overwhelming majority of those voting decides that all members of the society must practice Lutheranism? What is to happen to Catholics, Jews, Muslims, Presbyterians, and atheists? At what point does the majority rule over the minority and over the individual? At what point does the individual have precedence over the majority's pleasure? At what point does "national security," or even clear national needs (such as a conscript army in time of war) precede individual rights? Also, given the vast power of the modern state, how can individual liberty be maintained? These are not easily answered questions for any political society, and they are particularly troublesome in a large, powerful nation committed from the beginning to the preeminence of the individual over the group.

Important in the American political system (and most Western systems) is the notion that our rights are stated *negatively*, that is, certain government actions are proscribed—the government cannot deprive us of due process or infringe our freedom of speech, for example. Rights are *not* granted to us *by* the state (as is the case in some nations, where there may be a long list of *positive* "rights" given by the state), for that would imply that our rights derive from the state and, theoretically, could be removed by the state. Instead, the Declaration and Locke both insist that our rights existed *before* the state came into existence. The state is to preserve and protect rights we enjoy because we are human beings, not by virtue of our being members of any particular state.

This is not to deny that, over time, certain "rights," which we might call

Constitutional Rights

Article I, Sections 9 and 10—Guarantee of *habeas corpus*, no bills of attainder or *ex post facto* laws, no state laws impairing the obligation of contracts

Article III, Sections 2 and 3—Right of trial by jury in federal cases, precise definition of treason

Article IV, Section 2—Guarantee that citizens of each state shall have all the privileges and immunities of citizens in all other states

Article VI, Section 3—No religious qualification to hold public office

Amendment I—Freedom of religious practice, no established religion, freedom of speech, press, assembly, and petition

Amendment II—The right to bear arms

Amendment III—No quartering of military personnel in private homes

Amendment IV—No unreasonable searches and seizures

Amendment V—Guarantee of grand jury in federal capital cases, no double jeopardy, right against self-incrimination, right to due process of law, compensation for property taken for public use

Amendment VI—Guarantee of fair procedures in federal trials

Amendment VII—Guarantee of trial by jury in federal courts

Amendment VIII—Prohibition against excessive bail and cruel and unusual punishment

Amendment IX—Rights not enumerated are retained by the people

Amendment X—Powers not enumerated are reserved to the states and to the people

Amendment XIII—Prohibition of slavery

Amendment XIV—States prohibited from abridging rights and immunities of citizens, depriving a person of life, liberty or property without due process of the law, or denying any person the equal protection of the laws

Amendment XV—No denial of right to vote because of race, color, or previous condition of servitude

Amendment XIX—No denial of right to vote because of sex

Amendment XXIV—No poll taxes or other taxes in national elections

Amendment XXVI—Right to vote of all citizens eighteen years of age and above

---

positive rights, have been extended to Americans chiefly as a consequence of legislative action. These include such things as Social Security for the retired and free education for the young.

Yet, the rights we have in the Constitution are almost exclusively guarantees against encroachment by government or public officials. Whatever extent our rights are protected against private individuals or detrimental social customs (racial segregation or sexism in hiring, for example) is a function of statutory law passed by Congress or state legislatures. The Civil Rights Act of 1964 or various affirmative action laws (discussed below) are examples.

We should note that although the Constitution in several places declares that we have certain rights against the national government, the courts have interpreted the Fourteenth Amendment as providing protection to us, for those same rights, against state governments as well.[1]

First Amendment Rights

We will look shortly at certain rights contained in the Constitution as it was originally drafted in 1787. Many founders believed that because the new government was granted *enumerated* (specifically stated or implied) powers in the Constitution, there was no need to restrain government authority over the individual because Congress, for example, was not granted the power to regulate religion or the press or other matters regarding traditional rights. But the demands for a bill of rights were so great that the Constitution would not have been ratified by the states had not promises been made to place amendments into the new document specifically detailing certain rights. This was done by 1791, and many of the liberties we enjoy today are those contained in the Bill of Rights. An important number of these are stated in the brief First Amendment. These are (1) separation of church and state, (2) freedom of religion, (3) freedom of speech, (4) freedom of the press, and (5) the right of assembly and petition.

We have dealt with the "establishment" clause in the last chapter.[2] Jefferson had spoken of a "Wall of Separation" between the government and religion, and the courts have tried to apply this principle in a number of contentious cases, including the 1962 case *Engel v. Vitale*, which outlawed official prayers in public schools, and, as we have seen in an earlier discussion, created a storm of controversy. However, though government is forbidden from aiding, encouraging, or supporting any religious activity, the Supreme Court has on occasion consented to special treatment, as when Amish children were allowed to follow their own form of public education,[3] and when public monies to private religious colleges were granted for purposes determined to be nonsectarian.[4] Nonetheless, despite these particular decisions and the apparent popularity of putting prayers back in the schools and in other public places, the remarkable doctrine of separation of church and state, an early and at that time unique statement of political secularism and commitment to a plural society, remains firmly in place.

The "free exercise" of one's religion is less controversial than is the establishment clause, but there have been court cases that deal with it. For example, in 1988 the Supreme Court let stand a lower court decision that certain Fundamentalist families in Tennessee were not denied their freedom

---

[1]See discussion of the Fourteenth Amendment, Chapter 6, pp. 160–161.
[2]See Chapter 6, pp. 161–162.
[3]*Wisconsin v. Yoder* (1972).
[4]*Roemer v. Board of Public Works* (1976).

of religious expression because their children were assigned certain readings (including *The Wizard of Oz*) in the public schools they attended. The parents had gone to court to have the books removed from the public schools because they thought these books contradicted the religious beliefs of their children.[5]

Still, one's religious beliefs (or nonbelief) are inviolable, and the government cannot compel anyone to submit to any creed. For example, religious oaths cannot be a condition of public employment,[6] and, according to Article VI, Section 3 of the Constitution, no religious test can be required to hold public office or to work for the government.

Almost all of us dutifully proclaim our support for freedom of expression, yet we often find those who disagree with us or seem opposed to our form of government to be irritating, if not dangerous. In fact, radical doctrines condemning our form of government or obscene literature sold in neighborhood bookstores have frequently led citizens to demand restrictions on expression. Nonetheless, we seem as a nation committed to the principle of free speech as defended by nineteenth-century English philosopher John Stuart Mill, when he argued in his *Essay on Liberty*, "The peculiar evil of silencing the expression of opinion, is that it is robbing the human race. If the opinion is right, they are deprived of the opportunity of exchanging error for truth; if wrong, they lose, what is almost as great a benefit, the clearer perception and livelier impression of truth, produced by its collision with error." Indeed, if there were no free speech, who would determine what is true and correct? the government? a religious hierarchy? One value of free speech is that the people, who are expected in a republic to make important decisions, can hear many sides to an issue. Another benefit is that we can learn new and important things only in a society that values free and open inquiry and full rights to expression. This is not to say that all opinion is wise, correct, or as good as any other opinion. It is only to say that where there is a monopoly of opinion or where only certain opinions are accepted, wisdom and truth are less likely to prevail than where there is freedom of expression.

But the courts have never been willing to protect all speech. For example, the court has ruled that speech may be limited where it poses a "clear and present danger . . . The most stringent protection of free speech would not protect a man in falsely shouting fire in a theatre and causing a panic."[7] This "clear and present danger" doctrine maintains that speech must be genuinely threatening in order to be suppressed. Otherwise, most speech is protected, even that considered potentially subversive. In 1957, the Court reversed the conviction of 14 communists who had been found guilty of violating the Smith Act of 1940, which had outlawed advocating or teaching

[5]The case was *Mozert v. Hawkins County, Tennessee.*
[6]*Torcaso v. Watkins* (1961).
[7]*Schenk v. U.S.* (1919).

The Pursuit of Happiness

the overthrow of the U.S. government, and in subsequent years the Court has continued to uphold the rights of expression even for communists.[8] In addition, the Court, citing freedom of speech and freedom of conscience, has on other occasions upheld the rights of the individual against the state. For example, the Supreme Court has ruled that the government cannot penalize people for refusing to say the pledge of allegiance to the flag. Justice Robert L. Jackson speaking for the court's majority wrote: "Freedom to differ is not limited to things that do not matter much. If there is any fixed star in our constitutional constellation, it is that no official, high or petty, can prescribe what shall be orthodox in politics, nationalism, religion, or other matters of opinion."[9] The flag salute became an issue during the 1988 presidential campaign when George Bush criticized Governor Michael Dukakis for having vetoed a Massachusetts law fining schoolteachers who did not lead the pledge every morning. Dukakis had sought an advisory opinion from the Massachusetts Supreme Court before acting on the legislation. That Court had ruled that the law was contrary to constitutional law and a violation of constitutional rights. Dukakis insisted that he was upholding the Constitution. Bush said he would have signed such a bill had he been governor.

Freedom of the press has implications beyond those of 1787. Today, with the mass media including not just the press but radio, television, movies, and innumerable magazines, critics sometimes speak of the media as a "fourth branch of government."[10]

Government can try to control the media in one of two ways: (1) by prohibiting the publication of something (called "prior restraint"; typically, this would require a court order, and it is very rarely done), or (2) by prosecuting persons after they have published something. In the early 1970s, the New York Times published the Pentagon Papers, classified documents detailing the government's actions and policies that led to the decision to escalate the Vietnam War. The Nixon administration tried to restrain the publication of these documents. Subsequently, the administration sought to prosecute Daniel Ellsberg, a former official for the Department of Defense, for "leaking" the papers to the press. In both instances the government failed. The courts ruled that publication of the papers was legal, and the Ellsberg case was eventually thrown out of court.[11]

There are legal restraints on what is considered libelous speech, that is, speech that injures or defames an individual.[12] But it is difficult to bring libel suits against media that criticize or invade the privacy of public officials or those considered "public figures."[13] In 1988, the Supreme

[8] Yates v. U.S. (1957). See also Chapter 6, p. 161.
[9] West Virginia Schoolboard v. Barnette (1943).
[10] See Chapter 11, "Media."
[11] See Chapter 3, pp. 65–66, and Chapter 6, p. 168.
[12] Chaplinsky v. New Hampshire (1942).
[13] New York Times v. Sullivan (1964).

Court overturned a jury's award of $200,000 to the Reverend Jerry Falwell, leader of the religiously conservative Moral Majority. Falwell had sued for "emotional distress" over a *Hustler* magazine parody that portrayed him as an incestuous drunk. Chief Justice William H. Rehnquist, considered an extremely conservative jurist, spoke for the unanimous court, saying that "graphic depictions and satirical cartoons have played a prominent role in public and political debate" and that the First Amendment protects even "vehement, caustic and sometimes unpleasantly sharp attacks."[14]

Americans have the right to assemble, peacefully, in public as well as private places, but we are not free to incite riots, block traffic, or hold parades during rush hour. This is to say the courts accept reasonable restrictions on the right of assembly.

A recent and interesting decision by the Supreme Court that dealt with issues of assembly and free speech was *Boos v. Barry* (1988), in which the Court ruled that protesters in Washington, D.C., may peacefully picket in front of foreign embassies. By a 5–3 vote the justices struck down a District of Columbia ordinance that allowed the police to arrest demonstrators who were within 500 feet of an embassy or a place where a foreign dignitary was speaking. The case took on added notice in that appeals court judge Robert Bork, who had been nominated by President Reagan in the fall of 1987 to ascend to the Supreme Court but had not been confirmed by the Senate, had previously ruled in the lower court that the ordinance was constitutional in establishing a "buffer zone" around embassies and ambassadors and that it was in keeping with international law. But the high court majority found that the nation's commitment to free speech superseded its international duty to protect the "dignity" of foreign ambassadors, thus overturning the decision of Judge Bork.

Equal Protection of the Law

A fundamental principle of American jurisprudence is equality under the law, but clearly our history has been marked by an effort to expand and clarify that equality. Certainly there have been people who have had every reason to proclaim that they were not treated equally under the law. Slaves, for example, did not benefit from the Declaration of Independence's announcement of equality. They had to await the Civil War before emancipation. Even then equality remained elusive. In 1896, the Supreme Court, in *Plessy v. Ferguson*, ruled that "separate but equal" facilities for blacks and whites conformed to the Fourteenth Amendment's requirement of equality under the law. This decision sanctioned racial segregation, which was not

[14]*Hustler v. Falwell* (1988).

1960s Civil Rights Lunch-Counter Sit-In at Segregated Restaurant. Jackson, Mississippi. *(AP Wirephoto.)*

overturned until the landmark 1954 decision, *Brown v. Board of Education*, struck down the "separate but equal" doctrine and called for desegregation of public facilities.[15] Resistance to this decision resulted in several complementary court decisions throughout the national court system, and also led to the use of federal power to enforce court mandates. In 1957, President Eisenhower ordered the Arkansas National Guard to enforce school integration in Little Rock, Arkansas, where Governor Orville Faubus had resisted a court order, and in 1962 President Kennedy used the army to enforce integration of the University of Mississippi. In the Civil Rights Act of 1964, Congress authorized federal agencies to withhold federal financial assistance to any state or person failing to comply with desegregation rules and went even further by prohibiting owners of restaurants, theaters, and most hotels and motels from refusing to serve individuals because of their race.

In addition, the Civil Rights Act of 1964, by forbidding all discrimination in employment because of race, color, religion, sex, or national origin, addressed the issue of equal protection for virtually all Americans. Further protections against discrimination were extended to those over 40 and under 65 years of age in the Age Discrimination Act of 1967, to the handicapped in the Vocational Rehabilitation Act of 1975, and to Vietnam veterans in the Vietnam Era Veterans Readjustment Act of 1974. Legislation and court orders have continued to seek to bring further equity to all Americans. One of the techniques used, which has become controversial, is so-called "affirmative action" programs designed to promote education, job training, and employment for previously excluded groups like blacks, Hispanics, and

[15]See Chapter 6, p. 161.

women. This has resulted in programs to recruit certain people for jobs or universities or scholarships who in the past may have been overlooked or ignored.[16]

In March 1988, Congress overrode a veto by President Reagan of a controversial Civil Rights bill extending antidiscrimination laws to all activities of any organization receiving federal aid. In a decision of 1984 (*Grove City v. Bell*), the Supreme Court had ruled that antibias laws involving recipients of federal funds applied only to the specific program or activity that received the aid rather than to the entire institution or corporation. Congress had passed legislation to rectify this situation by extending rights. Under the law thus passed, antidiscrimination standards were to be enforced against an entire college, for example, even though only the athletic department had received federal funds. Despite President Reagan's veto, the support of that veto by Vice President Bush, and the outpouring of pressure to sustain the veto from religious Fundamentalists led by the Moral Majority, Congress overrode the president, thus turning back the first presidential effort to block a major civil rights law in more than a century. The consequence was the expansion of the scope of protection of equal rights for minorities, women, the handicapped, and the elderly in virtually all federally funded programs.

Life, Liberty, and Property

Returning to John Locke for a moment, we must remember that he asserted certain rights as unalienable and natural. These included "life," which is of course fundamental to the notion of rights; that is, no other agency has a right over our life. It is ours, and thus the foundation of our "liberty," which in turn is ours alone, and to be protected. The right of property for Locke was a bit more complex. In the state of nature property was held in common, but when individuals agreed, *via* a social contract, to come together into civilization, property as a private possession and right was created. This was because individuals utilizing their *labor*, which was an extension of their liberty, would cultivate property formerly held in common. Thus, what had before been commonly held but not cultivated now would be privately held *and* cultivated. Indeed, the *right* to property, according to Locke, derived from the mixture of an individual's labor with the land. Property was not granted, it was earned. Moreover, in the state of society (or civilization) as contrasted to the state of nature where all property was held in common, there would be more things—material things—because all were encouraged to produce and cultivate and thus expand the

[16]For further information regarding affirmative action, see the discussion regarding the Bakke case in Chapter 6, p. 165.

amount of property. Because we must assume that individuals would make more than they needed, they would provide, usually using a monetary exchange system, some of this surplus to others, who would likely also have a surplus they would like to exchange so as to gain more and different goods. The protection of individual rights now provided by the government would extend to individual private property, which by definition was *cultivated* property, which in turn could provide more material goods for the entire society.

The founders of the U.S. Constitution certainly wanted to protect property rights while nonetheless providing the public sector the power to tax, which of course is a right to take property for the public as contrasted to the private good. So in the Constitution the founders placed important safeguards for property, including the provision in Article I denying any state the right to impair "the obligation of contracts." The sanctity of contracts remains, but the courts have made certain adjustments over the years. In 1934, for example, the Supreme Court upheld a state law declaring a moratorium on the foreclosure of certain mortgages.[17]

From the late nineteenth century until the 1930s the Supreme Court tended to interpret the due process clause of the Fourteenth Amendment to prevent state legislation that invaded property rights. Thus the court frequently struck down state government attempts to regulate industry and business. Today, the Fourteenth Amendment is used, as we have seen, for quite different purposes, and, beginning in the 1930s, the Court has confirmed the right of both the national and state governments in a variety of economic regulations, including the establishment of minimum wage and maximum hour laws, the regulation of labor-management relations, and the imposition of environmental protection requirements on private industries.

There are also restrictions on the power of *eminent domain* in the Fifth Amendment. The federal government is prevented in this amendment (and the states are prevented by virtue of the Fourteenth Amendment) from taking private property for public use without just compensation and without proof of some public good resulting. Thus, governments build schools, roads, and public buildings and renew urban areas, but only after paying the former owner of the property a just price for it.

Process and Rights

Thus far, for the most part, we have been discussing *substantive* rights, that is, the substance or content of rights, rather than the *manner* in which rights are administered. The guarantee that the rule of law will protect our rights is the guarantee of correct procedure.

---

[17]*Home Building and Loan Association v. Blaisdell* (1934).

Several *procedural* rights were included in the original Constitution. These included the right to a *writ of habeas corpus*, which is a court order mandating that an officer of the state inform a person why he or she is being held. If a judge finds that a person is being held unlawfully, he may order the prisoner released. According to Article I, Section 9, this right can be suspended only "when in case of rebellion or invasion the public safety may require it," and it is on this basis that Lincoln did, in fact, suspend habeas corpus during the Civil War.

The Constitution also forbids *ex post facto* laws, retroactive laws establishing a crime after the crime has been committed, and *bills of attainder*, legislative acts inflicting punishment without judicial trial on individuals or groups specifically named.

The Fourth Amendment protects the people against "unreasonable searches and seizures," which means that a search warrant must be issued to an officer of the state, and only for probable cause, and only for a designated place and for something described in the warrant.

The right of privacy is not specifically guaranteed in the Constitution. But it has emerged as a right as a consequence of judicial elaborations of other rights, including the right against unreasonable searches.[18] Moreover, other rights in the Constitution seem to lead to a conclusion that we have rights to privacy. These include rights found in the Fourth and Fifth Amendments, the rights of belief and speech in the First Amendment, and the due process clauses of the Fifth and Fourteenth Amendments, plus the rights reserved to the people by the Ninth Amendment. Combining these various constitutional elements, the Court has determined that there is a right to privacy, although it is not clearly defined.[19] The culminating case utilizing the right of privacy was *Roe v. Wade* (1973), which upheld the right of women to abortion.[20] Even Justice Rehnquist, disturbed by the abortion decision, acknowledged the right of privacy. When Judge Robert Bork, appointed by President Reagan to fill a vacancy on the Supreme Court, testified in the fall of 1987, he revealed his own view that there was no constitutional right of privacy. His contention played an important role in convincing the majority of the Senate to deny approving him to ascend to the Supreme Court.

Finally, the Fifth Amendment provides freedom against self-incrimination. By using the Fourteenth Amendment, the Court has extended this right against states as well as against the federal government. This has established the so-called rights of the accused as explained in Chapter 6. The key decision was *Miranda v. Arizona* (1966), which established various

<hr/>

[18]*Katz v. U.S.* (1967).

[19]*Griswold v. Connecticut* (1965) emphasizes "a right of privacy older than the bill of Rights."

[20]See *Roe v. Wade* (1973) and Chapter 6, pp. 163–164.

procedures that any agency of a state would have to provide to an accused person once detained.[21]

As we have indicated, the idea of a free society that recognizes and respects certain fundamental human "rights" or "liberties" is historically a relatively new concept. It was championed in America by liberals such as Thomas Jefferson and James Madison, who were the guiding forces behind the Bill of Rights. More than two hundred years later, some politicians still use "liberalism" as an epithet, reaffirming the truth of the often-quoted but too often ignored adage, "Eternal vigilance is the price of liberty."

From the moment of our birth as a nation, we have been committed to the primacy of the individual. In fact, it is arguable that the meaning of the American experiment in government is to elevate the individual above any institution, including government. We accord to the individual dignity, worth, and thus rights. Yet three questions have always intruded into our regard for the individual: (1) How do we expand rights so that all are included? This has been a historic quest that continues. (2) At what point does the common interest prevail over the individual? (3) Does committing a nation to the fundamental importance of the individual over other, perhaps more valuable aims of government—glory, public purpose, esthetic or scientific or intellectual accomplishment, salvation, or survival of the human species—create a sullen and selfish people, unaware and uninterested in things outside themselves?

The challenge that has been with this country from the beginning is to have our rights but have our greatness too. It is a difficult challenge.

[21]See Chapter 6, p. 162.

8

The Art of Politics:
Parties and Elections

> **Politics is the art of creating wonder out of emptiness.**
>
> **Anonymous**
>
> **The best politics is poetry rather than prose.**
>
> **Richard Nixon, 1988**

Politics has been defined as a business, a profession, a sport, a calling, a science, and a racket. It is also an art, for, as with literature, painting, or music, it contains an element of unpredictability, mystery, and creative intuition. As with the artist, the successful politician somehow appeals to fundamental human emotions and stirs the passions of the people. Often such a person speaks in a language that transcends logic or reason. Talented politicians may use their gifts for noble or ignoble ends, arousing what is worst or best in people. Among the most successful politicians of the twentieth century have been individuals as dissimilar as Adolf Hitler and Benito Mussolini; Mao Tse-tung and Franklin D. Roosevelt; and Winston Churchill and John F. Kennedy. They were vastly different kinds of human beings, with varied, often directly antithetical, political philosophies. What they had in common was the ability to move people.

In the early 1930s, the United States and Germany—both heavily industrialized nations, both republics, each possessing a well-educated and technically competent population, each believing itself to be a civilized and moral nation—found themselves plunged into an economic depression. The German people responded to the depression by electing a spellbinding orator, Adolf Hitler, to lead their country. The Americans responded by electing another gifted speechmaker, Franklin D. Roosevelt, to lead them. Hitler took his country down a path that led to dictatorship, genocide, war, and perhaps the most evil orgy of hate that the world has ever witnessed. Franklin D. Roosevelt led his country into domestic and economic reform, culminating in prosperity and leadership of the Western world. Hitler came to power at a time when many Germans hated the Jews who lived among them. He exploited this bigotry and used it to establish his control of the German state. Roosevelt came to power at a time when many Americans were prejudiced against black people. He began a long, slow, and still not altogether successful process of raising the status and economic well-being of blacks in American life. Despite his lack of dramatic success in these attempts, FDR won the love (and the votes) of most black Americans and the enmity of most white racists for his efforts.

What kept the American people from turning to a Hitler as the solution to our depression and the Germans from finding an FDR to solve theirs? Luck? The character and culture of the peoples concerned? The nature of the political system extant in Germany and in the United States?

A politician once remarked, "God looks after drunkards, children, and the United States of America," which is another way of saying that historically we have been a relatively "lucky" nation. The United States has suffered no dictators, famines, or devastating plagues. No American city has been devastated by bombardment; the country has not been invaded by a foreign army since 1812. Is this, indeed, "luck," or have other factors been responsible for the durability and relative success of the American political system?

At least a partial answer to this question may be found in an analysis of that often maligned word *politics* and of the way in which politics works in America. Certainly, whatever definition or definitions one gives to politics, most Americans would prefer that political gifts be used for noble rather than ignoble purposes and would thus prefer the historical example of Roosevelt to that of Hitler. Moreover, in the end, FDR's policies proved more enduring and more successful. Finally, Roosevelt's successes were due to more than just luck. They were due to the skillful use of politics. In this respect FDR was similar to those figures in our history to whom we attribute moral leadership, such as Lincoln and Jefferson. At least one distinction these three men shared was that they were very good politicians.

What Is Politics?

Most people view their own lives as being lived on two levels. There is their private life: the life shared with friends and family and the life of schools, work, and play. Then there is public life: the life as citizen, a member of a larger community whether that community be a city, state, nation, or the world. Politics occurs in both realms of life, for it is a process by which we settle conflicts and distribute scarce resources (status, power, economic rewards) without resorting to violence. (Violence may be used by a stronger party to try to dominate a weaker one through force. An alternative is solving a problem or conflict through the give and take of politics.) Thus there is "politics" in families (in which siblings compete for familial affection), in school (in which students seek recognition from teachers), and in work (in which individuals seek promotion and higher income).

Nonetheless, we typically use the term *politics* to refer to the public life, in which politics concerns itself with such matters as how people live together in large groups; it establishes the ground rules for the buying and selling of labor and goods in the marketplace, and attempts to guide and control the social behavior of people. There is politics at the national level of government at which presidents and members of Congress are elected, and bills are passed and treaties concluded. Likewise, there is politics at the state and local level, at which governors, city council members, and school board trustees are elected and must deal with controversial issues and resolve them in one way or another. Thus politics, even in its more precise definition as a public endeavor, touches virtually every aspect of our lives.

People who say that they "take no interest in politics" imply that they are absorbed in their own private lives, that they lack the time, interest, or imagination to concern themselves with the problems or the destiny of the society in which they live. A person who lives, say, in the city of Los Angeles might follow the fortunes of the city's athletic teams, such as the Dodgers, with passionate intensity; be knowledgeable about the players, their performance, even their salaries; and argue vehemently for or against a given strategy, the wisdom or folly of trading this or that player. But that same person may barely know the name of the mayor of the city and probably will not be able to recall the names of most of its council members.

There are good reasons for this contrast. Sporting events are relatively simple, focusing on direct physical conflict. Politics, on the other hand, is complex, involving subtle, abstract, half-hidden conflicts of ideas, social and economic interests, and issues. The irony is that athletic fans so often seem unaware that although sports may give them pleasure and touch their imagination, politics controls their lives. The wages or salary that we earn for our labor, the profits that we reap on our investments, and the amount that we are permitted to retain after taxes for either or both are largely determined by politics. The quality of the air we breathe and the food we eat, the nature of the courses that we take in school, and the determination of who shall be allowed to teach and/or study them, how we drive our cars and whether or not we are allowed to drive at all, how much we pay for these cars and for the fuel that powers them—that is, virtually everything touching our lives as members of a social group—are ultimately shaped by politics. Thus, as Pericles noted of his fellow Athenians 2,500 years ago, "We regard the man who takes no intest in politics not as harmless, but as useless." The uninvolved nonvoter is the fifth wheel of democracy, asking society to provide nourishment and protection and offering nothing in return but an occasional platitude: "It's all politics," "They're all a bunch of crooks." Or as the lady polled by a CBS news team as to how she had voted in a recent election replied, "I never vote; it only encourages them."[1]

But because government goes on whether or not the ordinary citizen knows or cares about it, the actual day-to-day practice of politics has tended to become the special preserve of the professional politician and a handful of courtiers, aides, and small groups (such as political science students or teachers or members of the press or political consultants) and lobbyists for various special interests whose economic stake in government warrants serious attention, time, and expense. Most of these people have a strong personal and often an economic interest in influencing, controlling, and holding public office—because people who hold public office have power.

[1]For a discussion of voting behavior, see Chapter 9.

Politics is often described as the art of determining "who gets the cookies."[2] It can be viewed as simply another phase of the economic struggle among individuals, groups, interests, classes, states, or nations. Most people, it is said, "vote their pocketbooks." We find such an explanation somewhat too simple. Although economics obviously plays a fundamental, perhaps even the most fundamental, role in politics, other concerns sometimes compete with or even transcend purely economic issues. For example, opposition to the war in Vietman in the late 1960s and early 1970s cut across social and economic classes and seemed to be rooted in a general perception of the war as essentially immoral.

In the 1988 primary campaign, the Reverend Jesse Jackson emerged as a major force in the Democratic party in part by focusing on the issues of drugs and education, neither of them, at least directly, an economic issue to voters (drug pushers and their clients presumably do not vote in great numbers). By the spring of 1988, national polls suggested that Jackson had hit a responsive chord among many voters as the drug question was ranked by Americans as the nation's number one domestic problem. So too in the 1968 election, Richard Nixon's campaign against "hippies" and "militants" may have given him the victory in a close contest. In 1976 Jimmy Carter's victory was strongly rooted in his appeal to the country to "trust me" following the Watergate debacle. And in 1980 and again in 1984, millions of Democratic working-class voters opted for Ronald Reagan because they liked him personally and felt he would give the nation strong leadership, despite the fact that in both campaigns union leaders endorsed the Democratic candidates.

If it is not possible to reduce all the complex behavior that we call politics to a single motive—self-interest—it may be more defensible to stipulate a single objective, at least among the dominant leaders of the two major parties that constitute the mainstream of American politics—and that goal is winning elections.

To paraphrase an aphorism of the sports world, "Winning isn't the most important thing in American politics—it is everything." In Europe, where political parties are organized around class and ideological factions, politicians may lose elections while retaining influence, prestige, and real power. (For example, the Communist party in Italy has never achieved enough votes to win control of the government but remains a potent political force. In America, a party that had not achieved power in over a quarter century would almost surely have disappeared or have been reduced to impotence.) Under the parliamentary system, a losing candidate for prime minister becomes the minority party's leader in parliament and in the nation, the leader of "the loyal opposition." In America, a person may be a major

[2]See Harold D. Lasswell, *Politics: Who Gets What, When, How* (New York: McGraw-Hill, 1958).

party candidate for president one day and, within a few weeks after defeat, be reduced to relative obscurity. (Such was the fate of Alf Landon and Thomas E. Dewey.) Harold Stassen's fate, going from a leading candidate for the presidency to a perennially unsuccessful also-ran, haunts many politicians.

An example of how quickly politicians can fade from the center of the national scene to virtual obscurity can be found in the losing Democratic opponent of Ronald Reagan in 1984, former Vice President Walter Mondale. For decades a leader in Democratic party and national affairs, Mondale played little or no role in his party's major policy struggles after his defeat, or in the presidential primary battles of 1988. The same was true of former President Gerald Ford in his party. (An important exception is Richard Nixon. No American politician in the twentieth century has proved quite as durable. Elected twice to the vice presidency and the presidency, after serving in both the House and the Senate, and then being driven from office, Nixon remained a major figure in the political landscape. As late as the spring of 1988, with George Bush's nomination to his party's leadership virtually certain, thousands of Republicans wore "Nixon in '88" lapel buttons at party gatherings throughout the primary campaign.) On the other hand, if the usual fate of defeated candidates in American elections is obscurity, losers in totalitarian societies may face more drastic consequences, including imprisonment, execution, and having their names expunged from history books, except for allusions to their "darkest deeds."

It follows that to the professional, the art of politics is almost synonymous with winning elections. If a scientific formula for winning elections existed and if it could be tested objectively and used under varying circumstances and conditions to obtain success, politics could accurately be called a science. As no such formula exists, politics remains an art.[3]

Of course, a certain degree of prediction and control—which is the essence of science—does exist within the American political system. Polls usually can predict the outcome of elections with a high degree of accuracy. Incumbents can, by and large, expect to be reelected. In most cases, the candidate who spends money lavishly will defeat a candidate who does not or cannot. On the other hand, surprises do occur. Senator George McGovern was given only a remote chance of winning the Democratic nomination at the beginning of his campaign in 1972. Everyone talks about Harry Truman's stunning upset victory over Thomas Dewey in 1948 ("Truman is the Short-enders deity; they invariably invoke him," observed A.J. Liebling in his book *The Press*). And Jimmy Carter's drive from relative obscurity to the presidency was unforeseen by most political experts.

---

[3]We should make clear the distinction between *political science*, which is the academic study of politics, and the *practice* of politics, which is being discussed here.

Politics and Issues

A few weeks before the presidential election of November 1976, the *Wall Street Journal*, noting a widespread negative reaction to the first two Ford–Carter television debates, the apparent lack of voter interest in the campaign, and the high percentage of "undecided" voters remaining at that rather late stage of the campaign, decided to give the candidates a bit of advice: "Whichever of the two, President Ford or Governor Carter, is willing to speak out clearly and forcefully on the issues before the country will probably swing the undecided voters to his cause and win the election."[4]

This suggestion would seem plausible enough, but there is evidence that exactly the opposite may be true. At least in the recent past, candidates, particularly presidential candidates, who have spoken out clearly and forcefully on issues have been defeated, often overwhelmingly. The best examples of issue-oriented candidates to go down to defeat were Senators Goldwater and McGovern, both by overwhelming margins. In the 1950s, most voters preferred President Eisenhower, who was rather fuzzy about most issues before the nation, to Adlai Stevenson, who was more eloquent and precise. The overriding "issue" in the John F. Kennedy–Richard Nixon debates was the question of what the United States would do to defend the tiny islands of Quemoy and Matsu should they be attacked by the People's Republic of China. The differences between the candidates were never really clarified, and few would argue that Kennedy's victory could be attributed to his stance on a given issue rather than to personal magnetism. Richard Nixon captured the presidency in 1968 while virtually refusing to discuss the most burning issue of the day: the war in Vietnam. He won again in 1972 largely by avoiding strenuous personal campaigning and using surrogates to attack Senator McGovern's record.

When in 1980 Ronald Reagan and Jimmy Carter faced each other in debate before a national television audience, Carter tried grimly to focus on specific issues such as the likelihood that Reagan's proposal to slash taxes while increasing military expenditures would lead to huge budget deficits, which indeed happened; or that Reagan's bellicose anti-Soviet rhetoric would lead to an increase in the danger of nuclear war. Reagan turned aside Carter's attacks with an "aw shucks" shrug, a bemused smile, and the offhand comment: "There you go again," as if to say to the audience, how could anyone believe that such an obviously pleasant man would be capable of such extremism? The public, judging by the postelection polls and the election results, seemed to prefer Reagan's posture to Carter's efforts to discuss the issues.

In the New York presidential primary of April 1988, three remaining

---

[4]*Wall Street Journal*, October 14, 1976, p. 22.

Democratic candidates were confronted by the emotional issue of Palestinian protest riots in the Middle East and the armed Israeli response. Candidate Albert Gore strongly supported the Israeli government; candidate Jesse Jackson argued for the creation of a Palestinian state, something vigorously opposed by the conservative Israeli government. Candidate Dukakis took a more elusive position, generally supportive of Israel but not closing the door to a Palestinian state. (In fact, throughout the 1988 primary campaign, Dukakis stressed "competence" rather than issues or programs.) Dukakis won the crucial primary.

Professional politicians are sensitive to the danger inherent in taking hard-and-fast positions on highly emotional and controversial issues. They know that the vote, gesture, or statement that makes a person look like a hero to a given group today may make that person appear villainous to the same people tomorrow. "Politics makes strange bedfellows" is not just a joke. It is a description of what usually happens as issues, events, and roles change, requiring that former friends become enemies, and vice versa. This is one reason that politics appears to many people to be "dirty" and politicians seem unprincipled. Although seeming to be "tough-minded" and "decisive" to the average voter, the politician must in fact be subtle, always mindful of the need for compromise, conciliation, and shifting alliances.

A century and a half ago an adviser to presidential aspirant William Henry Harrison offered some sage advice to Harrison's campaign managers:

> Let him say not one single word about his principles, or his creed—let him say nothing—promise nothing. Let no committee, no convention—no town meeting ever extract from him a single word about what he thinks now, or what he will do hereafter. Let the use of pen and ink be wholly forbidden as if he were a mad poet in Bedlam.[5]

Harrison followed this advice and won the election of 1840. Although such recommendations have certainly not always been heeded (recent political figures such as Jimmy Carter, Edward Kennedy, Ronald Reagan, and Jesse Jackson have staked out recognizable positions on several major issues), the injunction highlights a truism of politics: Often in American elections, issues are less important in determining victory or loss than are other factors, such as the personalities of the candidates, the traditional voting habits of the people, and such imponderables as what effect Gary Hart's romantic interlude had on the ultimate result of the presidential campaign of 1988.

[5]Quoted in Arthur M. Schlesinger, Jr., *The Age of Jackson* (Boston: Little, Brown, 1945), p. 211.

Parties and Politics

As we have noted, one of the functions of politics is the elimination of violence and the solution of conflict among contending elements of society. Through much of history, and in many nations even today, differences of opinion about public policy are settled with guns, not votes. The strong have their way simply because they are the strongest. Consequently, competing political parties that legally and openly contend for public favor have emerged slowly and with some difficulty. Even in the Western world they are relatively recent innovations.

The Founding Fathers of the United States distrusted party politics and hoped that the nation could be governed without recourse to "faction."[6] There is no reference to political parties in the Constitution. The first political parties took shape in the United States by 1800, when the supporters of Thomas Jefferson (eventually called Democrats) banded together to oppose the ruling Federalists. It is ironic that Jefferson, among the founders of the nation who warned Americans against the dangers inherent in factions, was responsible for the formation of the nation's oldest and strongest political party.

Why has the two-party system become so dominant in American politics? Why not many parties, as in most European nations, or one, as in much of the rest of the world? The *Los Angeles Times* has suggested that "there will always be a two-party system in the United States simply because it works well to get two names on the ballot for every office."[7] Some Americans look upon the quadrennial presidential battle between two major candidates as a kind of sporting event, a political version of the Superbowl or the World Series. If politics is about winning and losing, then there is an obvious aesthetic tidiness in having one big winner and one big loser.

Students of the American political system have suggested other reasons for the curious persistence of the two-party system. One is that we elect people from single-member districts, and so there is only one winner. (There is no proportional representation by which, for example, a party receiving 10 percent of the votes would get 10 percent of the seats in a legislature.) Likewise, the presidential race is a winner-take-all election, and thus it is difficult for smaller parties to sustain long-term support. Also, Americans generally do not tend to seek out a candidate who champions a given political philosophy or view of public policy; they seem to prefer a more pragmatic approach. They do not ask, "Which candidate will better reflect

---

[6]This was George Washington's view as well as that of others. James Madison in *Federalist* 10 admitted that violence among factions was a great danger but that because factions could never be eliminated, the solution was to spread them out in a large federal republic in which none could dominate.

[7]*Los Angeles Times*, October 28, 1974, sec. 2, p. 6.

my political philosophy?'' but rather, ''Which candidate will better serve my interests and those of the nation?'' or even, ''Which candidate seems to be the nicer?'' Most minor parties depend on ideological commitment for long-range support. Finally, the federal system, with its dispersal of power, makes a one-party rule difficult to achieve and a multiparty system difficult to sustain because patronage and money, the ''mothers' milk of politics,'' are hard for minor parties to come by. Even when a strong regional third party emerges, such as Robert La Follette's Progressive party in 1924 or George Wallace's American Independent party in 1968, it is usually unable to build a national base. Wallace, for example, moved back into the Democratic party's ranks in 1972. Ronald Reagan, often mentioned as a Conservative party candidate in 1976, chose instead to seek the Republican party nomination and announced his intention of staying in that party, regardless of the outcome of his bid for the party's presidential nomination. Serious professional politicians, who seek to win elections rather than simply to raise issues, usually elect to stay within the two-party system.

Even when one of the two major parties collapses, as happened to the Whigs and the Federalists, it is simply replaced by another party incorporating elements of the old party and some new elements. From the time that the Jeffersonians formed the Democratic party until the 1850s, the Democrats dominated American politics. By the 1850s, a new party, the Republicans, had emerged, organized around the issue of slavery. The new party was antislavery. It was also probusiness, favoring land grants to railroads, a new banking system and protective tariffs, and a homestead law to provide cheap land for farmers in the West. After the Civil War, black voters joined the business–farming coalition, and the Republicans became the dominant party until the 1930s. Although the numerical strength of the two parties, Democratic and Republican, as reflected by registration figures, was about even, the Republicans in fact dominated American politics during most of the last half of the nineteenth and the first third of the twentieth century. During this period, the Democrats elected only two presidents—Grover Cleveland and Woodrow Wilson—in each case as the result of a split among Republicans. The GOP (Grand Old Party—the Republicans) dominance came about because the party had led the country successfully through the Civil War and had become identified (outside the South) in the minds of most voters with the ''respectable'' elements of American society: the business community and the independent farmer, the older and hence better established WASP (White, Anglo-Saxon, Protestant) families, the growing financial and corporate elite, the solid citizens and ''100 percent Americans.'' The Democrats, on the other hand, were characterized by one GOP critic as the party of ''Rum, Romanism, and Rebellion.'' It was, of course, a partisan overstatement, but it contained an element of truth, for with the Republicans representing the nation's established and successful people and institutions, the Democrats moved to organize the poor and the excluded. They built a curious alliance of sharecroppers and Jewish, Italian, and Irish immigrants who were concentrated in ghettos in the large eastern cities. New York's Tammany Hall became the prototype of the big-city political machine, and the big-city political "boss" emerged as a distinctive new American political type. The bosses were not interested in ideology or political rhetoric; they were interested in votes, which could be translated into money and power. Barely concealed corruption became a fixture of American political life.

While enriching themselves and providing high-paying, easy jobs for their relatives, cronies, and sycophants, the men who ran the big-city machines maintained their power by providing indispensable services to the millions of immigrants pouring into America. They met the immigrants almost as they stepped off the boats, usually arriving poor and frightened, speaking little or no English, and coming from lands wracked by famine, war, and oppression. Organizations such as Tammany Hall helped people find jobs, houses, and relatives and even acted as marriage brokers for young immigrants seeking spouses. They provided loans and a friend at City Hall in times of trouble. In short, they acted as a sort of unofficial welfare agency, run by local politicians called *ward heelers* (because they were usually walking the streets of the ward, or local political district) rather than welfare workers. It is debatable whether the largely uneducated ward heelers may not have done a better job at less cost to the taxpayers than today's welfare workers trained in sociology, counseling, and psychology.

During the Great Depression of the 1930s, the American business and political establishment was shaken. Hundreds of millions of dollars in paper wealth disappeared as the stock market sank to record lows. Thousands of banks failed and, at a time when there was no federal deposit insurance, took with them the life savings of millions of people. Of the American working force, 25 percent were unemployed. Bread lines appeared in the streets of every American city. Even members of the solid middle class—doctors, lawyers, druggists, business executives—lost their homes and businesses; the "tramp" who once was a business tycoon became part of the folklore of American life and the song "Brother, Can You Spare a Dime?" almost the national anthem.

The Republican party, which was supposed to have been managing the nation's affairs, was held responsible for the calamity of the Depression, and in 1932, Democrat Franklin D. Roosevelt was swept into office with vague promises of a "new deal" for the American people.

While setting in motion a host of measures designed to provide immediate relief from the most paralyzing effects of the Depression, Roosevelt also began to forge a new political coalition that would result in the Democrats', rather than the Republicans', becoming the dominant American political party for the next four decades. It included the traditionally Democratic South and added the urban workers, who under the Wagner Labor Relations Act of 1935 formed labor unions, which became a new source of power in American political and economic life. Many farmers and small business owners, ruined or at least badly frightened by the Depression, threw their support to FDR. So too did millions of black people, who had traditionally voted Republican, largely because of memories of Lincoln's role in emancipation. Blacks, the first to be fired and the last to be hired in American business, were among the most important beneficiaries of New Deal relief efforts. Also, they sensed a friend in FDR and particularly in Mrs. Roosevelt, who outraged many white people by her public concern for blacks, including young black men who had been sentenced to long prison terms on what she felt were unjust or baseless charges. Another important element in the new Democratic coalition was the intellectual community. The nation's artists, writers, teachers and professors, journalists, and the growing army of welfare workers and planners shifted toward liberalism and the Democrats. They did so partly because the Democrats, rather than the Republicans, increasingly reflected their own economic and social interests and because they came to believe that the Democrats were the party of progressivism, whereas the Republicans were portrayed as the party of business and narrow conservatism. Not until the 1960s—when figures like William F. Buckley, a literate, intelligent, and urbane spokesperson for the new conservatism, and economist and Nobel prize winner Milton Friedman began to emerge—were conservative Republicans able to mount a serious intellectual challenge to the dominant New Deal ideology.

Although the Republicans managed to elect two presidents—Dwight D. Eisenhower and Richard M. Nixon—during the four decades of Democratic dominance of the electorate, neither was able to make a significant shift in the balance of power in American political life in the way that Roosevelt had. Both faced predominantly Democratic legislatures during all or most of their terms in office. Eisenhower, a popular war hero, had a personal disdain for party politics and left party affairs largely to subordinates. Nixon was a partisan, and members of the Nixon administration talked vaguely about "our revolution," meaning a fundamental shift in the American balance of political forces in favor of the Republicans, which they hoped would take place during Nixon's second term. However realistic these plans may have been, the Watergate scandal effectively wrecked any chance of accomplishing them, so that in the congressional elections of 1974, the Democrats emerged with new gains approaching the political majorities they had enjoyed during the early days of the New Deal. And in the following elections the Democrats continued to have a majority in Congress.

By the end of the 1970s polls indicated that only about one American voter in five, just over 20 percent of the people, was willing to call himself or herself a Republican, whereas close to 50 percent labeled themselves Democrat, and about 30 percent preferred to call themselves independent, thus indicating at least some degree of displeasure with both the major parties.[8]

[8]*Gallup Opinion Index*, July 1979, p. 34.

Political Party Affiliation			

QUESTION: In politics, as of today, do you consider yourself a Republican, a Democrat, or an Independent?

	Dec. 1986–April 1987 (Personal)		
	Republican	**Democrat**	**Independent**
NATIONAL	**30%**	**40%**	**30%**
SEX			
Men	32	36	32
Women	29	43	28
AGE			
18–29 years	32	34	34
18–24 years	33	31	36
25–29 years	30	37	33
30–49 years	27	39	34
50 & older	33	44	23
50–64 years	31	43	26
65 & older	34	46	20
REGION			
East	32	39	29
Midwest	28	35	37
South	31	43	26
West	31	39	30
RACE			
Whites	33	35	32
Nonwhites	9	70	21
Blacks	7	77	16
Hispanics	25	46	29
EDUCATION			
College graduates	37	33	30
College incomplete	33	37	30
High school graduates	29	39	32
Not high school grads.	25	49	26
OCCUPATION			
Professional & business	38	30	32
Other white collar	29	40	31
Blue collar	24	42	34
Skilled workers	28	37	35
Unskilled workers	21	47	32

Political Party Affiliation continued			
	Dec. 1986–April 1987 (Personal)		
	Republican	**Democrat**	**Independent**
NATIONAL	30%	40%	30%
HOUSEHOLD INCOME			
$40,000 and over	38	32	30
$25,000–$39,999	34	34	32
$15,000–$24,999	28	40	32
Under $15,000	23	50	27
RELIGION			
Protestants	34	38	28
Catholics	27	44	29
LABOR UNION			
Labor union families	23	46	31
Nonunion families	32	38	30

Note: Excludes persons who said they belonged to other parties, or had no party allegiance.
Source: Gallup Report, May 1987.

Even following Reagan's victory in 1980, few voters identified themselves as Republicans. As Reagan's first term drew to a close, polling data showed that 45 percent called themselves Democrats, 31 percent independents, and only 24 percent Republicans. By the time President Reagan had served for a full eight years, the number of registered Democrats still outnumbered those of the GOP. At the same time that Reagan retained considerable popularity, most state legislators, most governors, and the majority in both houses of Congress were Democrats. This raised a question as to whether Reagan's victories in 1980 and 1984 represented an important and relatively permanent shift in sentiment, away from the liberal Democrats and toward the conservative Republicans, or simply a temporary aberration in the "normal" Democratic dominance. Although these figures suggested to some observers that America was indeed ripe for a new political shift of forces, similar to those that occurred after the Civil War and during the Great Depression, a shift toward what and whom remained in doubt. Other scholars saw the political situation of the 1980s as one characterized by party *dealignment*[9]—that is, a period not of ideological shifts or changing political party loyalties but, rather, a period when increasingly voters do not

[9]See Walter Dean Burnham, "The Eclipse of the Democratic Party," *Democracy*, July 1982: 7–17.

identify with one political party but vote for individuals who represent specific interests or simply want a change from the recent past, rather than supporting candidates from parties with broad general programs.

At any rate, the victories in recent years of Republican presidential candidates, often by overwhelming margins, while Democrats continue to win in most other elections has thrown the traditional alignments of the parties into some confusion. Essential to the achievements of political parties in the past was the ability to win and maintain the support of an alignment of disparate groups in American society. The New Deal Democratic party, as we have noted, won over blacks, Jews, ethnics, white Southerners, Hispanics, Roman Catholics, and intellectuals. In recent years Southerners, Catholics and ethnics (the term usually refers to people of eastern or southern European heritage) began increasingly to support GOP presidential candidates while retaining their loyalty to congressional and local Democrats. There have been various explanations for this phenomenon, including the charge that the Democrats' national candidates (like George McGovern in 1972) were simply too liberal for rank-and-file Democrats, that issues like the war in Southeast Asia split the party apart, and that it was impossible for a national candidate (such as Walter Mondale in 1984) to appeal to all the various interest groups in the party without being seen as a tool of "special interests." Another plausible explanation is that many members of the groups who were among the poor and excluded during the New Deal days have become relatively prosperous, middle class, and hence more conservative in their choice of presidents while still preferring to identify themselves as Democrats because of family loyalty and tradition.

Two groups that have remained consistently Democratic in both national and local elections are blacks and Jews. These two groups are now the equivalent of what once was the "solid South" basis of the Democratic party—a core of commitment comparable to Big Business support of the Republicans. However, in recent years this alliance, which also played a key role in winning civil rights legislation in the 1960s and 1970s, has begun to crack. Some black spokespersons (such as Nation of Islam leader Louis Farrakhan) have become openly and virulently anti-Jewish (Farrakhan reportedly referred to Judaism as a "gutter religion"), and some Jewish leaders have become equally hostile to black political aspirants (for example, during the primary campaign in the spring of 1988, New York's Mayor Edward Koch proclaimed that a Jew would be "crazy" to vote for candidate Jesse Jackson). This is but the most serious example of a dilemma that Democrats, unlike Republicans, continue to confront. The party's success depends on its ability to hold together the increasingly disaffected elements of the old New Deal coalition. When the coalition holds, Democrats tend to win national elections, as did Franklin Roosevelt, Truman, Kennedy, Johnson, and Carter. Unhappily for the majority party, the Democrats do not unite in support of their party nominees with anything like the loyalty and discipline that usually characterizes the GOP.

What Parties Do

Historically, what do parties do? There are several functions we may attribute to the two-party system:

1. Parties offer choices and simplify issues, which makes the voter's job easier. Parties sift through all the issues to find the most popular ones, and via a variety of techniques, they sift through all the candidates and, in each case, offer us alternatives.

2. The selection of candidates is a job in itself. Initially, parties chose candidates in meetings called *caucuses*, which at first were closed meetings of party leaders. Later, beginning in the 1830s, the party convention was adopted and is still used by the national party to nominate presidential and vice presidential candidates, as well as to debate, draw up, and adopt a platform. During the early twentieth century, various states began to adopt the direct primary as a means of nominating candidates. The direct primary allows every voter of the party a chance to participate in choosing the nominee. In many states, candidates for all offices—local and state—are chosen in this manner, and some states use a primary election for determining the choice for president among that state's party members.

3. In the general election itself, parties play a crucial role. They raise money for their candidates, campaign for the candidate, provide poll watchers, and mobilize volunteers. There is, needless to say, plenty of work for volunteers, and almost anyone interested in party work will be welcomed. In this way, of course, the rank-and-file party members can influence their party.

4. Parties, some believe, help shape public opinion. Each of the major parties has a national committee, with publicity divisions constantly propagandizing in the party's favor. Perhaps more than offering worthwhile information, the parties simply stimulate interest.

5. The party in power is expected to develop policies and govern. This is particularly true when the executive and legislative branches of government (whether at the state or the national level) are controlled by the same party.

6. The party out of power is expected to criticize the party in power. Thus in 1988, Paul Kirk, chairman of the national Democratic party, appeared on television and in the press criticizing the policies of Republican presidential incumbent Ronald Reagan and insisting that a Democratic president would do things differently and better. Republicans acted similarly when Democrat Carter was in the White House. Likewise, the minor-

ity party may be expected to develop alternative policies and advertise them publicly and even present them to legislatures.

7. The political party is an organization that allows like-minded and public-spirited people to meet, socialize, and perhaps get started in a career in politics.

8. Some scholars maintain that the two-party system helps keep the country unified, because in seeking to win elections, especially presidential elections, the party must appeal to as many geographic and ideological interests as possible. Thus the parties tend to keep politics in America moderate, because both parties seek to be middle-of-the-road in order to win elections.

Third Parties

What role, then, do third parties have? By definition, a third party is a party outside the two major parties that is unable to mobilize a majority of votes in elections.

1. Their major function, it has been argued, is to bring attention to controversial issues that the major parties often ignore or on which they seek to compromise. In 1968, the American Independent party under George Wallace, for example, was segregationist in domestic politics and hawkish in foreign policy, whereas the two major parties straddled those issues or were not identified with them.[10]

2. Third parties can allow an expression of political discontent. The American Independent and the Peace and Freedom parties in 1968 are examples of this.

3. A third party's candidate for president might influence national politics by gaining so many votes in the electoral college that no one candidate receives a majority. Thus the election would be thrown into the House of Representatives. The third-party candidate, using the electoral votes of the states that he or she had won, could bargain with the two candidates of the majority parties. Perhaps the third-party candidate could receive a cabinet post or a promise by one of the two major candidates to follow a certain policy. Governor Wallace may have hoped to do this in 1968. (This eventuality has not yet occurred.) Also, a third party may win enough of the popular vote in a presidential election to allow a minority party to gain a majority of electoral votes, as was the case in 1912 and 1968.

4. Third parties might have an effect on subsequent political programs. For example, Wallace's strong showing in 1968 may have influenced Presi-

[10]See Daniel A. Mazmanian, *Third Parties in Presidential Elections* (Washington, D.C.: Brookings Institution, 1974).

dent Nixon's so-called Southern strategy; that is, partly to attract more Wallace-like Southern votes to the Republican party, Nixon nominated Clement Haynesworth and G. Harold Carswell, both Southern conservatives, to the Supreme Court. (As it happens, however, neither nominee was confirmed by the Senate.)

5. Some third parties seek to counter third parties of the opposite ideological persuasion. For example, the leftist Peace and Freedom party argued in 1968 that it needed to gain official sanction to counterbalance the more right-wing American Independent party. Otherwise, the Peace and Freedom people maintained, the whole political spectrum would move to the right.

6. Finally, some third parties, not hoping to win elections, have worked to educate the electorate. Norman Thomas, who last ran as the Socialist candidate for president in 1932, had this goal in mind: to present voters with clear programs that might eventually be accepted by the major parties. Former Senator Eugene McCarthy's 1976 campaign was largely motivated, he claimed, by an effort to "open up" the American political system to new ideas. McCarthy, for example, advocated a four-day workweek as a solution to the unemployment problem. We should add that the proposals initially advanced by a third-party candidate that seem bizarre or radical to one generation sometimes become accepted national policy in the next. Norman Thomas used to point out that many of the ideas he advocated in his perennially unsuccessful bids for the presidency as a Socialist gradually became the law of the land. (The eight-hour workday is one example.)

But no third-party candidate has ever won the presidency. Although Republicans emerged in the 1850s as a new party, they quickly displaced the Whigs, so that by the time of the 1860 election they were part of the two-party system. Indeed, for a third-party candidate even to make a good showing, certain conditions seemingly must be met: There must be an intense feeling and disagreement over fundamental issues such as peace or war, integration or segregation. The two major parties must avoid taking a stand on these issues or alienating a minority by their stands, and there must be a personality with some following in order to lead the new party. All these conditions need not arise at once. Apparently the most important is the last, the strong political personality. For example, in 1912, Theodore Roosevelt, running on the Progressive ticket, actually came in second to Woodrow Wilson. And in 1924, Robert La Follette garnered millions of votes running on a third-party ticket. Likewise, John Anderson's popularity as a third-party alternative in 1980 rested more on his personality than on controversial issues outside the mainstream. But the 1968 election, which we have already noted, presents a classic case. Not only was there a noteworthy third-party candidate (Wallace), but there also were intense feelings and disagreements on basic issues (race and war), and the two major parties avoided or rejected segregation in domestic affairs and at the same time promised (however vaguely) to end America's prosecution of the war in

Vietnam. Thus those who favored segregation and a hawkish position on the war could vote for Wallace–Le May, and about 13 percent did.[11]

Are the conditions necessary for a successful third party present today? Will they be in the near future? What chance, if any, does a new party have of displacing one of the older parties? We shall return to these questions later when we discuss the concept of a "critical election."

The System Changes

The parties have changed over the years. For example, although there remain a few urban political machines (notably in Chicago), most tightly run machines have disappeared. Nationally regulated welfare programs, initiated during the New Deal period, replaced the kind of aid that local ward heelers gave to prospective voters. Civil service jobs at the city and county levels have removed the tool of patronage by which political parties rewarded party workers, and some cities, especially in the West, have legally made local elections nonpartisan, thus attempting to remove party influence altogether.

Another change has been the emergence of a two-party system where there used to be only one. In some Southern and border states, such as Oklahoma, Texas, and South Carolina, Republicans now offer a challenge and not infrequently win elections where the Democrats formerly had almost complete success. Moreover, in some northeastern states, Democrats are much more powerful than they were a few years ago. Maine, for example, has traditionally been solidly Republican yet now has a strong Democratic party.

Finally, as we noted, there is much less political loyalty among American voters than in the past. Recent research has suggested that voters increasingly, and sometimes calculatedly, cross party lines, believing that opposition parties in the executive and legislative branches represent a healthy balance.[12]

This decline in party loyalty is viewed by some scholars with anxiety.[13] They see the parties as the agents that can mobilize large numbers of the individually powerless against the relatively few powerful special interests. Others see the party structure as the necessary institution that aids the workings of a separation-of-powers government. Certainly, for example,

[11]These themes are developed in Mazmanian's book.

[12]Nelson W. Polsby, "What Do the Voters Want?" *Newsweek*, October 20, 1975, p. 15. Also see Gerald M. Pomper, "The Decline of the Party in American Elections," *Political Science Quarterly* 92 (Spring 1977): 21–41.

[13]See Everett Carll Ladd, Jr., with Charles D. Hadley, *Transformations of the American Party System*, 2nd ed. (New York: Norton, 1978), pp. 14–19.

parties are crucial to the organization of legislatures.[14] Thus a disintegrating two-party system, some observers fear, would result in special interest politics rather than in broadly based programs, elections based on personalities rather than on programs for which parties stand, and an inability to get anything important done in the legislative branch because representatives would be more loyal to special interests than to the larger political party.

What's Wrong with the Two-Party System?

Several reasons are frequently cited to explain the dissatisfaction with the two-party system. Some of these are the following:

1. *The parties are just alike.* A major complaint about the two parties is that they are really not very different. Both try to appeal to the moderate, middle-of-the-road voter, and each party includes both liberals and conservatives. Lowell Weicker, former liberal Republican senator from Connecticut, is ideologically far removed from conservative Senator Jesse Helms, and the Democratic party has such diverse personalities as Edward Kennedy and conservative Senator Hal Heflin from Alabama. What kind of sense does this make? European critics have long marveled at America's "absurd" system and regularly predict a fundamental realignment of American parties. Yet there are clearly ideological differences. Democrats, as a rule, tend to be more liberal and Republicans more conservative. Many of the major political figures in each party underscore this assessment. Michael Dukakis, Jesse Jackson, and Edward Kennedy are considered liberals; Jesse Helms, Robert Dole, and Ronald Reagan are conservatives. Moreover, Americans are becoming aware of the ideological differences of the parties.[15] Thus an intriguing question is raised. If voters are more aware of ideological differences and if, as the Gallup Poll suggests, most Americans call themselves "conservatives," why are there so many more registered Democrats than Republicans? Probably the answer is that the simple terms *liberal* and *conservative* are inadequate to explain an individual's understanding and perception of politics. It might be more informative to ask what a person's view is regarding environmental, energy, tax, and foreign policies, or what she or he thinks about congressional reform and defense spending. Does the success of Democrats in winning control of the House of Representatives suggest that voters favor liberal, Democratic positions on these issues? Part of the reason for Democratic success may lie in the differences between the major parties. Such differences can be found in the

---

[14]See Chapter 5.

[15]Gerald M. Pomper, "From Confusion to Clarity: Issues and American Voters, 1956–1969," *American Political Science Review* 66 (June 1972): 415–428.

kinds of people who normally support the parties with both their votes and their money, in the historical experience of the two parties, and in their stance on the issues. We must keep in mind, however, that when we are talking about groups of tens of millions of persons, there are bound to be many exceptions to the general rules.

Generally, the Democrats attract people who are not white-skinned or whose ethnic background often places them psychologically outside the American mainstream, such as blacks, Jews, and to a lesser extent many Roman Catholics. Most labor unions and hence most union members support Democrats. Democrats usually carry the big cities. Artists and intellectuals and people active in the communications industries, such as journalism, also lean toward the Democrats.

On the other hand, white business and professional people are more often Republicans. So are older voters, wealthy people, suburbanites, and Protestants (particularly if they are both suburban *and* Protestant). People in the West, where there are more suburbanites and residents of wide-open spaces than in the densely crowded Northeast, have been voting Republican more often than not in recent national elections.

Ideologically, the Democratic party nationally is normally liberal, whereas the Republican party nationally is usually conservative. But do these terms have any useful meaning today?[16] Partly, they arise from historical experience, particularly in Europe. Traditionally, the conservatives represented the hereditary landowning aristocracy of Europe. They enjoyed positions of great power, wealth, and prestige; hence they were interested in preserving the existing rules of society. Liberals, on the other hand, represented the rising business and industrial class, which was challenging the traditional prerogatives of the nobility; hence they stood for change and social innovation. At the far left stood the radicals, such as the communists, who demanded nothing less than the complete overthrow of existing social institutions with the aim of establishing perfect equality among all persons. At the far right were the fascists, urging violence as a means of crushing any dissident forces. Fascists raise traditional aristocratic values such as war and blood superiority to a kind of political religion.

Such designations fit uneasily into the American social and political scheme because here there was no landowning class of aristocrats. Instead there developed large corporations, run by boards of business executives, who generally became the dominant conservative force in American life. Here wealth and race, and more recently age, tend to differentiate conservatives and liberals rather than class (although some argue that wealth and race frequently amount to class).

The terms *left* and *right* in politics, corresponding roughly to *liberal* and *conservative*, originated in the seating arrangements in the first French

[16]See Andrew Kopkind, "Liberal or Conservative: Irrelevant Answers to the Wrong Questions," *Hartford Courant*, February 23, 1979.

National Assembly following the successful revolution against Louis XVI. Generally, the more radical members sat on the left side of the hall, the more conservative on the right. The terms have somehow stuck.

With respect to issues, liberals (hence normally Democrats) stress full employment as a matter of national concern. Republicans give first priority to controlling inflation. Thus liberals prefer fiscal and monetary policies favoring expansion of the economy, whereas Republicans worry about the growing national debt and the printing of "paper money" (although debt soared during the Reagan administration). Liberals condemn "tax loopholes," which conservatives often defend as "tax incentives" necessary to stimulate private investment. In a straight business–labor confrontation, liberals usually tilt toward labor, conservatives toward management.

Liberals tend to support government spending on social programs; conservatives look more kindly on spending money on national defense and on such things as highway building, which is a kind of subsidy to the auto industry. Liberals usually argue that ethnic and religious minorities have been discriminated against and that the government has a responsibility to help such people overcome unfair handicaps. Conservatives are more inclined to believe that the government should not interfere much in telling people who they may or may not hire or associate with and that although inequalities may exist, they can be overcome by individuals who are willing to work hard and "lift themselves up by their own bootstraps."

Liberals tend to stress individual liberty, particularly on matters of civil rights and social and aesthetic behavior. Conservatives talk about the need for social order and stability but emphasize free enterprise, or *economic* liberty.

In foreign policy, it is more difficult to tell the two apart because the nation has had, by and large, a bipartisan foreign policy since the end of World War II. Generally, the *rhetoric* of foreign policy debate, which is not always the same thing as the actions of those in power, indicates that liberals are more disposed to talk and conservatives are more disposed to exercise a military option. On the other hand, Lyndon Johnson and John Kennedy were certainly not doves, whereas Richard Nixon astonished many people, after a lifetime of "tough" rhetoric, with his opening up of negotiations with China and the Soviet Union.

Finally, conservatives tend to see themselves as the "real" Americans— true descendents of the Founding Fathers in appearance, values, and style. Liberals see America as a complex, diverse nation and doubt that members of any group (except, perhaps, Native Americans) qualify as "real" Americans.

2. *Parties are run by an elite.* Another criticism of the parties is that they are responsive not to their members but to party hacks and large contributors. Because most Americans take no part in party activity, pay no dues, and, at best, simply register in that party, it would not be surprising if the average voter had no input in party decisions. Yet the charge is not al-

together fair. Recent state and federal campaign laws have tried to restrain some of the influence of large monied interests; the parties use political polls to get an impression of grass roots attitudes; and, finally, many states use the direct primary, in which all members of a party may vote to nominate candidates. Moreover, there has been a dramatic change in the past few years in the method of nominating presidential candidates. During the 1980s, more rank-and-file party members than ever in history voted in presidential primaries. Some scholars have even argued that the nominating process has become *too* democratized, resulting in party fragmentation and disunity and the inability of parties to govern effectively once in office.[17]

3. *Parties obscure issues.* A constant charge against political parties is that they oversimplify issues and do not take clear stands. Vague and insubstantial party platforms and rambling, unspecific speeches by politicians leave us scratching our heads as to what the party and its candidate really intend to do. This, of course, is the characteristic practice of a party more interested in winning than in logic. For what good is logic if you have no power? As we have seen, parties and candidates who take clear-cut positions on the issues often do not win. Despite the rarity of obvious divisions on specific issues that characterizes most American elections, some party differences do exist and are probably perceived by most voters.[18]

In 1988, for example, although both parties tended to converge toward a middle ground, substantial differences remained between the leading representatives of the two major parties. Republican rhetoric remained hawkish about Nicaragua and support for the Contras (guerrillas fighting the government in that country). Democrats tended to look for a negotiated settlement of the issues that divided the Contras and the Sandinistas (who controlled the government), and opposed further military aid to the Contras. Although President Reagan had dropped his "evil empire" hostility to the Soviet Union, his party remained suspicious of Soviet motives, but Democrats were more apt to look upon Mikhail Gorbachev's peace efforts as sincere (hence, the most serious opposition to ratification of the Soviet-U.S. agreement eliminating intermediate-range nuclear missiles from Europe came from Republican conservatives like Senator Strom Thurmond). Democrats criticized President Reagan's "supply-side economics," which tended to emphasize lower taxes and greater freedom for business, and focused instead on programs designed to aid the disadvantaged. Republicans favored greater defense spending, Democrats preferred spending on domestic programs like education and rebuilding the nation's infrastructure (roads, bridges, public buildings). The GOP opposed compulsory national health insurance and timely warnings to workers of plant closings. Democrats favored both. Republicans often sided with Fundamentalists, who

[17]See Nelson Polsby, *Consequences of Party Reform* (New York: Oxford University Press, 1983).

[18]Pomper, pp. 416–420.

urged prayer in schools and opposed the right to abortion; Democrats were usually on the other side. The GOP had reservations about various social welfare and affirmative action programs designed to enhance opportunities for minority groups and women. Democrats tended to support these programs. Thus, whereas the major parties are not as sharply divided as those commonly vying for power in some other countries, their differences are still substantial, and these differences are most clearly drawn in the party platforms adopted every four years at the national conventions.[19]

Party platforms, of course, are not binding on anyone. They usually represent a compromise of the views and interests of the dominant party factions and individuals. Party platforms are not solemn pledges to be enacted to the letter by whichever party wins the election. (Once in office, Ronald Reagan, for example, presided over an economic policy that resulted in the highest federal deficit in history.) But neither are they wholly meaningless. They simply tell voters what the party would like to accomplish and what the leaders think the people would like to see accomplished.

In the post-World War II period, the nation tended to turn to the Democrats as the party of change and innovation when it felt the need for leadership in active and energetic new directions. (JFK's slogan, "Let's get the country moving again," although largely rhetorical, was probably perceived by most people as an alternative to the somewhat staid Eisenhower years.) On the other hand, when what was wanted was a firm, fiscally conservative, no-nonsense president, the people turned to Republicans Eisenhower and Nixon. Thus, Kennedy's election in 1960 seemed to spark action and changes in American society—the civil rights movement, for example, and later the youth movement—whereas Nixon's election eight years later signified to many people that the nation had tired of years of tumult and social experimentation and wanted to return to traditional values and forms of behavior. Interestingly, Reagan's election in 1980 may have signaled a shift in the perceived roles of the two parties, for Reagan, though appealing to a return to traditional values, worked hard to change existing domestic and tax policies (see Chapter 12) and defense and foreign policies (see Chapter 13), thus presenting himself as an active president moving the country in new directions different from those of the recent past (which he associated with a static Democratic party).

Comparison of the symbolic postures of the two parties, or at least of the parties' best-known leaders, may help explain the fates of the parties over the last four decades. Whereas the Democrats have seemed inclined to attract the new forces that have emerged in American social and economic life, the Republicans often have seemed to give a chilly reception to cries for fundamental change in America's social and political structure. Thus, in the last few decades, as blacks fought for an end to segregation, they found Democratic leaders, such as Lyndon Johnson and John F. Kennedy, often

[19]See *New York Times*, August 17, 1988, p. 12.

supporting at least their more moderate objectives. Famous Republican leaders, such as Gerald Ford and Barry Goldwater, were not so receptive. As a member of the U.S. Senate and the likely presidential candidate of the Republican party in 1964, Goldwater voted against the Civil Rights Act of 1964. Ford spoke out frequently and vigorously against busing both while a member of Congress and as president. Three decades earlier the GOP was no less cool to the emergence of organized labor as a power in American economic life, as we have previously noted.

In the 1970s the women's movement emerged as a growing new force in America. Jimmy Carter campaigned actively in support of the movement's primary goal—passage of the equal rights amendment, a constitutional amendment guaranteeing equal rights for women. On the other hand, Ronald Reagan opposed its passage. In 1984, Democratic candidate Walter Mondale sought and gained the support of major women's groups, including NOW (National Organization for Women). Thus the Democrats tend to succeed in politics when they can draw together a coalition of various interest groups (such as labor, blacks, and women), whereas Republicans tend to succeed when the electorate desires a return to traditional values, away from social reform.

Elections

Elections are the hallmark of a democratic society. It is through elections—not coups or civil wars—that we determine our leaders and our policies. Yet it may surprise most Americans to know that there are more elections in countries that we would consider undemocratic than there are here. The difference is that in the United States we expect to have a choice between candidates or issues, whereas in many parts of the world, elections take on the character of plebiscites (in which voters approve or disapprove an action already taken).[20]

In the United States there are over eighteen thousand governmental units, from the executive branch of the national government down to sheriffs' offices and local city councils. This means there are many more than eighteen thousand elected officials and even more individuals who run for office. Some elected positions are *partisan*, meaning that the political parties nominate candidates to run for election, such as is the case with the president. Others are *nonpartisan*, and aspirants run not as nominees of the party but directly for the office, as is the case in many municipal elections in the Western states.

Virtually all candidates for president, U.S. Congress, governor, and state legislature are first nominated by their party (usually in the spring or

---

[20]Guy Hermet, Richard Rose, and Alain Rouquie, *Elections Without Choice* (New York: Wiley, 1978).

The three candidates for the Democratic presidential nomination in 1984 square off for a debate at Columbia University in New York City (March 28, 1984). Left: Walter Mondale; second from left: Jesse Jackson; right: Gary Hart; moderator Dan Rather with his back to the camera. *(AP/Wide World Photos. Reproduced with permission.)*

summer of each election year). The choices of the parties then compete against one another in the general election (usually the first Tuesday after the first Monday in November of election years). Most nominations are now made in *primaries*—elections in which all registered members of a political party may vote for the candidate of that political party that they prefer. Thus a general election for office should not be confused with a nominating primary.[21] The presidential campaign is an illustration of these distinctions and deserves careful explanation.[22]

The way in which our president is chosen has changed considerably since 1968.[23] Whereas in the past there were only a handful of preferential primaries (17 Democratic and 16 Republican in 1968), in 1988 there were 34 Democratic and 35 Republican primaries (including one each in the District of Columbia and Puerto Rico). There were, as well, early caucus states, such as Iowa, that held precinct meetings (*caucuses* of party activists) to

[21]See *primary, convention,* and *electoral college* in the Glossary for clarification.

[22]See Stephen J. Wayne, *The Road to the White House: The Politics of Presidential Elections* (New York: St. Martin's Press, 1980).

[23]Changes in the Democratic party are detailed in William J. Crotty, *Decision for the Democrats: Reforming the Party Structure* (Baltimore: Johns Hopkins University Press, 1978); and Polsby.

choose delegates committed to the preferred presidential hopeful. Thus serious candidates had to begin campaigning well in advance of the general election. This system hardly confirmed the oft-stated complaint that party bosses and special interest groups met secretly and determined who the next president would be. On the contrary, to be nominated, candidates must campaign exhaustively for a large number of individual votes within their party and in states all across the nation.

In 1988, certain changes in the rules of both parties, but particularly in the Democratic party, attempted to return more power to party activists and encourage a more conservative electorate to participate in the nominating process. Thus, in the Democratic party, 645 of the 4,162 delegates chosen for the Atlanta convention were so-called "super delegates," picked from Congress and previous Democratic officeholders rather than as pledged delegates elected in popular primaries. These delegates were not pledged to a particular contender but were expected to vote in the convention for the person they deemed the most appropriate candidate. Also, for the first time, some 16 primaries, most in the Southern states, were bunched together on March 8, Super Tuesday. The idea was to make the nomination procedure less dependent on small, individual states (like Iowa and New Hampshire, which, though not really representative of the nation, had been unusually important because of their early caucus and primary) and also, by holding so many primaries on one day early in the campaign and in the South, to give conservative voters more weight in the nominating process. As it happened, George Bush swept Super Tuesday for the Republicans, and, contrary to earlier expectations, in the Democratic primaries of March 8, two liberals, Jesse Jackson (a black) and Michael Dukakis (a Northeastern governor), scored the most impressive victories.

Delegates committed to certain candidates are thus chosen at primaries and caucuses. These delegates then attend a national convention of their party during the summer of the election year. The number of delegates from each state is determined roughly on the basis of the population of that state (consequently California had the largest number of delegates at both the Republican and Democratic conventions in 1988). At the national convention, the voting takes place, and the candidate who receives a majority vote of all the delegates wins that party's nomination. Typically, as a result of the primaries and caucuses, one candidate has a majority of the delegates committed to her or him before the convention. If no candidate is able to muster a majority on the first ballot (the first time that each of the states' delegates vote), subsequent ballots are held until a winner is determined. Usually those candidates with little support release their delegates to vote for someone else. However, no convention vote has gone over one ballot since 1952.

The nominees of the two major parties then campaign for election. The winner is the candidate who receives a majority of the vote of the *electoral college*—a body of electors who actually choose the president and vice president. Each state is assigned a number of electors equal to its total of U.S. representatives and senators (in addition, the District of Columbia has three electoral votes). Currently, the candidate who wins the most popular votes (not necessarily a majority) in a state receives all that state's electoral votes, and the candidate who wins a majority of the *electoral* vote is elected president. This cumbersome means of choosing our president has led some critics to advocate the elimination or reform of the electoral college. On a few occasions in our history, the candidate with the plurality of popular votes has actually lost the election in the electoral college. But this has not happened during the twentieth century, and despite attempts to abolish or substantially change the electoral college, Congress does not seem disposed to tamper with it.

However, another reform has been introduced in recent years that has affected presidential (and all other) campaigns: the establishment of a public financing system, enacted by Congress and used in 1976, 1980, 1984, and 1988. Candidates have the option to participate in the system but are nonetheless restricted by a law limiting individual contributions to no more than $1,000 and donations of political action committees to no more than $5,000. In the primaries, candidates must raise $5,000 in small contributions in 20 or more states to qualify for federal financing. During the general election campaign, public financing is also available. The rationale behind this reform, of course, was to eliminate the influence on candidates of a few wealthy donors. Much nonpublic fund raising comes from *political action committees* (PACs), independent funding organizations that invest in candidates on behalf of groups of special interest contributors. PACs expanded their activities as a consequence of the 1970s campaign reform laws. As we have seen, they are limited to no more than a $5,000 contribution to any candidate; yet they proliferated from 600 in 1974 to 3,400 by 1982—an increase of over 500 percent—indicating a growing influence of special interest groups outside the regular party structure. This is just another indication that despite reform attempts, raising money continues to be one of the most important features (if not the dominant feature) of electoral politics. In 1980, $1.2 billion was spent in all elections, representing an increase of 759 percent over 1952.[24] And in 1988, candidates for the U.S. Senate, the Congress, and the presidency raised and spent more money than ever before in history, continuing the spiraling expense of American campaigning.

Finally, we should note the recent growth in campaign management and campaign consulting, likewise outside the regular party structure and requiring large sums of money. Professional consultants utilize all the latest techniques of polling, computerized mailings, direct-mail fund raising, and television advertising. This has resulted in the replacement of traditional

---

[24]See Sara Fritz, "Changing Roles in Game of Politics Shaping Races," *Los Angeles Times*, December 22, 1983, pp. 12–13.

seat-of-the pants politics with space age expertise and has, some scholars contend, further weakened the political party system.

The Election of 1988

If, as we have previously argued, American presidential elections have increasingly come to resemble a kind of political Super Bowl, the 1988 campaign was a contest in which the hype proved more interesting than the game itself.

George Bush and Dan Quayle were elected president and vice president by a substantial but not overwhelming 54 to 46 percent of the voters. Bush was the first sitting vice president to be elected since Martin Van Buren in 1836, and this was the most overwhelming *first* run for the Presidency since Eisenhower in 1952 (Reagan had only attracted 50 percent of the popular votes in 1980). At the same time the Democrats slightly increased their already solid margins in both the House of Representatives and the Senate. Since the campaign tended to focus on marginal or irrelevant "issues," no clear or decisive meaning or direction for the future could be gleaned from the results, unlike the 1980 campaign when Reagan was elected after emphasizing his promise to slash taxes, increase American military power, adopt a more aggressive posture toward the Soviet Union and international communism, and "get the government off the backs of the American people." Perhaps because of the failure of the voters to give any firm indication of what they wanted their government to do or not do in the coming four years, the days following the election were marked by sharp drops in the international value of the dollar and a decline in stock market prices, unusual in the wake of the election of a pro-business administration.

The election was frequently read as a victory for complacency and mediocrity. Consider the following items:

1. Fully half of those who were eligible to vote chose not to. This was the lowest turnout since 1924.

2. Of those who did vote, one-third told pollsters that they did so more in sorrow than enthusiasm for either of the two leading candidates.

3. The most widely discussed "event" of the campaign was the launching of a blizzard of "attack ads" on television by the Bush campaign, highlighted by an ad featuring a black Massachusetts convict who had raped and murdered a white Maryland housewife while on furlough from a life sentence in prison.

4. The most common and pervasive public response to the campaign was disgust with the negative manner in which it was conducted. Postelection pundits commonly characterized the campaign as "demeaning," "vulgar" and "mean-spirited," and fervently hoped that it would not prove a model for the future, while admitting that it probably would.

Yet the election seemed to reflect a vote for continuity in government. An

1988 Presidential Election Results (270 electoral votes needed to win)					
	Electoral Vote			**Electoral Vote**	
State	**Dukakis**	**Bush**	**State**	**Dukakis**	**Bush**
Alabama		9	Montana		4
Alaska		3	Nebraska		5
Arizona		7	Nevada		4
Arkansas		6	New Hampshire		4
California		47	New Jersey		16
Colorado		8	New Mexico		5
Connecticut		8	New York	36	
Delaware		3	North Crolina		13
District of			North Dakota		3
Columbia	3		Ohio		23
Florida		21	Oklahoma		8
Georgia		12	Oregon	7	
Hawaii	4		Pennsylvania		25
Idaho		4	Rhode Island	4	
Illiniois		24	South Carolina		8
Indiana		12	South Dakota		3
Iowa	8		Tennessee		11
Kansas		7	Texas		29
Kentucky		9	Utah		5
Louisiana		10	Vermont		3
Maine		4	Virginia		12
Maryland		10	Washington	10	
Massachusetts	13		West Virginia	6	
Michigan		20	Wisconsin	11	
Minnesota	10		Wyoming		3
Mississippi		7	Totals	112	426
Missouri		11			

improved international climate and a widespread sense of prosperity resulted in a vote to keep the GOP in control of the White House (*and* the Democrats in Congress). For Ronald Reagan, Bush's victory was undoubtedly a personal triumph. Iran-Contra and a historic national debt notwithstanding, he clearly retained the esteem and affection of the American people and was able to transfer this good will to his chosen successor. These proved decisive, perhaps insuperable, advantages for Mr. Bush in the campaign.

For the Democratic party, the election was not without its compensations, despite a bitter defeat in the presidential race. Democratic standard-bearer Michael Dukakis waged an uncertain and curious campaign. With a huge early lead in the polls, he chose to ignore Bush's attacks throughout the late summer and early fall. Instead, he spent time in Massachusetts, fulfilling his obligations as governor of that state while his lead slipped away. He seemed unable or unwilling to confront Bush and Reagan's attack on "the L-word" (liberalism) until late in the campaign, when he finally dropped the aura of a cool technocratic manager and accepted the liberal tradition of the modern Democratic party. At that point he closed the margin, particularly in the large, industrial states, sufficiently to make the election reasonably close, certainly closer than in 1984. Moreover, Dukakis attracted a much larger proportion of young voters than had Mondale four years earlier (about 51 percent to 40 percent in 1984) and a slight majority of women voters (about 52 percent compared to 44 percent for Mondale). The Democratic ticket continued to win the overwhelming support of blacks (at a 9 to 1 margin), Latinos (over 2 to 1) and Jewish voters (2 to 1), and considerably improved support from Catholics. Finally, Dukakis won the electoral vote in Oregon and Washington and only narrowly lost California. Thus, with the significant exception of the South, he exerted a broader-based national appeal than had been the case for the Democrats throughout the 1980s.

But 1988 left both parties in an ambiguous position. Democrats had firm control of both houses of Congress and most of the state governorships and legislatures, plus virtually all of the large city mayoralties. Yet Republicans had won five of the last six presidential elections. The Democrats appeared to be the nation's majority party but without the ability to control the nation's most important office or set a national agenda, particularly in foreign affairs. Some scholars suggest that voters like deadlock and see some wisdom in the Constitutional system of checks and balances; it seems to keep those folks in Washington from getting out of hand. Or perhaps like Arthur Miller's Willy Loman, both parties were liked but not well liked.

A Theory of Critical Elections

Although candidates usually avoid discussion or debate about substantive issues, there periodically arises in American politics an issue or a crisis so overwhelming (such as slavery or the Great Depression) as to force a realignment of political parties based on new coalitions of groups demanding a response to the crisis. Such a coalition formed the basis of the Republican party in the 1850s, as we have noted, and led to a fundamental change in the Democratic party in the 1930s.

Some scholars refer to elections such as those of 1860 (won by Lincoln) and 1932 (won by Franklin Roosevelt) as *critical elections*.[25]

[25]See Walter Dean Burnham, *Critical Elections* (New York: Norton, 1970); and V. O. Key, "A Theory of Critical Elections," *Journal of Politics* 17 (February 1955): 3–18. For criticisms of this theory, see Ladd and Hadley, *Transformations of the American Party System*; and Allen J. Lichtman. "Critical Elections and the Reality of American Presidential Politics, 1916–1940," *American Historical Review* 81 (April 1976): 317–348.

First and foremost, a critical election responds to a profound, revolutionary change in the nation's way of life and in the balance of political forces. After 1860, the Republicans ended slavery, successfully led the nation through the Civil War, and went on to preside over the transformation of the nation from a "prairie democracy" into an industrial giant.

Second, a critical election draws together a new coalition, resulting in a new balance of political power. Thus the Republicans became dominant after 1860 and the Democrats after 1932 because they were able to draw new and substantial support from new combinations of elements in the population. The Republicans combined business executives, Western farmers, and virtually anyone opposed to slavery. During the 1930s, the Democrats brought together a diverse coalition, including Southern whites, blacks, labor, farmers, urban ethnic groups, and intellectuals. Many of these were new voters.

Third, a critical election is characterized by the importance attached to an issue or a group of related issues. This does not mean that either Lincoln or FDR ran issue-oriented campaigns. What it does mean is that by using historical hindsight, we can see that the election of these men signaled a decisive new turn of events. As we have said, politics often is devoted to winning elections. By and large, the surest way to win an election is to appeal to the values of the voters. Most voters acquire their basic values when they are young. Thus there is normally a certain element of nostalgia in any political campaign. Politicians do not "tell it like it is"; they much prefer to tell it like it was. For example, the campaign of 1964 gave the voters an opportunity to redecide the issues that had been settled when the New Deal took power in 1932, 32 years earlier. President Johnson ran as a disciple of FDR (he even cultivated a certain physical resemblance to FDR), and his Great Society was in part an extension of Roosevelt's New Deal. Senator Goldwater, on the other hand, seemed to be campaigning against FDR, asking: Should we continue with welfare and Social Security? Should the TVA (Tennessee Valley Authority) be sold to private business? The election was fought out on these issues, and the New Deal won still another resounding victory. But the reality of American life had to do with much different issues. What would happen in Vietnam? What did the candidates propose to do about racism, urban decay, inflation? Could the Affluent Society go on without ruining the environment or running out of energy? These issues were on the horizon in 1964. But the major party candidates felt, probably correctly, that most voters were not interested or would much prefer to hear still another campaign on the now familiar topic of whether or not the New Deal revolution had wrecked or saved the nation.

One could cite evidence of issue dodging in other major political campaigns. As we have noted, the famed Nixon–Kennedy presidential debates of 1960 turned, in the last few encounters, on the burning question of what America was going to do about the islands of Quemoy and Matsu. In 1968 candidate Nixon ran for the presidency in the midst of a raging war in

Vietnam, promising to "end the war and win the peace" but refusing to say how or when. Questioned about this, Nixon insisted that his plans must be kept secret. Thus one might say that it is normal for political rhetoric to concern itself with the burning issues of three or four decades earlier, while ignoring the realities of the moment.

However, in the elections of Lincoln and Roosevelt important issues surfaced that resulted in new policy directions. Lincoln's election was followed by the legal termination of slavery and the federal government's support of business (such as tariffs and land grants to railroads). Roosevelt's election heralded the establishment of an activist state responsible for the good health of the economy (for example, Social Security and laws establishing minimum wages and maximum hours of work).

The new coalition created by a critical election must be enduring. For example, the coalition that carried Eisenhower to two terms in the White House collapsed when he left office, whereas FDR's coalition transformed the Democrats from the minority to the majority party. In 1969, many Republicans, such as Kevin Phillips, a columnist and GOP strategist, believed that the Nixon victory in 1968 would lead to a new and decisive shift in the power balance of the two major parties.[26] These Republicans urged a "Southern strategy" that would, in essence, add to the normal Republican vote those whites—largely but not exclusively in the South—who supported Governor Wallace, to create a "new majority" of predominantly conservative voters. The possibility of such a coalition may have existed, but if it did, the Nixon administration obviously failed to unify it.

In the mid-1970s, William A. Rusher, editor of the conservative journal *National Review*, argued for a new conservative party.[27] Noting that the polls showed that a majority of Americans identified themselves as "conservative," Rusher called for a party that would be more aggressively anticommunist in foreign policy, by junking détente, for example, or by giving more support to Taiwan and showing less friendliness to the People's Republic of China. On domestic policy, conservatives attacked the welfare state. Rusher wanted to see a new party formed around the "producers" in America, mainly working people and those in business, as opposed to the "consumers": welfare recipients, civil servants, and bureaucrats.

In a sense, Rusher's proposals were logical. But his logic did not prevail over the simple realities of American political life. The politician he had targeted to lead his new party, former California Governor Ronald Reagan, chose instead to remain in the Republican party.

On the liberal side, there has also been much talk of a new coalition. Senator McGovern's strategists in 1972 believed that the senator would be

[26]Kevin Phillips, *The Emerging Republican Majority* (New Rochelle, N.Y.: Arlington, 1969).

[27]"A New Party: Eventually, Why Not Now?" *National Review*, May 23, 1975, pp. 550–555.

carried to victory on the impetus of the votes of 15 million young people, believed to be overwhelmingly liberal, who would vote for the first time as the result of a constitutional amendment lowering the voting age to 18. But young people did not vote in great numbers, and those who did seemed only slightly more partial to McGovern than their elders were.

Have recent elections been "critical elections"? Are we about to have another period of such elections? Will there be, in the next few years, a new alignment of the political parties? Will the Republican party become the majority party, or will the Democrats claim more voters? Or have we entered a period of "dealignment" in which neither party dominates? We are too close to the present situation to answer these questions with clarity. But there is some evidence to suggest that the current two-party system will continue essentially as it is for the foreseeable future.[28] Nonetheless, almost every new administration sweeps into office believing that it is about to embark on a historic and wondrous adventure. Even the staid and conservative Eisenhower regime pictured itself as a "crusade for freedom." John Kennedy spoke of conquering the New Frontier. Lyndon Johnson sought to create a Great Society. Richard Nixon's supporters believed that his election signaled the emergence of a "new majority." Reagan's admirers were certain that he had brought the Republicans *and* the conservatives into prominence.

Although there is an element of mere electioneering rhetoric in all such claims, the rhetoric probably reflects the hope that each new administration represents a kind of "new dawn" in American life rather than simply a change in party, personnel, and/or policy. Each new administration hopes, and its strongest supporters believe, that it will indeed prove "critical," just as most human beings believe that their own lives will have importance.

Events, rather than the character and the policies of a given administration, help decide whether such expectations are fulfilled. If there had been no Civil War, Lincoln's administration might not now be regarded as quite so important. The Great Depression and World War II provided the context for the unfolding of FDR's New Deal.

Simply stated, the theory of critical elections (and that is just what it is—a theory) offers the possibility that America can adapt to rather abruptly changing conditions and new demands via its two-party system.

Politics Reconsidered

We have reviewed a number of definitions of politics—a technique of moving people, a way of settling conflicts and distributing scarce resources as a substitute for violence, a means of promoting self-interest, and the winning of elections. None of these definitions is sufficient in itself. Human

[28]See Ladd and Hadley.

beings, Aristotle insisted, are by nature political. To the extent that human beings in an organized society can achieve a better life, politics is the essential tool.

Of course, it may be true that politics is sometimes a dreary and dirty business (although probably no drearier or dirtier than most other businesses). Too often politics in America comes down to a matter of ambitious and unprincipled individuals seeking power or an easy life at the expense of the taxpayers. Much that passes for political action is a matter of artfully and often deceitfully manipulating the many while pandering to the wealthy and powerful few.

On the other hand, one should consider the millions of individuals who have engaged themselves wholeheartedly and unselfishly in the political arena, attending local city council meetings, campaigning for statewide issues, or supporting national figures of such diversity as Adlai Stevenson, John and Robert Kennedy, Jesse Jackson, Barry Goldwater, and Ronald Reagan—to name a few recent leaders with an extraordinary ability to arouse great energy and loyalty on behalf of their ideas. The people who have campaigned for school boards, or who marched with Jackson, or who rang doorbells for Reagan were not all fools, nor were they saints or martyrs. They were individuals who had found an exhilarating cause, something that helped give their lives meaning and purpose. They were also patriots, in the best sense of that much abused term, for they were prepared to sacrifice time, energy, and money and to set aside purely personal indulgences and ambitions to join with other, like-minded citizens and go out and do battle for their vision of the future of this republic. Whether they won or lost the battle, whether their champion prevailed or not, they shared in one of the richest and most deeply satisfying experiences available to free men and women. For Hamletlike, political beings are always and forever ambiguous, doomed to crawl in the dust, and yet how like an angel in their apprehension of a better world.

9

Who Rules America? The Elite, the Interests, and the Voter

- Democracy: Rule by the People -
- Making Public Policies -
- Pluralism: Rule by Interest Groups -
- Elitism: Rule by the Powerful -
- Voting -
- Political Socialization -
- Apathy and Anger -
- The Attentive Public -

> What's good for the country is good for General Motors and vice versa.
>
> **Charles Wilson**
> **Former President of General Motors,**
> **former Secretary of Defense**

> And this our form, as committed not to the few, but to the whole body of the people, is called a democracy [in which] there is visible in the same persons an attention to their own private concerns and those of the public; and in others engaged in the labor of life there is a competent skill in the affairs of government. For we . . . think him that does not meddle in state affairs—not indolent, but good for nothing.
>
> **Pericles**
> *On the Causes of Athenian Greatness*

Democracy: Rule by the People

There can be no question as to who is supposed to rule the United States of America. The premise of Abraham Lincoln's Gettysburg Address—that this is a "government of the people, by the people, for the people"—is the foundation of virtually all official political rhetoric. The only source of legitimate power in the United States is the people. As sociologist C. Wright Mills pointed out rhetorically, "No American runs for office in order to rule or even govern, but only to serve."[1]

Supreme Court Chief Justice Earl Warren believed that the most important judgment handed down by the Court in his tempestuous era was the *Baker v. Carr* decision of 1962. In this decision, the Court established the principle of "one-person, one-vote." So, too, President Lyndon Johnson believed that the decisive weapon in the struggle of black people to gain equality was the passage of the Voting Rights Act of 1965. Given the right to vote, Johnson argued, blacks would use their political power to overcome any economic, social, or educational disadvantages.

The key assumption of both these judgments is that America is ultimately ruled by decisions made at the ballot box. This is an appealing idea and part of every American child's most elementary education in citizenship. But is it true? Many think not.

In politics, as in many human endeavors, there is often a difference between theory and reality, between what is said and what is done. There is evidence that millions, perhaps tens of millions, of Americans, ranging from Marxists on the left to the John Birch Society on the right, simply do

---

[1]C. Wright Mills, *The Power Elite* (New York: Oxford University Press, 1956), p. 17.

not believe that ours is a government of, by, and for the people. Perhaps never before in our history have so many been willing to believe that they are being misled by so few. New candidates for the role of the "real rulers" or the "secret government" of America seem to arise almost weekly. Among those most frequently mentioned are the "Eastern Establishment," the military-industrial complex, big labor, the Mafia, the Jews, the Kennedys, the WASPs, Wall Street, the Council on Foreign Relations, the Tri-Lateral Commission, the media, the CIA, "America's 60 families," the oil cartel—one could go on almost indefinitely. There is hardly a group of Americans so poor and so powerless that someone is not willing to accuse them of being the secret rulers of America.

In the search for these hidden masters, some have even delved into feudal lore, tracing conspiracies back to such arcane (or nonexistent) groups as the *illuminati*—a group of exceptionally tall people who supposedly came from another planet to rule the world. (Lyndon B. Johnson was very tall, and so was Charles de Gaulle—obviously they were part of a conspiracy by the tall to dominate the rest of us.)

It is easy, almost too easy, to dismiss all such notions of a conspiratorial secret government as part of the prevailing paranoia. But where there is that much smoke, might not one expect to find some fire? The very fact that so many people refuse to believe that the American political system works the way it is supposed to work suggests that the question of who has power in America is worth considering.

Let us define power simply as the ability to decide how the resources of the nation, the energy of the people, and the apparatus of the government shall be used. Likewise, we should consider *for whom* power is being exercised. Whereas power can be exerted in a corporation or a group or a family, it becomes of widespread interest when it is exerted by government. In this regard we are interested in *public policies*—how they are formed and what their impact is on us.

Making Public Policies

Public policies are long-term commitments of governments and their bureaucracies to certain patterns of activity.[2] For a long time we had a *policy* toward the People's Republic of China. This was a policy of nonrecognition and hostility that affected other actions of the government; for example, to contain the Chinese enemy we armed the island of Taiwan (off the coast of China) and fought a war in Vietnam (on China's southern border). During the 1970s certain *decisions* were made regarding China—our Ping-Pong

[2]See Charles E. Lindblom, *The Policy Making Process* (Englewood Cliffs, N.J.: Prentice-Hall, 1968).

team and President Nixon visited there, and gradually relations began to improve—and now the policy toward that country has changed rather dramatically.

What people, or events, most influence the formulation and conduct of public policies, and who benefits most from these policies? These are questions that attract a variety of opinions. Let us appraise the questions in a historical context, as it is easier to judge policies and events that can be seen in a perspective of time and with some knowledge of their consequences.

As was discussed in Chapter 3, the American Revolution was not a result of a spontaneous uprising of the great majority of the people who lived in the 13 colonies. It is impossible to know just what percentage of the colonists supported rebellion and independence, but historians have variously estimated the number, some as being as low as 10 percent and few placing it higher than one-third of the total population. (Perhaps another third opposed the revolution, and the rest of the people apparently preferred not to get involved.) In fact, the revolution was largely the work of a group of political activists, mostly young and many of them lawyers, who took it upon themselves to act in the name of the people. Moreover, strictly speaking, the Constitutional Convention of 1787 was of dubious legality and had no clear mandate from the majority to establish a national government.[3] Thus some students argue that power in America from the very beginning of the nation's history was wielded largely by an elite—leaders like Jefferson, Washington, Madison, Franklin, and the Adamses.[4]

By the time of the Civil War, two groups had emerged to compete as arbiters of power in America: the planter aristocracy of the South and the business executive–politicians of the North. The Civil War settled the issue in favor of the Northern businessmen and politicians. From the Civil War until the Great Depression brought Franklin Roosevelt's New Deal to power, the businessman, now usually referred to by somewhat grander titles in keeping with his exalted status—such as "industrialist," "tycoon," "corporate magnate," and "robber baron"—had things pretty much his own way.

As William Randolph Hearst, himself a tycoon of no mean proportions, pointed out in a letter to Arthur Brisbane written in 1906:

> We still maintain the republican form of government, but who has control of the primaries that nominate the candidate? The corporations have. Who controls the conventions? The corporations. Who count the votes to suit themselves. The corporations. Who own the bosses and the elected officials?

[3]Of course, before going into effect, the Constitution was approved in state conventions chosen by citizens of the states.

[4]See Thomas R. Dye and L. Harmon Ziegler, *The Irony of Democracy* (Belmont, Calif.: Wadsworth, 1970).

Are they representatives of the people or the corporations? Let any fair-minded man answer this question truthfully.

    If the corporations do all this—and they surely do—can we maintain that this is any longer a government by the people?[5]

By the 1920s, perhaps the high point of unchallenged business power in America, President Coolidge could observe, with little fear of contradiction, "The business of America is business."[6]

The worldwide capitalist crisis of the Great Depression of the 1930s brought an end to this era in America. In totalitarian states such as the Soviet Union, Germany, and Italy, political functionaries became the prime decision makers and true rulers, even though in the fascist states, business people continued to own their property and often enjoyed great personal wealth. The real power to set production schedules and to determine prices and wages and other fundamental prerogatives of ownership was in effect usurped by party bureaucrats.

In America, the New Deal created another means of redistributing the power and prestige lost by the business classes in the wake of the Depression. Economist John Kenneth Galbraith described this as a system of "counter-vailing power."[7] Labor unions, for example, were deliberately encouraged and strengthened as a counterforce to the power of the great corporations. Government bureaucrats also acquired new powers to limit, control, and direct economic activity.

Pluralism: Rule by Interest Groups

By and large, the Roosevelt innovations were created pragmatically as specific responses to specific problems and injustices rather than as the result of an ideology, as was the case in the totalitarian states. Only after the fact did a philosophy arise that attempted to explain and justify the Roosevelt revolution. The doctrine has come to be known as *democratic pluralism*. Pluralism insists that power in America is shared by various interest groups, each attempting to influence government and direct the nation's affairs in a manner congenial to themselves. Such groups are usually perceived to be competing with one another for power, and this competition is considered healthy because it is consistent with both our capitalistic and our democratic traditions.[8] Typical of such interest groups are labor unions,

[5]Oliver Carlson, *Hearst, Lord of San Simeon* (New York: Viking, 1936), p. 140.
[6]Speech to the Society of American Newspaper Editors, January 17, 1925.
[7]J.K. Galbraith, *American Capitalism* (Boston: Houghton Mifflin, 1956), chap. 9.
[8]See Robert A. Dahl, *Pluralist Democracy in the United States: Conflict and Consent* (Chicago: Rand McNally, 1967).

business and manufacturers' associations, and ethnic blocs like the National Association for the Advancement of Colored People (NAACP). Special interest groups are normally defined as organizations, formal or informal, with a particular concern, such as the National Rifle Association (guns) or Common Cause (political reform).

These groups may play a critical role in policy decisions by government and in elections, contributing money and work to their chosen candidates. Once they have elected their candidates, they expect to receive their loyalty and support for their concerns, sometimes despite the wishes of a majority of the people that the politician is supposed to represent. For example, polls have indicated that for many years most Americans have favored some form of a national health insurance program run by the federal government. (The cost of medical care for the average American family reached about 10 percent of family income in 1980, far higher than that in any other Western nation.[9]) But the American Medical Association opposes such legislation, and many physicians are substantial political donors. Their view has prevailed. The same point could be made about labor organizations, such as the Teamsters Union, which though engaging in practices that many people think should be regulated, usually has sufficient political muscle to block hostile legislation.

In addition to indirect influence over legislators and sometimes over members of the executive branch (the secretary of agriculture, for instance, is unlikely to propose policies disliked by most farmers), interest groups often hire lobbyists directly.

According to the legal definition of the Federal Regulation of Lobbying Act of 1946, a lobbyist at the national level is any person who solicits money or anything of value to be used to influence the defeat or success of legislation in Congress. Most important American organizations have lobbyists in Washington, from the American Medical Association to Ralph Nader's groups.

Lobbyists can use a variety of techniques to affect government. They can try to influence legislators through personal contact; they can provide campaign contributions and other favors such as expense-free vacations at plush resorts; they can encourage the membership of their group to write and call legislators; and they can testify before congressional committees.

How effective lobbyists can be depends on many factors, not the least of which is the intensity of feeling that a group has about a particular matter. For example, although public opinion polls have for some time shown that the majority of Americans favor gun control legislation, the National Rifle Association has thus far been successful in thwarting substantive control laws. This success can be explained in part because the NRA is more intensely interested in the issue and more active than other groups and thus has an impact disproportionate to its total numbers. The NRA effectively

[9]*Los Angeles Times*, July 17, 1983, p. 2.

uses its lobbyists and at the same time mobilizes its membership to flood lawmakers with calls and letters. On the other hand, members of the NRA may have an opinion but little interest in a labor law, whereas the AFL-CIO will be very interested and may affect such a law's defeat or passage.

Some Americans believe that lobbyists are a threat to democracy. Others believe that they are indispensable. If you are president of General Motors and you influence the government to establish a tariff making it more expensive for Americans to buy foreign automobiles, you may argue that that is good for America because it will result in more jobs in domestic car manufacture. If you are a member of a consumer advocacy group, you may believe the General Motors lobbyist to be antithetical to the interests of the typical middle-class American. However, if your advocacy group influences the government to lower tariffs on foreign automobiles so that you will pay less for whatever car you choose to buy, you might reason that your lobbyist has acted in the best interests of the country. It is important to remember that groups normally have more power than individuals do and that you will agree with the aims of some groups and disagree with others.

Pluralism maintains that interest groups are beneficial. It is to be expected that organizations will develop to protect specific interests in public policy. If certain organizations gain too much power (as may corporations), others will emerge (such as labor unions and consumer groups) to counterbalance that power. According to pluralism, we all are, in a sense, somehow connected with interest groups, and our relationship to politics is very much influenced by the relationship of our interest group to government. For example, we may be students; thus our interests frequently coincide with those of other students, and we probably would oppose a tuition increase of 100 percent. We may be members of a labor union; thus we, along with other labor union members, might be keenly interested in a piece of labor legislation. The same might be said about those of us who are homeowners, taxpayers, and so on. Those interest groups that best represent us and have the most power are the ones that are the best organized. These would include such groups as the National Association of Manufacturers, the AFL-CIO, the Sierra Club, the American Civil Liberties Union, Common Cause, the National Organization for Women, and the NAACP. Because each of us can identify with an interest group, each of us can be represented. Thus power in America rests neither in the "people" nor in a single monolithic hierarchy. Rather, according to pluralism, there are "multiple centers of power, none of which is wholly sovereign," which will check excessive power, secure common consent to government policies, and provide the possibility for settling conflicts peacefully.[10]

Pluralists do not deny that there are "elites" in America, but they challenge the idea that there is a *single* elite (see the "power-elite" argument that follows). Rather, pluralists argue, it is possible, on the basis of merit,

[10]Dahl, p. 24.

talent, and hard work, for a person from any socioeconomic background to rise to a position of authority (that is, an "elite" position) within one of the several groups who compete for power. Thus the late George Meany, hardly an Ivy League aristocrat, became longtime president of the powerful AFL-CIO national labor federation.

Pluralism, then, accepts the idea of "multiple" elites but reaffirms the belief in upward mobility and an open leadership system that enables a significant number of Americans to rise to the top and influence public policies.

Elitism: Rule by the Powerful

If power in America was substantially diffused during the New Deal, the onset of World War II required that it quickly be concentrated again in the process of mobilizing the nation for war. The industrialist, scorned by Roosevelt in the early New Deal days as an "economic royalist" and a "malefactor of great wealth," was courted once again. Invited to come to Washington as "dollar-a-year men," many of the nation's foremost business executives found themselves working with the visionary New Dealers that they had regarded as enemies a few years earlier. By the time America emerged victorious from the war, the public had largely forgotten the bitterness against business that followed the 1929 stock market crash, and America's leading corporations trumpeted their war record in full-page newspaper and magazine ads proclaiming that "free enterprise won the war." But if business executives had successfully returned to the center of American life and power, they now found themselves in mixed and—from their standpoint—often dubious company. The politicians and bureaucrats' power had also swollen enormously, and they found the change agreeable. Organized labor, too, had played a key role in the war years, holding down strikes and excessive wage demands. The triumvirate of "big business, big labor, and big government" became a common catchphrase in the writings of those who chronicled the shifting balances of American power in the immediate postwar years.

But there was still another element of American society that emerged from the war with far greater power and prestige and income than would have seemed imaginable a decade earlier: the military-industrial complex, often referred to simply as the MIC. This term refers to an ostensible alliance between the military establishment and certain large corporations (such as McDonnell Douglas, Northrop, and Lockheed) whose business is sustained by contracts from the government to produce goods for military use (planes, rockets, and so on). President Eisenhower shocked many of his conservative and military supporters by including in his farewell address to the nation a warning against the growing power of the MIC.

Traditionally, Americans like to think of the United States as a peace-loving democracy. In theory, the common people had the most to lose and the least to gain from war. Therefore, it was assumed that a democracy would naturally be antimilitary. Wars, it was argued, were started by ambitious generals, greedy munitions makers, and arrogant kings and dictators. For most of the nations of the world throughout history up to and including the modern age, an essay on who rules would be an exercise in elaborating the obvious. The military—that is, the people who have the most efficient and destructive weapons and the men to use them—rule.

The Founding Fathers were aware of this and debated long and hard about how to prevent military preeminence in the United States. Some suggested that the only safe course was to abolish the professional military class altogether; the new country would do without a standing army or navy and rely on the patriotism of the people to defend it. Ultimately it was decided that a military force was essential, but the authors of the Constitution took the precaution of making the president the commander in chief, an unusual arrangement (because most presidents obviously would not 'be professional soldiers), as a means of ensuring that the military would remain subordinate to the civilian government.

Thus John Adams wrote that Americans

> believing that in the long-run interest, not violence, would rule the world, and the United States must depend for safety and success on the interests they could create, were tempted to look upon war and preparation for war as the worst of blunders; for they were sure that every dollar capitalized in industry was a means of overthrowing their enemies more effective than a thousand dollars spent upon frigates or standing armies.
>
> *American Ideals*

Through most of our first century and a half of national life, this principle was rarely challenged. Avoidance of foreign wars and the maintenance of a relatively small and weak standing army and navy were thought to be among the secrets of prosperity in America, especially when it was compared with European states, which, in the American view, were almost perpetually recovering from the last war or preparing for the next one, with the result that the people were impoverished by a rapacious military establishment.

The Japanese attack on Pearl Harbor brought an end to a majority support for this idea. Within the next four decades, the United States became the strongest military power on earth, fought three wars, and engaged in numerous "minor" military actions, such as the landing of American troops in Lebanon during the Eisenhower and Reagan administrations and the Mayaguez incident under President Ford. In fact, American troops were stationed more or less permanently in 40 to 45 countries, and the nation spent well over $1,000 billion on weapons during the cold

Who Rules America? The Elite, the Interests, and the Voter

233

war era. As a result, the MIC became a new power center in American life, controlling millions of jobs and many of the nation's largest businesses. Indeed, the Pentagon has become the largest single purchaser of goods and services in the United States, and, during the 1980s, defense spending accounted for nearly half of the nation's general tax revenues, with projections that its share would be nearly 60 percent by 1986. Moreover, one job in ten in the United States depends on defense contracts, and 30 percent of America's mathematicians and 25 percent of its scientists and engineers work for the Department of Defense or for defense contractors, which results, some critics point out, in siphoning off talent and money that could be invested in the private sector to help us compete better with other industrialized nations. Yet Congress is hardly interested in reversing this trend. Understandably, most members of Congress want to obtain defense contracts and jobs for their districts, not restrain the military-industrial complex.[11]

Moreover, the tremendous growth of the defense industry since World War II raised serious concerns regarding fundamental precepts of American democracy. Critics of the MIC were reminded that whereas the nation's founders certainly wanted to have a government with energy and authority, capable of protecting its citizens, excessive reliance on the military might well be dangerous. As Alexander Hamilton, an advocate of a strong government and a strong military, admonished in *Federalist* 8, "The violent destruction of life and property incident to war, the continual effort and alarm attendant on a state of continual danger, will compel nations the most attached to liberty to resort for repose and security to institutions which have a tendency to destroy their civil and political rights. To be more safe, they at length become willing to run the risk of being less free."

Thus, in his farewell address warning of the growing influence of the MIC, President Eisenhower restated a concern as old as the nation.

The growth of the MIC required a reassessment of who has power in American life, and the seminal work in this field was by sociologist C. Wright Mills.[12] Mills began by affirming what has become the common complaint of many people. Ordinary citizens have little real impact on decision making in the government or in the larger society. (Who decided to go to war in Vietnam? What role did the average citizen play in Watergate? Did the people choose to have a stock market crash in 1987?) Rather, Mills argued, the people are in fact manipulated by forces they can neither understand nor control. Mills called these forces the *power elite* and pointed out that a relatively tiny handful of people in the government (largely the upper echelon of the executive branch—Congress he considered irrelevant),

[11]See the special report "Servants or Masters? Revisiting the Military Industrial Complex," *Los Angeles Times*, July 10, 1983, p. 6.
[12]See Mills.

the leadership of the large corporations, and the top brass of the military, in fact, run the country. Moreover, he suggested that these three hierarchies frequently interlock so that the same people or groups float among the general staff, the corporate boards of directors, and the command positions in the White House and the president's cabinet. Mills went on to state that the men (and they are virtually all men) who rule America are not usually "the best and the brightest" but more often the most ruthless, the most selfish, and in a certain sense among the least enlightened of our citizens:

> In so far as the elite flourishes as a social class or a set of men at the command posts, it will select and form certain types and reject others. The kind of moral and psychological beings men become is in large part determined by the values they experience and the institutional roles they are allowed to play. . . .
>
> The men of the higher circles are not representative men; their high position is not a result of moral virtue, their fabulous success is not firmly connected with meritorious ability. Those who sit in the seats of the high and the mighty are selected and formed by the means of power, the sources of wealth, the mechanics of celebrity. . . . Commanders of power unequalled in human history, they have succeeded within the American system of organized irresponsibility.[13]

Later theorists have elaborated on Mills's beginnings. Thomas R. Dye extended the hierarchies to include other important institutions like the "newsmakers" (those corporations whose concentrated power is in the mass media), the "superlawyers" (with offices in New York and Washington, work occasionally in the executive branch of the federal government, and whose clients are among the largest corporations in the world), the foundations (such as the Ford and Lilly foundations), and the presidents and trustees of the top private universities in the country such as Harvard, Yale, Columbia, and the University of Chicago.[14]

In contrast with the pluralists, who believe that there is upward mobility into positions of authority, power-elite theorists argue that the path to such power is blocked to all but a select few. There are, for example, few blacks in positions of power. The first black four-star general in American history, Air Force General Daniel James, Jr., was not appointed until 1975, and only a few other blacks (such as Thurgood Marshall on the Supreme Court and Andrew Young, Mayor of Atlanta and former ambassador to the United Nations) can be counted as members of the ruling elite. Likewise, women are seriously underrepresented in the top positions of authority. Fewer than 5 percent of the nation's top institutional leaders are women, and only a third of the boards of directors of the 100 largest industrial corporations have

---

[13]Mills, p. 15.

[14]See Thomas R. Dye, *Who's Running America?* 3rd ed. (Englewood Cliffs, N.J.: Prentice-Hall, 1983).

female members. In government, women hold fewer than 10 percent of the key positions.[15]

Other than being male and white, the power elite, according to these theorists, is well educated and usually comes from major urban centers.

An interesting addition to the elite theory was made by sociologist G. William Domhoff, who studied the social backgrounds of these powerful men. He discovered that they attend the same universities, belong to the same clubs, are directors in the same corporations, and tend to vacation at the same resorts.[16]

Domhoff's studies suggest further the interlocking nature of this elite. It appears that a few men circulate among and serve in most of the hierarchies referred to. Two examples may suffice:

1. Caspar Weinberger, President Reagan's secretary of defense, graduated from Harvard Law School, was vice president of the Bechtel Corporation, and served on the board of directors of Pepsico and Quaker Oats. He was associated with the Council on Foreign Relations, the Trilateral Commission, the American Enterprise Institute, and the Bohemian Club and served in several high posts in past administrations.

2. President Carter's secretary of state, Cyrus R. Vance, was a senior partner of Simpson, Thacher and Bartlett law firm and a director of Pan American World Airlines, Aetna Life Insurance Company, IBM, the Council on Foreign Relations, the American Red Cross, and the Rockefeller Foundation. He was also a trustee of the University of Chicago and was chief U.S. negotiator at the Paris peace talks on Vietnam under President Johnson.[17]

Although the theory of the power elite was originally developed by a leftist professor, it proved attractive and popular enough to be expropriated in somewhat altered form by the right wing of American politics. But instead of seeing an unholy alliance of business, the military, and government as the true rulers of America, conservatives pointed to the "eastern liberal establishment" as the new power elite. They professed to see an alliance of left-leaning intellectuals and liberals, government bureaucrats, labor leaders, and the media as the focus of American power. They pointed to the power of the great foundations, the television networks, and such chummy groups as the Council on Foreign Relations as the true manipulators of American life.

By 1964, Senator Barry Goldwater had become the Republican candidate for president in a campaign whose central theme was a demand that the liberal establishment be turned out of power. His principal opponent in the Republican primaries was New York Governor Nelson Rockefeller. When Rockefeller rose at the Republican convention in San Francisco to attack

[15]Dye, pp. 195–197, 201–205.

[16]G. William Domhoff, *Who Rules America?* (Englewood Cliffs, N.J.: Prentice-Hall, 1967). Also, see the same author's *The Higher Circles* (New York: Vintage Books, 1971).

[17]Dye, pp. 68–69, 76.

Goldwater's ideas, he was roundly booed and prevented for many minutes from speaking. This proved to be the beginning of the end of Goldwater's hopes for attracting broad mainstream support for his campaign, and the Rockefeller family has ever since been regarded by the Republican right wing as the very embodiment of the eastern liberal establishment that they believe is systematically undermining traditional American values in favor of the "Rockefeller interests."

In 1972, Democratic candidate Senator George McGovern, although not embracing the power-elite thesis in so many words, sounded very much like someone who had read and agreed with Mills when he promised to cut the military budget by 50 percent and transfer both income and power from the rich and privileged to the poor, the young, and the powerless. He was beaten even more decisively than Goldwater.

Thus both major political parties have put forth a candidate who embraced some form of the power-elite thesis and failed to win election. Yet it remains a popular point of view, particularly among intellectuals. Many Americans apparently agree with C. Wright Mills that somehow, some way, the people are no longer in control (if they ever were) and that most of the nation's large and powerful corporations, unions, and the government itself have become enemies of the common person and the commonweal.

We have considered three reputed sources of power in American society: the people, pluralism, and the power elite. A plausible case can be made for each. The will of the people does count for *something* in America. (For example, when public opinion turned against the war in Vietnam, the politicians and the generals began to search for a way out.) President Nixon may have believed himself to be a "sovereign" after his sweeping victory in the 1972 presidential election, but he soon found himself under siege by the press, then the courts, and finally the Congress, and his resignation would seem to reaffirm the premise of pluralism, that power is shared by many competing groups in America under our federal system. Nevertheless, the power-elite thesis does seem to present a coherent and reasonable explanation of our foreign policy, which does not really change very much, regardless of who wins the elections.

How one feels about this question is probably related to how one judges American society and one's role in that society. Those who view America as "a noble experiment" will probably hold to the notion that the people, after all, do rule. Those who see America as having abandoned its stated ideals will tend to embrace one form or another of the elitist theory. Although it is beyond the purview of this book to attempt to convince the reader of the correctness or falseness of any of these viewpoints, the fact is that regardless of who ultimately rules, power in America can be legitimized only through the ballot box. If we are being manipulated, the manipulators must somehow affect our decisions as voters. Thus how and why we vote as we do, and whether or not we bother to vote at all, is important.

Voting

The most direct, clear, and understandable way that most individuals can influence the acts of their government is by voting. Voting is the fundamental political act in a democratic nation. Only the vote of the people can bestow legitimacy and legality on government. People who consistently refuse to exercise their franchise, either because they "can't be bothered" or because "it doesn't matter who I vote for, they're all a bunch of politicians and crooks," have in effect abandoned the idea of self-government. This attitude is most prevalent among young people, the great majority of whom did not bother to vote after the Twenty-sixth Amendment lowered the voting age to 18 in 1971.

To speak of voting is to speak of the individual citizen. When the country was founded, many doubted the ability of ordinary Americans to choose their own leaders through the ballot box. In response to a Jeffersonian plea to trust the people, Alexander Hamilton reportedly said, "The people, Sir, are a great beast." Few would dare echo this sentiment today,[18] at least not in these words, but there are some who still agree with the fundamental premise: The average citizen is too ignorant, self-centered, and irrational to be trusted to choose his or her own leaders. One such voice was that of H. L. Mencken, who for three decades wrote a newspaper column for the *Baltimore Sun* containing some of the most caustic criticisms of American society as well as some of the best political reportage ever published:

> Of the two candidates that one wins who least arouses the suspicions and distrusts of the great masses of simple people. Well, what are more likely to arouse those suspicions and distrust than ideas, convictions, principles? The plain people are not hostile to shysterism save it be gross and unsuccessful . . . but they shy instantly and inevitably from the man who comes before them with notions that they cannot immediately translate into terms of their everyday delusions; they fear the novel idea, and particularly the revolutionary idea, as they fear the devil. . . . This fear of ideas is a peculiarly democratic phenomenon, and is nowhere so horribly apparent as in the United States.[19]

Conservative columnist George F. Will put a positive face on this criticism of the average voter. Granting that voters were uninterested in and uninformed about the issues, Will said, "Voters do not decide issues, they decide who will decide issues." In short, they vote for the person, not the

---

[18]In fact, Hamilton very likely never uttered such a statement. See William A. Smith, "Henry Adams, Alexander Hamilton and the American People As a 'Great Beast'," *New England Quarterly*, June 1975.

[19]Malcolm Moos, ed., *On Politics: A Carnival of Buncombe* (New York: Vintage Books, 1960).

Declining Voter Participation	
Presidential Election Year	**Percentage of Eligible Voters Voting**
1988	50.0
1984	53.1
1980	52.8
1976	53.5
1972	55.2
1968	61
1964	62
1960	63

program.[20] But in voting for the person, they often in fact wind up voting for an image that has been carefully manufactured and artfully sold.

Partially because of such doubts about the ability or the inclination of the voters to choose wisely, the authors of the Constitution left to the states the authority to establish qualifications for voting. But gradually a series of constitutional amendments and statutory acts has eliminated most restrictions on the franchise:

1. By the late 1820s, most states had eliminated property qualifications for white males.
2. In 1870, the Fifteenth Amendment to the Constitution forbade states to deny the right to vote because of "race, religion or previous condition of servitude."
3. Women gained the right to vote with the Nineteenth Amendment in 1920.
4. In 1964, the Twenty-fourth Amendment prohibited states from requiring a poll tax in order to vote.
5. The Voting Rights Act, passed by Congress and signed by President Johnson in 1965, provided for the replacement of local election officials by federal registrars in areas in the South where blacks were often denied their right to vote.
6. The Twenty-sixth Amendment in 1971 forbade states to deny the vote to any citizen 18 years of age or older.

Consequently, in the almost two hundred years that our Constitution has been in effect, the franchise has expanded to include virtually everyone over 17 years of age. Yet, as we have seen, not everyone who is eligible actually votes. In fact, there has been a steady decline in voter turnout in recent presidential elections.

[20]"In Full Cry," *Newsweek*, March 8, 1976, p. 92.

Who then does vote? Two important factors answering this question are education and occupation. The higher a person's educational level, the more likely she or he is to vote. Moreover, the higher the status and income of the person's job, the greater the likelihood that he or she will vote.

Although these are the key factors, other influences may be important. For example, people may be more likely to vote if they think the election will be close; that is, voters may be more likely to vote if they think their vote can be effective.[21] Finally, those most interested and informed are more likely to vote.

This is not to suggest that the American voter is rational. Although we might expect the citizen to arrive at a voting decision by thoughtful judgment, most studies of voter behavior belie this expectation. Indeed, an eminent group of scholars suggested that America has "an electorate almost wholly without detailed information about decision making in government . . . almost completely unable to judge the rationality of government actions."[22] Rather than reasoned decision making, voters seem to act out of sentiment, mood, and disposition.[23]

Although fuzzy about a given candidate's specific stand on specific issues, voters often seem to be drawn toward candidates whose *values* reflect their own. This is particularly the case in primaries. Given a choice, a farmer will vote for another farmer more often than not. Catholics who deserted the Democratic party in droves to vote for Eisenhower returned to vote for Kennedy, a Catholic. Jimmy Carter, a "born-again" Christian, scored most heavily among rural Protestants (although he also drew strong support from black voters). In the 1980 Democratic primaries Senator Edward Kennedy, an urban dweller, carried most of the large cities. In the 1950s, two-time presidential candidate Adlai Stevenson, considered an intellectual, drew strong support from academics. To some extent, voters seem to ask themselves, consciously or unconsciously, "Which candidate is most like *me*?" and vote accordingly. However, this theory would seem to be contradicted by the success of Ronald Reagan, who is a former movie star and a fairly wealthy person. But part of Reagan's appeal may have been that he had successfully portrayed, in film and in politics, the part of an average, concerned citizen.

[21]Angus Campbell, Philip E. Converse, Warren E. Miller, and Donald E. Stokes, *The American Voter* (New York: Wiley, 1960), chap. 5. This last generalization does not always apply. For example, in 1948, the presidential election was close, with Harry Truman edging challenging Republican Thomas E. Dewey. There were also two other candidates: Henry Wallace, a liberal progressive, and Strom Thurmond, a states-rights "Dixiecrat." Yet, despite the variety of views in the campaign, the intense rhetoric, and ultimately, the closeness of the outcome, the voting turnout was the lowest for a presidential election in the last half century (51.5 percent).

[22]Campbell et al., p. 543.

[23]See Bernard R. Berelson, Paul F. Lazarfeld, and William N. McPhee, *Voting* (Chicago: University of Chicago Press, 1954), chap. 14.

Political Socialization

The factors that influence the way we vote normally have little to do with rationality. To a large extent, we are *socialized* into voting behavior, just as we are socialized into other human behavior.[24]

The first agent of socialization affecting virtually all of us is the *family*. Some sociologists maintain that the family is still the most important influence on our behavior, which would be true of voting behavior and political party identification. On the whole, people tend to identify with the political party of their parents.[25] By the time a growing child reaches adolescence, she or he begins to be influenced by *peer groups*, an influence that will continue throughout life. In the United States, children seem to be spending increasing amounts of time with their peers, as much as twice the time as with their family. The impact of this development on political behavior is as yet uncertain, for young people tend not to be interested in politics.[26]

School is also of some importance in socialization. School, of course, is where the young child usually first encounters peer groups outside the family. Moreover, some scholars see the school as a primary instrument of political learning, using flag salutes, national holiday celebrations, and the hierarchical and authoritarian organization of the school to foster conformity and obedience.[27] Other scholars discount such an influence on the part of the schools, and still others point out that at the college level of education, students may actually experience a significant and lasting shift in political attitudes.[28]

Finally, the impact of the *mass media* as a political socializer may be important, but it is difficult to assess. We shall discuss the media in Chapter 11. At this point, suffice it to say that politicians *believe* that the media have an effect on voting behavior, at least as measured by the enormous sums of money spent on political advertising. Also, when politicians speak of *image* and *momentum*, they are usually referring to how their campaigns are being presented to voters through the media. For example, in the 1964 campaign, political strategists presented President Johnson in the image of a warm-

[24]See Richard E. Dawson and Kenneth Prewitt, *Political Socialization* (Boston: Little, Brown, 1969); and Anne E. Freedman and P. E. Freedman, *The Psychology of Political Control* (New York: St. Martin's Press, 1975), chap. 4.

[25]See M. Kent Jennings and Richard G. Niemi, "The Transmission of Political Values from Parent to Child," *American Political Science Review* 62 (March 1968): 169–184. For a revisionist view of the impact of the family, see R. W. Connell, "Political Socialization in the American Family, the Evidence Re-examined," *Public Opinion Quarterly* 36 (Fall 1972): 323–346.

[26]Freedman, pp. 103–104.

[27]See Robert Hess and Judith V. Torney, *The Development of Political Attitudes in Children* (Chicago: Aldine, 1967), pp. 93–115.

[28]Kenneth Reich, "Students Cast Liberal Votes Survey Shows," *Los Angeles Times*, January 22, 1973, Sec. 1, p. 21.

hearted, humane man and a masterful politician—in the tradition of FDR —whereas his opponent, Senator Barry Goldwater, was widely perceived as a rather headstrong, reckless man. Johnson won overwhelmingly. Eight years later, the Democratic nominee, Senator McGovern, developed an image as a well-meaning but inept and unrealistic man, whereas the incumbent, Richard Nixon, was portrayed as a practical statesman. In this case, Nixon won overwhelmingly. In retrospect, most people would now be willing to acknowledge that these oversimplified "images" of all four men were distortions.

In the 1980 and 1984 primary campaigns for the presidency, the term *image* began to yield to a new word: *momentum*. The candidates who won the early primaries or even the early straw polls were considered more seriously by the media, and a certain mystique began to develop around them, with the result that their opponents quickly found funds, support, and media attention difficult to come by. Thus in 1980 a relative political unknown, John Anderson, gained early primary votes and media exposure, and stayed in the race far longer than did more nationally known Republican candidates such as Howard Baker and John Connally, and in 1984 Senator Alan Cranston, unable to make a strong showing in early primaries, was unsuccessful in raising funds and faded from the picture. He *lost* momentum.

This glance at factors influencing our socialization suggests those people and events that teach us about politics. As youngsters, we learn about politics from those in authority over us—our parents and our teachers. Later we learn from those in positions of equality to us—our age peers, our friends, and, still later and importantly, our work associates.[29] We also learn about politics from the media.

Finally, we might learn from and slightly change our attitudes because of political experiences themselves.[30] For example, we know that there were significant shifts in political loyalties and attitudes toward government as a consequence of the Great Depression; a larger number of people came to believe that government had more responsibility to regulate the economy than had so believed before. Many people came to consider themselves as Democrats rather than as Republicans. So although political ideas, and thus political behavior, are usually passed on from one generation to another, significant alterations in political attitude may occur as a consequence of experiences. In part, this happens because the real political world rarely operates in as perfect a way as the young citizen expects. Some disillusionment sets in, and some alteration of political attitudes takes place. When the young person then becomes an adult, this slightly altered political belief is transferred to the next generation.[31]

[29]Dawson and Prewitt, pp. 203–215.
[30]Campbell et al., p. 17.
[31]Dawson and Prewitt, pp. 203–215.

Apathy and Anger

Despite all, the basic characteristic of the American voting population seems to be apathy. It is well known that a smaller percentage of eligible voters votes in the United States than in any other industrialized, democratic nation. What causes this political apathy?

For one thing, political activity is somewhat threatening.[32] Many of us, wanting to be well liked, abide by the famous dictum to avoid discussions of politics and religion so as not to endanger our relations with our friends. Moreover, we may fear that we will reveal our ignorance if we launch too seriously into a political debate or activity. Finally, sometimes we feel that political activity might threaten our job security.

Another factor causing apathy is the feeling that political activity is futile.[33] Study after study has demonstrated the widespread feeling of political powerlessness on the part of many Americans.[34] Why get involved in or be concerned with politics when politicians do not really care about us, when political decisions are in the hands of powerful, anonymous forces, and when government has grown too complicated to understand, anyway?[35] Moreover, there seems to have been in recent years a loss of confidence by Americans that government can really accomplish anything worthwhile and a feeling that it in fact is basically corrupt and unworthy of concern.[36]

There may be simply too few influences or stimuli to get people involved in politics.[37] Political institutions deal with the total society; thus they seem abstract and impersonal, if not dull and remote. Political activity yields little in the way of immediate satisfaction, and politics does not seem to meet our daily concerns: for example, whom will I go out with this weekend, can I get my car serviced in time, and when should I study for the midterm exam? Even those people who might be interested in political activity are too frequently not contacted by friends, activists, or party organizations. Also, a number of Americans insist that they are simply not interested in politics.[38] Last, some potential voters may refuse to exercise the franchise merely as a way of protesting against the government and a political process they believe are beyond their control.[39]

---

[32]See Morris Rosenberg, "Some Determinants of Political Apathy," *Public Opinion Quarterly* 18 (Winter 1954): 349–366.

[33]Ibid.

[34]See Robert S. Gilman and Robert B. Lamb, *Political Alienation in Contemporary America* (New York: St. Martin's Press, 1975), pp. 14–18.

[35]Gilman and Lamb, p. 18.

[36]See Donald W. Harward, ed., *Crisis in Confidence: The Impact of Watergate* (Boston: Little, Brown, 1974).

[37]Rosenberg, p. 361.

[38]Gilman and Lamb, p. 96.

[39]Michael Parenti, "The Harvesting of Votes," in *Democracy for the Few* (New York: St. Martin's Press, 1988).

On the other hand, political apathy in the United States might reflect a basic satisfaction with things as they are. Moreover, if increased numbers of voters became agitated and excited about politics, would that not mean that an increasing number of ill-informed voters would be going to the polls and making irrational judgments? Indeed, political scientist Angus Campbell showed that when a smaller percentage of voters votes, it is usually the best informed who do vote and that a large turnout usually means an increase in uninformed voters.[40] This finding would seem to suggest the wisdom of *limiting* the number who can vote! Such a policy would be based on the traditional arguments that historically have kept large groups from participating in government. The British cited "virtual representation" to deny American colonists representation in Parliament, insisting that the views of the Americans were always presented in London. Such arguments have been used to exclude blacks, women, and young people from voting. Yet our history has gone in the opposite direction, opening ever wider the opportunity to vote. Recent evidence suggests that we may have to deal with a larger and heightened interest in politics on the part of Americans. If one's educational level is a determinant of one's political interest, then the increasing percentage of Americans going to college should result in less political apathy. In fact, some evidence suggests that although American voters have indeed grown more dissatisfied and disillusioned with politics, they are nevertheless increasingly less apathetic and less passive than formerly believed. Rather, the voter is more aware of and sensitive to political issues and more likely to cross party lines than in the past.

Additionally, according to an important study,[41] the American electorate has become much more politically aware and sophisticated since World War II. It has been shown that, contrary to past studies, voters can identify the ideological differences in candidates, relate presidential candidates to a basic framework of ideas (defining them as "conservative," "liberal," and so on), and understand what these categories mean in terms of specific issues. Thus there appears to have been considerable improvement in the ability of the general public to assess political parties, candidates, and issues.

Surely these are hopeful signs. Our dedication to democracy demands a great deal of us as individuals. It demands that we be part of an informed, enlightened, and active body politic. How much power over us that elites or anonymous forces have probably depends on how informed, enlightened, and active we are.

[40]Angus Campbell, "Voters and Elections: Past and Present," *Journal of Politics* 26 (November 1964): 745–757.

[41]Norman H. Nie, Sidney Verba, and John R. Petrocik, *The Changing American Voter* (Cambridge, Mass.: Harvard University Press, 1976).

The Attentive Public

We should note that "the power elite," if it in fact exists, is probably dynamic rather than static. Few observers of the American scene would have listed the military establishment as a decisive element in the power structure during the 1920s or 1930s. Organized labor, certainly not part of the power structure before the 1930s, might have to be included today. Even the most celebrated newspaper and radio commentators and reporters prior to World War II probably had nothing like the influence that their counterparts wield today. Intellectuals, too, would appear to have much more voice in the affairs of state these days, if only because there are so many more of them and because they speak with and for an infinitely larger clientele. Certainly, one of the dominant themes of politics in recent years in America has been a determined challenge by men and women whose roots are in the intellectual and/or protest communities, such as Ralph Nader and John Gardner, rather than the more traditional business executive–politicians who normally decide things in this country.

Summing up the national scene with one of those gaudy, sweeping generalizations he was so fond of, H. L. Mencken concluded that American life "is in three layers—the plutocracy on the top, a vast mass of undifferentiated human blanks bossed by demagogues at the bottom, and forlorn *intelligentsia* gasping out a precarious life between."[42] A more precise characterization of the participating citizen was suggested by the studies of two prominent political scientists, Kenneth Prewitt and Sidney Verba.[43] They described six kinds of participants in American politics: (1) *Inactives*, who account for about 22 percent of the population, rarely vote, and are involved in no type of political activity; (2) *Voting Specialists*, who only vote and make up about 21 percent of the population; (3) *Parochial Participants*, about 4 percent of the people, who regularly contact public officials but usually for personal reasons only; (4) *Communal Activists*, about 20 percent of Americans, who join civic groups, work in all kinds of community, and essentially nonpartisan, activities; (5) *Campaign Activists*, who regularly participate in political campaigns and make up about 15 percent of the population; and (6) *Complete Activists*, the 11 percent who are active in every way.[44] This last 11 percent we shall call the "attentive public."

These are the people who read the news magazines, the political columns, and even the editorials in the press, watch the public affairs shows regularly

[42]See H. L. Mencken, "The National Literature," *Yale Review* 9 (July 1920): 804–817.

[43]See Kenneth Prewitt and Sidney Verba, *Participation in America* (New York: Harper & Row, 1972), especially chap. 4.

[44]See Gabriel Almond and Sidney Verba, *The Civic Culture* (Princeton, N.J.: Princeton University Press, 1963), especially chaps. 6 and 7.

Who Rules America? The Elite, the Interests, and the Voter

245

on television, perhaps read nonfiction books dealing with current events, and participate in community affairs and political campaigns, and always vote. Despite their relatively small number, these people may play an important and, at times critical, role in politics.

First of all, although a president may require the votes of tens of millions of what Mencken called "undifferentiated human blanks" to get elected, in the day-by-day operation of the office, he deals with a much different and more sophisticated audience. The Washington press corps, students and teachers of politics in and out of the academy throughout the nation, plus well-informed professional politicians and activists weigh the president's words and judge his deeds against their own, often sophisticated, knowledge of events and issues. The same pressures from the attentive public are exerted on Congress and on state and local governments.

The attentive public can also prove decisive in a more positive role. Students, teachers, and political activists transformed Senator Eugene Mc-Carthy from a lonely crusader to a major candidate for the presidency in 1968. They played an important part in bringing Senator McGovern from the point at which he was favored by 1 or 2 percent of the Democratic voters in the national polls early in 1972 to his party's nomination that summer. John Maynard Keynes observed many years ago that abstract theories written in little-read journals and books by economists of one generation become the slogans of the "man in the street" in the next generation. Ideas that the average person takes for granted today—the right of working people to form unions, the right to public education, medical insurance, Social Security, the 40-hour workweek—all were proposed by theorists at one time or another and only gradually permeated the thinking of average citizens to the point that they became politically popular and feasible.

The same principle may often be seen at work in foreign affairs as well. For several decades following the victory of the Communists in China, discussion of a possible détente between the leaders of China and the United States was limited almost exclusively to a small circle of liberal intellectuals, most of them involved professionally in education and/or communications. This remained the case until President Nixon, once a foremost critic of those who preached any sort of accommodation with China, deemed the time right to go to Peking. The general public, which had supported the anti-China policy of the government for decades, now did a quick about-face and supported the new policy.

Who, in fact, was responsible for the change in America's policy toward China? Henry Kissinger, who made the initial diplomatic overtures? Richard Nixon, who made the actual decision? The professors who had been agitating for decades for just such a change? The military-industrial complex, which saw China as a potential ally in the continuing struggle against the Soviet Union and as an enormous potential market for American goods? The American people, who voted Richard Nixon into office?

Perhaps a whole series of events—such as the need to find a negotiated settlement to the war in Vietnam, President Nixon's desire to make the theme of "a generation of peace" the keystone of his 1972 campaign for reelection, and the recognition by cold war strategists of the increasing possibility of playing China off against the Soviet Union—combined to make a change in policy diplomatically desirable and politically possible. The failure to deal realistically with China was at least partially responsible for America's becoming embroiled in two wars in Asia in the past two generations. A new and different policy held out at least the hope for less tragic and bloody consequences. Finally, the people themselves, both the apathetic and the attentive alike, seemed to be ready for a change in our policy toward China, and they endorsed the new policy with votes for Nixon in 1972.

Moreover, if the new policy succeeded, the American people would benefit from expanding trade and friendship with one of the world's oldest and greatest civilizations. They would also pay the price if it failed. That remains the one compelling and unanswerable argument in favor of the democratic principle of one person, one vote. For regardless of who makes the decisions, it is the people who will either be its beneficiaries or bear its consequences.

Finally, the question of who rules America is not necessarily answerable. Because a person is elected to the highest office in the nation does not mean that from the moment of election, she or he is the sole determiner of its destiny. Such may be the case in a monarchical or totalitarian state, but in a republic the responsibilities of individual citizenship are much more demanding. Dedicated individuals, working separately and in groups, may influence the direction of political events. Preservation of the democratic system requires that they try.

10

The Bureaucrats:
Attendant Lords

- Bureaucrats -
- The Nature of Bureaucracy -
- The Federal Bureaucracy -
- History and Reform -
- The Bureaucracy: An Evaluation -

> I am no world reformer. I was the district doctor and did my duty. . . . I was badly paid yet generous and helpful to the poor.
>
> Franz Kafka
> *The Country Doctor*

> No! I am not Prince Hamlet, nor was meant to be!
>   Am an attendant lord, one that will do
>   To swell a progress, start a scene or two,
>   Advise the prince; no doubt, an easy tool,
>   Deferential, glad to be of use,
>   Politic, cautious, and meticulous;
>   Full of high sentence, but a bit obtuse;
>   At times, indeed, almost ridiculous—
>   Almost, at times, the Fool.
>
> T. S. Eliot
> *Prufrock*

Bureaucrats

Between the brave speeches of politicians and the lives of ordinary Americans falls a certain shadow—the shadow of millions of men and women, some highly placed and privileged, others obscure and seemingly unimportant, who make up the bureaucracy that operates federal, state, and local governments. Most Americans rarely or never see a president, a senator, or a representative in person. When they have any contact with the government that controls much of their lives, it is with a mail carrier who delivers their bills, an IRS agent who checks their tax forms, or a Social Security claims officer who computes their retirement benefits. The power of these officials is often immense, because they are the people who finally implement the laws passed by Congress and the policies enunciated by the president and his cabinet officers. They decide whether or not farmers facing bankruptcy are to be given another chance to preserve their farms or be ruined; whether a jobless woman with children receives welfare benefits; which firm is awarded a multibillion dollar defense contract providing thousands of jobs; whether a young couple will obtain a home loan; whether a student is eligible for a loan that will permit continued education; whether or not the food we eat is safe.

Indeed, it is no exaggeration that most major actions of our lives ultimately depend on the approval or disapproval of some anonymous bureaucrat.

"I'm sorry, dear, but you knew I was a bureaucrat when you married me."
(From The New Yorker, *March 3, 1980, p. 61.)*

Bureaucrats are not held in high esteem. Few of us take comfort in the fact that so much of our life depends on others. Unlike Blanche DuBois in Tennessee Williams's *Streetcar Named Desire*, we do not much like depending on the kindness of strangers. No one wins elections promising to improve the lot of bureaucrats. When we see them in films or books, they are usually portrayed as dull, mechanical little people enmeshed in senseless regulations who spend their lives counting paper clips. Poets denounce them as "hollow men." This is true not only in the United States but virtually everywhere else on earth. Soviet leader Mikhail Gorbachev has made them the prime targets of his efforts to revitalize the Soviet Union's economy. In France there is a common joke about the minister of education who can look at his watch at a certain hour of the day and tell you which page from which book every third grader in the country is reading at that moment. The German bureaucracy is legendary for its diligence in controlling even the minutiae of daily life.

And yet both France and Germany are excellent examples of stable, affluent, free societies, which is probably not a coincidence, for there is no surer sign of a nation in deep trouble than a bureaucracy that is corrupt, sloppy, and indifferent or habitually exceeds its proper authority. In many countries it is impossible to transact even the smallest item of business without "the envelope" changing hands. In the United States not so very long ago, there was a price list for anyone aspiring to a civil service job in most of the nation's big cities. If a well-run army and navy are essential to the defense of a nation, a well-run bureaucracy is no less indispensable to the conduct of civil affairs.

Politicians, although absolutely dependent on the bureaucracy if they are to do the job for which they were elected, are aware of the public view of these civil servants, and they often portray themselves as "outsiders" who, if elected to office, will "clean up the mess in Washington." One of the ironies of democracy is that so many politicians seek to win election to important government posts by denouncing the institution they wish to serve. That government is "part of the problem, not the solution" to many of our national ills was a standard refrain, for example, of President Reagan. One of his most effective and charming gambits was to make fun of, tell outlandish stories about, and generally denigrate the government that he led for eight years.

Reagan's predecessor, Jimmy Carter, likewise considered himself an "outsider," a "man of the people," and carried with him to the White House a widely advertised antipathy to "Washington insiders," an antipathy that critics of his administration felt contributed to an unfortunate tendency to involve himself too deeply in the particulars of government affairs down to personally writing and supervising the rules for using the White House tennis courts.

As a self-proclaimed foe of the Washington bureaucracy, Republican Ronald Reagan left too much in the hands of his associates—at least this was the judgment of the Tower Commission Report on the Iran-Contra scandal. As a self-proclaimed outsider, Democrat Jimmy Carter tried to do too much in the judgment of most political observers. What Carter and Reagan shared was an aversion to using those people and institutions that were created to deal with the nation's problems.

An important part of the growing mythology about the Washington bureaucracy has been the increasing references, by politicians and pundits alike, to the Washington "Beltway mentality." The notion of a unique Washington mentality stems from the fact that, unlike most other major capital cities, Washington is a one-industry town with only one abiding interest and passion—politics. Hence, those who live and work in and around the capital quickly absorb certain values and ideas unique to that city, notions that ordinary, sensible people who live in Cedar Rapids or San Jose know to be nonsense. That almost everyone with real power in Washington was born, educated, and raised somewhere in the hinterlands presumably grants little or no immunity to the beltway mentality.

A dispassionate look at the evidence, however, suggests that the exact opposite is more likely to be true. Few people on earth are more sensitive to the shifting winds of public opinion than politicians and the government bureaucrats who work under them. For example, during the 1980s, a Congress controlled by Democrats nevertheless voted to slash domestic spending, cut taxes, particularly for wealthy individuals and corporations, and enormously increase military expenditures—all apparently in opposition to Democratic party philosophy and the party's official platform—because many members of Congress were convinced that the public supported President Reagan, who wanted these things done. And they were done, bureaucrats and Washington mentality notwithstanding.

On the other hand, when political figures and/or bureaucrats do things that they know very well the public will not support—like the Watergate burglary and cover-up or the secret sale of arms to Iran—they do so in secret, but not because a "Beltway mentality" has misled them as to the true desires of the American people.

The subjects of Watergate and Iran-Contra lead to another question regarding certain bureaucrats. Both Presidents Nixon and Reagan have steadfastly maintained that they simply did not know nor did they authorize the acts that precipitated the greatest crises of their respective administrations. No one can say with certainty precisely how these blunders happened or who initiated them. All we know is that two relatively unknown public servants, G. Gordon Liddy, an attorney working on security for President Nixon's campaign staff and a former White House Staff member, and Lt. Col. Oliver North, an official of the National Security Council, were the "point men" in carrying out these assignments. Although unlike each other in some respects, Liddy and North had in common reputations as "can do guys." They were trusted to carry out their assignments with complete devotion and zeal, without permitting the niceties of bureaucratic procedure (or even the law) to stand in the way of accomplishing an assigned task. In short, they were the opposite of the bureaucratic stereotype.

No one doubts that highly placed but anonymous bureaucrats, particularly if they happen to work in or near the White House, have enormous power. But how much power should they have and how are they to be held accountable to the people, especially when they act in secret? Although spelling out the limits to the powers of Congress, the president, and the courts rather specifically, the Constitution is essentially silent on the power of the bureaucracy. Perhaps as a consequence, many of the scandals that rocked the country for the past few decades—the U-2 incident late in President Eisenhower's second term, the Bay of Pigs fiasco and, of course, Watergate and Iran-Contra—have all *seemed* to originate with some act of arrogance on the part of obscure bureaucrats committed while the president and Congress were ill-informed or uninformed.

An example of a bureaucrat ranging far outside his official responsibilities (and constitutional limitations) can be found in accounts of the activities of the late CIA director William Casey. The outlines of these activities were suggested during the Iran-Contra hearings in 1987 and further elaborated in a book, *Veil*, by Washington *Post* reporter Bob Woodward, published shortly after the hearings. Casey, a high-ranking official and close adviser to President Reagan, may have been more important in the Iran-Contra affair than was Col. Oliver North. According to Woodward, the director apparently used the CIA to conduct a personal and secret foreign policy different from the official policy of the administration and Congress. Among Casey's innovations was the notion of an "off-the-shelf" set of proposals to conduct secret wars and plots unknown to Congress or other high officials of the government. Had the director lived into the summer of 1987 (he died of a brain tumor the preceding winter), he undoubtedly would have been a key witness before Congress and a major focus of attention of the independent counsel investigating the Iran-Contra scandal.

What should be noted is that bureaucrats who do their job quietly, professionally, and intelligently do not usually wind up in newspaper headlines or televised hearings. When President Franklin Roosevelt set about to reconstruct a devastated national economy in 1933, he relied on workers who were described as having a "passion for anonymity." Thousands of government officials fanned out across America bringing food to the hungry, shelter to the homeless, jobs for the jobless, and hope for many who had almost abandoned hope. Interestingly, government officials were usually portrayed in the books and films of those days as decent, compassionate people doing everything they could to help unfortunate victims of economic catastrophe, which to millions of Americans was as incomprehensible as an earthquake or a hurricane.

A few years later, during World War II, another army of government employees was faced with the unprecedented task of converting the nation's economy from peace to war while holding prices in check and striking a balance between the essential needs of wartime production and the civilian economy. And they succeeded. Their names, like the names of those who have made the Social Security system a bulwark against the most disastrous consequences of growing old or the highway system a marvel of coast-to-coast travel are not celebrated in song or story.

The Nature of Bureaucracy

We remain uncertain about the value of bureaucracy and there are reasons why. Between 1969 and 1973, the Federal Bureau of Investigation (FBI), using female informers, spied on women's liberation groups throughout the United States. In response to a Freedom of Information Act request in 1977, the FBI made public fully 1,377 pages of information obtained in such covert activities. This federal agency compiled data on the political beliefs and the sexual habits of individual women and learned that most of them wore faded blue jeans.[1] It remains a mystery what possible usefulness

[1]*Los Angeles Times*, February 6, 1977, Sec. 1, pp. 1, 8.

The Pursuit of Happiness

such data could have had in combating crime, which is the FBI's mission. In fact, it appears that this spying on American citizens was carried out on the unilateral order of former FBI director J. Edgar Hoover. Of course, there are other agencies of the federal government—an important one is the Internal Revenue Service—that compile all kinds of information on Americans, and we have been told that there are enormous data banks that know everything about us.

But who is in charge of all this information? What is it used for? Such questions have led some observers to argue that America is not run by elites, interests, or the people but by administrators (like Hoover) in the government bureaucracy, responsible to no one in particular and without any general idea of where the government is going or what it should do. One student of administration observed that "government agencies are all becoming autonomous ends in themselves" and that because of "administrative incompetence," "modern government has become ungovernable."[2] More simply, the late philosopher Hannah Arendt called bureaucracy "rule by Nobody."[3]

Such comments will come as no surprise to many Americans. We deal on an almost daily basis with state or federal government bureaucracy, from the mailing of a letter to the renewal of an automobile license and the paying of taxes. We frequently find that bureaucracy difficult to understand, irritating, and unhelpful. But it is large and it is important: About one-fifth of our national income is taken in taxes by the federal government to provide us with certain goods and services. This money is used to defend the country (indeed, about one-third of the full-time civilian employees of the federal government work for the Defense Department), deliver the mail, operate parks, finance research into malnutrition, pay farmers not to grow crops, and a host of other things. The agencies that administer these activities are part of the bureaucracy, and although the term *bureaucracy* has taken on a negative connotation, it is a necessary fact of life.

All large organizations are "bureaucratic," which means simply that they must be administered. Most bureaucracies have certain fundamental characteristics. A university is an example of these. First, a university, like most organizations, is *hierarchical*. It has a president, a vice president, academic deans, department chairpersons, faculty members, and students. Each person more or less knows who the "boss" is and what responsibilities she or he has. Second, there is a *division of labor*. Individual jobs require certain tasks, no matter who holds the position: the president calls deans' meetings, the dean's office is responsible for class scheduling, the faculty are responsible for meeting classes and advising students, and so on. Third, there is a kind of *formalization* of activity; that is, communication in

---

[2]Peter Drucker, *The Age of Discontinuity* (New York: Harper & Row, 1969), p. 200.

[3]Hannah Arendt, *Crisis of the Republic* (New York: Harcourt Brace Jovanovich, 1972), p. 137.

bureaucracies tends to be in writing. Thus, within a large university there are a number of memos written from one position to another. Deans write memos to chairpersons, who in turn write memos to faculty, and so forth. In addition, written rules, regulations, and guidance are contained in the university's catalogue, in documents about student aid, in charts about pay scales for faculty and staff, and in organizational charts outlining the colleges and departments of the university. These written documents are stored somewhere and available to all members of the university community. The purpose of such formalization is clarity and the desire to specify what is to be done under all circumstances. Fourth, as in most bureaucracies, in the university there is the assurance of *tenure*, that after holding the job for a certain amount of time and demonstrating competence, a faculty member can be fired only for some serious cause.

The Federal Bureaucracy

The bureaucracy at the federal government level has grown immensely during our history. When Thomas Jefferson was president the federal government employed only about 2,000 people. There are currently nearly 3 million employees in the bureaucracy working in various kinds of agencies. These include the organizations that work within each of the 13 *cabinet departments* (see Chapter 14), which are directly responsible to the president.

Cabinet departments are headed by secretaries (except for the Department of Justice, which the attorney general administers) who are directly responsible to the president. The size of each of the departments varies considerably, but their organization is similar. Usually, they have an undersecretary—the person just below the secretary—and a number of assistant secretaries for specifically assigned responsibilities within the department (as, for example, an assistant secretary of state for Central American Affairs in the Department of State). The departments are usually subdivided further into bureaus and smaller units.

Other agencies are also part of the federal bureaucracy. Numerous independent *executive agencies* report to the president but are not part of the traditional cabinet departments. Examples of such agencies are the National Aeronautics and Space Administration, the U.S. Arms Control and Disarmament Agency, the Central Intelligence Agency, and the U.S. Information Agency. Independent *regulatory agencies* are not in the chain of command leading to the president. They regulate private businesses and activities, thus representing a compromise between "socialism" and unregulated— sometimes cutthroat—competition. Although the president appoints the members of regulatory agencies, once they are in office they serve for a set term and are independent of the traditional branches of government. Some of the more important of these agencies can be seen in the accompanying table.

The Pursuit of Happiness

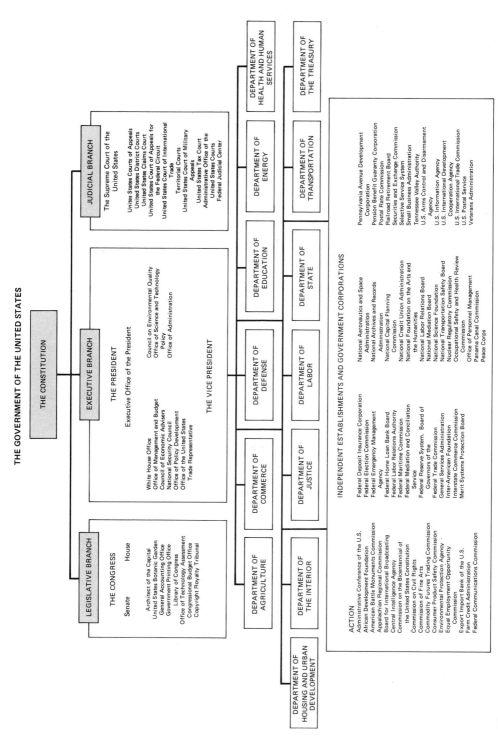

THE GOVERNMENT OF THE UNITED STATES

THE CONSTITUTION

LEGISLATIVE BRANCH

THE CONGRESS

Senate   House

Architect of the Capital
United States Botanic Garden
General Accounting Office
Government Printing Office
Library of Congress
Office of Technology Assessment
Congressional Budget Office
Copyright Royalty Tribunal

EXECUTIVE BRANCH

THE PRESIDENT

Executive Office of the President

White House Office
Office of Management and Budget
Council of Economic Advisers
National Security Council
Office of Policy Development
Office of the United States
Trade Representative

THE VICE PRESIDENT

Council on Environmental Quality
Office of Science and Technology
Policy
Office of Administration

JUDICIAL BRANCH

The Supreme Court of the
United States

Unites States Courts of Appeals
United States District Courts
United States Claims Court
United States Court of Appeals for
the Federal Circuit
United States Court of International
Trade
Territorial Courts
United States Court of Military
Appeals
United States Tax Court
Administrative Office of the
United States Courts
Federal Judicial Center

DEPARTMENT OF
HOUSING AND URBAN
DEVELOPMENT

DEPARTMENT OF
AGRICULTURE

DEPARTMENT OF
THE INTERIOR

DEPARTMENT OF
COMMERCE

DEPARTMENT OF
JUSTICE

DEPARTMENT OF
DEFENSE

DEPARTMENT OF
LABOR

DEPARTMENT OF
EDUCATION

DEPARTMENT OF
STATE

DEPARTMENT OF
HEALTH AND HUMAN
SERVICES

DEPARTMENT OF
ENERGY

DEPARTMENT OF
THE TREASURY

DEPARTMENT OF
TRANSPORTATION

INDEPENDENT ESTABLISHMENTS AND GOVERNMENT CORPORATIONS

ACTION
Administrative Conference of the U.S.
African Development Foundation
American Battle Monuments Commission
Appalachian Regional Commission
Board for International Broadcasting
Central Intelligence Agency
Commission on the Bicentennial of
the United States Constitution
Commission on Civil Rights
Commission of Fine Arts
Commodity Futures Trading Commission
Consumer Product Safety Commission
Environmental Protection Agency
Equal Employment Opportunity
Commission
Export Import Bank of the U.S.
Farm Credit Administration
Federal Communications Commission

Federal Deposit Insurance Corporation
Federal Election Commission
Federal Emergency Management
Agency
Federal Home Loan Bank Board
Federal Labor Relations Authority
Federal Maritime Commission
Federal Mediation and Conciliation
Service
Federal Reserve System. Board of
Governors of the
Federal Trade Commission
General Services Administration
Inter-American Foundation
Interstate Commerce Commission
Merit Systems Protection Board

National Aeronautics and Space
Administration
National Archives and Records
Administration
National Capital Planning
Commission
National Credit Union Administration
National Foundation on the Arts and
the Humanities
National Labor Relations Board
National Mediation Board
National Science Foundation
National Transportation Safety Board
Nuclear Regulatory Commission
Occupational Safety and Health Review
Commission
Office of Personnel Management
Panama Canal Commission
Peace Corps

Pennsylvania Avenue Development
Corporation
Pension Benefit Guaranty Corporation
Postal Rate Commission
Railroad Retirement Board
Securities and Exchange Commission
Selective Service System
Small Business Administration
Tennessee Valley Authority
U.S. Arms Control and Disarmament
Agency
U.S. Information Agency
U.S. International Development
Cooperation Agency
U.S. International Trade Commission
U.S. Postal Service
Veterans Administration

The government of the United States. *(From U.S. Government Manual, 1987–1988, Washington, D.C.: U.S. Government Printing Office, 1988.)* (Not included in the diagram is the Department of Veterans Affairs, which was created in 1988 and began to function in 1989.)

The Bureaucrats: Attendant Lords

Important Regulatory Agencies		
Agency	Date Established	Functions
Interstate Commerce Commission	1887	Regulates railroads, oil pipelines, bus lines, and so on.
Federal Trade Commission	1914	Prevents unfair competition, price fixing, false advertising, and so on.
Federal Power Commission	1930	Regulates interstate utilities and energy businesses.
Federal Communications Commission	1934	Licenses and regulates TV and radio stations.
Securities and Exchange Commission	1934	Regulates stock exchanges.
Civil Aeronautics Board	1938	Regulates airlines.

Finally, some *government-owned and -operated corporations* are under presidential control. The latest of these is the U.S. Postal Service, and other examples are the Federal Deposit Insurance Corporation, established in 1933, which guarantees bank deposits, and the Tennessee Valley Authority, also created in 1933, which generates hydroelectric power.

Although presidential appointments fill some of the important posts in this giant bureaucracy, most jobs are filled by civil servants. Individuals gain employment by taking scheduled civil service exams and are then appointed on the basis of merit. The merit system is supervised by the U.S. Civil Service Commission and has been in effect since the passage of the Pendleton Civil Service Act in 1883. This act considerably modified the patronage system by which federal jobs were given as political favors.

History and Reform

When the U.S. government began under President Washington, appointments were made by the president on the basis of ability. As partisan politics became increasingly important, succeeding administrations abandoned the practice of appointment on the basis of merit alone and instead chose government workers according to political allegiance. By the time of Andrew Jackson's presidency, when democracy was fully entrenched and the president insisted that any American could do an effective job in government work, the so-called "spoils system" of appointment ("to the victor go the spoils") became the rule. This system reached its apex during the presidency of Abraham Lincoln, who complained that he could hardly find time to do what he was elected for because he was so busy appointing political followers to government posts. Americans became convinced that the system was out of hand when, in 1881, President James Garfield was assassinated by a disappointed office-seeker. Congress responded to public clamor for reform by passing the landmark Pendleton Civil Service Act of 1883, which, as we have seen above, brought the merit system into being and created the U.S. Civil Service Commission, which is a clearinghouse for recruitment into the civil service, examines applicants for jobs, and appoints government workers. Today, over 90 percent of all civilian employees of the federal government are in the merit system.

Another important congressional act regulating the bureaucracy was the Hatch Act of 1939, which made it illegal to dismiss nonpolicymaking officials working for the federal government (that is, those below cabinet and subcabinet rank). The Hatch Act also restricted government employees from active participation in partisan politics.

In 1970, the Office of Management and Budget (OMB) was created to serve as a coordinating staff to connect the president with the numerous agencies of the administrative branch of government. The OMB is now part of the executive office and, with a director and several budget examiners, attempts to tighten up the management of the federal government.

Nevertheless, most Americans remain suspicious of the federal bureaucracy specifically and of all bureaucracies in general. A popular and satirical assault on the bureaucratic mind was embodied in "Parkinson's law": "Work expands to fill the time available for its completion."[4]

Indeed, one of the outstanding features of bureaucracy is that it tends to engulf and dominate an expanding number of human activities. We are surrounded by bureaucracies from the moment of our birth (which must be immediately recorded—and that certified record retained throughout our life) to our death (which must be officially registered).

In theory, the enormous bureaucracy at the federal level is under the control and direction of the president, but this control is far from complete, because programs are very large and often continue through several administrations. Moreover, bureaucratic resistance often checks presidential initiative.[5] Congress, of course, creates the bureaucracy by way of statutory law, and Congress theoretically instructs the bureaucracy in legislative acts. Also, in hearings Congress can investigate activities by government workers. Still, the bureaucracy is large, tends to be secretive, and is not easily controlled by Congress on a day-by-day basis. The courts, too, using the power of judicial review, can supervise administrators and determine whether a government worker has broken the law. But the bureacracy, virtually by its nature, seeks to maintain its survival and expand its functions. In a growing nation, where demands on the government are always

---

[4]C. Northcote Parkinson, *Parkinson's Law* (Boston: Houghton Mifflin, 1957), p. 2.
[5]Richard E. Neustadt, *Presidential Power* (New York: Wiley, 1976).

Government Employment and Population, 1957–1987

Fiscal year	Government employment				Population	
	Federal Executive Branch[1] (thousands)	State and Local Governments (thousands)	All Governmental Units (thousands)	Federal as Percent of All Governmental Units	Total United States (thousands)	Federal Employment per 1,000 Population
1957	2,391	5,380	7,771	30.8	171,984	13.9
1958	2,355	5,630	7,985	29.5	174,882	13.5
1959	2,355	5,806	8,161	28.8	177,830	13.2
1960[2]	2,371	6,073	8,444	28.1	180,671	13.1
1961[2]	2,407	6,295	8,702	27.7	183,691	13.1
1962	2,485	6,533	9,018	27.6	186,538	13.3
1963[3]	2,490	6,834	9,324	26.7	189,242	13.2
1964[3]	2,469	7,236	9,705	25.4	191,889	12.9
1965	2,496	7,683	10,179	24.5	194,303	12.8
1966	2,664	8,259	10,923	24.4	196,560	13.6
1967	2,877	8,730	11,607	24.8	198,712	14.5
1968	2,951	9,141	12,092	24.4	200,706	14.7
1969[4]	2,980	9,496	12,476	23.9	202,677	14.7
1970[2]	2,944	9,869	12,813	23.0	205,052	14.4
1971[2]	2,883	10,372	13,255	21.8	207,661	13.9
1972	2,823	10,896	13,719	20.6	209,896	13.4
1973	2,775	11,286	14,061	19.7	211,909	13.1
1974	2,847	11,713	14,560	19.6	213,854	13.3
1975	2,848	12,114	14,962	19.0	215,973	13.2
1976	2,832	12,282	15,114	18.7	218,035	13.0
1977[5]	2,789	12,704	15,493	18.0	220,904	12.6

Year					
1978	2,820	13,050	15,870	17.8	223,278	12.6
1979	2,823	13,359	16,182	17.4	225,779	12.5
1980[2]	2,821	13,542	16,363	17.2	228,468	12.3
1981[2]	2,806	13,274	16,080	17.5	230,848[6]	12.2
1982	2,768	13,207	15,975	17.3	233,184[6]	11.9
1983	2,819	13,220	16,039	17.6	235,439[6]	12.0
1984	2,854	13,504	16,358	17.4	237,663[6]	12.0
1985	2,964	13,827	16,791	17.7	239,951[6]	12.4
1986	2,967	14,190	17,157	17.3	242,222[6]	12.2
1987	3,030	14,451	17,481	17.3	244,425[6]	12.4

Source: Executive Office of Management and Budget, U.S. Government, *Special Analyses, Budget for Fiscal Year 1989*, Washington, D.C.

[1]Covers total end-of-year civilian employment of full-time permanent, temporary, part-time, and intermittent employees in the executive branch, including the Postal Service, and, beginning in 1970, includes various disadvantaged youth and worker-trainee programs.

[2]Includes temporary employees for the decennial census.

[3]Excludes 7,411 project employees in 1963 and 406 project employees in 1964 for the public works acceleration program.

[4]On Jan. 1, 1969, 42,000 civilian technicians of the Army and Air Force National Guard converted by law from State to Federal employment status. They are included in the Federal employment figures in this table starting with 1969.

[5]Data for 1957 through 1976 are as of June 30; for 1977 through 1987, as of Sept. 30.

[6]U.S. population data for 1981–1987 are the latest available from the Census Bureau.

increasing, the bureaucracy takes on an ever more permanent and powerful role.

In his campaign for the presidency, Jimmy Carter promised that he would reorganize the federal bureaucracy to make it more humane and efficient. In fact, he made several changes. Two new departments—Energy and Education—were added to the president's cabinet, and perhaps more significantly, Congress in 1978 passed the president's Civil Service Reform Act. This reform represented the most extensive revamping of the civil service system since it was established in 1883. Included in the new law are prohibitions on reprisals against employees who "blow the whistle" on government wrongdoing, provisions making it easier to fire incompetent employees, establishment of a merit pay system for certain federal employees (rather than automatic raises), an annual ceiling on the total number of federal employees, and the legal right of government workers to join labor unions and bargain collectively.

Whereas criticism of the federal bureaucracy was an important but somewhat muted element in President Carter's administration, it became a dominant theme of Ronald Reagan's presidency. Reagan promised to "get the government off the backs of the American people," and many found the rhetoric appealing. Most people assumed the president wanted a more modest, limited, and less expensive government. But in fact, government budgets soared under President Reagan, and the deficit approached a stratospheric $200 billion annually, even as Reagan asked for a constitutional amendment that would make such deficits illegal.

With respect to the federal bureaucracy, the more fervently we denounce it and vote for leaders who promise to cut, slash, and prune it to the bone, the more it seems to grow. The problem is a classic confrontation between abstract rhetoric and concrete facts. An important part of the federal government budget goes for Social Security. Few Americans want it cut, and fewer still want it eliminated. An even more important element is military spending. While proclaiming the wickedness of Big Government, President Reagan was in the forefront of those fighting for increases in military appropriations. American farmers think of themselves as independent, self-reliant individualists, but they depend on farm subsidies. The government seems to grow because the American people depend on it. In fact, although total public employment (at the state *and* national level) remained fairly constant in the 1970s, and the proportion of public employees in the entire work force declined slightly during that period, there began to be a perceptible increase in national government employment during the Reagan administration as a consequence of hiring in the Defense Department.[6]

The bureaucracy, whatever its size, plays a crucial and unique role in

6*Los Angeles Times*, August 21, 1983, Sec. 5, p.1.

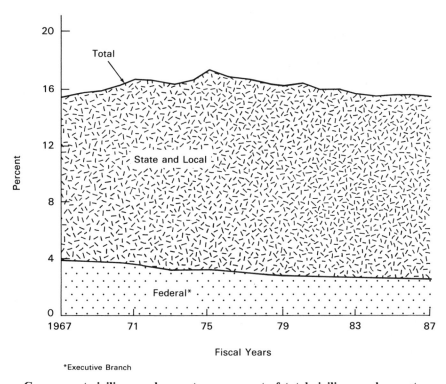

20

16

Total

12

Percent

State and Local

8

4

Federal*

0

1967   71   75   79   83   87

Fiscal Years

*Executive Branch

Government civilian employment as a percent of total civilian employment.
(From the Executive Office of Management and Budget, U.S. Government,
Special Analyses, The Budget for Fiscal Year 1989.)

formulating and *implementing* policy.[7] The various government agencies mobilize their employees on an annual basis to draw up preliminary plans and proposals for their department and develop a budget to carry forth these plans. The department then makes a presentation to Congress. Then, the bureaucracy has the important function of translating into action the policies mandated by congressional legislation. Often civil servants must interpret legislation and fill in details not specified by Congress.

The Bureaucracy: An Evaluation

Whether the bureacracy is responsive to the people's needs and accountable to elected officials remains an ongoing question. We can say some things about the bureaucracy that seem to contradict conventional wisdom. For example, only about 12 percent of career civilian employees work in Wash-

[7]See Chapter 9, pp. 227–228.

ington, D.C. Most are spread throughout the country. A very small part of the bureaucracy (less than 15 percent) works for welfare agencies; about half the civilians work for the Army, Navy, Air Force, or other defense agencies. Indeed, the largest agencies are the Army, Navy, Air Force, Postal Service, and the Veterans Administration—not those agencies typically associated with social and welfare activities. As the figure on page 263 illustrates, the federal bureaucracy, in terms of civilian employment, has remained fairly stable for a number of years and has actually leveled off in comparison with employment at state and local levels. The traditional bureaucracy may, indeed, be more rational than those who attempt to bypass it. For example, the CIA in the early 1960s advised against placing ground troops in Vietnam; cabinet officials opposed the sale of arms to Iran in the 1980s. In both instances the bureaucrats seemed right; those who tried an end run around the bureaucrats seemed wrong.

However, perhaps the ultimate question regarding the bureaucracy is how consistent it is with principles of democratic government. As German scholar Max Weber noted, the bureaucratization of government and politics clashes with the idea of popular rule.[8] Democracy emphasizes plurality, bureacracy seeks unity; democracy stresses equality, bureacracy insists on hierarchy; democracy means that new people come into office on a regular basis, bureaucracy needs duration in office; one is elected in a democracy, appointed in a bureaucracy; we praise equal access in democracy, authority and limited access in bureaucracy.

Yet a massive bureaucracy is indispensable to a large, modern nation (as it is to a large, modern corporation). Railing against its existence is rather like the king who gave orders that no dog shall bark while he slept. In the Philippines, shortly before the fall of Ferdinand Marcos, even the newsboys on the street had to pay a bribe to some petty official to sell their papers. That is usually a harbinger of a country ripe for revolution. On the other hand, the ability of ordinary citizens to turn to their government for help in meeting the problems of daily life and to receive such help without reservations as to their station in life or influence or politics is a commonplace of virtually all stable, democratic societies.

[8]Max Weber, *Essays in Sociology* (New York: Oxford Univ. Press, 1958), p. 228.

11

Media,
the Shadow Government:
Power and the Press

> The duty of the press is to print the truth and raise hell.
>
> Mark Twain
>
> Education is civil defense against media fallout.
>
> Marshall McLuhan

When asked to account for the enduring success of the *Reader's Digest* (which for many decades has been the world's largest-selling magazine), former editor DeWitt Wallace responded, "We sell hope." It was Wallace's way of pointing out that his magazine is not simply in the business of publishing stories and word games; rather, it brings to its tens of millions of readers throughout the world a certain view of life. Standard *Digest* fare includes such titles as "How One Town Solved Its Juvenile Delinquency Problem," "Ten Ways to Increase Your Word Power," "What America Means to Me," and "The Joys of Sexual Renewal." What all these seemingly disparate subjects have in common is that they tell a story of people triumphing over life's everyday problems by the use of common sense and traditional values, all told in simple sentences and short words.

So, too, almost any successful magazine, newspaper, or television or radio program brings to its audience not only information and entertainment but also a version of reality.

There was a time when most people depended on experience with life itself, careful observation of nature, and myth makers and religious and political leaders to define and create the world around them. Increasingly, the mass media have assumed this function. The myths of our day deal with celebrities, not demigods. Celebrities are created by the media. People once tried to foretell tomorrow's weather by looking at the sky; now they watch a TV weather reporter. In much the same way, the media have replaced the prophet, the priest, and the prince.

Media

Media refer to the variety of means by which technology transmits to us information and entertainment. Thus, in its broadest sense, *media* include newspapers, television, movies, radio, books, and magazines. *Mass media* specifically refer to those publications and programs that attempt to serve most or all the people in a given market. Commercial radio and television networks are mass media. Most "public" radio or television stations, which usually seek a selected audience, are not. *People* is a mass-media magazine, but the *New Republic* is not; yet both are part of the media. Finally, although "the press" normally refers to newspapers, it may also include other forms of media. Thus, when the president has a press conference, journalists from various media will ask him questions.

What Is News?

Hardly a man takes a half hour's nap after dinner, but when he wakes he holds up his head and asks, "What's the news?" As if the rest of mankind had stood his sentinels. . . . After a night's sleep the news is as indispensable as breakfast. . . .

Henry David Thoreau
Walden

One function of the media is to bring the world and all its infinite variety to the attention of the average citizen. A war in Asia, a famine in Africa, an election in Italy, a scandal in Washington, a coup in Latin America, a new film in Scandinavia, a new fashion in Rome, the price of meat in supermarkets, or the rate of exchange between the dollar and the mark—these are the commonplaces of media news. But of course, it is impossible to compress everything unusual or important that happens anywhere in the world into a 30-minute TV news broadcast, a daily newspaper, a magazine, or all three combined. Thus the media, in a sense, have a Herculean responsibility that they can never really hope to completely fulfill. They can only try. This means that they must select from the almost limitless number of happenings—some important, some trivial—those that they believe to be of interest and importance to their audiences.

There have been many attempts to define *news*. Perhaps the most satisfactory is an old bromide of the city room: "News is whatever the editor thinks it is." The consequences of that editor's decision go beyond whether or not the reader's or viewer's interest is aroused or satisfied. The power to decide what is news is the power to define reality for many people.

A distinction should be made between "hard news" and opinion or commentary. In theory, hard news is an objective report of factual events—what Dan Rather, for example, does on the evening news. Opinion is reserved for the editorial pages and columnists in the print media. On television it is the prerogative of commentators such as Mike Wallace on "60 Minutes." Although most working members of the press believe in and try to conform to this difference, in practice it is difficult to do so. For one thing, as we have noted, there is an element of subjectivity in the mere selection of what is or is not news. In the early months of the 1976 presidential campaign, for example, much media attention was given, usually good-naturedly, to President Ford's frequent mishaps, with respect to both physical and mental lapses. This helped create an impression of Ford as a not-too-bright and hence not very effective leader, which unquestionably damaged Ford greatly. The press might have chosen to ignore Ford's mishaps, just as it ignored the fact that Franklin D. Roosevelt had been crippled by polio. Ford's bumping his head was news because reporters and editors subjectively believed it was an important key to his performance as president. Roosevelt's polio was ignored because most reporters and editors deemed it irrelevant.

Events, Personalities, and the Media

Through much of American history the media did not feel constrained to probe too closely into the personal lives of prominent politicians, including presidents. But in the wake of the war in Vietnam and the Watergate scandal the press became much more aggressive in its coverage of both the personal and political lapses of public figures. American involvement in Vietnam set the stage for this change. In the early years of the war most of the press faithfully reported the government's version of both the causes and the course of that conflict. But as years passed and American involvement grew steadily from a few thousand to over a half million troops, and as casualties mounted to the tens of thousands, both the media and large elements of the public became doubtful of optimistic predictions by politicians and military leaders that victory was imminent. The "light at the end of the tunnel" kept receding as the same time that the body bags returned from Vietnam in growing numbers. Coverage of the war by reporters in the field became more skeptical until, in the later years of the longest war in U.S. history, the American people were confronted by two contradictory versions of what was happening in Vietnam. At one point CBS news anchorman Walter Cronkite, reputed to be the most trusted man in America, who, as had most of his colleagues, began as an ardent supporter of the war, concluded that it could not be won. It was then that President Lyndon Johnson is said to have concluded that the war was indeed lost, because the country simply would not support the commitment of additional troops that would be needed to gain victory.[1]

The Watergate scandal during President Nixon's term heightened the tension between the media and public officials. Following a break-in at the Democratic headquarters in the Watergate hotel in Washington, D.C., during the campaign of 1972, reporters began a long and detailed investigation into the complicity of the president's reelection committee in the affair. Subsequently, there were charges that the White House had ordered a "cover-up," that is, done what was necessary to avoid public exposure of the involvement of the president's people in the break-in and in a series of other shady dealings. Ultimately, as we have seen, the president had to leave

[1]See David Halberstam, "CBS: The Power and the Profits," *Atlantic Monthly*, February 1976, pp. 52–91.

The Pursuit of Happiness

office. Throughout his career, Nixon had frequently found himself the target of unfavorable press coverage, and he tended to regard reporters as enemies. His famous "enemies list," which came to light as the result of the Watergate investigations, was studded with the names of prominent newspaper and television reporters and editors. What was to be done with these "enemies" was unclear, but among the remarks made by the president in the Watergate tapes (tapes made in the White House and later released to the courts) was the promise that after being reelected he would "get" Katharine Graham, publisher of the Washington *Post*, perhaps his most relentless critic.

In the wake of both Vietnam and Watergate, the relationship between government and the media changed, perhaps forever. The darkest suspicions and worst allegations that the press had hurled at a whole gallery of prominent political and military leaders—including two presidents—appeared to have been confirmed by events. The government had simply misled the American people. And the press had done its job in trying to find and disclose the truth. Honors, promotions, and, in some cases, considerable wealth (as the result of royalties from best-selling books and films) flowed to the reporters who had taken the lead in revealing the truth. A new term, *investigative reporting,* became the rage in journalism. Rather than simply reporting the obvious and reproducing government statements and handouts, reporters, newspapers, and television news bureaus vied with one another seeking to dig out the reality behind the press releases.

When in the late 1980s it became known that the United States was secretly shipping arms to Iran at a time when the Iranians were publicly denouncing the United States as "the Great Satan" and playing an active role in the kidnapping and murder of Americans in the Middle East, the press sensed another scandal of Watergate proportions. And when further revelations suggested that profits from the sales of those arms were illegally funneled to the U.S.-backed Contras in Central America, even Watergatelike names were splashed on the front pages of newspapers, in magazines, and on TV ("Irangate," "Contragate"). In this case, however, President Reagan did not suffer in the same way as had President Nixon, for no "smoking gun" was found (that is, no definitive evidence that the president had knowingly broken the law).

A by-product of this relatively new, adversarial relationship between the press and the president was an increasing willingness by the media to look carefully at the personal lives of the nation's leaders. Senator Ted Kennedy was an early casualty of this trend. His involvement in the death of a young woman following a beach party at Chappaquiddick, Massachusetts, in 1969 almost surely cost him his party's nomination for the presidency. Moreover, the memory of his brother, President John Kennedy, was clouded by a series of highly publicized allegations, none proved in court, that the president had had numerous affairs while in office.

In the race for the presidency in 1988, Democratic Senator Gary Hart was an early favorite for his party's nomination. Rumors about Senator Hart's penchant for attractive young women were common in Washington gossip and some of these began to appear in print. Senator Hart then held a press conference, accompanied by his wife, at which he denied all the rumors and challenged the press to follow him. The Miami *Herald* took the Senator at his word and assigned reporters to watch the candidate's personal as well as political activities. In May 1987, the *Herald* broke a highly embarrassing story, charging that Hart had had a liaison with an attractive model while his wife was away from Washington. The senator withdrew from the race, changed his mind a few months later, and finally dropped out after dismal showings in early primaries. For the second time a leading candidate for the presidency was forced to withdraw as the direct result of media disclosures of personal improprieties.

In separate and unrelated incidents, two prominent television ministers, Jim Bakker and Jimmy Swaggert, also became the subjects of sensational media coverage relating to sexual lapses. The cumulative message was clear. The nation's most respected and admired leaders, from the presidency to the pulpit, could no longer assume that they were immune from the prying eyes and ears of the media.

One effect of the scandals that seemed to enliven, titillate, and degrade the political process in recent decades has been to make the issue of "character" a dominant one in the nation's quadrennial process of electing a president. Increasingly, the personal qualities of candidates, rather than their political philosophy or stand on any given issue, seemed to dominate elections. An obvious example of this was President Reagan. Throughout most of his eight years in office, with the exception of a brief period during the height of the Iran-Contra affair, Reagan enjoyed the strong support of most of the American people. At the same time, the people elected a Democratic Congress and Democratic governors, mayors, and legislatures by substantial margins. Moreover, public opinion polls demonstrated time and again that a preponderance of the voters did not agree with Reagan on certain fundamental issues like military aid to the Contras, cuts in assorted domestic programs, and a massive military buildup. Perhaps because of Reagan's "hands-off" style of management, he seemed to be the most poorly informed president the nation had had in some time. Often presidential speeches or press conferences were followed by "explanations" emanating from the White House staff disclosing that the president had not meant what he said about a particular issue. The corrections frequently concerned matters of fact, not opinion. Reporters like ABC's Sam Donaldson repeatedly took the president to task during press conferences for these lapses. As a result, Reagan simply stopped having press conferences except on rare occasions. Instead he made presidential pronouncements in the form of casual quips in response to shouted questions taken under the roaring blades of the presidential helicopter. All this was in sharp contrast to President Jimmy Carter, one of the best-informed presidents in modern times. Carter welcomed press questions and held frequent press conferences. He even hosted radio "talk shows" during which the public was invited to question their leader. Carter's answers tended to be long, detailed, and perhaps a bit boring, but accurate. Reagan's were quick, simple, and often funny (if too frequently wrong). Voters preferred Reagan. This struck many foreign observers and reporters as curious and perhaps an indication of the average American's lack of information. More likely it reflected a belief on the part of many Americans that certain personal characteristics—optimism, courage, good humor—are more important qualities in a leader than knowledge of the details of public policy; and the media readily captures these characteristics.

Also, every president and the people who make up his administration quickly assume a kind of dramatic persona that tends to dictate how the media, and therefore the nation, view the continuing drama. There are heroes (FDR, Eisenhower, Kennedy, Reagan), villains (Nixon, Edwin Meese), clowns (Billy Carter), and heroines (Jacqueline Kennedy, Betty Ford). Sometimes understudies are elevated to stardom that rivals that of the principal players. Henry Kissinger was a kind of foreign policy genius, at least for a while, in the eyes of the media, a true superstar. Each new president is assigned a kind of public role. FDR was a buoyant leader; Harry Truman the pugnacious but honest average man; Eisenhower the benign and wise father figure; Jack Kennedy Prince Charming; LBJ the wily and masterful politico; Richard Nixon the Godfather; Jerry Ford the well-intentioned but clumsy Good Guy; Jimmy Carter the earnest but ineffectual wimp; Ronald Reagan the Star.

All of this, of course, is an oversimplification, and many of the examples cited above are outright distortions of reality. But they reflect a powerful need the media have to simplify lest they bore and thus lose an easily distracted audience.

The Media's Audience

Studies show that over half the population depends on mass media, particularly the electronic media (television and radio), for information about the world in which they live.[2] Although it is true that these people can select from among competing media, typically on any given evening, almost all daily newspapers across the United States choose to headline much the same story or stories, and thousands of radio and television stations follow suit.

Traditionally, we consider indispensable to a democratic society the ability to read the written word and hence to root out information and opinion

[2]The Roper Organization, "What People Think of Television and Other Mass Media, 1959–1972," Roper Public Opinion Research Center, Williamstown, Mass., May 1973.

for oneself. If as some recent studies indicate, both the ability and the inclination to read and ferret out the truth for oneself are in decline, the prospects for democracy are not good.

There are different audiences, however, for the mass media, particularly for television. For many Americans, TV and radio news broadcasts, with perhaps an occasional glance at the day's headlines in the newspapers (almost half of American families no longer take a daily newspaper), represent the only source of information and opinion about the government and its leaders. Moreover, most of us use the electronic media more as a source of entertainment than as a source of information. Thus the Nielsen ratings usually show that sporting events, situation comedies, and movies gain the widest TV audiences.

For those we have called the "attentive public" (see Chapter 9), however, there are other sources of information. First, these people usually have some knowledge of history, and so they can judge current happenings in context rather than as inexplicable events. Second, the attentive public read books and serious magazines on current affairs, which offer various and frequently conflicting points of view. Third, they watch public affairs programs on television and often listen to both radio and TV talk shows. Finally, many are active themselves in political affairs and hence have personal and specialized knowledge.

Of course the number of Americans interested in news matters may change over brief periods of time. For example, during the winter of 1979–1980, while American hostages were being held in Iran and Soviet forces fought in Afghanistan, Americans demonstrated considerable interest. Public opinion surveys showed that over 90 percent of the population was familiar with these events, and a late-night ABC news show dealing with the Iran and Afghanistan crises actually attracted more viewers than did the perennially popular Johnny Carson.

The News Business[3]

American journalism evolved out of two impulses: the need to advertise goods and services, which is why the front page of most early American newspapers contained advertising exclusively, and the desire to educate or propagandize (depending on your point of view) the people. Thus Ben Franklin began his *Almanac* (which later became one of the nation's first mass magazines, the *Saturday Evening Post)* with the statement that he had become a publisher not so much to spread wisdom and enlightenment but because "my wife needs new pots." The shrewd Franklin understood that

---

[3]For an illuminating discussion of the American press before 1960, see A. J. Liebling, *The Press* (New York: Ballantine, 1961).

the hardheaded farmers who were to be his audience might not respond favorably to a publication presuming to improve their minds but, rather, preferred a sound commercial motive.

Thus, unlike Europe, where many newspapers and magazines were subsidized by political factions and religious, social, and artistic movements, the American press was first and foremost a business, like any other business, that existed to sell advertising. (Although the press does obtain revenue from circulation, this is usually an expense rather than a profit to the publisher. Paid circulation is important because it offers the most convincing proof to advertisers that a publication is being read.)

Through most of America's history, the business community has been conservative politically, and the press, with few exceptions, has followed suit. One exception occurred briefly during the early days of the Great Depression, when something akin to panic seized American business leaders, causing many business executives and some newspapers (such as the then influential Hearst press) to desert the Republican party and support Franklin D. Roosevelt. By 1936, however, the panic had eased sufficiently to find both business and the overwhelming majority of American newspapers and magazines solidly behind the Republican candidate, Alf Landon, who, nonetheless, was defeated in the election.

Another important exception to the general rule of a largely conservative and compliant press occurred during the early part of this century, when a few audacious publishers, such as William Randolph Hearst and Joseph Pulitzer, engaged in *yellow journalism*. They created newspapers, usually tabloid sized, designed to be sold for a penny or two to subway-riding working people. The success of such newspapers depended on creating an aura of excitement and crusading zeal, together with the stock ingredients of big, splashy photos and plenty of sex, violence, and gossip. Occasionally, these papers would engage in a struggle on behalf of the "common man" against such interests as private utilities, great trusts, and corrupt political machines. In the end, however, the successful tabloids, once firmly established, settled down to a cozy relationship with their advertisers and used their editorial crusades to champion those businesses beleaguered by "bureaucrats" and tax collectors.

As Joseph Patterson, publisher of America's largest-selling newspaper, the *New York Daily News*, noted, "Newspapers start when their owners are poor, and take the part of the people and so they build a large circulation, and, as a result, advertising. That makes them rich and the publishers naturally begin to associate with other rich men . . . then they forget all about the people."[4]

By World War II, the United States, unlike most European nations, had developed a press with an almost exclusively regional base. The nation's two most politically influential national publications were *Time* and *Life* maga-

[4]Liebling, p. 19.

zines, owned by Henry R. Luce. Luce, the son of an American missionary, who grew up in China, developed two ideas that were to have a profound influence on his magazines and, through them, on the nation. One was his unshakable belief that America's destiny was to spread Christianity and capitalism (which were virtually inseparable in his eyes) around the world. The other was a morbid hatred of communism.

Luce saw journalism not merely as a means of amassing wealth or as a vehicle for giving information to the American people but as an instrument for spreading the gospel of Americanism. As he once observed in a letter to the senior editors at *Time* magazine who had complained about the magazine's lack of objectivity, "Within our company there is some confusion on this score. For example, there is a persistent urge to say that *Time* is 'unbiased,' and to claim for it complete objectivity. This, of course, is nonsense. The owners make no such fantastic claim." Later Luce added, "Our great job at *Time* magazine is not to create power, but to use it."[5]

By 1940, Luce believed that America would soon enter World War II and foresaw the probability that the United States would emerge from that conflict as the dominant power of the noncommunist world. In a widely discussed editorial entitled "The American Century" (which Luce paid to have published in many leading American newspapers as well as in his own magazines), Luce argued, "The complete opportunity of leadership is *ours*." He urged that in the postwar years America undertake to feed and care for all friendly peoples and governments but "take a very tough attitude toward all hostile governments." America must become the world's greatest economic and military power and pursue a policy of unrelenting opposition to any who dared defy that power. Although Luce's views drew a varied response at that time, ranging from support from business and conservative interests to strong attack from liberals (including a speech by Vice President Henry A. Wallace entitled "The Century of the Common Man"), in fact he had outlined the essential elements of what would become America's postwar foreign policy under both Democratic and Republican leadership.

Luce was a tireless foe of both Franklin D. Roosevelt and Harry S Truman. Roosevelt was able to go to the people directly via radio, over Luce's head as it were. (He once "awarded" Luce a Nazi Iron Cross for giving "aid and comfort to the enemy.") But Truman, a poor radio and television speaker, was effectively portrayed as "a little man" and a political hack—an impression that dominated the public image of Harry Truman until his reputation experienced a recent revival to the point that he has become something of a folk hero. John C. Merrill wrote a now classic study of how *Time* successfully stereotyped Truman by comparing its coverage of HST with that afforded Dwight Eisenhower, a Luce favorite. For example, according to *Time*, Eisenhower was

[5]W. A. Swanberg, *Luce and His Empire* (New York: Scribner's, 1972), p. 246.

a smiling warm-hearted, sincere leader. . . . A patient and peaceful man, who wanted to keep his campaign promises. A president who moved quietly . . . who loved children, who was forgiving and religious . . . who was cautious, warm, charitable, modest, happy, amiable, firm, cordial, effective, serene, frank, calm, skillful and earnest . . . who spoke "warmly" and chatted "amiably."

On the other hand, Truman was

a bouncy man, sarcastic and shallow; very unpopular, a "little man" . . . a President who condoned "shabby politicking" . . . a man who practiced "government by crony." A petulant, stubborn man with "shoddy friends."

Eisenhower "said with a happy grin"; Truman "barked." Eisenhower "paused to gather thought"; Truman "grinned slyly and avoided answering." Eisenhower folded his "long and reflective fingers"; Truman's fingers were "blunt."[6]

When John Kennedy was nominated as the Democratic candidate for president in the summer of 1960, his father, Joseph P. Kennedy, was watching the event on television with Henry Luce at the Luce suite in the Waldorf Astoria Hotel in New York City. The elder Kennedy, a longtime friend of Luce (dating back to the time before the war when both had briefly admired the Nazis for their resistance to communism), sought to win Luce's favor for his son's cause by affirming, "Henry, you know goddam well that no son of mine could ever be a goddam liberal." Luce demurred, pointing out that JFK would inevitably have to court the traditional Democratic liberal vote on domestic policy. That, Luce went on, was not really serious. "But if Jack shows any sign of going soft on communism (in foreign policy) then we would clobber him."[7]

John Kennedy was mindful of the Luce threat and took it very seriously indeed. For example, with respect to China, he confided to foreign policy advisers Adlai Stevenson, ambassador to the United Nations under Kennedy, and Chester Bowles, undersecretary of state, that he agreed with them that the U.S. policy toward China (that is, pretending that the Chiang Kai-shek government-in-exile on Taiwan was the representative of China) was "moonshine."[8] Sooner or later, U.S. policy toward China would have to be changed. But Kennedy added, "If Red China comes into the U.N. during our first year in town, they'll run us both out." By "they" Kennedy principally meant the *Time–Life–Fortune* Luce empire.

---

[6]John C. Merrill, "How *Time* Stereotyped Three U.S. Presidents," *Journalism Quarterly*, Autumn 1965, pp. 563–570.

[7]Swanberg, p. 576.

[8]Swanberg, p. 581.

Presidents and the Media

Historian and journalist Theodore White pointed out,

> The power of the press in America is a primordial one. It sets the agenda of public discussion. Today, more than ever, the press challenges the Executive President, who, traditionally, believes his is the right to set the agenda of the nation's action.
>
> The Making of the President, 1972

Both Lyndon Johnson and Richard Nixon believed that their right to govern the country after having been elected president was, in part, subverted by the press. Johnson stated repeatedly that his Texas accent and style, particularly following John Kennedy's high Harvard glitter, doomed his presidency. Describing his doubts about running for a full term in 1964, after having succeeded the assassinated Kennedy a year earlier, Johnson expressed his belief that the nation could not be united around a Southern president. "I was convinced," said Johnson, "that the metropolitan press would never permit it." Subsequent events persuaded Johnson that he had been right all along. Nixon carried on a lifelong battle with the press. Columnist Jack Anderson said, "Nixon came to power with the conviction that he had gotten there by circumventing the press and could govern successfully only so long as he continued to do so."[9]

In a sense, both Johnson and Nixon were right. They began their political careers and achieved great power and prominence when the press had had a different and more modest role in national affairs than it assumed during their presidencies. What happened in the interim was the brief era when John Kennedy was president. Kennedy changed the relationship between the government and the media in a way that neither Johnson nor Nixon fully understood or accepted.

Kennedy, of course, was not the first president to manipulate the media to achieve both personal and political goals. Franklin Roosevelt made masterful use of the radio. President Eisenhower led a charmed life insofar as criticism of him or even of his administration was concerned. Fulminations against the presidency seemed tasteless and ill-mannered during the eight years of Eisenhower's administration. On the other hand, Eisenhower's opponent in two campaigns, Adlai Stevenson, a charming, witty, and eloquent man who today would surely be a great favorite of the media, was sometimes treated like a pariah for presuming to run against the great war hero. Questions put to President Eisenhower during his press conferences were respectful and usually intended to be helpful. Stevenson, on the other hand, was sometimes greeted with hostility and often downright rudeness, to the point that he noted, more in sorrow than in anger, that the press

---

[9]Jack Anderson, *The Anderson Papers* (New York: Ballantine, 1973), p. 19.

seemed to react to a Democratic presidential candidate the way dogs react to cats: "They invariably want to chase us down an alley."[10]

What was unique about the Kennedy administration was not that Kennedy enjoyed a largely favorable press (Eisenhower's was perhaps more adoring) or that he used television to charm the voters (FDR used the radio even more skillfully) but that he deliberately attempted to make the press a vital part of his administration, and in the process he gave it a kind of legitimacy and power that it had never before enjoyed. Kennedy elevated the press to a fourth branch of government, equal and in some ways superior to the presidency, Congress, and the judiciary. Neither of Kennedy's two immediate successors could accept the new status of the press as an accomplished fact.

Kennedy and the Media

There is evidence that John Kennedy deliberately set out to shift the balance of media opinion from Republican to Democratic, conservative to liberal, and specifically to create a countervailing power to the influence of the Luce magazines. Kennedy did this with no more of a congressional or constitutional mandate than Lincoln had had for freeing the slaves or Wilson had had for attempting to draw a blueprint for world peace after World War I. He did it by making reporters, columnists, and editors part of his administration and by deliberately cultivating close personal friendships with important figures in the major media. He used these men and women as both advisers and sounding boards. Often sympathetic reporters, editors, and media executives played a more important role in his policy decisions than did members of his official cabinet. Members of the press knew that this was happening, and despite some misgivings about where their loyalties were supposed to lie, they loved it and in time came to accept it as perfectly natural. When the doors to the Oval Office, which had been open to the press during the Kennedy years, closed during the Johnson and Nixon eras, the press reacted with predictable hostility.

The Kennedy administration invented the term *news management*. This meant using the powers and prerogatives of the presidency to control the flow of information and commentary going to the American people through newspapers, radio, and television on a day-by-day and even an hour-by-hour basis.

Kennedy accomplished this control not simply by being charming and making himself available for interviews or by issuing judicious invitations to Jacqueline Kennedy's dazzling White House parties but to a considerable

---

[10]Labeling candidate Stevenson "an egghead," *Time* went on to define the term as "an intellectual educated beyond his intelligence."

degree by becoming a student of American media. Thus someone like Benjamin Bradlee, then *Newsweek's* White House correspondent and now editor-in-chief of the Washington *Post*, found to his astonishment that Kennedy knew more about the Washington press corps—who the correspondents were, what publications or broadcasting stations they represented, and what the circulation, financial, and political problems of those publications and stations were—than Bradlee himself knew.[11] According to Bradlee, Kennedy genuinely liked reporters, had once been one himself, and planned to enter journalism when he retired from the presidency.

More important, Kennedy not only knew the personalities and the day-to-day problems of the working press, he also understood the inherent limitations of the mass media.

As Bradlee wrote,

> Kennedy worried out loud about the widening gap between the people who can discuss the complicated issues of today with intelligence and knowledge, and those he later referred to as "the conservative community" . . . the great majority who just don't understand these issues and hide their lack of understanding behind the old clichés.

Kennedy sometimes complained that the major media were compelled to please their audiences by oversimplification and "entertainment values." He made this the theme of a major address at Yale University. Kennedy carefully thought through the role of the media in a mass society. He also read many newspapers and magazines, as well as nonfiction literature, and there is evidence that this kind of activity influenced his presidency.

Two important examples can be cited. Perhaps the most celebrated came during the Cuban missile crisis, when the president was under considerable pressure from most members of the National Security Council, particularly the representatives of the military, to take direct military action against Cuba and/or the Soviet Union. Although never closing the military option, Kennedy delayed, hoping for the diplomatic triumph that ultimately materialized. In doing so, he referred on several occasions to a book he had recently read, *The Guns of August*, by historian Barbara Tuchman. Tuchman's work traced the outbreak of World War I in a manner that left the reader with the impression that this war and all its attendant agonies could be traced largely to the rigidity and the incompetence of the leaders of the European powers. Kennedy told his closest advisers that if World War III were to begin as the result of the impasse between the Soviet Union and the United States over Cuba, he did not want some future Tuchman to lay the responsibility at his door.[12]

The Kennedy administration also credited a book, Michael Harrington's

[11]Benjamin Bradlee, *Conversations with Kennedy* (New York: Norton, 1975).
[12]Robert F. Kennedy, *Thirteen Days* (New York: Norton, 1968), p. 40.

The Other America, with having provided the initial impetus for what Lyndon Johnson later called the War on Poverty.

Thus two important decisions made during JFK's brief tenure in office were influenced by writers rather than by generals, economists, bankers, labor leaders, or politicians—whose views are customarily sought by presidents regarding important policy decisions.

Kennedy cultivated the friendship of the moderately liberal publishers of the Washington *Post* and *Newsweek* magazine, Phillip and Katharine Graham. When JFK took office, the *Post* was simply a good Washington newspaper, and *Newsweek* was a poor and distant second to *Time* in the field of weekly news magazines, rumored to be facing imminent sale or suspension. By the end of the decade, the *Post* was a serious rival of the *New York Times* for the role of the nation's most influential newspaper, and *Newsweek* had caught up to *Time* in prestige and advertising. This development was certainly helped by the friendship of Kennedy, Bradlee, and the Grahams.[13]

Another, less direct, example of this impact on a major American newspaper was the transformation of the *Los Angeles Times* from a solidly Republican, strongly conservative newspaper to a position much closer to the center of the American political spectrum, which occurred at about the same time. The *Times*—for decades the all-powerful voice for the most conservative elements in California, the richest newspaper in the country, and the arbiter of the Republican party in California—suddenly began a series of changes in both personnel and political philosophy. The *Times* also entered into a loose editorial agreement with the liberal Washington *Post*—something that would have been impossible a few years earlier—whereby the two newspapers traded certain services and had the right to print each other's columnists.

The *New York Times*, although nominally a Democratic newspaper for many decades, met the challenge of the *Post* and the *Los Angeles Times* by moving significantly to the left. The *New York Times* became an early and powerful opponent of the war in Vietnam and endorsed four Democratic presidential candidates in a row: Kennedy, Johnson, McGovern, and Carter.

Nixon and the Media

It was the decision of the *New York Times* editors to publish the Pentagon Papers that brought open confrontation between the Nixon administration and the press. The Nixon–Agnew administration felt that its ability to govern the nation and successfully prosecute a war was being frustrated by what the vice president called the "nattering nabobs of negativism." For

---

[13]This is clearly implied in Bradlee's book.

their part, many prominent figures in the press felt threatened by the government. (Thus the managing editor of the *New York Times* publicly announced that he expected to go to prison for his decision to publish the Pentagon Papers if Nixon and Agnew were reelected in 1972.) As president, Nixon believed that he was entitled to the same respectful treatment that had been afforded President Eisenhower. He seems to have believed that newspapers should naturally be supportive of the government and that their failure to be so was a kind of treachery.

Convinced that the press was an opponent (as we have seen, many of the people on Nixon's so-called enemies list were from the media), the president counterattacked by authorizing Vice President Agnew to launch an unprecedented assault on the nation's press. One of the revealing comments on the Watergate tapes was Nixon's promising to "get" the Washington *Post*, to which a still subservient John Dean replied, "What an exciting prospect."

Agnew charged that the press was now dominated by "eastern establishment liberals," and he directed his attack particularly at the highly vulnerable television networks as well as at the *New York Times* and the Washington *Post*. Despite the heavy-handed Nixon–Agnew assault on the press, the vast majority of American newspapers that editorialized in favor of a presidential candidate in 1972 supported Nixon. Moreover, if the press ever had a liberal candidate to support, surely it was the president's 1972 opponent, Senator George McGovern. Yet the major media virtually ignored Watergate during the 1972 campaign and concentrated instead on McGovern's difficulty in finding a running mate, his proposal to give every American $1,000, and his troubles controlling a young and inexperienced staff. McGovern's problems were publicized to the point that millions of Americans became convinced that he was a bumbling fool.

Meanwhile President Nixon was portrayed as bringing peace to the world through personal diplomacy in China and the Soviet Union. On the other hand and at the same time, the unraveling of the Watergate story, which would destroy the Nixon administration, had begun.

As chronicled in the book and film *All the President's Men*, the investigation into Watergate was spearheaded by two young police reporters for the Washington *Post*, Bob Woodward and Carl Bernstein, covering a "routine" burglary. What became a journalistic coup was, then, the work of two obscure reporters, not regularly assigned to politics. Why wasn't the story unearthed by one or more of the famous and well-paid reporters assigned to cover Washington politics? Perhaps the press was intimidated by the Nixon–Agnew attack; perhaps experienced political correspondents were leaning over backward to avoid even the appearance of conducting a vendetta against the White House. At any rate, the Watergate story remained muted until the Woodward–Bernstein revelations made this virtually impossible.

The "Woodstein" phenomenon may have opened an entirely new phase in the history of American print journalism. For many years it has been the custom of Washington correspondents to maintain a sort of "old boy" code regarding the exposure of certain indiscretions by prominent politicians. But shortly after Watergate, two of the most prominent men in Congress, Wilbur Mills and Wayne Hays, found their private love affairs splashed across the nation's front pages. In pre-Watergate days, such stories would have been ignored or displayed far less prominently. Such investigative reporting continued. The widely publicized book by Woodward and another Washington *Post* writer, Scott Armstrong, entitled *The Brethren*, probed in tedious detail the private lives, idiosyncracies, and personal dislikes of members of the Supreme Court.

Carter and the Media

The Carter administration, likewise, became an early victim of the media's post-Watergate taste for personal scandal. Early in his administration the president's close friend and adviser, Bert Lance, was forced to relinquish his post as director of the Office of Management and Budget as the result of certain financial irregularities in his past. The president's brother Billy became something of a national joke and a continuing embarrassment.

Carter's own relationship with the media was ambiguous. Unlike Nixon or Johnson, he did not seem to believe that he was the victim of unrelenting hostility and obstruction. He did complain, and the evidence was on his side in this matter, that the media were often simply uninterested in substantive issues and instead were preoccupied with gossip and recording who was in and who was out, who was winning and who was losing in the political games of Washington. In short, the news media, except for an overwhelming event like the Iranian crisis or the gas crunch of 1979, appeared to be bored by politics. It was as if sports writers were to focus not on the game itself but, rather, on the salaries of the players, which player was sleeping with whom, and who was the current locker room favorite.

Until the Iranian crisis of 1979, Carter was seen as simply a failure, a good man who tried but somehow could not get the hang of whatever mysterious qualities it took to capture the nation's attention and assert leadership. The crisis in Iran, however, produced a sudden, almost miraculous change. The media, no less than the public, were outraged and sought to rally around a patriotic symbol. Given the American political system, Carter was the only person around whom the nation *could* rally. Although his handling of the affair was not particularly masterful or brilliant, and even though a case could be made that the president had brought the matter on himself by allowing the deposed shah of Iran into the United States for medical treatment, suddenly news coverage of President Carter took a distinctly more respectful turn. Carter's standing in the polls shot up. It was during this early stage in the Iranian crisis that Carter won several important primary battles against Senator Edward Kennedy, enabling him to hold off a late surge by the Massachusetts senator. But as the Iranian crisis dragged on month after month, what had been a source of sudden popularity for Carter became an increasingly heavy burden. It was, once again, the phenomenon that had become manifest many times during the Johnson–Nixon years. The president takes a decisive military action (escalate the bombing, invade Cambodia), and there is an immediate surge of support and popularity. But when the "decisive action" leads to still more frustration and stalemate, the president's popularity drops even more sharply than it had earlier climbed. In the end, Carter's inability to resolve the Iranian crisis played a major role in his defeat by Ronald Reagan. Carter, who was originally portrayed by the media as an honest, deeply moral, and intelligent antidote to the paranoid manipulations that characterized the Nixon administration, was seen simply as a loser.

Reagan and the Media

In many respects the success of Ronald Reagan represents the most conspicuous example of the impact of the media on politics. Reagan was for many years a professional actor, starring in several movies and television shows. His emergence into national politics was via a celebrated televised speech in 1964 calling for the election of Senator Barry Goldwater, the Republican candidate for president. Delivered with a trained actor's style and voice, the television message, although not electing Goldwater, immediately made Reagan the favorite of conservative Republicans. He was subsequently elected governor of California in 1966, reelected in 1970, and began his long pursuit of the presidency, all along the way skillfully using the media. Reagan occasionally wrote newspaper columns, and for years he had a regularly broadcast radio commentary by means of which he kept himself and his views before the public. In his frequent appearances on television, he always appeared relaxed and likable, conveying an image that other politicians, less familiar with the media, simply were incapable of matching.

President Reagan may well be remembered as a kind of ultimate practitioner and beneficiary of an increasing tendency by the American people to confuse politics with show business. Almost from the beginning of his administration, Reagan's policies, anathema to confirmed liberals, were regarded skeptically by middle-of-the-road and middle-class Americans. In foreign affairs, the polls suggested most Americans were uneasy about the possibility that his decision to involve actively American armed forces in Central America and the Middle East might lead to another Vietnam, and there was fear that his tough rhetoric vis-à-vis the Soviet Union could lead to a nuclear confrontation. Even President Reagan's most conservative admirers wondered aloud why American marines were losing their lives in Lebanon and the government seemed powerless to do anything about it. Yet there was clearly nothing like the general revulsion that emerged from the failure of Jimmy Carter to win release of American hostages in Iran, even though not one hostage's life was lost.

So too in domestic policy there was a general sense that the president had gone too far in granting tax cuts to business and the wealthy, while greatly increasing arms budgets and saddling the government with enormous deficits, and a lingering suspicion that though the country had indeed begun to recover from the deep recession of the early 1980s, the depth of the trauma and the suffering it entailed were not necessary. Yet President Reagan personally continued to gain high marks from the American people. Although the public may not have agreed with Reagan's policies, approved of his nominees for high office, or admired the skill with which these policies were carried out, they still liked Ronald Reagan.

As did Presidents Roosevelt and Eisenhower before him, Reagan seemed to have developed his own channels of communication with the people and to have transcended the press's criticism of him and/or his administration. Liberal critics, of course, excoriated the president as heartless, lazy, uninformed, and lacking even an ordinary curiosity about policies that affected the lives of millions. Even conservative intellectuals found much about Reagan that displeased them. William Safire, a nationally respected conservative columnist, urged Reagan not to run for reelection. Richard Viguerie, a right-wing political activist, kept hinting that conservatives should find a candidate closer to their own hearts. But none of this seemed to matter a great deal alongside the fact that Reagan's familiar, jaunty wave on television's evening news was somehow friendly and reassuring or that on interview shows with gentle probing from genial hosts like Merv Griffin, he radiated the kind of reasonable, nice-guy image that had made him for two decades a star of B-grade movies, pictures in which the hero was not Hamlet or even James Bond, but just a decent, well-meaning, good-neighbor type of fellow you would like to have escort your daughter to the senior prom.

An example of Reagan's unique ability to rise above mere facts could be found in the history of the brief invasion and conquest of the tiny Caribbean island of Grenada in October 1983. For several years this island had been under the control of a Marxist government that was much closer ideologically to Cuba and the Soviet Union than to the United States. When the Grenadans elected to build a major airstrip, which they insisted was being constructed to accommodate commercial jets to enhance their tourist trade, but which American military leaders feared might become a possible base for Cuban or Soviet aircraft, the United States began to consider military intervention. An internal coup that toppled the popular, elected Marxist leader was the event that triggered U.S. action. Present on the island were several hundred American medical students. Using their presence and the possibility that the new, more radical regime might take the American students as hostages (as was done with American diplomats in Iran), American forces invaded the island with the avowed purpose of rescuing the students and, not incidentally, toppling the communist rulers of Grenada in favor of a regime more congenial to the United States. The U.S. Army's crack infantry assault unit, numbering several thousand troops, was chosen to mount the invasion. Opposed to them were a few hundred poorly armed and trained Grenadan soldiers, and several hundred Cuban construction workers who were in the country to help build the airstrip, but who may also have had arms and military training.

The day after the invasion, President Reagan and Secretary of Defense Caspar Weinberger went on television to claim that the invasion was a great success. The students had been rescued without harm, the government of Grenada was in hiding, and American forces, showing outstanding skill and courage, were mopping up what little scattered resistance remained. Because the U.S. government had placed an unusual two-day news blackout on the invasion and followed that with restrictive coverage for three more days, there was no one to check the official version of events. (This represented a break with American tradition and produced a good deal of angry but ineffectual protest from the nation's press.) The president's bold action and the military's victory in Grenada helped the American people forget the disastrous loss of life by U.S. Marines in Lebanon earlier that fall and became a key element in the president's reelection campaign in 1984. Most Americans never did learn the facts about the Grenadan invasion, which were decidedly different from the version the president and the secretary of defense had presented. In fact, the invasion was a military fiasco, so badly managed that some of the ranking army officers were reprimanded and/or transferred to other units as the result of their troops' poor performance. Casualties among American soldiers were far higher than they should have been, many of them mistakenly inflicted by our forces on each other. Faced with weak, sporadic sniper fire, the crack 82nd Airborne did not attack or advance, but dug in and waited for aerial or artillery fire to remove the obstacle. As a result an operation that should have been over in hours took most of a week. The troops involved were confused about their purpose and objective. They complained about poor leadership and worse intelligence. (Several days before the invasion began, the army asked the CIA for military maps of Grenada that were in the CIA's possession, because a possible attack had been under discussion for months. The CIA, for reasons never explained, did not deliver the needed maps. Instead, combat troops and their officers were furnished with tourist guides that had originally been printed and distributed by the Grenadan Chamber of Commerce and that pointed out the best restaurants and beaches but were, of course, silent about military installations.) It was finally revealed that even as the president and the secretary of defense were proclaiming the rescue of the students, hundreds of them were in fact still in hiding, most of them in the homes of local citizens in areas still under the control of the Grenadan government. Fortunately, there had been no effort to harm the students or to take hostages, although that easily could have been done. On returning home many of the students interviewed by the media insisted that the only danger they were ever exposed to came from possible errant bombs launched from U.S. aircraft.

Here again was another example of the Vietnam syndrome: the government claiming a great victory, the press reporting a story of mismanagement and blunders that happened to turn out well only because there was no real resistance. But the president's version was announced in the heat of a breaking story with all the nation's attention focused on this obscure little island. The press version came out slowly and gradually, much of it weeks and months after the event and long after most Americans had lost all interest. Some time after the event, the army quietly announced that it was revising its training procedures for jungle warfare.

In short, the triumph of Reaganism seemed to reaffirm once and for all the view of those who loudly and long have insisted that issues are less important than are images. No president before Reagan had ever so successfully managed to wrap hard, conservative doctrine into a soft and amiable package. The media, to their consternation and perhaps dismay, may have found themselves irrelevant to Ronald Reagan's success or failure as president.

At one point, during the depth of the recession of 1982, with over 10 million Americans unemployed, the CBS network television news ran a nightly series showing the impact of the recession on working-class families throughout the nation's industrial heartland. As the nightly horror show continued, President Reagan was finally moved to call CBS and ask why their reporters could not for once interview someone who had a job.

CBS, of course, gleefully reported the incident. It was proof that the president feared and respected the power of its news program. But the last laugh may have been on CBS. As the economy began to recover, the people seemed to conclude that although President Reagan had made mistakes, he was a nice man, doing his best, and he certainly looked a lot more like a president than that Carter fellow did.

Bush and the Media

For most of his public career, George Bush had served others (as Republican Party Chairman, Director of the CIA, and Vice President). Thus, as the campaign for the Presidency commenced in 1988, he was seen by many as a passive, "wimpish" follower of the popular President Reagan. However, by utilizing the expertise of media experts with uncommon skill, Mr. Bush transformed his image from one of an elite, preppy underling "born with a silver spoon in his mouth," to one of a likable, forceful leader. This was in large part because he placed himself in the hands of ex–Richard Nixon adviser Roger Ailes, a master of television advertising (including negative ads). Perhaps Mr. Bush's best moment in the 1988 campaign occurred during the second presidential debate. Appearing relaxed, natural, and competent, he clearly performed better than expected, thus blunting what many thought was the last chance for Mr. Dukakis to regain momentum in the campaign. Above all, what Bush seemed to grasp better than most political personalities was what President Reagan had been able to accomplish as a professional actor. Like Reagan, Bush played on television the role of a loving grandfather, a kindly person one would want to have as a neighbor, and as a "likable" guy. There was little in the way of substance in what Bush said he would do to address the challenges confronting the nation, and the media seemed perfectly willing to emphasize personality over substance. Thus the ad makers and the pollsters, not Dan Rather, Tom Brokaw, or Peter Jennings, set the agenda and determined the course of the 1988 campaign. Will this become the pattern in Presidential politics?

As Mr. Bush prepared to assume the Presidency, author Joe McGinnis, commenting on the change in public image that the President-elect had undergone, suggested that "The American people are beginning to view the presidency as just one more aspect of show business."

Television

It has been estimated that the average high school graduate has watched between fifteen thousand and eighteen thousand hours of television, and at the same time he or she has spent about twelve thousand hours in school. Such data cause Americans to believe that this important medium has somehow changed us. But there is little evidence that television has caused us all to conform to a common standard of behavior, as some early critics feared. Likewise, television has eliminated neither radio nor reading, both of which are flourishing. Some worry, however, that excessive TV viewing by the young has been a major cause of the decline in literacy in the country. It is clear, as we have suggested, that television is an influential, perhaps the most influential, medium in America. But the nature of that influence remains uncertain.

One thing does seem clear, however, and that is that mistakes on television tend to prove very damaging indeed. Nixon's apparent loss of the first TV debate to Kennedy in 1960 is usually credited with having turned the campaign in Kennedy's favor. George Gallup asserted that President Ford's remark about Poland's not being dominated by the Soviet Union, in the course of the second debate between Ford and Carter, was the critical element in giving Carter the victory in the very close election of 1976.

The free-swinging Democratic conventions televised in 1968 and 1972 almost certainly contributed to Richard Nixon's victories in those two campaigns. The combat between Governor Nelson Rockefeller's forces and those who supported Senator Barry Goldwater in the Republican convention of 1964, also televised to millions, probably paved the way for the GOP's defeat in that year.

The leaders of both parties have learned these lessons well and have sought to avoid televised dissension during the party conventions. The need to present an image of party unity on television is one reason that major party candidates have usually been chosen on the first ballot ever since the advent of TV coverage of party conventions. Thus, although television began by covering the national political conventions, now the conventions are largely managed for television.

Although still a relatively new and dimly understood force in politics, television has amply demonstrated its power to shape events. The first dramatic evidence of this came in the 1950s with the live broadcast of the Senate hearings into charges that Senator Joseph McCarthy had been exerting pressure on the U.S. Army on behalf of a young staff assistant who had been drafted. McCarthy responded to these charges with his now familiar allegation that high-ranking army officials were coddling communists. A fascinated public watched what became a mortal struggle. By the end of the hearings six weeks later, McCarthy's power to rally support from the people and hence to intimidate important public officials had been broken. In a sense, the press created McCarthy, but television destroyed him.

Another highlight of television's impact on politics came with the first Nixon–Kennedy debate in 1960. Nixon had been favored to win the election, but his poor performance in this debate is generally credited with having turned the tide in Kennedy's favor.

In the spring and summer of 1973, the nation watched a Senate select committee, led by Senator Sam Ervin, investigate a range of presidential abuses generally grouped together under the heading of Watergate. Support for President Nixon, which was substantial at the beginning of the hearings, seemed to erode with each day of the investigation. Television had, in effect, prepared the nation for Nixon's resignation.

In January 1977 a televised version of Alex Haley's book *Roots* absorbed the nation's attention for a total of 8 evenings and 12 hours and garnered the largest television audience until that time. Although it is too soon to judge the political consequences of this event, many, including author Haley, have expressed the belief that the TV program "Roots" may prove as important to race relations in America in this century as the novel *Uncle Tom's Cabin* was in the nineteenth century.

In late 1979 Iranian radicals stormed the U.S. embassy in Teheran and took hostage the embassy staff there. For weeks tens of millions of viewers watched on television as crowds of Iranians condemned the deposed shah and criticized the United States. It was as though the event had been created for television.

In November 1983, ABC's television movie "The Day After," graphically depicting the gruesome aftermath of a nuclear exchange, attracted an enormous television audience and launched innumerable discussion groups around the country and on nationwide television, debating the social and political implications of nuclear war, as well as the impact of television on our political views.

During the summer of 1987 large audiences watched the televised hearings conducted by special committees of both houses of Congress investigating the Iran-Contra affair. Numerous witnesses were called before the committees: Retired General Richard Secord and businessman Albert Hakim, who had purchased U.S. arms from the CIA, sold them to Iran, placed the funds in private Swiss bank accounts, provided a portion of the funds to the Contras (the funding of which was at the time outlawed by congressional act), kept most of it in Swiss bank accounts, and then announced that they were serving the foreign policy interests of the United States; members of the National Security Council (Robert MacFarlane, John Poindexter, and Col. Oliver North), who planned and coordinated these activities out of the White House; and high-ranking cabinet officials (including Secretary of Defense Weinberger and Secretary of State Shultz), who insisted that they had always opposed such an initiative, and in any case knew very little of the details. Although serious questions of violating the law, the Constitution, and the doctrine of checks and balances (see Chapter 3) were raised, many viewers found themselves favorably attracted to some of those testifying before the television cameras. This was particularly true of Col. Oliver North, who became an instant celebrity. "Ollie For President" T-shirts sprouted up around the country as a large viewing audience saw in this brash officer a "can-do" kind of he-man usually seen only in Clint Eastwood or Sylvester Stallone movies. As the improprieties of Col. North's activities became more evident, however, his popularity began to wane, so that by the time of his indictment in March 1988 by an independent counsel appointed to investigate wrongdoing in the Iran-Contra scandal, there was hardly a whimper from the general public. Nonetheless, the summer of 1987 proved that Americans were as interested in televised political drama as they were in fictional soap operas.

Few serious students of politics, and even fewer politicians, doubt the power of television not only to portray but also to shape events. But that power can be used negatively as well as positively. An example of how the voters can be manipulated by sophisticated exploitation of television's inherent tendency to focus on image rather than on substance is detailed by Joe McGinniss in *The Selling of the President, 1968*. McGinniss describes a strategy to sell a "New Nixon" (the old one had been somewhat tarnished by his defeat in the presidential campaign of 1960 and a subsequent loss to Governor Pat Brown of California in 1962). The essence of this strategy was outlined in a memo circulated among Nixon's close advisers written by Raymond K. Price, who subsequently became a presidential speech writer.

I AM LOVED.

PEOPLE NEED ME, WORSHIP
ME, CAN'T LIVE WITHOUT ME—

GO CRAZY WHEN I DON'T
COME ACROSS WITH WHAT
THEY WANT.

I SHAPE LIVES. I TEACH:
HOW TO SHOOT. WHAT
TO BUY.

I DRAIN EMPTINESS
FROM LIVES. FILL THE
VOID WITH JUNK. PEOPLE
ARE GRATEFUL.

I AM THE GIVER OF
NEWS. OPINIONS DON'T
EXIST WITHOUT ME.

I AM THE INSIDES
OF YOUR HEAD.

IF YOU WANTED A GROSS
NATIONAL PRODUCT, YOU GOT IT.

(Copyright © 1976 by Jules Feiffer.)

The natural use of reason is to support prejudice. (The Nixon campaign should focus on a) gut reaction . . . unarticulated, non-analytical . . . it's not what's there that counts, it's what's projected . . . voters are basically lazy, basically uninterested in making an effort to understand.

Hence, Price urged, the Nixon campaign should concentrate on an emotional appeal, "saturation with film" that "can be *edited*" (italics ours). Price concluded, "So let's not be afraid of television gimmicks . . . get the voters to like the guy and the battle's two-thirds won."[14]

In all fairness, Nixon was certainly not the first or the only presidential candidate to rely largely on "gimmicks" and "prejudice" or to assume that most voters are intellectually lazy. Virtually all nationally prominent politicians strive to create a favorable "image" and seek to use television's power to communicate on a nonverbal level. Thus President Carter was reported to have instructed his speech writers to try to limit the words used in his speeches to the vocabulary of a ninth grader.

As Niccolo Machiavelli said long ago in *The Prince*, "Everyone has eyes to see but few are capable of understanding." Or as Marshall McLuhan more recently noted, the rule in television is "describe the scratch but not the itch." That is, tell what happened, but not *why* it happened.[15]

The great television networks are in the entertainment business. They earn hundreds of millions of dollars annually, and their executives enjoy a measure of fame and high social status, principally by giving the people a constant diet of innocuous melodrama, game shows, music, and comedy. Their income comes not from the viewers but from advertisers, almost always large, conservative American corporations that prefer not to be involved in any sort of controversy that might result in lower sales or unpleasant political flak. Moreover, the networks, unlike the print media, are not specifically covered by First Amendment guarantees of freedom. On the contrary, they are licensed by the government, and what government gives, government can take away. Also, they are subject to all manner of government regulations, so that even a relatively minor policy change by the Federal Communications Commission (appointed by the president) could cost the networks millions of dollars.[16]

For all these reasons the policy of network television toward news has been to regard it as a necessary evil, a dangerous and highly vulnerable threat to a profitable entertainment business. Usually, the networks have tried to select as news "anchor" people figures like Walter Cronkite or Dan Rather, who project an air of both objectivity *and* authority. The rule is and

[14]Joe McGinniss, *The Selling of the President, 1968* (New York: Trident, 1969), pp. 30–33.

[15]Marshall McLuhan, *Understanding Media* (New York: McGraw-Hill, 1964).

[16]The FCC-imposed "family hour," requiring programming "suitable for family viewing" during the key prime-time hours of 7 to 9 P.M. resulted in many major problems for the networks, among others, a multimillion-dollar lawsuit from Norman Lear (producer of "All in the Family" and "Mary Hartman, Mary Hartman").

has been that if the audience can tell whether the anchor person is a Republican or a Democrat, a liberal or a conservative, then he or she is not suitable for the job.

But television is such an inherently powerful medium that despite the frantic efforts of executives not to influence public opinion ("There is always a vice president in charge of fear," notes critic David Halberstam) particularly on political matters, the slightest half-smile, the lifting of an eyebrow, the choice of a given word or phrase can and does have consequences—which is to say that television newscasters are human beings, after all, and cannot help but react to the events they describe for the American people, and occasionally some of that reaction slips through the supersensitive eye of the camera. Thus when Walter Cronkite was broadcasting the 1968 Republican convention in Miami, he began unconsciously and repeatedly using the word *erosion* in describing the support for a plank in the platform. A note came down from the executives, nervously instructing Cronkite to stop using the word *erosion*. Whereupon the exasperated Cronkite wrote a note in reply that simply said, "I quit," and he began to dismantle his earphones and prepared to leave on the spot. Frantic executives prevailed upon Cronkite not to walk off in the middle of the broadcast.[17]

In recent years television viewing possibilities have been enhanced by the growth of cable television. Today most Americans have access to scores of stations ranging from local public service outlets and religious channels to national public affairs stations and all-news cable networks. Viewers can watch, at virtually any time of the day, congressional sessions, full State Department press briefings, and most major speeches given in Washington as well as sophisticated and constantly updated news from around the world. And the evidence is that American viewers are taking advantage of these expanded opportunities.[18]

The power of television has transformed American politics and American society. A film such as *Broadcast News* satirized this and, at the same time, raised serious questions about the future of an industry that increasingly dominates the nation's collective vision of itself and of its leaders. Can and should such power continue to be exercised by a small group of private individuals operating on the basis of largely commercial motives?

The Fourth Estate: An Assessment

Early in his presidency Jimmy Carter made it clear that he would seek to have an "open administration" and made good on this promise by frequently holding televised press conferences. At one point the president's

[17]Halberstam, p. 78.

[18]See Ernest Leiser, "The Little Network That Could," *New York Times Magazine*, March 20, 1988, pp. 30–38; and "Who watches C-Span," *C-Span Update*, March 7, 1988, pp. 4–5.

press conferences were coming so rapidly and seemed to have so little interest for the country that one reporter asked the president if he did not fear the danger of "overexposure." The president, somewhat irritated, replied, "Attendance at press conferences is not mandatory." The exchange may have highlighted the nature of the media–president relationship during Carter's term. Carter was cooperative and available enough to satisfy most reporters. The problem was that he was not very interesting.

Whether or not it is important for a president to be interesting to the media is one of the questions raised by the altered political environment in the late twentieth century. For a president to be honest, well-informed, reasonable, and decent in his conduct of the nation's affairs would seem to be very formidable virtues indeed. But the role and power of the media in America today require something more. Some critics believe that President Carter's major problem was his inability to move the American people to care deeply about the issues of the hour, something that we expect to be done through the mass media. This would appear to be the only effective way in which the president can define and create a strong national will and identity in the face of the various personal, sectional, and private interests continually pulling the country in various directions, sometimes to the point that the nation itself seems incapable of rational action. For example, since the oil embargo of 1974, it has been clear that the United States required a national energy program that would, at a minimum, include a program to develop alternative sources of fuel, expand mass transit, encourage conservation, and bring about a fundamental shift in both the way we use automobiles and the kinds of automobiles we use. Despite brave words from three presidents—Nixon, Ford, and Carter—very little has been done. (President Reagan showed very little interest in the subject.) At least a major part of the problem has been the inability of presidents to communicate the urgency and gravity of the crisis to most Americans. By way of contrast, within two or three years after America's entry into World War II, virtually the entire U.S. economy had been altered and mobilized for the war effort. Of course, mobilizing a nation for war is obviously more easily accomplished than meeting a problem as inherently less tangible and dramatic as the energy crisis. The point is that FDR managed to convince the nation that personal and provincial interests had to be sacrificed to the larger national cause. Perhaps this was an unusual moment in our history, when most Americans perceived a common danger. Yet the long-run problems of energy might well pose an equally serious danger. It is arguable that the modern president will have to understand how to rally the nation through the use of the media to lead in times of crisis.

If the media are, then, this important and if they have become a de facto "fourth branch of government," should not their powers be defined and regulated by law, as is true of the other three branches? Not everyone agrees that the media should be free to "print the truth and raise hell," as Mark Twain urged. In only about 20 percent of the countries of the world are newspapers and radio and TV stations even marginally free. Third World countries, by and large, do not believe that their countries can be developed while the people are permitted the luxury of a free press. They have even sponsored a UN resolution that would make each nation's government "responsible" for what its newspapers print and its radio and TV stations broadcast. This resolution would put the United Nations in the position of officially advocating that the press be controlled by the state. In totalitarian states, of course, the government runs the media, and in those states virtually nothing can be printed or broadcast that runs counter to the wishes of the ruling clique. Even among those who remain committed to the idea of free expression of opinion, there is a serious, perhaps growing criticism of what the media actually do. Among the most common complaints are the following.

Particularly in the post-Watergate era, although the media do a generally good job of investigative reporting, they remain largely hostile to serious ideas. For example, television, by its very nature, tends to stress the physical at the expense of mental activity. The printed press, which might do otherwise, is infatuated with headline-making "hard news" and often does a very shabby job of explaining the meaning of that news. Early in the 1976 campaign, then Georgia Governor Carter told *Playboy* interviewer Robert Scheer, "The traveling press has zero interest in any issue unless it's a matter of making a mistake . . . there's nobody on the back of this plane who would ask an issue question unless he thought he could trick me into some crazy statement." Carter's observation turned out to be an accurate forecast of how the media handled the 1976 campaign, with their extraordinary emphasis on the candidates' occasional gaffes rather than on the substance of what they were saying, a process that Pulitzer Prize winner Harry Ashmore summed up in the *Los Angeles Times* as "the trivialization of the campaign."

A related problem is the media's preoccupation with the "star system." Certain individuals are deemed by the media to have "star quality" and are made into virtual demigods. An example was Secretary of State Henry Kissinger, who was treated as a diplomatic superman by the media until about the time of the fall of Richard Nixon. Later the press apparently tired of him, as it often does with stars who are overexposed, and there was very little that Kissinger could do that seemed to be right. Still later the former secretary of state became again a celebrity appearing on entertainment talk shows on TV and appearing in gossip-oriented tabloids. In short, the media too often seem to try to measure the people who hold the nation's most awesome responsibilities by the same standards used by groupies in judging rock musicians.

The most omnipresent medium, television, remains essentially committed to "entertainment values," even in its handling of news. A recent fad, perhaps still another overresponse to the "bad news" of Vietnam and Watergate, has been the spread of "happy news." Under the happy news formula, two or three attractive young people try to joke with one another and generally look cheerful while reporting the latest round of famines, murders, and political scandals. It is a formula for reducing the news to what Shakespeare called "a tale told by an idiot, full of sound and fury signifying nothing."

Edward R. Murrow was one of the first to see and effectively use the power of radio, and then of television, to enlighten and inform the American people about the people and events that controlled their lives. He saw television as a means to "alter and illuminate our times." During and after World War II, where his coverage of the European theater had made him the nation's most famous and respected reporter, Murrow gathered about him at CBS News perhaps the most distinguished group of correspondents in the history of journalism. (Among them were Eric Sevareid, Howard K. Smith, Charles Collingwood, and Cecil Brown.) Murrow's news broadcasts and even more his weekly public affairs programs were classics of journalistic clarity and intelligence. But the audience for his public affairs programs remained small, whereas another Murrow program, which featured the reporter engaged in trivial gossip with celebrities, mostly movie stars, was a popular success.

In 1954, Murrow made broadcasting history when he attacked Senator Joseph McCarthy on CBS. McCarthy received equal time, which he used to imply that Murrow was a communist. Although Murrow's broadcast is often credited with having marked the beginning of the end for "McCarthyism" in America, it also represented a turning point in his career and in television history. As the result of this broadcast Murrow became "controversial," therefore tainted from the standpoint of CBS, and his influence steadily declined until he quit broadcasting to join the Kennedy administration.[19]

To be sure, there have been some excellent special news broadcasts, from those done by Murrow down to the present. But perhaps too often the bland, noncontroversial aura that characterizes other TV programming influences TV news. A serious but characteristic example of this deficiency took place in 1967, when CBS decided not to broadcast live former Ambassador George F. Kennan's critical views on Vietnam before the Senate Foreign Relations Committee and instead provided viewers with a rerun of the "I Love Lucy" comedy series.[20]

An example of how television's sins by omission can lead to serious distortions of events and/or manipulation of the public can be seen in the furor that arose after the shooting down of a Korean passenger plane by the Soviet Union on September 1, 1983. When the event occurred, and for several weeks thereafter the media accepted the American government's official version of the event: The Soviets had shot down an innocent, unarmed passenger plane and then lied about it with characteristic "brutal

---

[19]See Alexander Kendrick, *Prime Time* (Boston: Little, Brown, 1969).
[20]Kendrick, p. 4.

disregard for truth and life," in the words President Reagan used to discuss the event before the United Nations. Later, in October, the press revealed that American intelligence sources had concluded that the Soviets probably had told the truth when saying that they believed that the giant jet was a spy plane involved in a hostile intrusion into sensitive Soviet territory and that this assessment of the incident was known in Washington as early as mid-September. Of course, none of this excuses a brutal action on the part of Soviet air defense, resulting in the loss of 269 innocent lives. Yet, no American television network (or spokesperson for the government) corrected the dominant impression in the minds of most Americans that the Soviets had deliberately shot down a civilian passenger liner. The implications are important, because if there is an unspoken assumption that the Soviets are capable of such a deliberate, brutal, and unnecessary act, then they are capable of anything, including perhaps starting World War III. Thus the media, rather than explaining an event, may have unduly added to a dangerous paranoia, worsening the tensions of the cold war. All this in stark contrast to the shooting down of an Iranian civilian airliner by U.S. forces in 1988. The U.S. media generally treated this as an "unfortunate mistake."

On the other hand, the media, which are nothing if not trendy, were quick to exploit the image of Soviet Premier Mikhail Gorbachev as a genial, reasonable fellow who sincerely wanted peace. After Gorbachev's historic meeting with President Reagan in the United States in December 1987, national pollsters discovered that the Soviet leader was more popular and better known among the American people than any of the leading Democratic candidates for the presidency, and only slightly less well thought of than President Reagan himself.

It should be added that television sometimes blurs the distinction between news and entertainment. Within a relatively brief period of time in the fall of 1979 three seemingly unrelated, shocking events occurred on the international scene. A group of "students" invaded the American embassy in Teheran and took 63 Americans hostage; Lord Louis Mountbatten, a British hero of World War II who had been retired from active military and political life for many years, was murdered while fishing in Ireland; and the most sacred shrine of the Muslim world at Mecca was invaded and held for several weeks by armed insurgents. What did these three events have in common? On the surface, nothing. On closer examination, however, there is a common thread. Murdering Lord Mountbatten accomplished nothing toward resolving the disputes in Northern Ireland. Obviously, his murder was designed to provoke rage and anger in the British public and to ensure maximum coverage in the mass media of the cause of the Irish revolutionaries. Taking American hostages did nothing for the Iranian people. (There was little hope from the outset that America would respond by returning the shah to Iran). Rather, it too was an act designed to provoke maximum frustration in the American people and to ensure that the world's attention would be riveted on Iran. The same can be said of the assault on Mecca: the attackers must have known that they would eventually be overwhelmed and executed.

All these events appeared to be "crazy," that is, pointless at least from the traditional view of power politics. They were not rational attempts to achieve a given national or group objective: to gain wealth or territory or political power. Rather, they were designed and executed as *media events*. The overriding objective in all these cases seems to have been to shock the world and force its attention on the cause of their perpetrators. More and more we live in a world in which the mass media do not simply "cover" stories. Stories are created so that they will be covered by mass media. Desperate acts, perhaps even including the possibility of igniting general war in an entire region, are taken to ensure a place on prime-time television and in the headlines of the world press. Sometimes the same motivation applies to happier, less bloody events. An early step in achievement of a peace treaty between Israel and Egypt came when President Anwar Sadat of Egypt indicated to an American TV interviewer that he would welcome an invitation to visit Israel.

In short, access to and control of the media have become not merely a means but an end of politics, nationally and internationally. The media no longer simply witness and report on the political life of a nation, they have actually become part of that process, their role still ill defined, but no less vital than that of the courts, Congress, or the presidency.

The effects of the media, particularly television, on political campaigns further illustrates the point. We have already discussed the growing use of preferential primaries for nominating candidates for office (see Chapter 8). These reforms have led many of us to assume that the nomination of candidates, and thus the influence on political parties, has been removed from party bosses and redistributed to the general electorate. But recent studies have suggested that, instead, journalists and the news media have emerged to make or break candidates, even during the primary campaigns.[21] (Senator Kennedy's troubles with the Chappaquiddick issue, discussed earlier, are an example of this thesis.) Thus the media seem to play a more important role in politics than do the traditional political parties. Also, parties must try to choose candidates who will have the appropriate television appearance. It is also of note that the expenditures for media exposure represent the major cost of most campaigns, and this has caused an enormous increase in campaign spending.

Despite the importance of the media, we should keep in mind the distinction between the government and the media or between politicians and reporters. Governments and politicians are directly responsible to their

[21]See James David Barber, ed., *Race for the Presidency: The Media and the Nominating Process* (Englewood Cliffs, N.J.: Prentice-Hall, 1979).

constituents, whereas the media are not. Media are private businesses, but government is the concern of all. We also should be aware of the overall influence of the media on our lives. It is worth recalling that a number of sociologists attributed to television the urban riots of the late 1960s. They believed that underemployed and poor blacks saw on television shows a style of life better than their own yet portrayed as typically American, that they were frustrated by this difference, and that they took out that frustration in riots. This may well be an exaggeration of the impact of television on social violence; nonetheless it underscores a pervasive belief that the media affect our expectations or, more precisely, our *rising* expectations. Certainly, advertisers, who sustain commercial television, radio, as well as magazines and newspapers, believe that they can convince us to want more things, whether these things are beer, cosmetics, cars, or a better life-style. Moreover, the media have likely had an impact on family relations, sexual roles, and race relations, among other things. The success of the magazine *Ms.* is illustrative. Although it cannot be considered part of the *mass* media, *Ms.* has been a very successful magazine aimed at a selected audience. Its message is the liberation of women; it has a sophisticated format; and it has many advertisers. *Ebony* magazine, directed chiefly to blacks, is likewise successful and important. These journals affect the views and expectations of important segments of the population.

Finally, we come to an interesting paradox. The past half century in America has led to a revolution in both the quality and quantity of political information available to the American public. Never before have so many people been bombarded by so much information, so many pictures and opinions and "inside dope." Contrary to what might have been expected, the result has been a steady decline in the percentage of Americans who bother to vote or who seem either well informed or passionate about political choices. At the same time, political leaders themselves have seemed to become less interesting, less articulate, and more slavishly devoted to the public opinion polls. A common complaint about the 1988 presidential campaign, for example, was summed up by the observation that the leading candidates were dashing to and fro across the nation, "stirring up apathy." For all its enormous coverage and technical complexity, its wealth of pseudoexcitement, the net impression left by the mass media of American politics was of the bland leading the bland.

The media cannot be fairly charged with the sole, or even the primary, responsibility for the enormous gap that seems to have developed between the leaders of American democracy and the people. But by too often reducing politics to another form of the show biz gossip business, the media have dealt the nation a serious blow.

The media penetrate most of the nooks and crannies of our everyday lives and have an overall social influence as well as a significant political influence. Although some critics fear that the media have begun to direct our lives, dictate our politics, and promote the views only of advertisers, we suggest that the American people can learn to use the media intelligently and skeptically. For interested, informed, and relatively enlightened readers or viewers, the media represent a source of information and an opportunity to become more aware of their government, society, and world that are unequaled in history.

12

Economics: The Prevailing Smell of Money

• Rich Man, Poor Man •

• Capitalism •

• Socialism •

• Social Democracy •

• The Best of Times, the Worst of Times •

• Welfare for the Rich or the Poor? •

• Is Less More? •

• Politics and the Economy •

• The New International Economy •

> What is all this growing love of pageantry, this effusive loyalty, this officious rising and uncovering at a wave from a flag or a blast from a brass band? Imperialism? Not a bit of it. Obsequiousness, servility, cupidity roused by the prevailing smell of money.
>
> George Bernard Shaw
> *Preface to Man and Superman*
>
> There is no free lunch.
>
> Bernard Baruch

The fundamental fact of economic life in the second half of the twentieth century has been an explosion of wealth unprecedented in the history of the world. Prior to World War II, there was only one country where a majority of the people enjoyed what today would be considered a decent standard of living—the United States. Even in the United States at that time, fully one-third of the nation was described by President Franklin Roosevelt as too poor to afford decent food, housing, or clothing. There were, of course, rich people even in those bleak times. But they were a tiny handful. There are probably more millionaires today in the city of Zurich, Switzerland (where one in every ten persons is said to be a millionaire) than existed in the entire world during the 1930s. The very rich were indeed so few and so special that their names and photos were known worldwide by school-children, newspaper readers, and radio listeners. Today there are billionaires who live in comfortable anonymity. By 1986, 18 of the 24 members of the OECD (Organization for Economic Cooperation and Development) had an average per capita income of more than $10,000, hence qualifying as members of a "rich man's club" according to *The Economist* magazine.[1] In addition, nonmembers with rapidly growing economies like South Korea, Singapore, and Taiwan were approaching the point where they would be as affluent as most OECD members. Indeed, some economists estimated that, at present growth rates, South Korea would have a higher per capita income than Great Britain, France, or Italy by the end of the century. In addition, there were the newly rich Middle Eastern nations, floating on a sea of oil, with per capita incomes far above that of the United States.

These rich two dozen or so nations account for less than 20 percent of the world's population but produce more than two-thirds of the world's wealth. Apart from a few countries whose wealth is derived from a single source—such as petroleum—the "rich man's club" members share certain characteristics: they practice relatively "free market" economics, although several

[1] *The Economist*, January 30, 1988, p. 58.

have a long history of socialist governments (see the discussion of these terms below). They have literate populations; most are relatively free and democratic societies; they have stable governments; and they are scientifically sophisticated. Many of the other 140 or so nations of the world continue to struggle with the age-old problems of poverty, illiteracy, disease, and unstable or oppressive governments. An average child fortunate enough to be born into almost any of the world's affluent nations can reasonably expect a long and healthy life, abundant food, decent housing, sufficient educational opportunity, personal freedom, and various other amenities that help make life more than an endless struggle for survival. For the rest, life remains, in the words of seventeenth-century English philosopher Thomas Hobbes, "nasty, brutish and short."

The United States, although no longer the richest nation in terms of per capita income, can take pride in being the largest and most influential affluent society. Ironically, although we early demonstrated the possibility of creating an economy in which the majority of the population could share in general and widespread abundance, we are one of the very few members of "the rich man's club" to tolerate poverty-stricken slums, high crime rates, and other familiar, painful maladies more characteristic of Third World than developed countries.

Yet it is not an exaggeration to assert that the past half century has seen an economic miracle come to pass in the Western world that seems likely to change the course of history. We know that poverty need not be the inevitable fate of most of the world's inhabitants. Indeed, we have a pretty good idea of how it can be eliminated, and in the case of the "rich man's club" we have various models of how this may be accomplished. Some people would dispute this, particularly in Third World countries. They continue to insist, and perhaps believe (although with diminishing conviction), that wealthy nations grow rich by exploiting the resources of their poorer neighbors. Yet former Third World countries, such as South Korea, Taiwan, Singapore, and more recently China and several Middle Eastern states, which have maintained a close tie to the affluent West, have in fact prospered and developed. Those with the least contacts with the West (Albania, Ethiopia, and Mozambique come to mind) remain wrapped in poverty (and in some instances in debilitating civil war).

Although exploitation of the poor and weak by the rich and strong remains a fact of international life, there is growing awareness that the path to international as well as domestic wealth lies in sharing affluence rather than seeking to impoverish one's neighbors. Just as the United States provided the economic engine that pulled much of Europe, Japan, and other parts of Asia from poverty to prosperity in the past few decades, so the rich two dozen may ultimately provide the model and the means for transforming the economies of the Third World. The poor countries are aware of this and, political rhetoric notwithstanding, are in many instances seeking to modernize themselves and change their political and economic ways. Among these are the two communist giants, China and the Soviet Union.[2] Since setting out on the path of modernization in the 1970s, China has undergone an economic revolution that has produced enormous benefits for its 1 billion people. Today China, with an annual growth rate of 9 percent, is the world's fastest growing economy and, if the present pace can be maintained, it may become an economic superpower in the next century. Meantime, the erstwhile arch-adversary of Western, capitalist democracies, the Soviet Union, has also decided it can no longer remain isolated from the growing power and wealth of the world's most successful economies. Under General Secretary Gorbachev, the Soviet Union launched a program called "*perestroika*" (reconstruction), an attempt to transform the sluggish Soviet economy. Although far from capitulating to capitalism, the Soviets have embraced such hitherto heretical capitalist notions as production for profit; encouraging limited private enterprise; rewarding the efficient and firing inefficient workers and managers; a much greater degree of "*glasnost*" or openness, with respect to the media and the public; arms reductions (partly to redirect investment into economic growth rather than arms production); and a host of other measures hardly reflective of the hardened Marxism–Leninism about which we used to be so concerned. The Soviets even applied for membership in the General Agreement on Tariffs and Trade (GATT) and offered to form partnerships between Soviet and Western corporations.

It is too early to judge the ultimate fate of Gorbachev's attempts to reform the Soviet economy (the Soviet people have not been overly enthusiastic, nor have many bureaucrats, who are being told to produce or lose their jobs). What does seem clear, however, is that a certain idea has permeated the consciousness of many if not most of the world's leaders. The idea is that it is no longer necessary for nations to be poor, and a path from poverty to prosperity has been cleared for those societies with the political will to walk down it.

For the United States too, the second half of the twentieth century has been a period of spectacular economic growth that has transformed the lives of Americans. Most of the people now at or approaching old age in this country were born and spent their childhood years in a United States that was characterized by massive unemployment (during the Great Depression), when it was common for people to spend years looking for a job, any job, which in those days meant not sending out resumés but standing in long lines hoping to be chosen among hundreds of applicants. Most people lived in small, rented apartments or rural towns. Such amenities as a telephone, a refrigerator, and a reliable automobile were symbols of success and uncommon prosperity. Very few could afford the luxury of travel. About 5 percent of young people of college age could afford any form of higher education.

[2]See Marshall I. Goldman and Merle Goldman, "Soviet and Chinese Economic Reform," *Foreign Affairs; America and the World, 1987/88*: Vol. 66, no. 3, 551–573.

Visits to a doctor or dentist were a rarity. Americans were thinner then, not because they were dieting or jogging, but because they ate less. Steak and chicken were luxuries consumed on special occasions. A visit to a restaurant was an event. Old age, for most, was an economic disaster that left people poor and dependent. Today most Americans live in relatively spacious houses equipped with an array of machines that keep us warm in winter and cool in summer, wash our clothes, store and cook our food, and entertain us with music, drama, and a flood of information, much of it in the form of advertising that urges us to strive for even greater heights of comfort and well-being and more elevated standards of consumption. Half of our college-age young are pursuing higher education. Six million Americans visit Europe each year. Many Americans now live in affluent suburbs close to shopping malls and supermarkets packed with goods and foods that are readily affordable. Two of our great national preoccupations are dieting and exercise, because we consume so much with so little expenditure of human energy. Most older people enjoy a comfortable and economically secure retirement. Everyday life has been transformed.

These changes did not occur accidentally or through some amazing streak of good fortune. In many respects they are the results of concrete economic policies and programs usually brought about after intense political struggle. Much of contemporary economic well-being can be traced to programs initiated during the New Deal era in the 1930s. New Dealers dreamed of an America of "garden towns" that would be made of neat little houses, each with a plot of land for gardening, of shopping arcades and parks with community recreation centers—all connected by nonstop superhighways— not so very different in concept from the reality of today's suburban America.

The general and widespread prosperity that occurred with mobilization for World War II provided another enormous stimulant to the economy. Among its attendant and probably unplanned benefits was that millions of blacks and women—hitherto considered unsuited for good jobs and decent pay—were pressed into the nation's economic mainstream by wartime labor shortages. The postwar G.I. Bill, providing homes and low-cost housing to millions of veterans, was still another milestone. The cold war and the space race of the next few decades pumped still more dollars into the American economy. The steady rise of affluence continued with only a few relatively minor interludes of inflation and recession until the 1970s. Then, for reasons which economists continue to dispute, there was a sudden and dramatic inflation that saw interest rates rise, housing prices soar, and an economy that seemed out of control. The election of Ronald Reagan to the presidency in 1980 was, at least in part, due to the "general malaise"—to use President Carter's term—that seemed to be rooted in a sense that old answers and economic prescriptions simply were not working anymore. One of the consequences has been an important debate and reevaluation of economic theory and economic policies, which we discuss below.

Rich Man, Poor Man

Scottish essayist Thomas Carlyle once called economics the "dismal science." Carlyle had been reading a treatise on economics and population growth, published by Thomas Malthus at the very end of the eighteenth century, that undertook to prove by means of mathematics and logic that efforts to improve the lot of the poor in Europe were doomed to failure.[3] As we have seen, the eighteenth century was generally a time of optimism in both Europe and America, an optimism rooted in the belief that through the use of reason and the relatively new insights and tools created by the natural sciences, it would be possible to create a more just and bountiful society.

There was a belief that science, the spread of education and knowledge, and the political liberation of the Western world from many ancient forms of tyranny over people's minds would result in a better, happier, and more productive future. European intellectuals of that era wrote the first dictionaries and encyclopedias, and crusading reformers created hospitals for the sick and penitentiaries for the wayward.[4] In America, thinkers like Benjamin Franklin concerned themselves not merely with politics and abstract philosophy but also with paving and lighting the streets of American cities, organizing fire departments and public libraries, inventing better stoves for housewives, and exploring the mysteries of that arcane and powerful but then useless new force called electricity.

The publication of Malthus's essay did not, of course, bring all such activity to a halt. But it had a sobering effect on many intellectuals, particularly in Europe. Malthus argued that the universe was arranged in a manner that made the idea of progress simply a short-term delusion. Improving the conditions of life for the masses, he asserted, must inevitably lead to an exploding birthrate. Because human beings increase their numbers geometrically, whereas the earth, the ultimate source of wealth, is finite, population growth must inevitably outrun economic progress, with the end result that "progress" will sooner or later lead to famine, war, and even greater misery for humankind. The logic of Malthusian economics was that it was better to leave the "poor and wretched of the earth" to their misery than to tamper with "natural law."

Until fairly recently, experience seemed to prove Malthus wrong. The world's population, for example, has grown from approximately one billion to about four and a half billion in the past century alone. This phenomenal growth has been accompanied, at least in most of the Western world and in

---

[3]Thomas Malthus. "An Essay on the Principle of Population As It Affects the Future Improvements of Society," 1789.

[4]The penitentiary was an eighteenth-century idea. It was conceived as a place in which criminals could be made "penitent" for their sins, rather than as a place of punishment.

such nations as the Soviet Union, China, and Japan, by an improvement in the material standards of life for most people. The "underdeveloped" world, rather than reject economic growth, has usually tried to follow in the path set by the richer nations.

But in one form or another the ghost of Malthus continues to haunt the fog-shrouded castle of economics, "Making night hideous; and we fools of nature. . . ." Malthus's ghost appears in the pages of books by a number of prominent ecologists, such as Paul Ehrlich (author of *The Population Bomb* and *The End of Affluence*), who warn that we are destroying the very environment that has sustained us. Malthus's chilling spirit, in a sense, hovered over all those Americans who impatiently waited in gas lines for a chance to pay almost any price for a few gallons of that increasingly precious fluid that kept their cars rolling a few more miles. Or his spirit may be seen in the steadily declining percentage of Americans, particularly young Americans, who can realistically expect to buy their own homes, or in the cold facts and statistics that emanate from various government bureaus, that tell of increasing U.S. dependence on foreign energy sources, goods, and capital; or of rising illiteracy rates, and standards of education that place us near the bottom of modern, industrialized societies; of acid rain and persistent pollution; or perhaps most ominously, of the depletion of the protective ozone layer surrounding the earth, caused by human-made chlorofluorocarbons[5]; that is, economic, environmental, energy, and educational concerns continue to raise questions about the most appropriate government policies to follow regarding the economy.

Before examining current economic, energy, and environmental issues, however, we shall define certain fundamental terms that dominate much of the public debate about these issues. Broadly speaking, economic "systems" exist among the developed nations of the world in the second half of the twentieth century: capitalism, socialism, and social democracy.[6] None of these systems is "pure." For example, there is some free enterprise in the Soviet Union. There are many nominally "socialist" (that is, publicly owned) institutions in the United States, like the army and the navy or the public schools. But most goods and services offered in the United States are produced by private companies and corporations. Thus we may speak of the Soviet Union as a socialist state and the United States as a capitalist state, although in this imperfect world, neither is a perfect example of either socialist or capitalist ideals and ideas.

[5]An international team of researchers headed by the National Aeronautics and Space Administration reported in March 1988 that the ozone layer had been depleted by over 2 percent *since 1969*, a loss twice as high as previously believed by scientists.

[6]Robert L. Heilbroner, *The Worldly Philosophers* (New York: Simon & Schuster, 1961) presents an excellent and highly readable introduction to the usually difficult subject of economic theory.

Capitalism

Capitalism, a complex concept referred to as *free enterprise*[7] by those who wish to stress its superiority to other, competing economic systems, is often confused with democracy or representative government. There is good historical reason for such confusion because the growth of free political institutions has frequently been associated with free trade. Democratic political institutions and traditions developed in France, in England, and in America side by side with capitalism, and hence it is not surprising that many people regard the two as inseparable. But strictly speaking, the two are not the same thing, because capitalism, like socialism, is primarily an economic system. *Democracy* and *dictatorship*, on the other hand, are political terms. Thus there are avowedly socialist states—Sweden and Norway, for example—that boast a highly developed political democracy, including such democratic characteristics as the multiparty system, free speech, a free press, and freedom from arbitrary arrest and imprisonment. On the other hand, there have been dictatorships, such as Nazi Germany or fascist Italy or Japan, in which the economic system was at least nominally capitalist.

Capitalism begins with the premise that humans are naturally acquisitive and competitive creatures, fundamentally motivated by self-interest. In seeking to gratify these instincts, people trade with others, hoping thereby to make a profit, that is, a net gain. The result of this trade will be the creation of a market. Because many individuals and companies (which in theory are simply groups of individuals banding together to trade more efficiently) will participate in this market, competing with one another as both buyers and sellers, those who produce the best goods at the cheapest prices will thrive, and the less efficient producers will gradually disappear. Thus the market is effectively governed by the law of supply and demand.

Freedom in the marketplace (freedom to buy and/or sell at the best price, terms, and conditions one can wangle) is the heart of capitalist economics. For the capitalist, profit is the reward for economic wisdom and efficiency and for having the foresight, the ability, or the luck to produce goods that other people want at a price they are willing to pay. To a capitalist, profit is good and healthy, the prime stimulant to economic activity and the driving

[7]There are distinctions that can be made between free enterprise and capitalism. Simply defined, free enterprise refers to the freedom of private individuals and businesses to compete in buying and selling goods and services without government regulation. Capitalism is likewise usually associated with a free market, but it also refers to an economic system with private and corporate ownership of the means of production and distribution, in which there is an accumulation of profits (thus capital) to be used for reinvestment into further production. Moreover, corporate ownership tends to become concentrated; thus large corporations or "conglomerates" frequently develop and may dominate the market even to the point of monopolizing it. Finally, capitalists may benefit by certain government regulations (as tariffs to protect a domestic manufacturer against foreign competition).

The Pursuit of Happiness

force that makes capitalist economies more productive and creative than their socialist rivals. Profit also provides the wherewithal for future investment to make the business enterprise larger, more productive and efficient, and hence even more profitable. Moreover, it is the emphasis on the free play of the market—that is, the myriad of individual and group decisions to buy and sell, invest or not invest, produce or not produce—as contrasted with economic decisions being made by the direction of the government, that sets capitalism apart from systems that emphasize planning. In 1776, Adam Smith, a philosopher and economist from Scotland, published the now classic work on the market system, *The Wealth of Nations*.

Proponents of capitalism argue that this system of economics is superior to its rivals because

1. Capitalism, particularly in the United States, has provided more people with more goods and services (hence a higher standard of living) than any other system has.
2. An economic system that honors and rewards private initiative and ownership of goods is conducive to personal freedom, free political institutions, and cultural and artistic freedom.
3. A system based on the private ownership of property is in keeping with human nature, and hence under it, more people will be happy and productive than under a system that compels them to practice an altruism that in fact can be imposed only bureaucratically and that would rob most people of any incentive to excel.

Critics of capitalism, on the other hand, contend that

1. Capitalism makes it impossible to approach the ideals of justice and equality for all people because those few who are able to amass great wealth will inevitably control the lives of those who do not.
2. The competitive ethic makes it impossible to build a society based on cooperation and neighborly love. Greed and selfishness dominate capitalist societies.
3. Although in theory capitalism is based on equal competition, in practice capitalist economies inevitably develop huge corporations that crush their competitors and control the market, manipulating prices and the flow of goods to their own advantage and thus robbing the general public.
4. Free, democratic government in capitalist states is an illusion, just one more variety of the consumer fraud that is normal in capitalist ethics. In advanced capitalist states like the United States and Japan, the government is in fact nothing more than "the executive committee of the capitalist class." Although professing to serve all the people, it acts solely in the interest of the corporate and financial elite.

Socialism

Although theories and forms of socialist thought have existed for many centuries, nineteenth-century German philosopher Karl Marx codified the principles of modern socialism and was the creator of communist economics. While a refugee from his native Germany living in London, Marx, a relatively obscure, ailing, and impoverished revolutionary, struggled to support himself and his family from sporadic earnings as a writer (including a brief term of employment as a commentator on the American Civil War for the *New York Tribune*) and with loans and gifts from his friend and collaborator, Friedrich Engels. Marx spent much of his time haunting the London libraries, studying not only economics but also history, philosophy, and virtually every other area of human culture. As a result, he created a body of ideas that has had an enormous and steadily growing influence on the course of history in the ensuing years. Two of the world's three great powers, China and the Soviet Union, today affirm that Marxism is the basis for the political and social organization of their societies. At the present moment, perhaps half the earth's population lives under governments at least formally committed to Marxist ideology. The triumphant sweep of Marx's ideas, particularly since the Russian Revolution of 1917, has had few parallels in human history. What are the essential Marxist ideas?[8]

1. *Scientific socialism.* Although socialist thought was not original with Marx, he was the first to attempt to build a coherent economic system out of socialist idealism. Using an intellectual formula borrowed from German philosopher Hegel (thesis versus antithesis equals synthesis), Marx proclaimed that he had discovered the key to history. For just as Newton's laws explained the movements of the planets and as Darwin explained the course of biological evolution, so Marxists believe they have discovered the principles that scientifically explain the course of human history. Marx rejected the idealism of earlier socialist writers, who essentially staked their hopes on persuading people that cooperation was better than competition, and attempted to prove scientifically that the triumph of Marxist socialism was inevitable. This sense of certainty about the ultimate victory of their cause has helped imbue Marxists with a sense of revolutionary zeal—comparable perhaps to the zeal of the early Christian martyrs, who were certain that they were destined to go to heaven—that has proved a powerful political weapon.

2. *Economic determinism.* Human history, Marx declared, is controlled not by ideas or ideals or spiritual, religious, or cultural values but by the "prevailing means of production," that is, economics. Human beings, Marx said, are economic animals. That is, before they are liberal or conser-

---

[8]Although Karl Marx's *Das Kapital* is the definitive work of Marxist economic theory, a shorter, more interesting, and less forbidding insight into Marxism can be gained by reading *The Manifesto of the Communist Party*, published by Marx and Engels in 1848.

vative, Catholic, Protestant, or Jewish, they are creatures who struggle for food, clothing, and shelter. The struggle for the necessities of life precedes, defines, and controls all other human behavior. It is not people's creeds that decide what they do, it is how they earn their livelihood. Thus the key to understanding human history can be found in what people must do to secure wealth, for in the long run, economic interests determine behavior, hence "economic determinism." Consequently, those forces in a society that control the means of production and the distribution of goods (the landed aristocracy in the Middle Ages, corporation capitalists in the modern Western world) are not only the wealthiest members of society and its upper classes, but they also determine the culture of society and dominate its social and political life to their own advantage.

3. *Class conflict.* Whereas the capitalists see economic struggle being waged by individuals in competition with other individuals, Marx saw people banding together into social classes. Throughout history, Marx stated, we are presented with a continuing drama: master against slave, lord against serf—and in the capitalist stage of production, owner against worker. Everywhere the picture is essentially the same: a small minority of powerful people band together into an upper class for the purpose of exploiting a vast and miserable lower class. The property-owning class owns virtually everything, including the government, which acts as their agent; the propertyless masses own nothing—not even the fruits of their own labor. Because this arrangement is inherently unjust, there is certain to be conflict between the privileged few and the impoverished many. Sometimes this conflict is half-hidden, as in labor-management "negotiations"; sometimes it flares into open combat, as in a strike or a food riot. But it always exists behind the veil of ruling-class propaganda and management's "employee relations."

From the Marxist standpoint, democratic politics is essentially a fraudulent con game designed to give the workers an illusion of power and to divert attention from their true condition of dependence on the ruling class. Religion too is "the opiate of the people." However, despite the efforts of the capitalists to conceal the reality of power from the people, ultimately the workers will cease to be fooled and will rise up in revolution, a revolution that *must* prove victorious because the workers are the immense majority.

4. *The theory of capitalist crisis.* Because all capitalist states are rooted in the exploitation of the majority by the minority, they contain inherent "contradictions." These contradictions must manifest themselves in periodic crises, such as depressions, wars, and civil conflict. With the passage of time, growing injustice and exploitation will result in greater and greater crises until the system itself faces collapse. At this point, modern Marxists argue, the capitalists will give up trying to fool the workers and will resort to naked force. Thus there will usually be a fascist interlude between the collapse of a capitalist state and the birth of a socialist society.

5. *The greatest good for the greatest number.* Although the Marxists

agree with the capitalists that business takes place as the result of a desire for profit, they regard the profit motive as inherently evil rather than as a force for good. To a capitalist, profits imply greater production and investment; hence they are necessary and useful to society. Marx saw profit as inherently unjust, derived through the monopolistic robbery of consumers and the exploitation of workers and by "grinding the faces of the poor." The ideal communist state would not allow profits to exist. Goods and services would be produced for the welfare of the whole community. Thus houses would be built because people need shelter, and the question of whether or not people could afford to pay for these houses would be irrelevant. The economic watchword of such a society, Marx proclaimed, would be "from each according to his ability; to each according to his need." (It should be reiterated here that recently the world's two great Marxist giants, China and the Soviet Union, have veered sharply away from classical Marxism, apparently because of dissatisfaction with the pace of economic development under rigid communist orthodoxy. Both have moved toward the Western economic models, seeking closer economic cooperation with their erstwhile capitalist enemies while introducing such previously disdained practices as production for profit and decentralized planning. Each insists that it has not and will not abandon communism, but their practices and policies suggest otherwise. In China, for example, a stock exchange has even been established.)

6. *The dictatorship of the proletariat.* Marxists foresee that during a period of transition from one economic and social system to another, there will be great confusion and struggle. The old ruling class will seek to reestablish its power (through counterrevolution). Many persons educated under the old bourgeois (business) system will be unable or unwilling to change to the new way of life. Hence, during this interval between capitalism and socialism, there will be a need to establish a temporary dictatorship of the proletariat (or working class). Marx was somewhat vague about how this dictatorship would work. His theory was further elaborated by the Russian revolutionary leader, V. I. Lenin. According to Lenin the Communist party, which is the party of the working class and the party that understands scientific socialism, is charged by history with leading the dictatorship of the proletariat. As "the vanguard of the working class," communists, who may represent only a small minority of the total population, must take the responsibility for directing the state, guiding the transition to true socialism, reeducating the people, and creating the new "socialist man."

Proponents of Marxist socialism believe that their system will prevail because

1. It is more "scientific" than capitalism and hence is destined to win out over a system based on superstition and ignorance.
2. It will provide a more just and equal way of life.

3. As socialist states, unlike capitalist states, are not engaged in competition for world markets and resources, there will be no reason for international war.
4. Under socialism, human values, culture, and the arts, will flourish because the artist and the intellectual will no longer be subservient to the wealthy. Art will become a "weapon of the people."
5. Economic distortions such as inflation and unemployment, caused by the inherent problems of capitalism, will not occur in socialist states.
6. Marxism, unlike other economic systems, offers a way for poorer, developing nations, lacking a large capital base, to avoid dependence on rich nations and to organize, plan, and consolidate what resources they do have for the purpose of modernizing and industrializing.
7. The socialist practices followed in the Soviet Union and China since their respective revolutions have resulted in incredible economic improvement for these countries as a whole, and for individual citizens as well. Although there are current economic problems, all nations face economic challenges, and given the low base at which both the Soviet Union and China began, their economic growth, improved prosperity, and general progress has been remarkable.

Critics of Marxism, on the other hand, argue that

1. History has proved Marx wrong. Capitalist states have not destroyed one another but are stronger and more prosperous than ever. The working classes in most Western capitalist societies have not been ground down by the capitalists to steadily deeper misery and deprivation but, on the contrary, have enjoyed rising incomes and more and more benefits (such as private autos, television sets, guaranteed pensions, and health care). In fact, Western Europeans and Americans enjoy a far higher standard of living today than do the people of the Soviet Union, seventy years after the Bolshevik Revolution.
2. The "temporary" dictatorship of the proletariat becomes the permanent dictatorship of the Communist party bureaucracy, which becomes, in effect, a new ruling class. In no communist country is there any sign that the party dictatorship is preparing to yield control of the state to the people through democratic and free elections, even though all communist states have constitutions that proclaim this to be their objective.
3. Socialist states are no less warlike and aggressive than are their capitalist counterparts. China and the Soviet Union are just as apt to go to war as any capitalist countries, and the Soviet Union today is as imperialistic and aggressive as was any nineteenth-century colonial power.
4. Marxist states dare not give their people the freedom to speak, to write, or to criticize the government. They wall in their people, will

not allow free emigration, and maintain prison camps and "psychiatric hospitals," in which dissenters are persecuted in a fashion that outrages any person with a sense of human decency and dignity. Minorities (such as Jews or Lithuanians in the Soviet Union) who wish to preserve their own cultural identity are persecuted.

5. The materialist interpretation of human history, which is the foundation of Marxism, is simply an inadequate explanation of the whole range and depth of human experience, in that it ignores or diminishes the spiritual, psychological, and cultural roots of human beings.

6. Seventy years after the introduction of the socialist system in the Soviet Union and four decades after it became the dominant mode of production in China and Eastern Europe, most of the communist world remains poor and backward compared with the United States, Western Europe, and Japan. In countries like Poland, the failure of the communist system has led to open rebellion by masses of the very workers that communism professes to serve—a rebellion contained only by the threat of massive Soviet military intervention if "counter-revolutionary" forces go too far. Evidence suggests that as a system for producing and distributing goods, "scientific socialism" simply does not work.

Social Democracy

There is an alternative to capitalism and socialism that has emerged in the twentieth century and characterizes much of Western Europe. It is variously referred to as the *welfare state, democratic socialism*, and *social democracy*. In essence, it is a mixture of what its proponents believe are the most desirable features of both capitalism and socialism. States that have embraced democratic socialism—such as Sweden, Norway, Holland and, to a lesser extent, Great Britain, Israel, Italy, France, and West Germany—are characterized by a democratic political and social life, including respect for most of the freedoms encompassed by the first Ten Amendments to the U.S. Constitution, plus a substantial degree of free enterprise operating side by side with public ownership of many basic industries, such as transportation, oil, the manufacture of automobiles, and coal and steel. A part of this system is the welfare state, under which the government takes responsibility for managing the economy and guaranteeing employment, health care, and pension programs for all.

In this country, social democracy is often associated with John Maynard Keynes,[9] an English economist, whose book *The General Theory of Em-*

---

[9]Strictly speaking, Keynesianism is not the same as social democracy. Simply stated, Keynesianism maintains that the government can use fiscal (taxing and spending) policies and monetary (banking and interest) policies to stimulate or cool off the economy.

ployment, Interest and Money[10] had had considerable influence on twentieth-century economic thought. Keynes traveled to Germany after World War I as part of a commission of British economic experts to help reorganize the shattered economies of the various nations of Western Europe. He returned home convinced that the victorious allies had made a mistake in seeking to impose a vengeful peace on the defeated Germans and to give themselves a competitive advantage as the result of their military triumph. His book argued that what the Allies had failed to grasp was that economically, Europe was a single community and that Germany was one of its most important members. If the German economy was deliberately weakened, the Allies would also suffer. When the Depression came, many, including U.S. President Franklin D. Roosevelt, were willing to listen to Keynes. Keynes proposed what was then considered a heretical notion for resolving the crisis. Nations should seek to spend their way out of poverty (rather than trying to save by cutting back on expenditures, as many were doing), if necessary on credit. The Depression, Keynes believed, had been caused by *too much saving*, thereby creating a lack of purchasing power; hence it could be remedied only by a governmental spending spree.[11]

Keynes's ideas were reflected in the general New Deal assault on the Depression and even more directly in the economic policies adopted by the nations of Scandinavia. World War II drove still another lesson home to many European and American economists. Nazi Germany, mobilizing for war, was able to achieve full employment and a generally rising standard of living for its people (at least until well into the war).[12] There was little or no unemployment or economic deprivation. In the United States, too, there was general prosperity during the years of World War II. Why couldn't a nation's economy be as prosperous in peacetime as it was in times of war?

In Western Europe, many states undertook to accomplish this. They set out to reduce or eliminate poverty and insecurity and to provide a new level of prosperity for their people. To a considerable extent they succeeded. In the United States too, an "affluent society" was created, but here it was based more on the production of goods for private consumption, such as autos and TV sets, plus enormous spending for defense. (One study estimated that "military spending never exceeded 1 percent of the gross national product before World War I." By 1970 it was about 10 percent of the total GNP.[13])

By the late 1970s, social democracy had become the dominant economic

---

[10]Keynes wrote to English dramatist George Bernard Shaw upon completion of his manuscript, "I have written a book . . . which will revolutionize the way the world thinks about economic problems." Quoted in Heilbroner, p. 234.

[11]Heilbroner, p. 237.

[12]John Kenneth Galbraith, *Money* (Boston: Houghton Mifflin, 1975), pp. 225–226.

[13]Michael Reich and David Fenkelhor, "Capitalism and the Military Industrial Complex: The Obstacles to Conversion," in David Mermelstein, ed., *Economics: Mainstream Readings and Radical Critiques*, 2nd ed. (New York: Random House, 1973), pp. 181–192.

system in Western Europe and was playing a steadily larger role in what most regarded as the earth's last bastion of capitalism: the United States. Even President Nixon, a lifelong voice for conservative business corporations in the United States, declared midway through his administration, "I am a Keynesian."[14]

Proponents of democratic socialism pointed out that in states like the Scandinavian countries and West Germany, productivity levels had risen steadily and that the per capita income in most of these nations had about equaled and in some cases exceeded that of the United States. There was, strictly speaking, no dire poverty in these lands anymore, no sprawling slums, no class largely excluded from the economic mainstream and struggling to obtain sufficient food or pay for decent shelter. Unemployment was minimal, far below that in the United States, and there was medical care for all. (And by such standards as the infant mortality rate, there was better medical care than most Americans could get at any price.) All this had been done without purges or the destruction of fundamental property rights, such as the right to own a home or to go into business for oneself. (Indeed, the percentage of people, relative to the total population, engaged in their own businesses was higher in most of the Scandinavian states than in the United States.) Finally, it was still possible for some people to become very rich.

But the welfare state had not achieved economic utopia. There were many who found the system oppressive for a variety of reasons. Perhaps the most persistent and serious problem afflicting those states committed to democratic socialism was inflation. For reasons not entirely understood, inflation tended to hold at or below a level of about 5 percent annually, considered by most economists to be troublesome but bearable. In the mid-1970s, however, inflation rates suddenly began to soar throughout the noncommunist world, perhaps touched off by a decline of confidence in the U.S. dollar, stemming from the Vietnam debacle, and aggravated by an oil embargo and then large increases in oil prices imposed by Arab states as a consequence of the 1973 Arab–Israeli War. Inflation rates in some of the economically weaker Western nations, such as Great Britain and Italy, soared to 25 percent and even 30 percent annually, reaching about half that in even the strongest economies. (In Israel, a welfare state, inflation soared to 100 percent in 1979.) At these rates, inflation threatened to destroy the economic and social gains made by Western Europe in the 30 years since the economic and social gains made by Western Europe in the 30 years since the Marshall Plan helped bring about recovery from World War II.

Another major burden of the welfare-state economic system is very high taxes. In return for "cradle-to-grave" security for all, productive citizens of

[14]James Tobin and Leonard Ross, "Living with Inflation," *New York Review of Books*, May 6, 1971, pp. 23–26.

the welfare state usually pay a larger portion of their income in taxes, and the rich often pay very high percentages.

Finally, an argument often heard in the United States is that life in the welfare states, such as Sweden and Denmark, has become drab, boring, and colorless because the incentive of people to work hard and make more money has been destroyed. President Eisenhower once ventured the opinion that the high suicide rates typical of Scandinavian nations were attributable to the fact that people were unhappy about having too much security. Scandinavians replied that perhaps the real reason they killed themselves more was because they killed one another less often than did Americans.

By the late 1970s, Great Britain's welfare state, which had been nurtured under both the Labor and Conservative parties, seemed to be an exception to the general improvement and growth of European economies. Racked by frequent strikes, poor management, and low productivity, Great Britain's economy was in decline with respect to its ability to compete with other industrialized nations. A low point was reached when London was forced to borrow funds from the International Monetary Fund, a world bank established by the rich nations primarily to finance economic development in the Third World. The English people turned to the Conservative party and in 1979 elected Margaret Thatcher prime minister. Thatcher proposed a rigorous dose of austerity and free-market economics to cure the nation's ills. As was true for the programs of her ideological soul mate in Washington, Ronald Reagan, Thatcher's programs first produced sharp recession, unemployment, and misery, particularly for the poor. But then began a steady recovery. The British economy has flourished. The public has responded to the upsurge in prosperity and pride by reelecting Thatcher twice, making her one of the longest-serving prime ministers in English history. Thatcher's successes have clearly influenced the rest of Europe. In West Germany, conservatives dominated politics and economic policy in the 1980s, and in France, a socialist president, François Mitterrand, actually moved his government more and more in free-market directions; Mitterrand was reelected overwhelmingly in 1988.

The Best of Times, the Worst of Times

When the stock market collapse of October 1987 struck, most people wondered if this was the begining of a 1929-style depression. The danger was (and perhaps still is) that the crash would set off a chain reaction of panic and fear starting in the financial community, then spreading throughout the economies of the world. In their efforts to reassure people, and themselves, that this would not happen, Wall Street gurus and government officials hit on a common theme: 1987 did not portend another 1929 because we had learned the lessons of that painful era. Now banks were regulated and deposits were insured by the government. The Federal Reserve System would increase the supply of money and lower interest rates to provide plenty of money to keep the economy going (the opposite of what was done after the 1929 crash). Finally, the economy of 1987, unlike that of 1929, had strong governmental support in the form of Social Security payments, defense expenditures, unemployment insurance, and more. Keynesianism, recently in some disrepute, was turned to as the best and surest defense in an hour of greatest need. That the market collapse of 1987 did not produce a major economic disaster is evidence that Keynes's prescriptions—for all their problems and detractors—still worked.

Economics is not an exact science and probably never will be, because its subject is human behavior. As Harvard economist John Kenneth Galbraith has frequently pointed out, if anyone could predict with certainty the behavior of markets, the trend in interest rates, and the precise effect of this or that economic policy, that person could quickly and easily become immensely rich and would in short time control most of the world's wealth. But to say that economists do not know everything is not the same as saying that they know nothing. In fact, history suggests that economists can and do help politicians achieve economic goals. In the decades that followed World War II, most Western nations resolved to keep unemployment to a minimum and to improve the material conditions of the average citizen. This was done not so much out of altruism or love for the common citizen but because two world wars and innumerable revolutions had convinced political leaders that unemployed and impoverished people are a form of social dynamite threatening the political and social fabric of a nation. As a consequence, by the late 1960s unemployment in Europe, for example, was negligible, whereas 5 percent in the United States was considered high.

In the past decade, economic policy has tended to shift its emphasis from aggregate demand (maintaining the purchasing power of the people) to supply side (increasing profits of corporations and the income of wealthy investors to encourage savings and thus increased investment in new plants, equipment, and research). As a result, in the 1980s profits climbed along with the incomes of the wealthy. In fact, according to a study done in 1988, the most affluent Americans (the top 5 percent) saw their incomes rise from 20 to 24 percent of the national income during the 1980s. The top 1 percent experienced an even greater rise in their proportion of the national wealth, an increase of 46 percent. The poorest Americans, on the other hand, saw their share of the economic pie cut by 8 percent. As a result of changes in the tax laws, the study indicates, there was also a shift in the total tax burden from the richest to those with average or below-average incomes.[15] At the same time, higher levels of unemployment than were once found acceptable

[15]Figures are from a Congressional Budget Office study for 1977 to 1988; cited by Michael Kinsley, *Los Angeles Times*, April 21, 1988, Sec. 2, p. 13.

were now common. By the late 1980s unemployment in Western Europe hovered around 10 percent in most countries and remained right at 6 percent in the United States. Although this represented a sharp decline from the 11 percent recorded during the severe recession of the early 1980s, the fact was that the unemployment rate at the end of Reagan's second term approximated the figure at the time he assumed the presidency; that is, even a 6 percent rate was high by earlier standards. And the rate of unemployment was particularly devastating for certain groups, notably black teenagers, where unemployment was persistently about four times as high as for the rest of the population.

Moreover, individual nations set economic policies and goals according to their tastes. In Japan average workers save about 15 percent of their income—about four or five times the savings of the average American. This provides the Japanese with abundant capital for investment and for the purchase of U.S. real estate and corporations. During the 1980s, the United States spent about 7 percent of its GNP on defense, Japan (whose defense forces are limited by law) about 1 percent. These figures have suggested to some economists that in the not too distant future Japan will pass the United States as the world's leading economic power.

Ever since the Great Depression of the 1930s, much of the economic planning in the Western world has been intended to reduce or at least contain widespread unemployment, a general collapse of purchasing power, and consequent deflation—in a word, depression. The tragedy of general economic collapse that threatened most industrial states in the 1930s helped the growth of fascism and communism and culminated in World War II.

When the war ended, capitalists and trade union leaders, conservatives and liberals, politicians and voters all agreed that the Western world must not permit another worldwide depression. The United States (with some variations) adopted Keynesianism in fact if not in theory. The formula for preventing depression was simple and direct: Prevent widespread unemployment by maintaining purchasing power. When possible, this should be done by encouraging high levels of spending, production, and demand and, therefore, jobs. The Employment Act of 1946 confirmed that the role of government would be crucial in this endeavor, and the Council of Economic Advisers was established to help the president plan a healthy economy. The government spent money and lowered (only sometimes raised) taxes to stimulate the economy, and the Federal Reserve System (which regulates the national banks) made certain that the money supply was sufficient to aid in this economic stimulation.

An important aspect of postwar economics was an expansion of credit. Whereas before the Depression most home buyers had to pay one-third to one-half of the house's total cost as a down payment, with the balance usually payable in no more than ten years, in the postwar era, homes have commonly been sold for as little as 5 to 10 percent down (and in some cases no down payment at all). Mortgages were stretched to 30 and 40 years. The same principle was applied to the purchase of automobiles and other consumer goods. Private individuals, families, and businesses financed purchases and expanded investment by going into debt. In fact, private debt in the United States has, for a long while, been higher than governmental debt.[16]

A second major impetus to the consumer society was advertising that, like the "buy now pay later" plan, was largely a creation of the American free enterprise system. Advertising, particularly on television, stimulated demand for a variety of products, such as deodorants, cigarettes, and flashy automobiles, that people might not have known they needed.

Finally, the development of international trade and travel and the general lowering of barriers to the movement of goods and people across previously closed national boundaries have brought about an enormous expansion in the demand for new goods and services. A phonograph record made in Los Angeles finds an audience all over the world, just as automobiles made in West Germany or Japan are purchased in southern California.

By the 1960s the new system seemed to be an unqualified success. In virtually every Western nation, more and more people shared in the abundance. Indeed, even as the 1980s began, Americans could cite some remarkably positive conditions in their economy: gross national product (the total value of all goods and services produced in the country each year) had for years grown steadily both in terms of *real* dollars as well as in current (inflated) dollars. Meanwhile, total personal income soared during the 1970s; that is, there had been a consistent growth in the U.S. economy, and large numbers of people benefited. Moreover, as 1980 began, the *proportion* of the population that was employed was higher than ever in history, surely a mark of a dynamic economy. Finally, the amount of Americans' earnings taken in taxes, *at least as measured against that in almost every other advanced Western nation*, remained low.

Tax revenue as percentage of GNP		
	1970	**1982**
Sweden	40.7	50.3
Holland	39.9	45.4
France	35.6	43.7
Great Britain	37.5	40.0
West Germany	32.8	37.0
Italy	27.9	33.7
USA	30.1	31.2
Japan	19.7	26.9

[16]Walter W. Heller, "Balanced Budget Fallacies," *Wall Street Journal*, March 16, 1979.

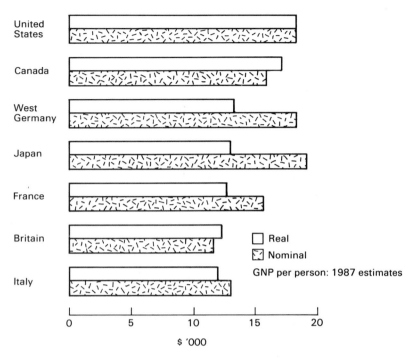

United States

Canada

West Germany

Japan

France

Britain ☐ Real
☒ Nominal

GNP per person: 1987 estimates

Italy

0   5   10   15   20

$ '000

Real = actual GNP per capita in dollars. Nominal = adjusted for cost of living. (OECD.)

Nevertheless, a great many business people and those who believed in the traditional values of the business class found the welfare state a mixed blessing. They disliked sharing the power to make economic decisions with government officials, whom they called bureaucrats. They disliked high taxes, implicit in social democratic economics, and the idea of government "entitlement" programs, ranging from Social Security to outright welfare grants, food stamps, and free school lunches.

As inflation began to race out of control in the late 1970s and unemployment started to grow ominously, anti-Keynesian conservative economists were accorded increasing respect. Milton Friedman, a Nobel prize-winning professor and an articulate champion of an economic philosophy called *monetarism* gained wider audiences. Friedman argued that the profligate Keynesians were pumping too much money into the economy, thereby feeding inflation. The remedies he proposed included "tight" money (making money scarcer by raising its cost, or interest rates), less government spending, and less manipulation of the economy in the interests of dubious social causes, and more freedom for private businesses to make economic decisions, on the lines of Adam Smith's traditional laws of supply and demand.

Another important contributor to this so-called neoconservative eco-

The rich—and the poor rich (GDP = Gross Domestic Product)				
	GDP 1986 $bn	GDP per head 1986 $	Employment in agriculture%	Exports* % of GDP
US	4,195	17,360	3.1	7.1
Japan	1,963	16,160	8.8	14.6
W. Germany	892	14,610	5.5	32.5
France	724	13,070	7.6	25.1
Italy	600	10,490	11.2	27.9
Britain	548	9,650	2.6	29.4
Canada	367	14,200	5.2	28.8
Spain	229	5,920	17.6	23.3
Holland	175	12,040	4.9	64.2
Australia	168	10,540	6.2	16.4
Switzerland	135	20,830	6.6	39.1
Sweden	131	15,700	4.8	35.2
Belgium	114	11,540	2.9	77.8
Austria	94	12,480	8.2	40.3
Denmark	82	15,990	6.7	36.9
Finland	71	14,320	11.5	29.8
Norway	70	16,730	7.2	47.2
Turkey	58	1,150	57.1	21.5
Greece	40	3,990	28.9	21.6
Portugal	29	2,830	23.2	38.5
New Zealand	26	7,900	11.1	31.2
Ireland	25	6,910	16.0	62.2
Luxembourg	5	13,243	4.2	10.4
Iceland	4	16,170	10.5	45.1

*Goods and services
Source: OECD

nomics was Professor Arthur Laffer of the University of Southern California, the inventor and champion of the Laffer Curve. Laffer argued that economic history demonstrated that when taxes were raised beyond a certain point, a law of diminishing returns sets in. Economic activity would decline rather than increase, and the government would end up receiving less rather than more revenue from its tax boost. The contrary, he urged, would also prove true. By cutting taxes, economic activity would increase, and the government would actually derive greater revenues.

Influenced by the new thought, the Reagan administration brought with it the first major economic policy changes since the New Deal days. Reagan asked for and got from Congress the largest tax cut in history. Two more landmark tax bills were passed during his presidency, and the tax policies implemented by these bills dramatically altered the tax structure. As noted

above, responding to supply-side theory (to increase savings and investment), they resulted in a considerable shift in income from middle- and
lower-income brackets to higher-income brackets. Who paid taxes differed
from the past as well. During the boom years of the 1960s, individual
taxpayers and corporations contributed about equally to the total amount of
federal taxes collected. By 1988, individuals were paying more than three
times as many tax dollars to the federal government as were corporations.[17]

At the same time that he sought tax cuts, Reagan convinced Congress to
support him in sharply increasing military spending and slashing or eliminating several of the welfare programs left over from President Johnson's
Great Society days. So President Reagan led policies to cut taxes and
increase expenditures (spending and taxing are called *fiscal* policies), which
would normally add to the fires of inflation by increasing taxpayers' dispos-
able income. Simultaneously, Paul Volcker, Chairman of the independent
Federal Reserve Board (Fed), the agency responsible for regulating the
nation's currency, banks, and interest rates (this is *monetary* policy), led
movement to keep interest rates high and the money supply tight. A consequence of these seemingly contradictory fiscal and monetary policies was
the worst recession since the grim days of the Great Depression. But inflation did subside and by 1983 the economy began a long, sustained period of
growth.

Economically, the Reagan years defied simple pronouncements, whether
for good or ill. For many—perhaps most—Americans, these would appear
to have been years of great, even unmatched prosperity. For others they were
years of neglect and hopeless struggle. Fashionable new automobiles of the
well-to-do glided past the homeless in the streets. Corporate towers staffed
by armies of well-paid stockbrokers and Yuppies cast shadows on spreading
urban slums, filled with the poor unable or unwilling to fit into the new
economics.

The confusion engendered by eight years of "Reaganomics" could be
measured concretely: inflation had declined precipitously from 18 percent
in 1980 to an acceptable 5 percent by 1988. Unemployment in 1988 was but
5.6 percent of the labor force, down from 11 percent during the depths of
the recession of the early 1980s. Indeed, during the Reagan years the
economy had created 14 million *new* jobs, more than the combined total in
Japan and West Germany. There had been steady gains in the GNP and, in
fact, the longest sustained period of growth without a downturn in the post-
World War II period. There were increases in worker productivity (output
per unit hour of work), profits, and, despite the volatility of the exchange
markets, in stock prices. And interest rates had come down significantly.

---

[17]*Los Angeles Times*, February 19, 1988, Sec. 1, p. 24. Some liberal-economists, like MIT
Professor Lester Thurow, oppose income taxes on corporations, seeing them as resulting in
double taxation—on shareholders and then on the corporation—and believe that corporations
simply raise prices to absorb the extra cost of the tax.

Good News

Economic Growth
(gross national product, after inflation)

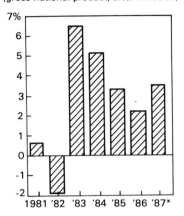

Unemployment
(yearly average)

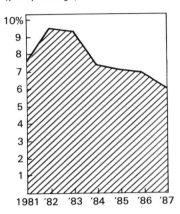

Inflation
(consumer price index, yearly average)

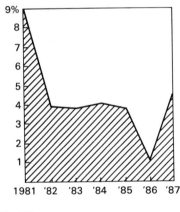

Interest rates
(bank prime rate, yearly average)

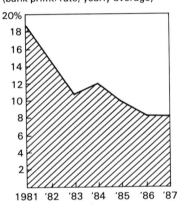

Bad News

Budget deficit
(fiscal years, billions of dollars)

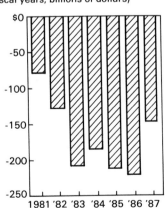

Trade balance
(billions of dollars)

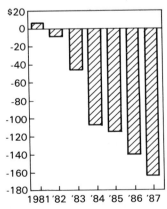

The 1980s Economy. *(Sources: Commerce Department, Bureau of Labor Statistics, Federal Reserve Board, Treasury Department.)*

Supporters of the president and his economic policies had ample reason to argue that the policies had worked well indeed.

But critics could marshal numbers as well. Average earnings of U.S. workers actually declined from 1981 to 1988. The trade deficit soared. The national debt doubled in eight years. Government deficits during the Reagan years exceeded the combined deficits of all other administrations in the two-century history of the nation, ascending astronomically from $1 trillion in 1980 to $2.6 trillion in 1988. As one consequence of these developments the United States changed from being the world's richest creditor nation in 1980 to the world's largest debtor nation by 1988. In the words of New York Senator Daniel Patrick Moynihan, "America gave a great national party, and we are sending the bill to future generations." Our leading economic competitors, principally Japan but also several European countries, bought into American corporations, banks, and prime real estate at the rate of $50 billion per year during the 1980s. And this is not to mention hundreds of billions of dollars of federal IOUs in the form of government bonds now held by foreign nationals as well as citizens of the United States.

Great questions of economic policy are rarely settled cleanly and decisively. People are still arguing about whether Social Security is a good idea (one Republican candidate for president in 1988—Governor Pierre DuPont —offered a plan to dismantle the Social Security system, albeit without much encouragement from the voters). It seems likely that we will be debating the effects of Reaganomics for some time. The programs and policies of the 1980s left the nation prosperous but badly in debt, in an economic resurgence but relatively weaker in competing with other developed nations for a share of the world's business, rich but with a growing army of homeless. The larger question is whether the economic miracle accomplished during the past five decades has about run its course, or whether we may indeed be on the brink of still greater advances that will leave the grandchildren of today's workers wondering how and why they accepted such a meagre existence.

Welfare for the Rich or the Poor?

There is perhaps no American institution more widely and vigorously condemned by political orators, more deeply resented by millions of people, or more frequently held up as prima facie evidence of the failures of American government over the past few decades than the welfare system. To say that the present welfare system is unpopular and unsuccessful is to exaggerate its achievements. *All* recent candidates for the presidency, regardless of party, have run for office promising a fundamental overhaul of the various welfare programs. That the nation's welfare program has failed is one of the few political propositions on which Senator George McGovern, Senator Barry

Goldwater, Gerald Ford, Jimmy Carter, and Ronald Reagan all would agree.

The welfare system is unpopular for a number of reasons. Working people resent having to pay taxes to support those who do not work. It is widely believed that self-reliance and economic independence (which to the average person means being self-supporting) are essential to the mental and social health of any individual physically and mentally able to work. Hence welfare often destroys the people it was intended to help. Finally, it is argued that welfare has become a way of life for millions of Americans, many of whom have been on welfare for two or three generations.

Defenders of the welfare system, growing fewer and perhaps less confident of their own cause each year, usually retort by pointing out that most of the people on welfare are the aged, the sick, children, and mothers of small children. Even the most severe efforts to "crack down on welfare chiselers" by the most conservative politicians have usually been at best marginally successful, sometimes totally unsuccessful.

Welfare for the poor is widely disparaged, not only because of the economic burden it imposes on the rest of society, but also because it is associated with failure and with ethnic minorities (although, in fact, the majority of America's welfare recipients are white). Perhaps it reminds too many Americans that their society is imperfect and damages the credibility of the myth of all-pervading affluence and opportunity.

Less widely advertised is what many call *welfare for the rich*, which enjoys a much more favorable image. For example, a study of the cost of sending a student to two kinds of public institutions for higher education in California in the mid-1960s revealed that the cost to the taxpayers per student was about $5,000 at a branch of the University of California and $1,000 per student at a typical California community college.[18] Similar studies have demonstrated that the average student at a state university tends to come from a relatively prosperous, upper-middle-class family, whereas the typical community-college student is more likely to be from a working-class family.

Translated from statistics, this means that a student who lives in plush Westwood, Bel Air, or Beverly Hills, California, and attends the nearby campus of UCLA is costing taxpayers five times more than does a student who lives in the barrio of East Los Angeles and attends East Los Angeles Community College. That example clearly constitutes a kind of welfare for the rich. Finally, there are those who simply cannot afford any form of higher education.

Another example of the same kind of subsidy to the affluent can be found at any airport. By and large, the business and professional classes use airports far more than do the unemployed or the hourly wage earner. But

[18]W. Lee Hansen and Burton A. Weisbord, *Benefits, Costs and Finance of Public Education* (Chicago: University of Chicago Press, 1969).

the cost of building and maintaining airports and keeping them safe is shared by all. As a result, there is usually little fuss made about proposals to improve and expand airports (except on environmental grounds). On the other hand, expansion of public transport, such as subways and buses, which serves primarily the less affluent, is almost invariably controversial.

Unquestionably the greatest and most flagrant example of government subsidy to those least in need of charity lies in the tax structure. By now it has become fairly common knowledge that there are hundreds of multi-millionaires and wealthy corporations that pay little or no taxes.[19]

The well-publicized case of President Nixon's paying a smaller percentage of his total income in taxes than do most Americans earning a fraction of his salary spotlighted this problem. The rich manage to pay a far smaller share of their taxes than do working people,[20] simply because they can afford to employ the services of lawyers, accountants, and tax consultants to take advantage of "loopholes" in the law *and because the laws are written in a manner designed to give them these advantages.*

Still another form of government compassion for those least in need can be found in various "subsidies." Large corporations and immensely wealthy individuals annually receive checks ranging from hundreds to millions of dollars as gifts from a grateful government for *not* growing certain crops on their immense landholdings. Finally, government grants to those corporations we have earlier described as being part of the military-industrial complex (see Chapter 9) result in large numbers of jobs for people not typically believed to be on welfare. None dare call that welfare.

Is Less More?

In 1958, John Kenneth Galbraith published *The Affluent Society*,[21] a book whose title became a synonym for the United States between 1950 and 1968. Galbraith pointed out that the overriding concern of America's economic planners, particularly since FDR, had been to increase the gross national product every year. Bigger was presumed better. As the torrent of goods coming from America's factories had to be purchased if they were to continue to be produced profitably, a system had been created, largely by the manipulation of credit terms, to enable more people to buy at nothing down or very little cash down. As a result, Americans were building and buying more and larger cars, houses, and appliances each year. At the same time, Galbraith noted, public services, supported by taxes, were being

[19]Phillip Stern, "How 381 Super-Rich Americans Managed Not to Pay a Cent in Taxes Last Year," *New York Times Magazine*, April 13, 1969, sec. 6, p. 30.

[20]Michael Parenti, *Democracy for the Few* (New York: St. Martin's Press, 1974), p. 87.

[21]John Kenneth Galbraith, *The Affluent Society* (Boston: Houghton Mifflin, 1958).

constrained. Hence the anomaly of the American family's going off to enjoy a vacation in a $10,000 air-conditioned mobile home with all the most luxurious amenities, only to fight for a place to park in an overcrowded campground alongside a polluted stream.

Galbraith was among the first to raise the "quality-of-life" issue ("The Gross National Product has gone up, but what of Gross National Pleasure?"), but other, more radical critics of capitalism and even of the whole idea of industrial civilization soon went far beyond him in their criticism. At the heart of the prevailing U.S. economy, charged such writers as Paul Ehrlich and Barry Commoner,[22] was the idea of growth. A capitalist economy, noted Keynes, was like a spinning top: It could accelerate and decelerate, but it could not maintain its equilibrium without a change in velocity. Because the innate tendency of the capitalist was to seek ever-greater profits, "pollution," concluded Commoner, "is an unintended concomitant of the drive to increase productivity." As our economic capital (gross national product) goes up, so our *biological capital* (pure air, clean water, minerals in the land, and so on) is diminished. Thus, despite "apparent prosperity," argued Commoner, "the system is being driven into bankruptcy." "Growth," noted Robert Theobald, "while essential to corporate profits, may not be compatible with the interest of society."[23]

"You [the United States] could very comfortably have stopped growing after World War I," noted British economist Ezra Mishan, "there was enough technology to make life quite pleasant. Cities weren't overgrown. People weren't too avaricious. You hadn't really ruined the environment as you have now."[24] Surveying the U.S. economy, a number of prominent British observers openly questioned the wisdom of Great Britain's attempting to follow a similar path. "Affluence creates more problems than it solves. . . . Little England would be a much better place to live than Great Britain," was a frequent response to governmental requests for greater efficiency and productivity.

More traditional economists responded with a vigorous defense of the social and political benefits of economic growth. Economic growth has, to some degree, become the modern psychic equivalent of the frontier in early America. It provides a safety valve, particularly for the poor. As the result of affluence, the number of Americans below the poverty level has diminished from one-third of the nation in FDR's era to less than one-fifth by the 1980s, and even these were probably better off in a material sense. After allowing for inflation, the bottom 10 percent of the population increased its income by over 55 percent since 1950. "Twenty more years of growth,"

[22]Barry Commoner, *The Economic Meaning of Ecology in the Closing Circle* (New York: Knopf, 1972).

[23]Robert Theobald, *The Challenge of Abundance* (New York: NAL, 1962), p. 111.

[24]See Peter Passell and Leonard Ross, "Don't Knock the $2 Trillion Economy," *New York Times Magazine*, March 5, 1972, pp. 14–15, 64, 68–70.

A tree struggling to survive in an atmosphere polluted by factory smoke symbolizes industrial America, as seen by many environmentalists. *(Photograph by Dean Immenschuh, Upland, California.)*

argued economists Peter Passell and Leonard Ross, "could do for the poor what Congress won't do."[25]

Moreover, the real victims of a "no-growth" policy in the United States and other industrialized states would be the underdeveloped peoples, who needed our tractors and technology and food far more than they did the pools of oil and mountains of ore buried in their earth. Because the West

[25]Passell and Ross, p. 70.

needed oil, the people of Kuwait, for example, were transformed in a single generation from impoverished nomads into the residents of an economic paradise, with free education, free utilities, no taxes, and the highest per capita income in the world. Other underdeveloped nations were not so fortunate, but most depended on the sale of their raw materials to the West for the wherewithal to meet the most fundamental human needs of their peoples.

In sum, a little- or no-growth economy seemed to contain certain social by-products perhaps as undesirable as pollution is to a rapidly growing economy. Among them are higher unemployment rates than had traditionally been considered acceptable to America; a lack of social mobility, particularly afflicting the least educated and least able to compete; and an end to the idea of continually expanding and improving economic life-styles. Some argued that it would mean the end of the dream of America as the land of boundless opportunity.

Politics and the Economy

In a speech delivered in the spring of 1977, President Carter declared the energy crisis and its concomitant by-product of inflation and unemployment (called by some *stagflation*) to be "the greatest challenge, with the exception of preventing war, our country will face during our lifetime." The press promptly dubbed the president's remarks his "Doomsday" speech.

The Carter administration proposed and carried out a number of activities to address the economic and energy crises, including an attempt to encourage voluntary wage and price restraint, trying (in cooperation with the Federal Reserve Board) to control the supply of money to cool off the economy and bolster the value of the dollar, moving toward less deficit spending and an eventually balanced federal budget, signing a world trade agreement that in the long run should aid U.S. exports, and perhaps most important, sponsoring a series of bills to implement a broad-based energy program. In 1978, Congress passed a comprehensive energy bill that deregulated the price of natural gas, encouraged conversion from petroleum to coal (which the United States has in abundant supply), reformed utility rates to encourage conservation of energy, offered tax incentives to individuals and businesses to conserve, and placed a progressively higher tax penalty on "gas guzzling" automobiles.[26] Congress passed an important addition to the energy program in March 1980, providing for the deregulation of petroleum prices. The bill was considered a major legislative victory for President Carter. The long-run effects of such an energy policy were intended to decrease our dependence on foreign energy supplies and encour-

[26]See *Energy Policy* (Washington, D.C.: Congressional Quarterly, 1979).

age conservation. Indeed, Americans began to conserve; automobiles became more efficient; and even by the early 1980s an "oil glut" developed—more petroleum was available than was in demand—causing gasoline prices to stabilize and in some instances to decline. This in turn helped cause the inflationary rate to decline.

President Reagan was less interested in government-directed energy policies and more concerned with encouraging the private development of energy sources. Nonetheless, he did not dismantle the new Energy Department, as some believed he might, and he certainly reaped some political rewards from Americans' conservation of energy and the consequent decline in prices.

In the face of scientific reports that manufactured chlorofluorocarbons (CFCs) were destroying the earth's protective layer of ozone, 24 nations plus the European Community concluded a protocol in 1987 providing for a freeze on the use of CFCs and an eventual cut in consumption, even though such action might cause temporary economic discomfort and dislocation to producers and marketers of these products. When a 1988 report of the National Aeronautics and Space Administration showed that depletion of the ozone layer was more serious than even had been previously thought, these nations accelerated their support of an international agreement mandating more stringent and more rapid curtailment of the use of CFCs. Thus international politics, as is true of domestic politics, can address the most crucial issues affecting collective human life.

The connection between politics and the economy is often difficult for us to make. Most people probably think of economics as the daily struggle to pay their bills. Yet the decisions made by government shape and direct our personal fortunes to an extent greater than we may recognize. Still, most of us find it difficult to come up with ideas as to what to do about inflation, unemployment, deficits, and energy crises, or how to balance the frequently antagonistic demands for increasing productivity and protecting the environment, helping the poor and protecting the rich, meeting increased world competition without destroying the delicate balance of world trade, and freeing ourselves from the stranglehold of the oil companies and OPEC without radically reorganizing the American way of life.

In attempting to solve, or failing to resolve, these problems in the years just ahead, the American people will inevitably have to rely on the wisdom of their political leaders and the integrity of their political institutions. Few if any of these problems can be solved by some magical economic gimmick (such as a return to the gold standard) or technical breakthrough (such as the oft-proclaimed invention of a one-hundred-mile-per-gallon carburetor).

It seems unlikely that the United State can or will embrace the Malthusian notion that improving the lot of humankind is simply not possible. On the contrary, it will be the test of statecraft in the decade of the 1990s to find a way to keep the U.S. economy strong and vital and its people working, while conserving existing sources of energy, developing new energy pos-

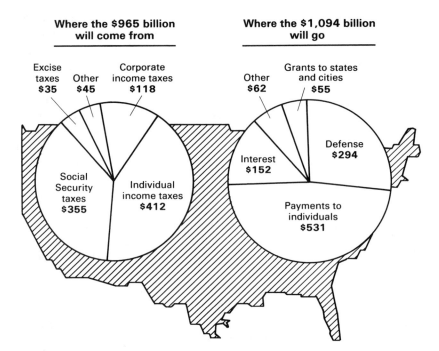

Where the $965 billion will come from

Excise taxes $35
Other $45
Corporate income taxes $118
Social Security taxes $355
Individual income taxes $412

Where the $1,094 billion will go

Other $62
Grants to states and cities $55
Interest $152
Defense $294
Payments to individuals $531

1989 Federal Budget. *(Office of Management and Budget.)*

sibilities, and, at the same time, halting or at least reducing the gradual degradation of the earth, water, and air that must determine our destiny.

The issues discussed in this chapter lead us to a fundamental question: Can corporate capitalism, as it has developed in the United States, meet our economic needs and problems? Can poverty be gradually eliminated and inequality of opportunity and environmental deprivation be brought within tolerable limits? Can we at least maintain a reasonably comfortable standard of living for the mass of Americans while remaining competitive with foreign nations and conflicting economic systems? A positive answer to these questions will require, at the minimum, equity in the tax laws, lower levels of unemployment, and far greater social, human, and environmental sensitivity on the part of both our political and economic leaders.

The New International Economy

As the twentieth century draws to a close, four recent developments are altering the world economy:

1. Japan has emerged as an economic superpower and has become a challenger to the United States as the dominant force in the world's

economy. Other Asian nations, some following the Japanese model, are developing economically at an unparalleled rate and may themselves soon challenge the traditional economic powers.

2. In 1992, Western Europe, pursuing an accelerated policy of economic and political integration, will become virtually a united free market, abolishing all barriers to trade, travel, and finance within the market. It is likely that Western Europe will then become the richest single market in the world, thus challenging the economic leadership of Japan and the United States.

3. The Soviet Union and China have shifted from strict Marxism–Leninism to much more pragmatic, market-oriented economies, and are seeking to participate in the world economy under the rules long followed in the West. The consequences of this change are likely to be profound.

4. The United States has suffered a *relative* decline in economic power, manifested by huge international debt, an unfavorable trade balance, and massive federal budget deficits. At the same time the American people have increased, rather than lowered, their consumption of goods, particularly foreign-produced goods. They have done this by borrowing from the surplus wealth of others, a condition that cannot continue indefinitely.

Shortly after World War II, the leaders of Western Europe, observing the devastation of their continent—40 million dead and uncounted millions of refugees in camps and bombed-out buildings—reflected upon what was once the richest and proudest continent, now utterly dependent on U.S. charity for survival and U.S. military might for protection. They decided to make some changes.

Perhaps the most important consequence of these changes has been the gradual unification of the economies of most Western European nations, including those of erstwhile implacable foes France and Germany. The ancient quarrel between these two peoples had caused, they believed, a series of wars that had brought Europe to its knees. The best hope of preventing future tragedies lay in creating a new European Economic Community. Almost half a century later, the French, Germans, and other Europeans move freely across almost open borders. Trade and travel flourish. French and German troops conduct joint maneuvers. The likelihood of war among the major European states is near zero. Europe has grown, by all previous standards, immensely rich.

Is this a pattern that may be repeated, if in a different form, by the great socialist and capitalist blocs? If it were possible, would it result in a flowering of mutual wealth, prosperity, and peace as has happened in Western Europe? The ultimate questions of future wealth or poverty will not be decided by economists, or business executives, or labor leaders. They will be decided by politicians—or generals.

13

Trumpets and Flourishes: America in the World

- Nationalism -
- War -
- Deterrence and Nuclear War -
- Foreign Policy and Diplomacy -
- Making Foreign Policy -
- American Diplomacy: Principles, Perceptions, and Policies -
- From Cold War to Realism -
- Foreign Policy Under Carter -
- Foreign Policy Under Reagan -
- Lessons from the Past -
- The Future of American Foreign Policy -

> Thou wretched, rash, intruding fool.
>
> Shakespeare
> *Hamlet*
>
> Justice is as strictly due between neighbor Nations as between neighbor Citizens.
>
> Benjamin Franklin

Some grandparents of today's college students grew up in a world dominated by Great Britain and France. London was the capital of the world's financial markets; the army of France was commonly considered the world's strongest. Between them, these two European powers controlled, or strongly influenced, the daily lives of many of the peoples of the earth, and each had vast colonial empires. The United States, although economically strong, was militarily weak and its influence was largely limited to the Americas and certain sections of Asia. By the time the parents of today's students were youngsters the world had changed completely. France and Britain were devastated and close to bankruptcy, dependent on the generosity of Americans to sustain their own people. Their empires were gone, their power sharply limited. From the remnants of these empires, dozens of new nations emerged, many of them destined to play an increasingly important role in the world's affairs. Now the United States and the Soviet Union had become superpowers. Between them these two nations dominated the world's political, economic, and military affairs. Although both vigorously denied it, they had, in fact, inherited the power of the old British and French empires, referring to their dependent nations as "allies" rather than colonies. Still, the facts were that important decisions made in Moscow or Washington now determined the lives of people throughout the world.

Approaching the last decade of the twentieth century, there was every indication that the world might experience a shift in the relative power and strength of the major international forces as significant as those of the recent past. Japan was in the process of becoming the prime mover of international trade and finance. The Soviet Union, its economy in disarray, seemed destined to retreat from a clearly overextended position. In 1992, most of Western Europe would become a single economic unit with total wealth far surpassing that of either the United States, the Soviet Union, or Japan. Looming on the horizon was China, with a billion people, a growing economy, and an ancient civilization advancing toward becoming a modern superstate. Not far behind was India, also progressing economically.

It seemed clear that all this meant that ordinary Americans, who had spent much of their lives in the secure belief that this country was "number one," would have to learn to think differently about relations with the rest of the world. The Soviet Union had learned that it could not impose its will on the people of Afghanistan and had begun to question how long it could continue to sponsor increasingly independent and possibly untrustworthy allies at the cost of untold rubles badly needed to keep the USSR itself from falling hopelessly behind other major industrialized societies. The United States could not impose its will on Vietnam and seemed to be learning the same lesson in tiny Nicaragua. U.S. politicians, like their Soviet counterparts, began to wonder how long we could afford to go on defending the "free world" while much of that world grew richer and we grew *relatively* poorer. How long would America continue to keep its soldiers and its most sophisticated, expensive weapons standing guard over Tokyo, the Middle East, Berlin, Rome, London—at enormous cost—while Japanese, Arab, German, Italian, and British firms returned the favor by buying our largest corporations and most valuable real estate?

A Canadian, asked to comment on the difference between our two countries (which are similar in many ways), observed, "Americans have this sense of being special, destined to shape the affairs of all the world, that Canadians simply do not share." Not long ago, it was possible to believe that we held "the whole world in our hands." If that idea is no longer tenable, we may find another, perhaps better role in international affairs than being "number one."

Nationalism

The fundamental fact of international life is the power of nationalism, reflected in the doctrine of the sovereignty of nations. Each nation is a sovereign power, at least in theory, with the almost absolute right to do whatever it pleases. Unlike civil life within the confines of a nation, in which the individual's behavior can be and often is guided, and if necessary forcibly restrained by such agencies as the police, the military, the courts and—perhaps more important than any of these—the tradition of respect for other human beings and the law, there is no comparable international police force, military organization, or court system. Respect for law and the rights of other nation-states is, unhappily, still a relatively weak factor in international affairs, although it may be increasing.

Examples of international lawlessness are easily found by glancing at the front page of almost any morning newspaper. An example occurred in late 1979 with the seizure of the U.S. embassy in Iran and the taking hostage of its staff by militant students. The Iranian government, committed by international law, custom, and its own private assurances to U.S. officials to guarantee the safety of the remaining U.S. diplomats in Iran, instead

(Drawing by Joseph Mugnaini.)

endorsed the action of the student-militants and supported their determination to hold the Americans until the deposed shah of Iran (and his wealth) was returned to Iran. For most Americans the action seemed parallel to a situation in which a wealthy family is taken hostage and held for ransom and the police join the kidnappers.

In seeking a peaceful solution to the crisis, the United States appealed to and won favorable judgments from both the World Court and the Security Council of the United Nations, both of which condemned the actions of the Iranian government and ordered that the hostages be released. The Iranians simply ignored both bodies, and the affair served to dramatize the impotence of international law and world opinion as forces capable of restraining the actions of even a relatively weak nation like Iran.

But Iran does not stand alone in this regard. Only a few weeks after the Iranian crisis erupted, the Soviet Union launched an invasion of neighboring Afghanistan, apparently because of the possibility that the already pro-Soviet leadership in that country might fall victim to another revolution led by devout Muslims. Despite international protest over the invasion of Afghanistan, including the refusal by the United States and some 60 other nations to participate in the 1980 Summer Olympic Games in Moscow, the Soviet Union persisted in its assault on the Afghan people. By 1988, the

Soviet Union had been fighting in Afghanistan longer than it fought in World War II. Unlike their earlier invasions of Hungary and Czechoslovakia, the Soviets this time appeared unable to secure control with a quick, decisive blow aimed primarily at occupying the major cities and centers of power. In 1988 the Soviet Union, under its dynamic new leader, Mikhail Gorbachev, began to withdraw Soviet forces, leaving behind a legacy of enormous casualties, both Afghan and Soviet, millions of refugees, and a devastated nation.

Both the U.S. government and American citizens were outraged at these examples of international misbehavior. But our own hands are not entirely clean in these matters. The U.S. invasion of Vietnam was remarkably similar in many respects to Soviet activity in Afghanistan. We too poured in troops and weapons of almost unbelievable ferocity in an attempt to protect a puppet regime created by and for the United States. And although we can find no excuse for the taking of innocent hostages, the fact is that the United States, for almost three decades, was deeply involved in the authoritarian regime of the shah of Iran and certainly bears some responsibility for the crimes that regime perpetrated against the Iranian people. Also in Nicaragua, the United States sponsored, maintained, and largely directed an armed rebellion against the government of the Sandinistas, often contrary to both international and—at times—our own laws. The point is that nations act first and foremost not out of commitment to international principles, but out of concern for their own perceived vital interests. (Sometimes, of course, they misjudge their true interests.) If they seem to be behaving in a high-minded concern for international principles of conduct it is often as an afterthought, or because adverse world opinion, conditioned by a ubiquitous world press and worldwide communications, has become so damaging as to compel a change in policy.

The most conspicuous examples of militant and mindless nationalism can be found in the operations of terrorists who murder innocent airplane passengers and schoolchildren. Committing atrocities usually against unarmed persons, terrorists typically hope to focus international attention on a cause or grievance that becomes an excuse for unbridled ferocity. Ironically, publicity—indeed, negative publicity—is almost invariably terrorism's only reward. The kidnapping and murder of American hostages in Lebanon by Iranian sympathizers has not softened or fundamentally altered U.S. hostility to Iran (the Iran-Contra scandal notwithstanding). Israel has grown stronger, not weaker, despite terrorist attacks for four decades. The Western European democracies and Japan have grown richer and stronger despite the outrages of various national and international fanatics. That these assaults almost never achieve anything but bloodshed leads to the lamentable but unavoidable conclusion that for international terrorists, murder is its own and only reward, although often perpetrated in the name of nationalism.

War

The most effective check on the behavior of nations is not fear of offending international opinion or UN sanctions but fear of war. Anytime that a regime chooses to "throw the iron dice," it is gambling with its own existence. Frequently the most serious casualties of wars are the governments that initiate them. The next most frequent casualties are the illusions of the people who support their government's decision to resort to force. The war in Vietnam offers an example. Both Presidents Johnson and Nixon can be regarded as indirect victims of their military actions in Vietnam. For millions of Americans, the war represented a lesson in the limits of American power. World War I brought about the liquidation of the czarist regime in Russia, the Kaiser's government in Germany, and the Austro-Hungarian Empire. It probably finished forever the centuries-old power of monarchs in Europe. World War II brought about a transformation of the social system in Europe, divided a Germany that had been unified for less than a century, helped usher in a communist regime in China, and destroyed the power of the ruling military class in Japan. Nothing is more likely to bring about a revolution in a nation than war, particularly if one happens to choose the losing side.

In addition to political changes, war usually results in social dislocation. Casualties, particularly in modern warfare, are enormous. Whole cities are destroyed, and there often is hunger, sometimes famine. All that people have spent a lifetime, even centuries, to construct may be destroyed in a few minutes. Now that at least a half dozen states possess nuclear weapons, any war however localized at first, may escalate into a worldwide holocaust that might end the precarious life of the human race on this planet.

Ever since the first atom bombs were dropped on Hiroshima and Nagasaki, Japan, in World War II, the existence of nuclear weapons has permanently altered the nature of war and, hence, of foreign policy. Although an all-out nuclear war might not be the end of human life on this planet (the experts disagree on this question), no one will really know until it is too late to worry about who was right and who was wrong. But certainly in view of what we know of the economic, social, and political consequences of the past two world wars, which were fought with conventional weapons, the survivors of a nuclear war would be condemned to living a life that we should be hard put to recognize as human, let alone civilized.[1] Even if the "optimists" are right and we could manage to rebuild civilization in a hundred or a thousand or a million years, it is, to paraphrase Shakespeare, "a consummation devoutly to be missed."

Few statesmen today speak glowingly of war. This was not always true. As recently as the pre-World War II era in Europe, Italy's fascist leader

[1]See Carl Sagan. "Nuclear War and Climatic Catastrophe: Some Policy Implications," *Foreign Affairs* (Winter 1983–1984): 257–292.

Benito Mussolini proclaimed that "war is the health of the state." Adolf Hitler asserted that war "was not forced upon the masses. It was desired by the whole people." Both statements contain important half-truths that have become somewhat obscured in recent years. In a certain sense, war is our oldest and most honored profession. Many of the figures that history labels "great"—Caesar, Alexander, Napoleon—were warriors whose "greatness" largely resided in drenching whole continents in blood. Shakespeare, who was not unaware of the terrible human cost of war, nevertheless described many of his heroes as "warlike"; and he meant it as a compliment.

War has been a popular and honored human activity, the ultimate sport of both kings and commoners. One of the great causes of tension in the modern world may be that technology has raised the price of war so high that nations can no longer indulge themselves in periodic bouts of bloodletting with anything like the old relish. One of humankind's favorite activities—the one that fills the pages of our history books, that suffuses the lyrics of national anthems, that thrills the imagination of poets, prophets, and politicians, and that is still the world's number one industry—is in some danger of being priced out of the market.

Deterrence and Nuclear War

Perhaps one of the more enduring contributions of President Reagan to world politics may have come about as an unforeseen by-product of the president's approach to foreign affairs. In the early years of the Reagan presidency, the president and members of his administration seemed to be competing with one another for the honor of denouncing Soviet wickedness. Important newspapers carried stories about the prospects for an American "victory" in a nuclear war. Civil defense proposals, usually involving fantastic mass evacuations of populated areas, were publicized and promoted as official policy. One official seriously suggested that Americans could improve their chances of surviving a nuclear holocaust by digging holes in their backyards and covering the holes with a door. The net effect of the administration's rhetoric, coupled with a massive military buildup and accentuated by a certain readiness to use force in Central America, the Caribbean, and the Middle East, created a sense of danger in Europe and among many Americans unmatched since the Cuban missile crisis of 1962. Serious critics in Europe and the United States began to consider the possibility that the administration, by design or accident, might actually lead the world into a nuclear war. Massive protests were mounted in Europe. A proposal to freeze nuclear weapons development and production in the United States and the Soviet Union was voted for by millions of Americans in statewide elections, despite the president's opposition.

People have lived with nuclear weapons ever since that day in August

1945 when the United States dropped the first atomic bomb on Hiroshima. Why did the issue become so urgent and compelling in the 1980s? In politics, as in physics, every force tends to generate an opposite force. In World War II, the threat of fascism created the United Nations. Expansive Soviet communism in Eastern Europe led to the formation of the North Atlantic Treaty Organization (NATO). The establishment of Israel stimulated Arab nationalism. The Vietnam War created the peace movement of the 1960s and early 1970s. The U.S.-led boycott of the 1980 Moscow Olympics resulted in the Soviet-inspired boycott of the 1984 Los Angeles Olympics. Similarly, President Reagan's commitment to a massive military buildup helped spark a worldwide apprehension about the danger of nuclear war. The danger, of course, had existed since 1945, but in the 1980s it seemed about to become the most compelling issue of the decade.

At the heart of the military buildup was the notion of *deterrence*, a policy of maintaining and increasing nuclear capabilities to convince one's opponent not to start a nuclear war. Deterrence is an idea simple enough for a child to understand. In fact, its proponents often use a childlike metaphor: school yard bullies pick on people who are too weak or cowardly to defend themselves. (However, this is often not true. In school yards, as anywhere else in life, people who look for a fight find one, and those who are more peaceably inclined usually manage to avoid conflict.) The theory of deterrence—that weakness invites and strength discourages attack—has become an unchallengeable cliché of American foreign policy. But the facts of life suggest the question may be more complex than the Department of Defense is likely to admit. Military weakness has not deterred the various Arab states from making war on Israel, or challenging American power, as in Lebanon. The "weak" Vietnamese drove the powerful Americans out of Vietnam. The weak Chinese did not hesitate to attack American forces when General Douglas MacArthur's armies approached China's border during the Korean War. During the immediate post-World War II era, the United States commanded a monopoly of nuclear weapons and a great preponderance of industrial and military power vis-à-vis the Soviets. Nevertheless, the Soviets have challenged us time and again, from Berlin to Cuba. In fact, the evidence seems to suggest that superior military strength, far from ensuring that one's potential foes will be cautious and well behaved, often has the opposite effect. Thus it seems that a country that faces an adversary that it knows to be militarily superior is apt to become more, not less, belligerent. This apparent irrational behavior is rooted in an irrational emotion—nationalism—which is simply a contemporary version of an old idea: that death can be made spiritual and meaningful. The debate over nuclear weapons, which ultimately is a debate over the life or death of the human race, was long overdue, and President Reagan, ironically, must be given credit for having ignited it.

Moreover, President Reagan and many of his supporters claimed an important victory for their policy of military buildup and confrontation with the Soviet Union when, after the advent of Mikhail Gorbachev to Communist party secretary, the USSR's foreign policy became decidedly less confrontational. After a series of meetings, the president and the Soviet leader reached important accords that altered international expectations and diminished the danger of nuclear conflict. Most of these agreements came about as the result of major Soviet, not American, concessions (for example, the treaty banning intermediate-range nuclear missiles in Europe required the Soviets to eliminate four or five times as many weapons as the United States). Whether these positive changes came about because of, or in spite of, the U.S. policy of deterrence reflected in the doctrine of MAD (mutually assured destruction) is a subject that hawks and doves will argue for years.

Foreign Policy and Diplomacy

Given the fact of international lawlessness, the human penchant to settle disputes by force rather than by reason, and the fundamental popularity of "patriotic wars" and national belligerence, the wonder is not that diplomats so often fail to keep the peace but that sometimes they succeed.

When diplomacy fails, the military takes over. In war, military leaders are charged with carrying out the orders of the government; in peace, it is the diplomats who must carry out their government's wishes, often a complex and sometimes contradictory set of short-term goals and long-range objectives. So *diplomacy* is what a nation uses in negotiating with other nations in the international community; it involves diplomats representing nations. A war may break out when countries cannot reach agreements by means of diplomacy. A *foreign policy* refers to a nation's aims within the international community—such as the containment of communism, the expansion of trade, and so on. A foreign policy normally is carried out by diplomacy, but it may be pursued through warfare, subversion, or other methods. For example, in the United States in the years since World War II, two of the government's most important foreign policy objectives have been to contain the spread of communism and to avoid war with the Soviet Union.

If the United States did not fear, or at least wished to avoid, war with the Soviet Union, our foreign policy would be much simpler and easier for the average person to understand: We would oppose the Soviets everywhere and, when we failed to get our way, use force. If, on the other hand, we were indifferent to the spread of communism and/or Soviet influence and power, there would be little basis for conflict. As matters stand, our diplomats must walk a careful line, trying not to precipitate World War III on the one hand, while maintaining U.S. power and prestige relative to that of the Soviets on the other. Thus the U.S. government since World War II has employed a variety of techniques, including limited warfare (Vietnam and

President Reagan and Secretary Gorbachev meet. *(White House photo.)*

Korea), propaganda (via the U.S. Information Agency), economic pressure (the Marshall Plan, the sale of food to the Soviet Union), subversion (in Chile and Guatemala), mutual-defense treaties (as NATO and SEATO [Southeast Asia Treaty Organization]), and diplomacy (as represented in the Helsinki agreement of 1975 or in arms negotiations)—all with the common objective of checking the growth of communism and/or Soviet power while avoiding a major war.

Making Foreign Policy

In the United States, there is a complex bureaucracy responsible for developing foreign policy and conducting diplomacy.[2] This bureaucracy and its activities are directed by the president, with varying—but normally limited—input from Congress. As we have seen in earlier chapters, Con-

[2]See John H. Esterline and Robert B. Black, *Inside Foreign Policy* (Palo Alto, Calif.: Mayfield, 1975); John Spanier and Eric M. Uslaner, *How American Foreign Policy Is Made*, 2nd ed. (New York: Holt, Rinehart & Winston, 1978); and James A. Nathan and James K. Oliver, *Foreign Policy Making and the American Political System* (Boston: Little, Brown, 1983).

The Pursuit of Happiness

gress declares war, appropriates money, and discusses foreign policy, but the president (or his designated agent) is the only person who can communicate officially for the United States with other nations. As chief diplomat and commander in chief of the armed forces, his power in foreign policy is immense.

The oldest agency responsible for conducting our diplomacy is the Department of State, and its head, the secretary of state, is considered the ranking member of the president's cabinet. The secretary is aided by diplomatic and consular establishments throughout the world. Normally, there is a single diplomatic mission in the capital of each of the countries recognized by the United States, and there may be several consulates in the same country.

Although the president, with the consent of the Senate, appoints the secretary of state and subordinate officers down to assistant secretaries (there are undersecretaries and then assistant secretaries who are divided geographically and functionally) and the heads of diplomatic missions (ambassadors), most other important jobs in the department are held by foreign service officers, who obtain their jobs by passing a difficult civil service exam. Foreign service officers work up in rank and are rotated among various posts about every three years.

Since World War II, the State Department has increasingly had to share its role of making and conducting policy with other agencies in the national bureaucracy. In 1947, Congress created the Department of Defense to absorb all the functions of defense and war making. The DOD now represents our largest bureaucratic entity, accounting for the largest number of those working for the federal government and absorbing by far the largest percentage of the national budget.

In addition, the Central Intelligence Agency, which coordinates all foreign intelligence activities, has come to be important in policy implementation. Going much further than simply gathering intelligence information, the CIA has been charged with covert activities to overthrow other governments and assassinate foreign leaders. Although in the 1970s, congressional revelations of these latter activities led to increased demands for more stringent controls over CIA operations, during the early 1980s the agency again expanded its covert activities around the world.

The National Security Council (NSC) coordinates all these agencies and activities under a presidential adviser for National Security. Formed by Congress in 1947, the NSC combines all the elements that go into the making and conducting of foreign and national security policy, pulling together the views of the departments of State, Defense, Treasury, and Commerce and the CIA and the Joint Chiefs of Staff. Before becoming secretary of state, Henry Kissinger presided over the NSC as President Nixon's special adviser on national security affairs. Because Congress does not confirm appointments to this post, Kissinger was able to conduct a vigorous and at times novel foreign policy outside normal constitutional

Mao Tse-tung, President Richard Nixon, and Henry Kissinger in China.
(National Archives.)

constraints. Such a development during the Nixon administration underscored the power of the president in making and conducting foreign policy.

Under President Reagan both the CIA and the NSC apparently expanded their powers to the point where they were making fundamental foreign policy decisions without the president's knowledge. (At least this was the president's claim during the Iran-Contra hearings.) Reagan was served by six National Security advisers—a historic high—during his two terms. Also, the NSC staff grew while Reagan was president, although important decisions apparently came to be made by ever smaller groups within the council. President Reagan's assertion that he simply did not know about various illegal schemes to help arm the Contras in their efforts to overthrow the Sandinista government in Nicaragua was supported by the congressional testimony of Admiral John Poindexter, former chief of the NSC, who indicated that *he* had taken unilateral responsibility to make these decisions. Other interesting disclosures surfaced during the Iran-Contra investigations concerning the activities of the late CIA chief William Casey. Colonel Oliver North testified to the existence of certain "off the shelf" plans for covert operations that Casey either planned or put into action without the knowledge or consent of either Congress or major cabinet officials within the administration. The Tower Commission, appointed by President Reagan to investigate the Iran-Contra affair, severely criticized the president's "laid-back" style of foreign policy formulation, which apparently permitted powerful and ambitious subordinates to behave as if they—rather than Reagan—had been elected chief diplomat and commander in chief.[3]

[3]See *The Tower Commission Report* (New York: Bantam Books and Times Books, 1987), especially part II.

The Pursuit of Happiness

American Diplomacy: Principles, Perceptions, and Policies

In 1939, the U.S. Army contained fewer than 200,000 volunteers. The United States had a defense budget of about $0.5 billion, no military alliances, and no American troops in any foreign country (although troops were stationed in U.S. territories such as the Philippines and the Panama Canal Zone). Today our army numbers over 1 million, and we have an enormous air force and navy, alliances with over two-score nations, military personnel stationed around the world, and an annual defense budget of about $300 billion.[4] Clearly, in the space of one generation, America's perception of its place in the world has changed considerably. So too has its foreign policy, and the traumatic events of World War II were at least partially responsible for these changes.

World War II had brought us into a struggle of great powers for a second time this century, but this time under different circumstances. The Axis powers—Germany, Italy, and Japan—all were dictatorships dedicated to values alien to the principles shared by the American people. The events leading up to World War II, climaxing as far as Americans were concerned with the Japanese attack on Pearl Harbor, convinced a generation of Americans that the war had been caused by the failure of free and democratic nations to stand firm against the challenge of the dictatorships. Americans renounced isolationism as unworkable and resolved never again to be "caught sleeping."

The image of World War II as a struggle between peaceful democracies on the one hand and fanatical dictatorships on the other was marred by one hard fact. The Soviet Union, certainly a dictatorship, was fighting on the side of the Allies. Moreover, the Soviets faced about two-thirds of the German army and suffered by far the heaviest casualties of the Allies in the war.

When the war ended, it was clear that the ranks of great powers had been thinned to just two nations, henceforth called *superpowers*: the United States and the Soviet Union. The Soviets had the largest, and most powerful army in the world, and the United States had at least a temporary monopoly on nuclear weaponry plus the world's strongest economy.

President Roosevelt hoped that the United States and the Soviet Union could find a means, despite their ideological differences, to work together peacefully. He proposed the United Nations, which would inevitably be dominated by the United States and the USSR, as an instrument for securing world peace and international order. However, FDR died shortly before the collapse of the Axis armies, and his successor, Harry S Truman, was less committed to U.S.–Soviet cooperation in the postwar world.

[4]See Stephen E. Ambrose, *Rise to Globalism* (Baltimore: Penguin Books, 1983), pp. 13–21.

President Franklin Roosevelt signs the Declaration of War on Japan. *(National Archives.)*

At about the same time, Soviet dictator Joseph Stalin, always suspicious of the possibilities of peaceful collaboration with capitalist states, appears to have concluded that postwar Soviet–American cooperation was not going to happen. (Whether or not either Stalin or Truman even *wanted* it to happen is a question that historians continue to debate.[5])

The Soviet Union, which suffered 20 million casualties in the war, was understandably determined never voluntarily to allow anti-Soviet regimes in that part of Europe through which it had been attacked twice in one generation. The Soviet regime now had the world's strongest army and decided that it would be prudent not to rely for its future safety on vague American promises of future friendship, particularly as America was now ruled by someone largely unknown to the Soviets. Instead it established in the various Eastern European nations that had been occupied by Soviet forces communist regimes dependent for their survival on Soviet power and closely following the Soviet model.

[5]The debate over the origins of the cold war has created an explosion of literature. A useful collection of conflicting views is Thomas G. Paterson, ed., *The Origins of the Cold War*, 2nd ed. (Lexington, Mass.: Heath, 1974).

The United States saw the establishment of this "buffer zone" as evidence that the democratic and capitalist world, now led by the United States, was threatened by another form of totalitarianism not very different from the Nazi dictatorship. There were fears that a communist tide might sweep over Europe. Moreover, the United States had emerged from World War II as virtually the only major power in the world whose homeland had not been devastated by the war. U.S. leaders foresaw that much of the Western world would inevitably become an economic dependency of American business, with only the spread of Soviet-led communism representing a major threat to American economic hegemony over much of the world.

Thus, for a number of reasons, the United States began to consider the world in *bipolar* terms; other nations were either on our side, and thus dedicated to democracy and some form of capitalism, or on the Soviet side, and thus (as with the East European countries) puppets of the Soviet Union. There was, then, a two-way struggle between a vaguely defined Americanism and international communism directed from the Kremlin. Because there was no shooting war between Moscow and Washington, we described this bipolar tension as a *cold war*. When in 1949 China came under the dominance of the Chinese Communist party and Mao Tse-tung, the official U.S. position was that the new Chinese regime was subservient to Moscow and that the real Chinese government was temporarily residing on the island of Taiwan. Thus we refused to recognize the government that in fact existed on the Chinese mainland. In varying degrees, the same sort of "temporary" position was accorded Fidel Castro in Cuba and Ho Chi Minh in Vietnam. For almost 25 years after World War II, this *cold war bipolar* view of the world was shared by virtually all political figures in the United States and by most of the American people. The only difference between so-called liberals and conservatives was in what to do about this situation. The liberals (normally Democrats) maintained that we should *contain* communism wherever it was and stop it from spreading to other countries, hoping that it would one day liberalize itself.[6] Thus the North Atlantic Treaty Organization (NATO), formed in 1949, was intended to hold the line in Europe; the Korean conflict, after some initial confusion, was explained as containing communism at the thirty-eighth parallel in Korea; and similarly, we contained communism at the seventeenth parallel in Vietnam. The conservatives, led by President Eisenhower's secretary of state, John Foster Dulles, and Senator Barry Goldwater, among others, talked about ultimate victory over communism and, in fact, the possibility of "liberating" the "slave peoples" behind the Iron Curtain.[7]

[6]The classic statement of containment was the article by "X," actually State Department member George Kennan, "The Sources of Soviet Conduct," *Foreign Affairs* 25 (July 1947): 566–582.

[7]See Barry Goldwater, *The Conscience of a Conservative* (New York: Hillman, 1960), chap. 10.

Nikita Khrushchev and President John Kennedy meet in Vienna. *(National Archives.)*

From Cold War to Realism

There were, of course, many problems with this analysis. For one thing, how was one to classify a revolution in a Third World country against a colonial imperial power? Or a revolution in a poor country for a larger economic share of that country's resources? John Kennedy shared most of the assumptions of the bipolar cold war view of the world, but he understood the implications of Third World revolutions and so sought a more imaginative solution to the problem, which he called *counterinsurgency*. This involved attempts to win over the people of a country to our side (or to the side of nationalist leaders favorable to us) by countering revolutionary forces with their own techniques. Thus he instigated the Green Beret program in Vietnam, where tough antiguerrilla American forces would go into the jungles and conduct covert activities against Southeast Asian revolutionaries.

But even this did not work, and Kennedy's successor, Lyndon Johnson, was forced to use much more power to thwart the "advance of communism" in Southeast Asia. As a result, by 1968, the United States had 525,000 ground forces in South Vietnam, costing the country close to $30 billion a year.[8]

A corollary to the bipolar cold war view of the world was the *domino theory*. As President Johnson's secretary of state, Dean Rusk, once said, "Aggression feeds on success."[9] Once an aggressor was at all successful, it would seek ever-more satisfaction. So as President Eisenhower emphasized, if Vietnam "fell" to the communists, so too, in rapid order, would other "free" nations in Southeast Asia, eventually Australia, and perhaps on and on until most of the world was engulfed.[10]

By the late 1960s, the evident failure of U.S. policy in Vietnam confronted policymakers with a dilemma. If the cold war bipolar perception of the world was correct, then the other side was about to score an important victory, the line had not been held, and other communist aggressions would surely soon take place. We had either to anticipate doom or change our perception of the world. We did the latter.

Henry Kissinger, a professor from Harvard, brought to the Nixon administration a different way of looking at the international scene. This view we shall call *realism*. It is associated with various academicians, perhaps the most famous (other than Kissinger) being the late Hans J. Morgenthau.[11] Although there are differences among realists, the essential lines of their thought are the following.

First, aggression on the part of one country against another country (like Germany's invasion of Poland in 1939) is different from a civil war (like Vietnamese communists fighting other Vietnamese *in* Vietnam).

Second, an international ideology, such as communism, may well not be as important a factor in motivating individuals and governments as we have thought. Indeed, the most important factor in the contemporary world may be *nationalism*, that is, the desire of a people to achieve national independence (whether from Western colonial powers or from others) and, if possible, national greatness. Maybe Vietnam was distinct from Moscow or Peking. In fact, among communist states themselves, there are great differences in both national aims and ideology. China and Russia, rather than being closely aligned because they are both ostensibly Marxist–Leninist states, actually are suspicious and fearful of each other. Indeed, some realists argue that the Soviet Union is more *Russian* in its aims than it is *communist*. For example, the Soviet invasion of Afghanistan in late 1979

[8]For details, see *The Pentagon Papers* (New York: Bantam, 1971).

[9]Dean Rusk, "Guidelines of U.S. Foreign Policy," *Department of State Bulletin*, June 28, 1965, pp. 1032–1034.

[10]*Public Papers of the President . . . Dwight D. Eisenhower, 1954* (Washington, D.C.: U.S. Government Printing Office, 1960), pp. 382–383.

[11]See Hans J. Morgenthau, *In Defense of the National Interest* (New York: Knopf, 1951); *Politics Among Nations* (New York: Praeger, 1967); and *A New Foreign Policy for the U.S.* (New York: Praeger, 1969).

might be explained as part of the historical thrust of Russia to the Indian ocean, a movement as characteristic of Russian czars as of Russian communists. Likewise, Soviet dominance in Eastern Europe more closely resembles past Russian aims than some vague Marxist mandate.

Third, according to the realists, a nation should pursue its *interests*, not conduct diplomacy on the basis of ideology. That is, a country should understand its limitations, its own economic and defense needs, and avoid a foreign policy based on "spreading democracy," "preserving freedom," or "fighting communism." These latter aims are vague and lead to bizarre and occasionally disastrous consequences. How, for example, could the United States legitimately say that it was upholding freedom and democracy by bringing the former dictatorship of Portugal into NATO or by fighting on the side of the corrupt government of South Vietnam?

Fourth, realists look at the world in terms of a balance of forces. Thus they tend to believe that arms agreements can succeed only if the countries negotiating them perceive that there is "parity" between them, that both sides have equivalent military strength. For example, the United States would probably not be willing to negotiate an end to the development of armaments if the Soviet Union had just demonstrated that it had military strength superior to that of the Americans.

Finally, some realists accept the fact and value of *spheres of influence*. They would concede Soviet dominance in Eastern Europe, understanding its importance to the Soviet Union, whereas in return the Soviets would be expected to sanction our influence in the Western hemisphere.

Ironically, Richard Nixon, one of the most implacable and vocal of the early cold warriors, became the first president to break with the old bipolar view of the world and, under the influence of Kissinger, proclaim realism as the basis of our foreign policy. An important 1970 speech to Congress by President Nixon marked this transition: "The postwar period in international relations has ended . . . international Communist unity has been shattered . . . by powerful forces of nationalism." From now on, "our objective in the first instance is to support our *interests*."[12]

When Nixon followed this speech with diplomatic trips to the Soviet Union (to begin negotiations for arms limitations) and China, the American people seemed to respond positively, demonstrating the popularity of the new approach in foreign policy. Particularly in our relations with the Soviet Union, we began to pursue a policy of *détente*, which simply means a thawing of the old cold war and a vigorous effort to achieve diplomatic understandings whenever possible rather than to seek success through threats. In the context of détente, the United States left Vietnam and, mainly because of the efforts of Henry Kissinger, launched an intense

---

[12]*U.S. Foreign Policy for the 1970's: A New Strategy for Peace.* A Report to the Congress by Richard Nixon, President, February 18, 1970.

diplomatic effort to begin solving the Mideast crisis. In each of these instances, we did so without having to invoke the old cold war bipolar slogans.

Foreign Policy Under Carter

Still, there were challenges in the contemporary world not addressed by either the cold warriors or the realists. For example, what should U.S. policy be toward the undeveloped Third and Fourth World nations, which are characterized by economic poverty? (Third World nations are "developing nations" such as most of the countries in Africa; Fourth World nations are those with so many problems—chiefly large-scale hunger—that for them even to begin "developing" seems impossible at the moment. Bangladesh is an example.) What should be U.S. policy toward energy-producing nations, such as the members of the Organization of Petroleum Exporting Countries (OPEC), which, though not economically developed as are Western nations, nevertheless have considerable influence over the flow of indispensable raw materials, especially oil?

Moreover, the emergence of a realist foreign policy did not end some of the more unacceptable techniques used by the cold warriors. For example, in the early 1970s, the CIA apparently spent large amounts of money to help overthrow the legitimate, constitutional government of Salvador Allende-Gossens in Chile. Allende's government was replaced, following his assassination, by a military dictatorship. Does this represent a pursuance of American "interests"? Where, indeed, do morality and a sense of values fit into foreign policy? "Morality" was one key to the cold war views of the world because we considered communism ruthless and immoral. Yet this view led us to drop napalm bombs and antipersonnel weapons on civilians in Vietnam. On the other hand, realists discount as unwise the insistence on morality in foreign policy and emphasize instead "interests." But should not our foreign policy be moral? President Carter insisted that we restore morality to U.S. foreign policy, and he emphasized the advancement of human rights as an aim of his administration's diplomacy. Certainly, the president's decision to speak out forcefully in favor of human rights was in keeping with the best American tradition. Yet, in the past, such pronouncements usually intensified the cold war. The Carter policy appeared to have strong support from the American people and Congress, but it touched a sensitive nerve in Moscow and almost certainly played a role in the Soviet Union's decision to let the first serious negotiations between the Carter administration and the Soviets (over arms reduction) lapse into failure. Presumably, Carter meant to apply this policy impartially to friends and trading partners as well as to less friendly states. What then of authoritarian nations such as South Africa or Zaire whose support may have been important to our national interests but whose human rights policies left much to be desired?

When Soviet troops invaded Afghanistan on December 27, 1979, the world suddenly seemed plunged once again into the cold war. The Carter administration removed from Senate consideration the SALT II agreement (the Strategic Arms Limitation Talks treaty concluded in 1979 between the Soviet Union and the United States but not approved by the Senate), suspended the trade of grain and high-technology exports to the Soviet Union, and announced an American boycott of the 1980 Summer Olympics in Moscow. Additionally, the president asked Congress to increase defense expenditures in fiscal year 1981. Obviously, the administration believed the Soviet move was a threat to our national interests in the Persian Gulf region, from where we received about one quarter of the oil we imported in 1979 (the proportion was even higher for our allies—two-thirds for Western Europe and three-fourths for Japan). The United States proceeded to increase its naval presence in the area and began negotiations to gain American access to additional air and naval facilities in countries in the region, and the president announced in early 1980 what came to be called the *Carter doctrine*: "An attempt by any outside force to gain control of the Persian Gulf region will be regarded as an assault on the vital interests of the United States of America, and such an assault will be repelled by any means necessary, including military force." Such ominous verbiage was reminiscent of the early days of the cold war, but the administration insisted that it was not returning to the earlier policy. Secretary of State Cyrus Vance stressed that "we seek no cold war, no indiscriminate confrontation." Rather, he said, we wished to have with the Soviet Union an appropriate and restrained competition in which each side recognized and appreciated the interests of the other.[13]

Indeed the Carter administration had taken advantage of the movement away from the cold war to realize some acknowledged achievements in foreign affairs. With little or no reference to the Soviet Union, the Senate approved the landmark Panama Canal treaties in 1978 (providing for gradual return of the Canal Zone to Panamanian sovereignty). Similarly, by early 1979, the president succeeded in obtaining the signatures of Israeli Prime Minister Menachem Begin and Egyptian President Anwar Sadat to two historic treaties, one establishing peace between the two countries and the other providing for an ongoing process to achieve a comprehensive settlement of the Middle East problem. Other achievements of Carter's foreign policy were the establishment of full diplomatic relations with the People's Republic of China in early 1979, the negotiated settlement of a civil

[13]See Cyrus Vance, *U.S. Foreign Policy: Our Broader Strategy* (Washington, D.C.: U.S. Department of State, Bureau of Public Affairs, March 27, 1980). This statement before the Senate Committee on Foreign Relations was a comprehensive outline of the Carter administration's foreign policy.

war in Nicaragua in mid-1979, and the peaceful transition of Zimbabwe-Rhodesia in 1980 from an African country ruled by a white minority to a nation with majority rule. (Although Great Britain took the lead in this latter affair, the Carter administration was very supportive and quickly announced its recognition of the government of Robert Mugabe, the black radical leader overwhelmingly elected prime minister in late February 1980.)

These successes were due in part to America's perceiving international affairs in a more complex way than the bipolar view of the cold war, and the results seemed eminently more attractive than what we gained (or lost) in intervening in Southeast Asia or in disrupting politics in Chile. Yet, as the 1980s began, serious problems remained: Comprehensive peace in the Middle East was still far from achieved; dangers persisted in the military buildup of the two superpowers and the proliferation of nuclear weaponry; economic disparity between poorer and richer countries continued to grow; and the worldwide competition for energy threatened to raise, not lower, international tensions. These concerns, along with frustrations over events in Iran and Afghanistan, led Americans to wonder which approach to the world—cold war, realism, or the demands of a growing peace movement in the United States and Europe—really best served our interests.

Foreign Policy Under Reagan

When he entered office, President Reagan was concerned primarily with his domestic legislative program, believing that he had a mandate to solve the problems of high inflation, low productivity, and economic stagnation. As we have noted, he proved successful in implementing his legislative program and apparently successful in his economic plans. His early concentration on domestic affairs may help explain some of the difficulties of his foreign policy. Apart from a strident rhetoric, there is little evidence that Reagan began his presidency with anything like Richard Nixon's understanding of or plans for the world arena.

As a candidate for president in 1976 and 1980 Ronald Reagan set himself apart from his competitors with his staunch opposition to the policies of détente (indeed, among his most frequent targets was fellow Republican Henry Kissinger). He was skeptical of improving relations with the People's Republic of China (going so far as to indicate during the campaign of 1980 that he would restore diplomatic recognition to the government on Taiwan); he vigorously campaigned against the Panama Canal treaties; he attacked the Carter policy of insistence on the upholding of human rights, agreeing with Professor Jeane Kirkpatrick (later Reagan's ambassador to the UN) that human rights violations should be condemned when taking place in "totalitarian" countries, like the Soviet Union, but ignored when perpetrated by friendly "authoritarian" regimes, such as the military junta in

Argentina (see the glossary for definitions of these terms); he opposed arms talks with the Soviet Union, such as SALT II, and urged instead a unilateral U.S. arms buildup; and he advocated a more vigorous interventionist policy in Central America.

Not only his rhetoric as a candidate suggested that he would return to a strict cold war posture once in office, so too did his early appointments of hard-liners, such as General Alexander Haig as secretary of state, Richard Allen as national security adviser, and Jeane Kirkpatrick as UN ambassador. Also, the harsh language continued, reaching an apex in March 1983, when the president delivered a bitter speech calling the Soviet Union an evil empire responsible for virtually everything that was wrong in the world. Then, by the fall of 1983, with American marines stationed in Lebanon (and suffering casualties), with the U.S. invasion of the Caribbean nation of Grenada, with American military maneuvers in Central America, and with the arms talks at a standstill, the president spoke to the nation, explaining that all of this was because America had to check the advances around the globe of the Soviet Union and its clients. U.S. foreign policy seemed to have come full circle, returning to a most implacable cold war bipolar view of the world.

Moreover, by early 1984 it became clear to the Democrats that Reagan, although popular, was politically vulnerable on foreign policy issues, because a large number of Americans, probably a majority, did not favor turning back the diplomatic clock. This political problem may help explain the ongoing shifts discernible in the president's foreign policy. For example, in the summer of 1982, the moderate businessman and economist George Shultz had replaced the flamboyant Haig as secretary of state. During 1981, serious strains plagued the NATO alliance as the Reagan administration, pursuing its anti-Soviet course, attempted to restrict U.S. suppliers from exporting to Europe the technology necessary to complete an oil pipeline from the Soviet Union to Western Europe. However, eventually—and quietly—the administration backed down from its position, perhaps assuaging somewhat the ill feelings of both Soviets and West Europeans. Meantime, Reagan's campaign remarks regarding China, the special military arrangements with Taiwan that Reagan supported, and some minor irritations of U.S. trade and financial policy resulted in a deterioration of relations with that country. But in early 1984, Chinese Premier Zhao Ziyang came to the United States in a highly publicized state visit; some trade arrangements were announced; the president subsequently visited China; and relations seemed to be back to the friendly status achieved when President Carter recognized the PRC.

Reagan had found distasteful President Carter's policy in southern Africa, which supported black majority rule, opposed human rights violations, and, as we have seen, helped bring an end to the white minority government in Rhodesia (now called Zimbabwe). Reagan and his chief African adviser, Chester Crocker, viewed the minority white-ruled government of the Republic of South Africa as a friendly ally and called for *constructive engagement*, by which they meant continuing to recommend reform within South Africa (including the gradual inclusion of black Africans in the political process), but doing this in a more friendly manner by encouraging U.S. firms to invest in South Africa and ceasing any form of overt pressure on the government there. The administration also believed that this policy would more quickly lead to the independence of Namibia (formerly South-West Africa), a country ruled by South Africa since it ceased being a German colony in World War I. Critics pointed out that the policy had led neither to black voting in South Africa nor to Namibian independence, but the Reagan administration pointed to the establishment in 1983 of a new constitution in South Africa allowing limited political participation for "coloreds" (those of mixed race) and "Asians" (Indians), although still excluding the majority black Africans from any participation in the government.

By the spring of 1988 the situation in southern Africa had changed little. *Apartheid* (a system of racial segregation) in South Africa had not been ended and Namibia remained under South African control. However, talks were under way among South Africans, the Angolan government (supported by the Soviet Union), Cuba, and the United States. These talks were encouraged by the United States and welcomed by the Soviet Union, one more indication of the desire of the superpowers to resolve regional differences between themselves. If successful, they could lead to removal of Cuban forces from Angola (invited there to help protect oil fields from attack by South African-supported guerrillas), and to eventual Namibian independence, because South Africa continued to insist on the evacuation of Cuban troops as a precondition for leaving neighboring Namibia.

The always perplexing Middle East proved no easier for President Reagan than it had for his predecessors. By 1984 the stationing of U.S. marines in Beirut, Lebanon, had become one of the most unpopular of Reagan's actions. Although he eventually removed these forces, the president insisted that their presence was necessary to help bring peace to that troubled and divided country, and for a while at least he continued to promote his own plan for a comprehensive Middle East settlement. This proposal, announced in a major speech on September 1, 1982, called for Israeli withdrawal from the West Bank of the Jordan River (taken during the war of 1967) and the establishment there of an autonomous Palestinian entity politically tied to Jordan. But neither Israelis nor Arabs would ultimately agree to the proposal, and U.S. initiatives languished until the outbreak in December 1987 of uprisings in the occupied West Bank and the Gaza Strip. These uprisings, which continued into the summer of 1988, featured Palestinians in the territories confronting Israeli security forces with rock throwing, boycotts, and other forms of disobedience. Worldwide television covered the uprisings and the subsequent Israeli efforts to contain them, often using harsh methods. Under the new circumstances, Secretary of State Shultz resurrected the moribund peace plan of 1982, added some new features to it (including a proposal for an international conference and a more rapid timetable for trying to meet Palestinian grievances), and set out on several trips to the Middle East. But the secretary's efforts seemed futile as Arabs resisted recognizing Israel's right to exist within secure borders and Israel refused to deal with the Palestinian Liberation Organization or agree to an international conference that would include Soviet participation. The only signs of progress by the summer of 1988 were the Soviet Union's kind words for Secretary Shultz's efforts and a willingness by members of the Israeli Labor party (part of the country's coalition government) to accept Shultz's proposals (whereas the more conservative Likud party refused).

Iran too proved a continuing headache for the United States. Iranian-supported, and probably sponsored, terrorists kidnapped and murdered Americans. Some 240 U.S. marines died in a single suicide bombing in Beirut in 1983, widely believed to have had Iranian complicity. Efforts to improve relations with Iran through secret negotiations initiated by then NSC Director Robert MacFarlane and later by Admiral Poindexter and Colonel North proved a political and diplomatic fiasco. Finally, the United States was forced to intervene militarily in the long war between Iraq and Iran by deploying large naval forces in the Persian Gulf, where the two belligerents were blasting each other's and neutral shipping. Mines planted by the Iranians led to reprisals and even battles between Iranian and U.S. forces at sea and in the air. Late in 1988, the end of the Iran–Iraq War raised at least the possibility of an improvement in U.S.-Iranian relations.

Central America also challenged the president. A U.S.-supported government in tiny El Salvador faced a vigorous guerrilla rebellion, and Nicaragua, run by Sandinistas—a leftist group named for a guerrilla fighter killed during the 1930s—was opposed by the United States, which supported the anti-Sandinista guerrillas. Polls showed that Americans were confused as to which government we supported and which revolutionary guerrillas were on our side. Partly to resolve the confusion but mostly to establish a bipartisan consensus on Central America, Reagan appointed a 12-member blue-ribbon commission, the National Bipartisan Commission on Central America, to study the area and make proposals. Headed by Reagan's erstwhile political enemy Henry Kissinger, the panel developed recommendations essentially in line with the president's tough policy. Insisting that joint Soviet and Cuban incursions in the area represented a strategic danger, the commission urged that financial aid amounting to $8 billion over a five-year period be funneled to friendly governments in Central America to help remove the social and economic distress that the Soviets and Cubans were exploiting. There were also recommendations to maintain, and even increase, military aid to the government of El Salvador and to the rebels fighting against the Nicaraguan government. In opposition to the views of both Reagan and Kissinger, the majority of the commission urged that aid be given to El Salvador only upon proof that human rights violations in that country were ceasing (there were allegations that the government condoned the activities of so-called death squads—right-wing military groups that traveled around the country summarily executing civilians suspected of guerrilla sympathies). The administration hinted that it might ignore this latter recommendation but accept the rest of the report. There were two aspects of this policy that disturbed a growing number of critics: first, that the administration showed a preference for military over diplomatic techniques in pursuing its policies and, second, that the policy seemed remarkably similar to the one followed so unsuccessfully in Vietnam. By 1987, as we have seen, the Iran-Contra scandal had severely damaged the administration's hard-line Central American policy. By summer of that year the president began a modest shift in his policy, accepting a peace proposal worked out by President Oscar Arias of Costa Rica and accepted by the presidents of all the Central America countries. The proposal called for an end to the fighting, cessation of outside military aid to guerrillas fighting existing governments, and talks between guerrillas and governments to resolve differences peacefully (this would include both Nicaragua and El Salvador). Indeed, for the most part, fighting did stop, and by summer 1988, despite the off-and-on nature of the talks, Sandinistas and Contras were discussing ways of ending the civil war that had so debilitated their country.

It was the relationship with the Soviet Union that most concerned the American people. Reagan's early rhetoric certainly helped sour the relationship, but in fairness, he rarely *acted* in a hostile manner. For example, following the clampdown of martial law in Poland in 1981 (encouraged by the Soviet Union), the United States gingerly imposed some trade and financial restrictions but by 1984 had lifted them and moved toward normal relations with the Polish government. After the Soviets shot down a Korean airliner in September 1983, killing 269 passengers (including a number of Americans), President Reagan lashed out in words but did very little in the way of concrete retaliatory action. Indeed, only a few weeks after this tragic event, the president delivered a rather conciliatory and well-received speech at the UN (an institution he once ridiculed), calling on the Soviets to join in serious arms talks. However, the Soviets were not all that helpful. At every hint that the United States was prepared to deal more constructively in this important relationship, the Soviets seemed to make some blunder. For example, the downing of the Korean airliner came on the heels of a negotiated arrangement to sell much-needed grain to the Soviet Union.

Nonetheless, it was the U.S. decision (along with that of its NATO allies) to deploy sophisticated intermediate-range nuclear missiles in Western Europe that caused the most concern in the Soviet Union. In the late 1970s, NATO discovered that a new-generation missile—the SS-20—was being installed in European Russia and aimed at Western Europe. By late 1983 there were over 300 of these, each with three nuclear warheads. In 1979, during the Carter presidency, NATO had decided to deploy 572 new missiles to counteract these SS-20s, while at the same time pursuing negotiations to cut back the so-called INFs (intermediate-range nuclear forces) on both sides. The Soviets and the Americans each made public proposals, but no serious negotiations ever transpired, and when the Western missiles began to be deployed in December 1983, the Soviets walked out of the INF negotiations (and began for the first time to deploy their missiles in Eastern European countries) and also left the START talks (Strategic Arms Reduction Talks, formerly called SALT) and the MBFR talks (Mutual Balanced Force Reduction talks, dealing with conventional weapons and standing armies in Europe). Meantime, Reagan announced in his 1985 budget an even larger increase in military spending than in the past. The arms race accelerated dangerously.

Yet, on January 16, 1984, Reagan delivered a conciliatory speech insisting that the United States was now stronger than ever and that consequently peace was more certain, and he called for the Soviets to reenter arms negotiations.[14] Subsequently, a number of U.S. officials indicated that the United States was prepared to be more flexible than ever in negotiations. This was followed by several other goodwill gestures. In his 1984 State of the Union Address, Reagan declared, in remarks directed specifically to the Soviet people, that "a nuclear war cannot be won and must never be fought."[15] Upon the death of Soviet leader Yuri Andropov, the president and other high officials in the government stressed their desire to enter a "constructive and realistic dialogue" to "build a more stable and more positive relationship" with the Soviet Union.[16] Vice President George Bush, attending Andropov's funeral in Moscow, brought to the new Soviet leader, Konstantin Chernenko, not only condolences but also this conciliatory message.

With the ascendancy of Mikhail Gorbachev to the position of party secretary in 1985, Soviet responses to these conciliatory American moves were quick in coming. Gorbachev, seemingly genuine in his desire to restructure the Soviet economy, liberalize the society, and diminish heavy-handed Soviet diplomacy around the world, moved rapidly in international affairs. He sought better relations with China, visited his Eastern European allies, where he encouraged more independent and liberal policies, and began the withdrawal of Soviet forces from Afghanistan. Most important, he developed an unusual (some might say close) relationship with the U.S. president. Reagan, criticized for years for being the first president since Hoover *not* to meet with a Soviet leader, ended up having more summits (four by the spring of 1988) than any other chief executive in our history. The relationship between the two superpowers was never so cordial (except

[14]For the text of the speech and an analysis of it, see the *New York Times*, January 17, 1984.
[15]*New York Times*, January 26, 1984, p. 12.
[16]These were the words of Secretary of State George Shultz. See the *New York Times*, February 11, 1984, p. 7.

perhaps in the darkest days of World War II when we fought together), a *disarmament* treaty (a treaty actually resulting in the destruction of a certain class of weapons) was achieved in the Intermediate Range Nuclear Forces agreement signed by the two leaders in Washington in 1987 and exchanged in Moscow in 1988, and prospects for further arms agreements were bright.

President Reagan's foreign policy had evolved dramatically. Yet there were ups and downs, and there remained serious questions as to whether this policy served our interests and those of the rest of the world. Thus there also remain unanswered questions about the principles, perceptions, and policies of our country's foreign affairs. How we got into this situation and where we might go from here can perhaps best be understood from a brief, impressionistic look at our history.

Lessons from the Past

Let us return for a moment to the definition of diplomacy. It means negotiating in the international community to get what you want, or at least as much as possible. Diplomacy may be the chief means used by nations to implement their foreign policy.

What does a country use to conduct diplomacy? There are three tools. First, physical power: you can threaten an adversary until you get your way. If you have superior military power, this may work. In the generation after World War II, cold warriors believed that this was the best means to achieve diplomatic goals. John Foster Dulles developed the theory of *massive retaliation*, which meant that if problems arose anywhere in the world, we would threaten the communist enemy with wholesale attack until the problem ceased.[17] Other examples are Kennedy's and Johnson's attempts to impose favorable solutions on Vietnam by using military force, and Reagan's policies in Central America.

A second tool is economic power. When the United States emerged as a rich nation in the early twentieth century, it frequently followed a policy called *dollar diplomacy*. President William Howard Taft used to talk about substituting "dollars for bullets." Thus, to maintain America's security in Central America, he sent U.S. bankers to various countries to control customs collections and national budgets there to thwart potential intervention by European powers. He also authorized the organization of a large group of American financiers to lend money to the Chinese government so that it, in turn, could build railroads and other public works and avoid influence from other great powers. In recent years, foreign aid programs have represented the U.S. attempt to use economic power to further diplomatic ends. The economic sanctions imposed on Panama in 1988 is another

[17]Ambrose, pp. 193–195.

example, as is the proposal of the Kissinger commission to pour massive financial aid into Central America.

But what if a country does not have a large, powerful, and threatening military establishment? Or what if the country is not rich, as was the case in Vietnam in the 1960s or the United States in 1776? What tools then can be used? The third tool is wily, wise, and skillful diplomats. That is what the Vietnamese had in Paris in 1972 and what the Americans had, also in Paris, from 1776 through 1783.

Let us look at American diplomacy in the first generation following our Revolution, when diplomats were used at least as much as other tools were. From 1776 to 1823, the United States' perception of its role in the world was based on certain principles, and it conducted its foreign policy on the basis of those principles and that perception.[18]

To be sure, Benjamin Franklin, John Adams, John Jay, and later, George Washington and John Quincy Adams had differences of opinion, but there were certain essentials in their foreign policy. For example, Americans believed that they could develop a new diplomacy based on the principles of the eighteenth century. The diplomacy of each of the states of Europe, not unlike that of the realists today, sought to further the interests of that nation, even (sometimes purposely) at the expense of other nations. On the contrary, Benjamin Franklin said that nations should conduct diplomacy with other nations in the same spirit as a person should treat a neighbor. Thus did Franklin create the concept of good neighborliness in diplomacy.

Moreover, the Americans believed that their most important asset was a potential, growing market, and so they encouraged trade among nations, in contrast with the typically mercantilist policies then in effect. Also, the Americans, who possessed a Puritan strain, believed that cunning, adventurous diplomacy was characteristic of a decadent government. John Adams was repulsed by secret maneuverings and espionage and preferred what has been called *shirt-sleeve diplomacy*, that is, diplomacy that is open and down to earth. Finally, the originators of our diplomacy were, in the best sense, internationalists. Franklin, for example, while in Europe, devised a scheme for international arbitration to replace warfare as a means of settling disputes among nations. He would have liked to establish such an ongoing, almost permanent, procedure of arbitration following the wars of the American Revolution.

---

[18]The following few paragraphs are based in part on material in Felix Gilbert, *To the Farewell Address: Ideas of Early American Foreign Policy* (Princeton, N.J.: Princeton University Press, 1961); Gerald Stourzh, *Benjamin Franklin and American Foreign Policy*, 2nd ed. (Chicago: University of Chicago Press, 1969); James Truslow Adams, *The Adams Family* (New York: Literary Guild, 1930); and Samuel F. Bemis, *John Quincy Adams and the Foundation of American Foreign Policy* (New York: Knopf, 1949). Also enlightening are the *Federalist*, nos. 3, 4, 6, 8, 11, 24, 25, 64, 66, and 75; and Richard B. Morris, *The Peacemakers* (New York: Harper & Row, 1965).

If we look at a few items of the period from 1776 to 1823, we can detect the characteristics of this early diplomacy. These items include the "model treaty" of 1776, approved by Congress, influenced by John Adams, and intended to be a guide for our relations with other countries; Thomas Paine's *Common Sense*, which influenced Americans' view of their place in the world; the two treaties with France in 1778, which created a trade relationship between the two countries and a military alliance (the latter was terminated officially in 1800—we did not join another military alliance until the twentieth century); the Peace Treaty of 1783 ending the Revolutionary War; Washington's Farewell Address of 1796; the Louisiana Purchase of 1803; and finally, the great accomplishments of Secretary of State John Quincy Adams: the convention with Great Britain in 1818, the Adams-Onis Treaty of 1819, and the Monroe Doctrine of 1823. Without attempting to explain each of these documents in detail, we merely note that they contain certain basic characteristics that define our early diplomacy.

First, with the exception of the French alliance, the United States acted in diplomacy *unilaterally*—that is, on its own—not in alliance with other nations. Second, in the items listed, the United States pursued a policy of *noninterference* in the internal affairs of other countries and *nonentanglement* in the affairs of other continents, particularly Europe. Third, the United States gave *de facto recognition* to governments—that is, we recognized the governments that in fact existed, whether or not we agreed with their form of government. Fourth, we pursued policies of *economic and commercial expansion* with as many portions of the world as possible. Fifth, we sought to solidify our *continental* boundaries, creating an empire to stretch across North America, but one (unlike that of Rome or Britain) that contained self-governing republics (states) of equal citizens rather than colonies. Finally, we sought to be an *example* to the world of a proper, republican form of government that other countries, on their own volition, would try to imitate.

In 1846, in violation of some of the principles of the early period, the United States went to war with Mexico, and by means of the Treaty of Guadalupe Hidalgo in 1848 ending that war, we appropriated half of what had been Mexico. Henceforth, the goal of American foreign policy was different. The continent was filled and America was growing more prosperous. Now we looked forward to an isthmian canal and, concomitantly, hegemony in the Caribbean and control of Hawaii. It was 50 years before these implications of 1848 were fulfilled, but as a result of the war with Spain in 1898, the United States eventually got its canal in Panama, gained control of the Caribbean, and annexed Hawaii.[19] Also, however, in contrast with our traditions, we annexed the Philippines, which threw us into the

[19]See Charles S. Campbell, *The Transformation of American Foreign Relations* (New York: Harper & Row, 1976).

cauldron of East Asian diplomacy. The world wars in the twentieth century and the subsequent cold war (as we have seen) drew America further into world affairs.

We should keep two things in mind about American diplomacy during all this history: First, the United States was never in any definable sense "isolationist" (we had normal diplomatic relations with other nations; we negotiated and signed many treaties; and we sought commercial expansion throughout the world). Second, we never avoided being involved in conflicts once they became international in scope. The American Revolution was itself a world war. The War of 1812 was a rump action in the international wars following the French Revolution. A century of relative peace in the world kept the United States and the rest of the world out of sustained warfare, but once war again became worldwide in the twentieth century, the United States became involved.

The Future of American Foreign Policy

Thus the crucial question is not whether the United States should be isolationist or internationalist. The former is and has always been impossible. The question is what our international role should be. Should we be cold warriors or realists? Or something else?

Radical critics of U.S. foreign policy find both cold warriorism and realism inadequate. Many of them argue that U.S. foreign policy is based not on ideology or vague "national interests" but on expanding the markets and the available resources for large U.S. corporations. We seek the overthrow of governments, as in Nicaragua, and the control of other governments, like those in the Caribbean, to protect and expand the interests of American corporate capitalism. Applying a kind of power-elite thesis to international affairs, these critics argue that U.S. foreign policy is chiefly influenced by and beneficial to big business, ignoring the needs of the people of other countries as well as those of the majority of Americans. Thus, to eliminate American imperialism, according to these critics, it would be necessary first to make fundamental alterations in the economic system in the United States.[20]

But as wholesale revision of the U.S. economy, on the face of it, seems unrealistic, how can the United States best pursue its interests without abandoning its sense of morality? Is there a foreign policy alternative to that promoted by cold warriors, realists, and radical critics?

One way of answering this question is by investigating once again the

[20]See Gabriel Kolko, *The Roots of American Foreign Policy* (Boston: Beacon Press, 1969); and Harry Magdoff, *The Age of Imperialism: The Economics of United States Foreign Policy* (New York: Atlantic Monthly Review Press, 1969).

principles, perceptions, and policies of the first generation of American diplomacy to see how appropriate some of them might be for our day.

1. As Benjamin Franklin might say, we should be good-neighbor internationalists. We could do this in a number of ways. For example, we could seek solutions to international problems, whenever feasible, through international organizations. Our economic policy could be to encourage international trade, and particularly we should be willing and able to export food to countries desperately in need of it. Also, we could end unilateral foreign aid programs (which were designed to create diplomatic allies in the cold war, not to aid countries) and encourage the substitution of an internationalized aid program. Thus each country would be taxed a small percentage of its gross national product, perhaps on a progressive scale (the richest nations would pay more—this is the case now anyway). The money thus accumulated would be administered by an international organization on the basis of need rather than on the basis of political alliance.

There are, of course, several formidable barriers to such international cooperation. First and foremost is the perennial problem of nationalism, which, as we have seen, militates against international law and collaboration. Moreover, as long as the world remains divided into two, three, or four blocs, each struggling for increased power and prestige for itself and a diminution of the power and prestige of others, any effective and sensible program of cooperation will be difficult to organize. But policies of confrontation and war have not solved world problems and, in some instances, have made them worse. The United States is a rich and powerful nation, born, after all, out of revolution against a colonial power. We have an obligation to keep trying international cooperation.

There are other elements of that first generation of U.S. diplomacy that may also be worthy of consideration.

2. We could return to the policy of recognizing countries *de facto* (those that actually exist) rather than *de jure* (those that we think should exist). De jure recognition has created enormous problems for the United States. From 1917 to 1933 we did not have an ambassador in Moscow. For a generation we refused to recognize China (though it contained about 20 percent of the world's population) and instead recognized the Chinese on Taiwan; we refused to recognize Ho Chi Minh's government in Vietnam and got bogged down in a disastrous war. In each instance, we may well have been better off to have recognized the real government. The normalization of relations with China and the recognition of the government of Zimbabwe represent a positive return to the policy of de facto recognition.

3. We could return to the earlier policy of noninterference in the internal affairs of other countries. American interventions in the twentieth century have frequently caused us difficulty and often have been harmful to our interests—in the Soviet Union from 1918 to 1920, in China in the late 1940s, in Cuba in 1961 (the Bay of Pigs invasion), and in Vietnam. The wrath that Iranians have display toward the United States has been in large part due to

their remembrance of American involvement in and support of the shah's government (the CIA helped set up the shah's regime in 1953).

4. We should limit considerably, if not end, certain international covert activities of espionage agencies. The accumulation of important and sometimes secret data is indispensable for framing and conducting foreign policy, but the surreptitious assassination of foreign leaders and the purposeful internal disruptions of other countries are questionable for a country dedicated to law and republican institutions.

5. We should rely more on diplomacy and less on military blustering to achieve our foreign policy aims. We have had some recent successes in this regard in the Egyptian-Israeli accords, the Helsinki agreement, and the INF treaty. The credibility of the United States as a leader in the international community would be greatly enchanced by our continuing in this direction.

6. We should return to the Founding Fathers' image of our being an example to the world rather than physically trying to create little (or big) American-style regimes around the world. As John Quincy Adams so well knew, if we kept our own house in order, others would be much more likely to follow our example.

These factors represent a framework for foreign policy activity based on a reconsideration of earlier American diplomacy. But what of specific problems and areas in the world?

If national survival is the first and most important goal of foreign policy, then our primary concern is our relations with the Soviet Union. Only the Soviets have the military power to destroy us, just as we have the power to destroy them. That has been the fundamental argument in favor of détente, which succeeded the policy of cold war because of the inescapable fact that the Americans and the Soviets, whatever their political, economic, and social differences, must either find a way to live together in peace or face mutual nuclear annihilation.

Thus, the world is *militarily* bipolar, but it is *politically* multipolar. This seems to be one lesson emerging from the most recent events characterizing Soviet-American relations. For although we certainly hope that the two sides can find a way of living together on the same planet without an arms race and without war, we should also note that where the two can work together to solve international problems (as in Afghanistan, Cambodia, Central America, or the Middle East) confrontation diminishes, peace tends to be more quickly and easily achieved, and the needs of the world's peoples more readily satisfied. Together the Soviet Union and the United States constitute less than 15 percent of the earth's population. The superior military capabilities of the two giants give them neither the right nor the reasonable hope of controlling the social, economic, and political affairs of the other 85 percent.

This leads to the question of future U.S. relations with other nations, ranging from firm allies like Great Britain to countries whose hostility to the United States stops just short of war, such as Iran. The United States needs to recognize that it has different responsibilities in different parts of the world. We are clearly involved with and committed to the survival of the world's remaining democracies, including most of Western Europe, Canada, Australia, New Zealand, Japan, and Israel. A threat to the survival and independence of these nations is like a threat to the United States itself. Second, we are also involved with and committed to a number of other nations, but in a way that is different from our relationship with Western Europe. This includes much of Latin America and several states in the Pacific area such as South Korea and the Philippines. The difference in these two categories of nations is that the first group tends to share our basic values and traditions, whereas the second may or may not. More precisely, sometimes they do, at other times they do not, depending on what type of leadership happens to be in power in those nations. Our commitment to nations like South Korea, or many countries in Latin America, for example, must be tempered by the fact that we cannot realistically hope to control domestic events in these societies, CIA plots notwithstanding.

We must also consider those nations with whom we are neither firm friend nor foe—the OPEC states, for example, or the Soviet Union's allies in Eastern Europe. The United States has little power to control events in these nations and therefore should not realistically be expected to shed American blood in defense of their governments from either foreign or domestic foes. Likewise, our relations with the so-called Third World nations should be based on positive bilateral relations and respect in international forums.

Three of the most humilating failures of U.S. foreign policy in the post-World War II era have come in three Third World countries—Cuba, Vietnam, and Iran. Although the circumstances varied, in all three cases we were kicked out of each of these countries after successful revolutions against governments that had become so identified with the United States as to lose the respect of their own people. In each case a traditional culture was in the process of being radically altered by an influx of both American political and military aid and business, social, and cultural values different from those of the local inhabitants. In short, policies to export the American way of life to underdeveloped nations have often failed miserably.

In dealing with these nations we all are prisoners of history. The Western states carry with them into conferences the vestigial remains of policies that were frankly racist and colonial. Other nations carry memories of exploitation and racial arrogance. The United Nations has grown from 51 member nations in 1945 to 159 today. Most of the states to join the United Nations in the past three decades were former colonies of Western nations. It would be unreasonable to expect delegates from countries that have emerged from a struggle against foreign domination not to view white faces and hear Anglo-Saxon voices with a certain suspicion. Moreover, the leadership of many of these states is Marxist because Marxist doctrine has often played a strong intellectual role in organizing resistance to colonialism, and the Soviet

Union has often contributed at least sympathy and sometimes material aid in the struggle for independence.

Thus we must realize that the nonwhite world, unlike many Western European nations, may not regard the United States as a generous, well-intentioned nation. Some see us simply as the current bosses of the same gang that stole their country centuries ago, enslaved or colonized their people, exploited their resources, and withdrew only when the business of international robbery (imperialism) stopped being a paying proposition.

The Soviet Union has, of course, succeeded in controlling not only the political and military but also the economic and social systems of most of its allies. But in most cases it has done so only by the use of force.

The United States has failed in such efforts because the total domination of one nation over another, even if the dominator is a vastly stronger and more modern state, cannot be maintained indefinitely without force—as Cuba, Vietnam, and Iran have made clear. In the end the United States has been unwilling or unable to apply sufficient force to maintain an empire. Even the ancient Romans understood that the best policy for an imperialist power is scrupulously to avoid interference in the culture, religion, and local affairs of its subject peoples. The British Empire was successful, in part, because British policy was to avoid contact with native subjects beyond that necessary to maintain efficient administration. But Americans are not Russians or ancient Romans or the nineteenth-century British. We seem incapable of going into such places as Vietnam or Iran without trying to "improve" these societies and bestow the blessings of American technology on the people. The results too often are resentment, then hatred, and finally revolution. At that point we face a painful choice: either use our advanced military technology to repress the people whom we thought we were be-friending or pack up our computers and go home. The latter is what we did, wisely, in Iran. In Vietnam we took the other course, with calamitous results.

The bipolar world of the 1950s and 1960s, dominated by the two super-powers, the United States and the Soviet Union, had changed fundamen-tally by the last decade of the twentieth century. Many Americans, and perhaps many citizens of the Soviet Union as well, might welcome this development. For the fact is that superpower status brings no great benefits to the common people. Although Great Britain dominated much of the world during the nineteenth and early twentieth centuries, average Britons remained notably poorer than their counterparts in Germany or France. Despite the Soviet Union's great military and political power, its people are still among the poorest in Europe. While the United States played the role of global policeman for four decades, its economy steadily lost ground to Germany, Japan, and other smaller nations in the competition for the world's markets.

There was evidence by the beginning of 1989 that the United States was beginning to understand these developments and alter its relationships with both friends and foes. Our friendship with China seemed secure and a probable result was peace for the United States in Asia. Our relationship with the Soviets may at last have taken a decisive turn for the better, opening up the prospects not only of an end to the arms race and the cold war, but also the possibility of cooperation in addressing the most intractable international problems. If our allies in Europe were showing signs of increasing independence, this was not so bad for the American taxpayer. Responsible allied leaders had begun talking of the need for "sharing the burden" of defending their own wealth and security. Relations with the Third World remained difficult, if only because the disparity in living standards between the wealthy West and the poor South grows steadily wider. Sooner or later the rich countries of the world will probably have to initiate some sort of global Marshall Plan, not out of charity for the poor and wretched of the earth, but in their own best interests. Even the age-old, implacable Israeli-Palestinian dispute might well be resolved if the wealthy nations, which depend on oil and therefore on peace in the region, were to devote a small fraction of their incomes to helping make a secure and prosperous Israel *and* Palestine possible.

These ideas may seem implausibly idealistic. But then, only a few years ago, so did the notion of friendship with China or arms agreements between Reagan and Gorbachev.

As is the world outside, the United States is made up of a diverse people—more diverse than that of virtually any other nation. Although that diversity is a challenge to us domestically, it is our great advantage in world affairs, for as we proceed to fulfill our own promise, so the world can better hope for progress in international relations. We are, Lincoln observed, "the last, best hope of the world." That is an audacious assumption unless we understand it in terms of trying to make our own society workable and just. In this way we can be the example that our founders wanted us to be. Our historic mission, if there is such a thing, can be understood only in this way. Thus, what is needed is a foreign policy that is finite, modest, and consistent with our traditions.

14

Politics and the Pursuit
of Happiness

- Government: The Cause or the Cure? •
- The Individual and Politics •
- Of Politics and Americans •

> If one really feared democracy, if one really feared the people, one
> would not waste time discrediting a Democrat against a Republican,
> a liberal as against a conservative; one would simply discredit them
> all. . . . One would impute base motives to the politicians and mun-
> dane motives to the people. One would teach them to despise them-
> selves . . . to have contempt for the political process [so that]
> something—anything—look[s] superior to the political motive.
>
> Henry Fairlie
> *New Republic*
> November 13, 1976
>
>
> Every country has the government it deserves.
>
> Joseph DeMaistre

History affirms that no human institution more quickly subverts an established and successful social order and political system than does war,
particularly an unsuccessful war. Marx notwithstanding, it was war, not
communism, that haunted and ultimately destroyed the social order of
nineteenth-century Europe.

Two unpopular and unsatisfactory wars and the four decades of tension
implicit in the cold war have left the United States with a cluster of related
problems, no one of which, perhaps, is as emotionally charged as was the
question of slavery in the nineteenth century, as catastrophic as the Great
Depression of the 1930s, or as militarily dangerous as the rise of fascism in
that same period, but which together do raise fundamental questions about
the continuing viability of American society.

The United States, which only three decades ago could easily command
support of the majority of representatives at the United Nations, now
frequently finds itself in the minority. As the leader of a shrinking bloc of
pro-Western states, the United States too often finds itself awkwardly alone
in international affairs. A gulf seems to have opened between the aspirations of a majority of humankind and the rhetoric of the U.S. government.
No leading American statesman has thus far proposed a coherent plan
whereby that gap might be closed. We must bear in mind that "isolationism" is not always a matter of simply trying to withdraw from the affairs of
the world. One can be isolated by too great a dependence on sheer military
and economic power. (Witness Nazi Germany, surely the strongest military
power on earth at a certain point in its history and also the most isolated.)

Domestically, the past four decades have left most Americans more
prosperous than ever before, perhaps freer to follow their own paths in daily
life, but visibly less certain of their own success as a society.

(Drawing by Joseph Mugnaini.)

Government: The Cause or the Cure?

It has become fashionable in recent years to argue that the government is (1) the cause of most of our problems at home and abroad and (2) utterly unable to propose and carry out any effective remedies for these problems. Those who so believe sometimes point to the failed Eighteenth Amendment to the Constitution (prohibition) as an example of a government that created a problem (illegal bootlegging by organized crime) by passing an unnecessary and unwarranted law and then failing in its efforts to enforce it.

There is another side of this issue. For example, Franklin Roosevelt's New Deal did help combat the Depression, and there have been beneficial effects of much government action, such as the GI Bill of Rights, which provided generations of Americans with affordable homes and higher education, and Medicare, which has protected millions of older Americans against at least some of the financial burdens of illness during old age.

Most of us want the government to act. At the local level we expect a city council either to approve or disapprove a zoning ordinance providing for industrial development. At the national level some people urge Congress to increase defense expenditures while cutting social programs, and others demand exactly the opposite action. The point is that we expect the government to do things. What it does will have consequences, sometimes good and sometimes bad.

Through wise and appropriate actions, the government has made and still can make decisions that will cause life to be better and fairer and that will create greater opportunities for the American people. Of course, by inadequate or unwise acts, government can likewise make bad situations much worse.

The policies we pursued in Vietnam and Iran, for example, were not preordained. We could have chosen not to participate in the civil struggle in Vietnam. The outcome might have been no different, but we would have saved many lives, tens of billions of dollars, and great national travail. Nor were we destined to become enmeshed in the domestic affairs of Iran. We could have bought Iran's oil, as others did, without becoming the shah's bulwark and mentor.

Political decisions with respect to purely domestic matters have been no less significant. Inflation for example, is not divinely ordained. Government decisions affect the price level as well as the ups and downs of unemployment. Even the energy crisis is not beyond the power of human beings to comprehend and resolve. Although sometimes differing among themselves on precise programs and remedies, members of the scientific community have been all but unanimous in urging the United States to turn to new, alternative sources of energy as an effective, long-term solution.

There are thousand-year-old cities all over the world with less crime, less poverty, and less evidence of decay and demoralization than is characteristic of many of America's great cities. A 30-year-old neighborhood does not have to become a slum.

In his book *The End of Liberalism*, political scientist Theodore J. Lowi argues that the crisis of American life "is at bottom a political crisis" stemming from the collapse of "interest group liberalism."[1] Lowi's thesis is that the result of many of the "liberal" programs of the government, such as housing, welfare, and highway building, has often been the opposite of what those who originally sponsored such proposals intended. These programs have tended to make the already prosperous and powerful more so and left the poor still poor. Lowi believes that what he calls *interest group liberalism*[2] has in fact already failed. Its programs survive not because anyone believes that they are working but because of bureaucratic inertia and the inability of politicians to think of something better to do about the nation's problems.

Even those who may not share Lowi's gloomy assessment of liberalism's failures might be inclined to acknowledge the decline of public support for

[1]Theodore J. Lowi, *The End of Liberalism*, 2nd ed. (New York: Norton, 1979).
[2]For a discussion of interest groups, see Chapter 9.

and patience with the liberal approach to government. Yet major challenges need to be met for the sake of the whole nation, and, in large part, by actions of the government: achieving peace without the sacrifice of fundamental American interests or principles, restoring health to the economy, reducing unemployment, reversing the decline of the cities, and preserving the environment.

One way these goals might be achieved is by reversing the perspective of many government programs of the past few decades. Liberals have tended to put their faith (and their resources) in programs—in dollars expended—rather than in people. Conspicuous examples are so-called urban renewal projects, which frequently turn out to be simply an excuse for large corporations to get federal help in building huge complexes of office buildings and shopping centers, while driving away the people who once lived there. An urban renewal program that begins with people, rather than buildings, might have happier results. The question is not how we can tear down all these depressing old stores and tenements and replace them with shiny new buildings—but how we can help the people of this area solve their problems and live better lives. That is, of course, a far more difficult question, which is perhaps one reason that we have tended to avoid it.

The federal government has spent substantial funds on education in recent years. Much of this has gone to pay for "pilot" programs, special equipment, new facilities, and more administrators. Critics, such as Christopher Jencks, have pointed out that more money has not always meant better education and that efforts to achieve equal opportunity through integrated education have proved disappointing.[3] This assessment has led other critics to support the premise that the government is impotent —that it cannot "do good" in the sense of solving our problems in the same way that it helped solve problems in the past.

We do not agree. If political decisions made by human beings have created or contributed to such national problems as educational inequality, urban decay, environmental pollution, unemployment, and crime, then surely other decisions made by other human beings can help remedy these problems. In foreign affairs, one has only to look at such matters as the reversal of America's cold war policy toward China to see a concrete instance of how a change in policy can produce, relatively quickly, a much improved relationship between ourselves and another nation. At home, government support for higher education has resulted in a growing proportion of Americans receiving a college education. Despite the uncertainty and the ambiguity implicit in every political problem, wise political policies can produce beneficial results. It is true, as many conservatives argue, that government cannot and should not try to do everything for everyone. There

---

[3]Christopher Jencks and Mary Jo Baine, "The Schools and Equal Opportunity," *Saturday Review of Education*, September 16, 1972, pp. 37–42.

are many areas of personal and social life that are none of the government's business. But government does influence certain directions of our national life, and hence of our personal lives as well.

The huge federal budget and how it is dispensed inevitably benefits some people more than others. A subtle change in tax policy may redirect billions of dollars in private capital from, say, housing to manufacturing, or vice versa. The most financially astute people in the nation, those who earn their living buying and selling on the New York Stock Exchange, ceaselessly search out the newest government statistics, examine statements by the president or his close advisers, and monitor the ebb and flow of federal monetary and fiscal policies, seeking to capture the slightest hints of future trends and policies. They do this because they understand that such things will likely have a decisive impact on the future of their investments. The average working man or woman will also be affected by such shifts.

The Individual and Politics

There are limits to the power of politicians. It is doubtful if even philosopher-kings or philosopher-presidents could make us happy and good. The Declaration of Independence speaks of the right of individuals to *pursue* happiness. The delivery thereof is up to the private person.

This, of course, is a tricky point. Can we all, equally, pursue happiness without getting in one another's way? Too often we expect the government to smooth the way for us, but not for our neighbor. *We* should get the tax break or the tax incentive, but others should pay the price, either in getting fewer services or in paying higher taxes. Still, we expect the government to run efficiently and justly (whatever our idea of justice is) and to allow all of us to compete. What we must emphasize is that the government, as important as it is, is nothing without us.

It is wise to remember a theme we earlier touched on: the concept of government as initially developed in America in the eighteenth century emphasized the rights and *responsibilities* of the individual. Contrary to fascist statism, our form of democracy ostensibly promotes the individual, not the state, as of the first importance. Thus a two-way relationship is implied. First, the state is here to promote the good of individuals (to aid us all, we might say, in pursuing happiness). Second and equally important, we as individuals have responsibilities to see to it that the state stays on the track.

The eighteenth-century philosophers believed that human beings were rational, that they could weigh evidence and make sensible judgments, and that they did not need to be told by abstract and mystical institutions what was right and wrong. Accordingly, enlightened individuals working together could further the progress of the society.

This is not such an old fashioned notion today. Whether we like or dislike Michael Dukakis or George Bush, we cannot sit back and wait to see whether they will save us. That is asking too much of them and, by implication, gives them too much power. We too have responsibilities. Politicians, properly, react to their constituencies, and a constituency of well-informed, sensitive, and broad-minded individuals is as significant a guarantee of what Jefferson meant by a "virtuous" government as is the election of a "good" president or a "good" member of Congress. Thus, the right to "pursue happiness" is more complex than it might originally seem, for it involves much more than the right to gain material well-being. It includes, above all, responsible participation in the important activities of one's society, including government.

Of Politics and Americans

Henry Fairlie, an English observer of the American scene, said "It is not in an art gallery, not in a church, not on a stock exchange, not even in bed, that man is whole. It is in the ballot box."[4] Fairlie felt that politics was more than an argument about "who gets the cookies." It is also about how human beings interact with one another; about people's capacity to create and preserve civilization; about our age-old, frustrating, and yet indomitable quest for justice; and about human efforts to make meaningful our brief sojourn on this earth. Aristotle stressed that "a state exists for the sake of noble actions." This is a lofty, if not a very modern, idea.

Clearly, however, not everyone who participates in the political process—whether as office seeker, activist, student, partisan, or simply sometime voter—is spurred by noble motives. Ambition, fear, and greed are common and powerful political impulses. Many enter actively into the political process because they find it an enjoyable pastime. Although the stakes are high—money, power, and even life or death—politics is a game that people play, like football, sex, or business. Winning, as we have noted, is important because it keeps you in the game. (The vice presidency has been described as a "splendid misery," not because the vice president is denied a handsome salary and other emoluments of high office, but because he is usually not permitted to participate fully in the day-to-day struggles of the administration.) Playing well, with verve, commitment, and style, is also important. Presidents who elicited strong emotional support (and dislike) from Americans, such as Franklin D. Roosevelt and John F. Kennedy, loved politics and took pleasure in high office, and they communicated that pleasure to the people. On the other hand, politicians who have fallen short of achieving the highest office—such as Senator Barry Goldwater and Senator Hubert

[4]Henry Fairlie, "Press Against Politics," *New Republic*, November 13, 1976, p. 12.

Humphrey, one a conservative Republican and the other a liberal Democrat—have also won a certain affection and respect for having devoted their lives to fighting hard and well for their respective causes and have seemed to enjoy themselves in the process.

One of the common characteristics of the political fanatic and the demagogue is a certain joylessness. It is hard to imagine the Ayatollah Khomeini of Iran laughing, particularly at himself. To be sure, tears and disappointments are part of politics, but joy and laughter are also indispensable to a humane politics.

If the aims and consequences of political action are important, the practice of the art on a day-to-day basis is also interesting. The rise and fall of certain individuals and factions, the making and unmaking of careers, the shifting alliances and changes in public opinion, the struggle to reach an easily bored and distracted people, the occasional success of a bold strategy, or the failure of prudent, careful planning—all these are a continuing source of interest, pleasure, and excitement to the political devotee. On one level, it is a kind of soap opera, and at times it achieves the authentic grandeur of high tragedy. Surely the assassinations of the Kennedys or Martin Luther King, Jr., lack only a Sophocles or a Shakespeare to make their stories as timeless and exalted as the death of Julius Caesar or the fall of Oedipus.

Through politics, the American people struggle to survive, to achieve social order and a measure of justice, and to express their values, fears, and aspirations. The successes or failures of 250 million Americans—in business, agriculture, sports, science, the arts, or education—may exist independently of government. Moreover, history, music, art, literature, gossip, myths, and popular culture may tell us a good deal about a given people, past or present. But none of these speaks quite so clearly as does how a people are governed and/or how they govern. Whether or not the United States is the "world's last, best hope," as Lincoln believed, or a "naked and arbitrary power intent upon enforcing crackpot definitions upon the world," as sociologist C. Wright Mills charged, remains arguable. What is not arguable is that this government has had and will continue to have enormous impact on the lives of its own people and on all humankind.

Appendixes

• Glossary •
• Suggested Readings •
• The Declaration of Independence •
• The Constitution of the United States •

Glossary

Within definitions, words in italics are also defined in the Glossary.

Affirmative Action: Requirement that businesses, government agencies, labor unions, or schools increase the number or proportion of women, blacks, Hispanics, and other minorities in their organization.

Aggression: An attack on one nation by another.

Alienation: A term used in the United States to describe those individuals who have psychologically "dropped out" of the political system. Persons who take no interest in working with others to solve common problems are "alienated."

Anchorperson: The central person responsible for coordinating and delivering the flow of news on television. See Chapter 11.

Appellate Jurisdiction: The authority of a court to try cases on appeal after they have been tried in a lower court. See Chapter 6.

Apportionment: The act of calculating the number of representatives in the House of Representatives each state is to have. Apportionment takes place every ten years and is based on the national census.

Arbitration: Resolving a dispute between two parties by appointing a third party to act as a judge or arbitrator.

Attentive Public: People who keep informed about public affairs, read newspapers and magazines, and occasionally communicate with lawmakers. See Chapter 9.

Authoritarianism: See *totalitarianism*.

Bicameral: Composed of two houses. The U.S. Congress is bicameral. See Chapter 5.

Bipartisan: Emphasizing cooperation between the major political parties.

Bipolar: A view of the world as essentially divided into two sides, ours and theirs. Also see Chapter 13 and *cold war*.

Bloc: A group of persons, political parties, or nations united for common action.

Bureaucracy: The institutions and people, usually within the executive branch, who administer the laws and services of the *government*. Bureaucrats sometimes acquire great power because they do not come and go, as elected officials tend to do. See Chapter 10.

Cabinet: The major departments of the *executive* branch of the *government*, such as the Department of State, Energy, Labor, and so on. The president chooses his cabinet with the approval of the Senate. See Chapter 4.

Capitalism: An economic system in which there is private and corporate ownership of the means of producing and distributing goods. See Chapter 12.

Caucus: A meeting of the leaders of a faction in the Congress (such as the

Black Caucus) or a meeting of all members of one party in the Congress to choose party leaders or decide on ways to conduct *legislative* business.

Charisma: Originally a term employed in Greek drama, the word has been widely used in politics to describe a certain "star quality" that is projected by some leaders, such as the late President Kennedy.

Checkers Speech: In 1952, vice-presidential candidate Richard Nixon was faced with the possibility of being dropped from the Republican ticket (headed by Dwight Eisenhower) as a result of the widespread publication of certain financial irregularities. Senator Nixon went on television and delivered an emotional speech, capped by a reference to "his daughter Trisha's dog Checkers, that succeeded in turning public opinion in his favor and saved his political career.

Civil Service: *Government* employees who obtain their jobs through examination rather than through political appointment. See Chapter 10.

Cloture: A technique used to limit or end debate in the Senate. See *filibuster*.

Coalition: A combination of several interest groups or factions for the purpose of achieving some political goal. Successful candidates for the presidency must attract a large coalition of diverse voters to win election.

Coattail Effect: The influence of a candidate (such as a presidential candidate) on the electoral success (or failure) of other candidates of the same party.

Cold War: The period between the end of World War II and the advent of a new *foreign policy* created by President Richard Nixon and Secretary of State Henry Kissinger in the late 1960s. Relations between the United States and Russia, and between the United States and China, were characterized by political, economic, and diplomatic hostility, often leading to the brink of an outbreak of military hostilities. See Chapter 13.

Communism: A social and economic system in which there is an absence of classes and a common ownership of the means of production and distribution. See Chapter 12.

Compact: An agreement between consenting parties. Comparable to a contract between individuals, a compact is normally an agreement between states or governing bodies.

Confederation: A system of political organization in which regional governments or states have ultimate *sovereignty*. The United States was a confederation under the Articles of Confederation. See *federalism* and *unitary government*.

Consensus: An attempt of conflicting parties and interests to agree on a common course of action. President Lyndon Johnson's supporters believed that he had achieved a national consensus after his great victory in the 1964 election. However, the consensus, if it ever existed, soon collapsed.

Conservatism: A point of view favoring political and social policies that preserve the existing order. See Chapter 8.

Constituent: A person living in a public official's district. A mayor's constituency is the population of the city, a Congress member's constituency is the population within the congressional district.

Constitution: A written law describing the organs of *government*, their power, limitations on them, and the relationship between citizens and the government. See Chapter 3.

Containment: The U.S. *foreign policy* of not allowing *communism* to spread. See Chapter 13.

Convention: Each of the major political parties holds a national party convention during the summer of every presidential election year. Here the party nominates its presidential and vice presidential candidates and draws up and approves a platform. Each state is represented at the convention by delegates. The number of delegates is determined by a formula that is based on the population of each state, the number of public officials in that state who are members of the party, and other criteria. Some delegates to the convention are pledged to particular candidates as a consequence of a state presidential *primary* or of a commitment made at a local *caucus* or state convention. The convention should not be confused with the *electoral college*, which elects presidents. See Chapter 8.

Counterculture: A term that became popular during the late 1960s. It was used broadly to describe large and sometimes quite different groups of Americans, such as *hippies*, radicals, or various exotic religious cults, who adopted a set of values and a style of life that rejected the established patterns and values of the American middle class.

Countervailing Force: A source of power that is opposite to and acts as a check on another source of power. For example, the Congress is often a countervailing force to the presidency. Labor is a countervailing force to corporations.

Critical Election: Election in which groups of voters switch party allegiances; then this new *coalition* lasts, as in the 1932 election. See Chapter 8.

Culture: The totality of socially transmitted institutions, beliefs, arts, and behavior patterns of a community. See Chapter 2.

Dark Horse: A person who receives unexpected support for nomination at a party *convention*; from the racetrack term for a little-known horse who does well in a race.

Demagogue: A leader who gains power by appealing to the prejudices and emotions of the masses.

Depression: See *Great Depression*.

Détente: A relaxing of tensions between nations. The Nixon-Kissinger policy opened the door to somewhat better relationships between the United States and the two communist superpowers, Russia and China. Under the policy, trade between the United States and the communist powers expanded, and cultural and other contacts were increased. Also, efforts were made to limit the arms race, particularly between the United States and the Soviet Union. See Chapter 13.

Deterrence: The policy of convincing an adversary not to launch a first strike nuclear attack, by threatening a devastating second strike. See Chapter 13.

Devaluation: A reduction in the relative value of one nation's currency in exchange for the currency of other nations. Devaluation lowers the value of a nation's products on the export market and concurrently raises the price of imported goods.

Diplomacy: The practice of conducting international relations. See Chapter 13.

Discharge Petition: A technique used in the House of Representatives to bring a bill out of committee and onto the floor. If a bill has been in a committee for thirty days and a majority of the House signs a discharge petition, the bill must come to the full House.

Dissidents: Those who disagree with the ruling powers.

Domino Theory: The belief that if communists took over one country they would shortly take over all adjacent countries. See Chapter 13.

Doves: Those favoring a peaceful solution short of military victory in the war in Vietnam. See *hawks*.

Due Process of Law: A clear, understandable procedure that must be undertaken before a person can be convicted of an offense or a crime. See Chapters 6 and 7.

Ecology: The study of the relationship between organisms and their environment.

Electoral College: A body of electors chosen every four years by the states and the District of Columbia to elect the president and the vice president. The framers of the Constitution, unwilling to have the president elected by the people as a whole or by the national legislature, settled on an indirect system. Each state would provide a method to select electors, who would meet in an electoral college and choose the president and the vice president. The system still exists. Each state is assigned a number of electors equal to its total of U.S. representatives and senators. The District of Columbia has three electoral votes. The candidate who receives a majority of electoral votes wins the presidential election. Currently it is the practice that the candidate who wins the most popular votes (not necessarily a majority) in a state receives all of that state's electoral votes. Thus it is possible that the candidate receiving the most popular votes nationwide could actually lose the election. On three occasions (in 1824, 1876, and 1888), this has happened. The electoral college should not be confused with national party *conventions*, which nominate candidates.

Elitism: See *power elite*.

Enlightenment: A period in the eighteenth century in western Europe of intellectual and critical examination of social and political institutions. See Chapter 3.

Escalate: In the 1950s and 1960s, a theory emerged from *Pentagon* war games called *escalation.* The theory held that international conflict, including war, could be held to manageable limits in a nuclear age by a process of gradual diplomatic, economic, or military pressure—as when the stakes are gradually raised by poker players until one party or the other is forced to quit. The theory had its greatest test in the war in Vietnam and did not work.

Ethnicity: Referring to the special racial, national, religious, or cultural features of a group of people.

Executive: Describing the authority to carry out the law. See Chapter 4.

Executive Agreement: An agreement made between the president and the leader of a foreign country that does not require Senate approval.

Executive Privilege: The claimed right of a president to withhold information or testimony from the courts or the legislature on the grounds of protecting national interest. Until so ordered by the Supreme Court, President Nixon refused to release the White House tapes, claiming executive privilege.

Existentialism: A philosophy currently popular among some twentieth-century intellectuals and artists. It stresses subjective rather than objective truth and the freedom to create the meaning of one's own life.

Faction: A group of persons forming a cohesive, sometimes contentious *interest group.*

Fairness Doctrine: A requirement of the Federal Communications Commission that broadcasters and telecasters must make every effort to ensure that differing points of view are heard.

Fascism: A theory of *government* developed by Benito Mussolini, dictator of Italy in the 1920s and 1930s, and later adopted by Adolf Hitler in Germany and the ruling military clique in Japan before and during World War II. The fascist state is characterized by *totalitarian* government, extreme *nationalism, racism*, militarism, and glorification of war and the merger of government and business leadership.

Favorite Son: A person nominated at a party *convention*, often as an honorary gesture, by the delegates from that candidate's home state.

Federalism: A dual form of government whereby *sovereignty* is shared by regional governments (such as states) and a national government. See Chapter 3 and *confederation* and *unitary government.*

Federal Reserve Board: A quasi-public organization largely made up of bankers whose chairman is appointed by the president. The Fed is charged with regulating the nation's money supply and defending the value of the national currency. Under the controversial leadership of Chairman Paul Volcker, the Fed has been alternately blamed for provoking the *recession* of 1980–1982 and praised for checking *inflation.* In fact, it helped do both.

Filibuster: Unlimited talking during debate in the U.S. Senate. Used to delay the passage of a bill that the majority favors. The House of Representatives does not allow filibustering. See Chapter 5.

Fiscal Policy: *Government* spending and taxing policy designed to manage the economy. See Chapter 12 and *monetary policy*.

Foreign Policy: A nation's aims and goals in relations with other countries and the international community. See Chapter 13.

Founding Fathers: The writers of the U.S. Constitution and early statesmen. See Chapter 3.

Free Enterprise: An economic system that has a free market and in which the laws of supply and demand determine prices and levels of production. See Chapter 12.

Gender: Classification according to sex, as male or female.

Genocide: The systematic destruction of a people or a race. The classic example is the Nazi government's efforts to impose a "final solution" to the "Jewish question" by annihilating the Jewish people in Europe.

Gerrymandering: Drawing *legislative* boundaries in ways that give special advantages to one political party or candidate.

GOP: Grand Old Party, the Republican party.

Government: The institution or authority that creates and administers public policy.

Grant-In-Aid: Federal funds granted to state and local government for use in specified activities, such as to build highways or finance education. See Chapter 3.

Grass Roots: Emerging from people at a distance from the major political center. A grass roots candidate usually has little official party support.

Great Depression: The period of high unemployment and lack of economic growth that began with the stock market crash in 1929 and continued into the 1930s.

Great Society: The slogan created by the Johnson administration designed to project an image of boundless achievement.

Gross National Product (GNP): The total value of all goods and services produced by a country in a year.

Habeas Corpus: A court order requiring an explanation as to why a person is held in custody.

Hawks: Those favoring strong military measures during the war in Vietnam. See *doves*.

Hierarchy: A system of leadership by which authority passes from the top down to the lower ranks, usually modeled in one form or another on the military.

Hippies: A widely used term in the late 1960s and the early 1970s, often used indiscriminately to describe young people who espoused alternative life-styles, including long hair, unkempt clothing, the heavy use of drugs, and a good deal of rhetoric about "peace" and "love." Most hippies were nonpolitical.

Honeymoon Period: After a new president takes office, there is traditionally a brief period, lasting from a few weeks to a few months, in which both the press and the opposition are expected to refrain from serious criticism and show a spirit of national unity.

Ideological: Based on a system of ideas, usually reflecting a coherent philosophy.

Impeachment: A charge of malfeasance in office, that is, an accusation of a public official. Only the House of Representatives can bring impeachment charges against a president (by a majority vote). Impeachment does not mean conviction. The president is then tried by the Senate, a two-thirds vote of the Senate being necessary for conviction and removal from office.

Imperialism: Domination of one nation by another, either directly through the use or threat of military force, or indirectly, as when economic, political, or *diplomatic* power are used to manipulate the affairs of a *sovereign* nation.

Implied Powers: Authority conceded to the *government* based on the Constitution, although not explicitly stated in the Constitution.

Incumbent: The person currently holding a public office.

INF: Intermediate-range nuclear forces, those that travel between 300 and 3,000 miles. In December 1987 the Soviets and Americans signed an agreement eliminating all INF launchers.

Inflation: A rapid rise in prices and hence a lowering of the value of money.

Interest Group: A group that comes together because of a common goal or interest and that tries to influence *government*. See Chapter 9.

Interstate Compact: An agreement between or among two or more states to act jointly in some matter of public policy.

Judicial Review: The power of the courts to determine whether or not a state law or *constitutional* provision or a federal law is in violation of the U.S. Constitution. Judicial review occurs only if a case is brought into court. The U.S. Supreme Court normally invokes judicial review only if a case is successfully appealed to that court. See Chapter 6.

Juridical: Of a legal nature.

Keynote Address: The opening speech at a political *convention*.

Lame Duck: A public official serving out a term after having been defeated for reelection, or not being eligible to run for reelection.

Left or Left-Wing: Very *liberal*. See Chapter 8.

Legislative: Possessing the authority to make law. See Chapter 8.

Liberalism: A point of view favoring political and social policies of non-revolutionary change, progress, and reform. See Chapter 8.

Limited Warfare: A conflict fought for certain specific and limited objectives and with something less than full force, such as the Korean conflict. In contrast, in World War II, for example, the Allies insisted on the unconditional surrender of enemies and used virtually every weapon available, including the two atomic bombs dropped on Japan.

Litigation: Legal action.

Lobbyist: A representative of an *interest group* who works in Washington or in a state capital and tries to influence *legislative* and *executive* action to the advantage of the interest group.

Marxism: A theory of history and a program of revolutionary *socialism* derived from the writings of Karl Marx (1818–1883). See Chapter 12.

Media: Mass communications, such as magazines, newspapers, radio, television, film, and books. See Chapter 11.

Military-Industrial Complex: Combination of the U.S. Department of Defense and large corporations that produce weapons under contract from the Defense Department. See Chapter 9.

Monetary Policy: A policy, usually carried out by the *Federal Reserve Board*, that affects the money supply and the availability of credit. See Chapter 12 and *fiscal policy*.

Nationalism: Devotion to the interests of one's nation above those of other nations. Also a desire for national independence from foreign political or economic domination. See Chapter 13.

New Frontier: The slogan created by the Kennedy administration to characterize itself and its legislative program. It intended to project an image of courage, action, and exploration of new ideas.

Oil Depletion Allowance: For many years, oil companies and others engaged in finding, developing, and marketing natural resources were allowed a special tax incentive based on the theory that they were selling a nonrenewable commodity.

Original Jurisdiction: The authority to try a case for the first time. U.S. district courts have original jurisdiction over cases arising under the Constitution. U.S. courts of appeal have no original jurisdiction. The U.S. Supreme Court has original jurisdiction over a very few specific kinds of cases. See Chapter 6.

Pardon: To exempt a person from punishment for an offense or a crime. The president has this authority.

Parliamentary System: A governmental system in which the parliament (or representative legislature) is the primary body and the *executive* function is carried out by the leader of the parliament, who is called the prime minister or the premier. This system is different from a presidential system, in which the executive function rests with a president chosen separately from the legislature.

Partisan: A strong supporter of a party, cause, person, or idea.

Patronage: Favors, such as jobs or contracts, given by successful political leaders to supporters.

Pentagon: The headquarters of the Department of Defense.

Philosophes: Intellectuals during the *Enlightenment*. See Chapter 3.

Plank: An article of a political platform, as a plank of wood is part of the floor of a building.

Platform: The formal declaration of the principles and policies of a group, such as a political party.

Plea Bargaining: Admitting to a crime in exchange for taking a lesser sentence than if one had been convicted in a regular court procedure. See Chapter 6.

Pluralism: The idea that public policy is influenced chiefly by many different *interest groups*. See Chapter 9.

Plurality: The number by which the vote of a winning candidate exceeds that of her or his closest opponent. A plurality may represent a majority of the vote, but not necessarily.

Political Actional Committee (PAC): A committee representing a special interest, a corporation, or a labor union that raises money and provides campaign contributions to friendly candidates.

Political Hack: A person who plods away at a political job, obeys the orders of superiors without question, and rarely or never deviates from the prevailing platitudes of his or her party.

Political Socialization: See *socialization* and Chapter 9.

Politics: An individual's or group's efforts to gain or exert power or influence, as in *government*. See Chapter 7.

Popular Sovereignty: The theory that *sovereignty* ultimately rests with the people.

Power-Elite Theory: The idea that public policy is chiefly influenced by very powerful persons in large corporations, the military, and the executive branch of *government*. See Chapter 9.

Pragmatism: An approach to life and politics that stresses practical results rather than *ideology*. Americans are often said to be politically pragmatic and hence nonideological.

Primary: A method of nominating, by popular vote, candidates to run for office. Normally, Democrats can vote only in Democratic primaries, Republicans only in Republican primaries, and so on. The candidate who wins the primary becomes that party's nominee to run for election. Many states use the primary system to nominate almost all local, state, and national candidates. In 1988 thirty-four states and the District of Columbia and Puerto Rico also held presidential primaries so that voters in those states could, in effect, choose delegates to the national *conventions* who were pledged to their favorite presidential candidate. See Chapter 8.

Prior Restraint: Generally there are two ways to punish people who insist on doing things you do not wish done: One is by prior restraint, that is, preventing them from doing the thing in the first place; the second is by punishment after the fact. The U.S. Supreme Court ruled in the Pentagon Papers case that the government could not prevent the *New York Times* from publishing excerpts from these documents but might proceed legally against the paper after publication.

Propaganda: Material (books, speeches, movies, and so on) intended to instill a particular set of values or beliefs or a certain version of reality in another's mind.

Pundits: A popular term used to describe political experts, such as newspaper and TV commentators.

Quorum: The minimum number of members of a *legislative* body necessary to conduct business.

Racism: The belief that one's race is superior and/or that certain other races are inferior and the social and political practices based on that belief.

Rank and File: From the term for common soldiers of an army, those who form the common and major portion of any group, as of a political party.

Reaganomics: Economic policies favored by President Ronald Reagan, sometimes called *supply-side economics*, because it supposedly emphasized investment in businesses that would create supplies of goods, rather than economic policies that encouraged consumption.

Realism: A *foreign policy* that emphasizes pursuing national interests as more important than fighting *communism*. See Chapter 13.

Reapportionment: Rearranging congressional and state *legislative* districts to accommodate population changes. Normally done every ten years, after the census. See Chapter 5.

Rebellion: Usually an unsuccessful attempt at political *revolution*.

Recession: A time of higher-than-normal unemployment and a slowdown of economic growth. See Chapter 12.

Republic: A nonhereditary government designed to serve the common interest. Frequently considered to be a representative *government* with a written *constitution*. See Chapter 3.

Revenue Sharing: The granting of federal funds to states with no qualifications placed on the grant.

Revolution: A sharp and fundamental break with established tradition.

Right or Right-Wing: Very *conservative*, perhaps reactionary, that is, favoring a return to a condition of the past. See Chapter 7.

Segregation: The system of separating white and black races that almost always involves placing blacks in an inferior or dependent position. In some American states this system was actually written into the laws. The U.S. Supreme Court and the Congress have declared segregation to be unconstitutional, but the actual practice still survives in many areas of American life.

Seniority: In the U.S. Congress, the rule that the person who has the longest continuous service on a congressional committee is the ranking member of that committee. See Chapter 5.

Socialism: An economic system in which there is *government* or group ownership or control of the production and distribution of goods. See Chapter 12.

Socialization: The conditioning of a person to behave in a certain way, one usually considered normal by that person's family, peers, and associates. See Chapter 9.

Southern Strategy: A strategy by which some of President Nixon's advisers believed that the president could transform the Republican party from a minority to a majority party by wooing the votes of *conservative* Southern whites who traditionally had voted Democratic.

Sovereignty: The power to command all others.

Star Wars: The label the *media* gave to President Reagan's proposal to seek to counter the threat of nuclear missiles by developing sophisticated weapons based on laser technology that will destroy the missiles before they reach their targets. Also called Strategic Defense Initiative.

START: Strategic Arms Reduction Talks. Negotiations between the United States and the Soviet Union to bring about limitations or reductions in long-range nuclear missiles.

Substantive: Having to do with the substance or content of an issue or a subject rather than with its appearance.

Subversion: An undermining from within.

Superpower: A large and powerful nation. Generally, the United States, the Soviet Union, and China are considered superpowers.

Supply-side Economics: (sometimes called *Reaganomics*) The theory that the economy will prosper if taxes and other restrictions placed on business and the wealthy by government are sharply reduced. This will stimulate the suppliers, the producers of jobs and wealth to be more productive.

Totalitarianism: The doctrine, propounded especially by *fascist* rulers such as Hitler and Mussolini, that an entire nation is a single organism, a totality, ruled by a single individual.

Totalitarianism versus Authoritarianism: An attempt to distinguish between two kinds of dictatorships: those of the right that are authoritarian because they practice repression and do not permit free elections and a free press but that do permit capitalism and some freedom of religion; and those of the left that are totalitarian because they attempt to control virtually all of the national life, including business, religion, and cultural expression, as well as politics. The conservative premise is that Americans should support the former but not the latter.

Unitary State: A political system in which the central government is supreme. Most nations—England and France, for example—are unitary. See *confederation* and *federalism*.

United Nations: International organization established after World War II, with worldwide membership, for the purpose of avoiding war and improving the condition of the world's peoples. See Chapter 13.

Veto: The power of the *executive* to kill a piece of legislation by refusing to sign it.

Vital Interest: A nation is presumed to have certain interests, such as its territorial integrity, the protection of which are important enough to warrant extreme measures, up to and including war.

War on Poverty: The term commonly used to describe President Lyndon Johnson's highly publicized *legislative* campaign to eliminate extreme poverty in America through various governmental programs.

Wasp: Literally, white Anglo-Saxon Protestant. In practice, the term usually is meant to describe the dominant English-speaking groups who often tend to assume that they are the "real Americans."

Watergate: A hotel-apartment complex in Washington, D.C., where burglars, associated with the Committee to Reelect the President, were caught breaking into the Democratic National Headquarters in 1972. It became a generic term used to describe the various offenses of the Nixon administration.

Witch Hunt: A term deriving from the practice of hunting down suspected witches in colonial America. Used as a synonym for baseless accusations of innocent but unpopular persons or groups.

Suggested Readings

The following suggestions, arranged by chapter, are intended only to whet the appetite of the serious student of American government, politics, and culture. The student should also refer to the footnotes in each chapter.

There are other aids as well. Periodicals are important. The *Reader's Guide to Periodical Literature* indexes popular magazines (such as *Time* and *Newsweek*). The *New York Times Index* is very useful, is organized yearly and by topic. Helpful scholarly journals, each with its own index, are the *American Historical Review, American Journal of Political Science, American Political Science Review, American Quarterly, Journal of American History, Journal of Popular Culture, Political Science Quarterly*, and *Public Opinion Quarterly*. The Congressional Quarterly, Inc., is an editorial research service that publishes yearly *Guides to Current American Government*, a *Weekly Report*, and several other publications of interest. Additionally, students will find useful the *United States Government Manual*, published annually by the office of the Federal Registrar, and the *Almanac of American Politics*, published annually by E. P. Dutton & Co., Inc.

Periodicals that provide intelligent commentary, original ideas, and uncommon insights into current political, economic, and intellectual affairs include the *New York Review of Books*, for a left-of-center approach to current politics and thought, and *Commentary*, for a neoconservative approach to the same subject matter; two longtime favorites of American liberalism are the *New Republic* (liberal) and *The Nation* (more radical). Closer to the center are the *Atlantic* and *Harpers*, and William Buckley's *National Review* covers contemporary issues from a conservative point of view. For a foreign viewpoint, students will find useful the London-based *Economist*.

Some scholars of political science believe that the serious student should start with the ancient Greek philosophers. Plato's *Republic* (trans. Benjamin Jowett [New York: World, 1946]) is a seminal work of political thought, written in the form of a dramatic dialogue. Aristotle's *Politics* (trans. Benjamin Jowett [Oxford: Clarendon Press, 1967]) is a classic examination of many themes still important to political scientists and politicians.

Of equal importance to an understanding of American government is the *Federalist*, essays written by James Madison, Alexander Hamilton, and John Jay to explain and defend the Constitution and currently available in several editions. Also useful and stimulating is the classic study by the nineteenth-century French visitor, Alexis de Tocqueville, *Democracy in America* (2 vols., New York: Random House, 1954).

The student should be alerted to two novels, often cited as the greatest works of American literature. Herman Melville's *Moby Dick* (New York: Dell Pub. Co. Inc., 1960) is, among other things, a prophetic song of an imperial democracy. Mark Twain's (Samuel L. Clemens) *The Adventures of Huckleberry Finn* (Glenview, Ill.: Scott, Foresman, 1960), although superficially simply a youthful adventure story, presents a powerful critique of American society and values. The Scott, Foresman edition contains critical abstracts designed to help the reader understand Twain's caustic views, which are often masked as frontier humor.

Other literary classics that will prove particularly helpful to the study of American government and values include Benjamin Franklin's *Autobiography* and *Poor Richard's Almanack*, both outstanding examples of the ideas and values associated with traditional Americanism; Thomas Paine's *Common Sense*, a radical view of the possibilities of American life; Ralph Waldo Emerson's essays, particularly *Self Reliance*, considered by many as the definitive statement of American individualism; Henry David Thoreau's *Walden*, still perhaps the best book ever written on the relationship between a man and his environment; Emily Dickinson's poetry, a delicate, insightful and strong statement of a woman in secret rebellion against Victorian chauvinism; Walt Whitman's *Leaves of Grass*, a lifelong effort to translate the democracy of everyday life into epic poetry; Ernest Hemingway's short stories, for a view of life known as "modern"; John Steinbeck's *Grapes of Wrath*, the best book on the Great Depression and an excellent vehicle for the student who wishes to understand that era.

Chapter 1: Shine, Perishing Republic

Carnoy, Judith, and Marc Weiss. *A House Divided: Radical Perspectives on Social Problems*. Boston: Little, Brown, 1973. Critical essays from the perspective of the political left.

De Grazia, Alfred. *Eight Bads, Eight Goods: The American Contradictions*. Garden City, N.Y.: Anchor, 1975. A putative series of lectures to a Chinese reader outlining the good and bad aspects of American culture and society.

Evans, M. Stanton. *Clear and Present Dangers: A Conservative View of America's Government*. New York: Harcourt Brace Jovanovich, 1975. A conservative criticism of contemporary America.

Hayden, Tom. *Reunion: A Memoir*. New York: Random House, 1988. Reminiscences by a major 1960s radical who now serves in the California legislature.

Kennedy, Paul. *The Rise and Fall of the Great Powers*. New York: Random House, 1988. A history of the fortunes of great nations during the modern period of history, with a theory about decline some public figures have found appropriate to America.

Putney, Snell. *The Conquest of Society*. Belmont, Calif.: Wadsworth, 1972. A somewhat unorthodox analysis of America, stressing that "systems" are no longer under the control of people.

Revel, Jean-François. *Without Marx or Jesus: The New American Revolution Has Begun*. Garden City, N.Y.: Doubleday, 1971. An upbeat assessment contending that the United States is leading a necessary, worldwide, and peaceful social and political revolution.

Wattenberg, Ben J. *The Real America*. Garden City, N.Y.: Doubleday, 1974. A criticism of the leftist lament over American society, stressing the positive features of American values and behavior.

Chapter 2: The Pursuit of Happiness

Bellah, Robert N. et al. *Habits of the Heart: Individualism and Commitment in American Life*. New York: Harper & Row, 1985. University of California study investigating the dilemma caused by the conflict between our fierce individualism and our need for community and commitment.

Bloom, Allan. *The Closing of the American Mind*. New York: Simon & Schuster, 1987. Best-selling critique of liberal arts college education for the last quarter of a century, by a University of Chicago political philosopher.

Burns, James MacGregor. *The Vineyard of Liberty*. New York: Knopf, 1982. First of a projected three-volume intellectual history of the United States entitled *The American Experiment*.

Commager, Henry Steele. *The American Mind*. New Haven, Conn.: Yale University Press, 1950. A classic account of American thought, literature, and political philosophy.

Feldman, Saul D., and Gerald W. Thielbar, eds. *Life Styles: Diversity in American Society*. Boston: Little, Brown, 1972. Essays emphasizing diversity rather than uniformity in America.

Friedan, Betty. *The Feminine Mystique*. New York: Norton, 1963. An important first book in the literature of the current women's movement.

Haley, Alex. *Roots*. Garden City, N.Y.: Doubleday, 1976. The personal history of a black family, beginning in Gambia, West Africa, in the eighteenth century, extending through slavery in America and Reconstruction, and ending with an explanation of the author's research.

Hall, James W., ed. *Forging the American Character*. New York: Holt, Rinehart & Winston, 1971. A compilation of classic and conflicting essays regarding the nature and origin of an American character.

Handlin, Oscar, ed. *Immigration As a Factor in American History*. Englewood Cliffs, N.J.: Prentice-Hall, 1959. Essays gathered by a major scholar.

Hirsch, E. D., Jr. *Cultural Literacy: What Every American Needs to Know*. Boston: Houghton Mifflin, 1987. Charges that there is no common cultural heritage in American education and offers suggested list of books all of us should be aware of.

Howe, Irving. *World of Our Fathers*. New York: Simon & Schuster, 1976. An account of the Jewish immigrant experience.

Manchester, William. *The Glory and the Dream*. New York: Bantam, 1975. Narrative history of America from the Roosevelt era to 1972, focusing on the interaction between politics and culture.

Miller, Perry. *Errand into the Wilderness*. Cambridge, Mass.: Harvard University Press, 1956. One of many important works by the most profound student of New England Puritanism.

Morgan, Edmund S. *The Puritan Dilemma*. Boston: Little, Brown, 1958. A short and insightful analysis of Puritanism via the biography of John Winthrop.

National Advisory Commission. *Report of the National Advisory Commission on Civil Disorders*. New York: Bantam, 1968. A comprehensive study of the problems and the promise of blacks in America.

Riesman, David. *The Lonely Crowd*. New Haven, Conn.: Yale University Press, 1961. The character and qualities of middle-class, suburban American life examined by a prominent sociologist.

Schrag, Peter. *The Decline of the Wasp*. New York: Simon & Schuster, 1970. An account, by a WASP, of the decline of WASP (white Anglo-Saxon Protestant) power in the United States.

Taylor, George Rogers, ed. *The Turner Thesis: Concerning the Role of the Frontier in American History*. Lexington, Mass.: Heath, 1972. Contradictory essays on the meaning and importance of the frontier. Includes F. J. Turner's seminal essay of 1893.

Whitman, Walt. *Democratic Vistas* (first published in *Galaxy* magazine shortly after the Civil War). Whitman undertook in this essay to evaluate the condition of democracy in America and ended by writing a prose poem of American idealism.

Chapter 3: The Constitutional Framework

Adair, Douglass. *Fame and the Founding Fathers*. Edited by Trevor Colbourn. New York: Norton, 1974. Seminal essays on the Founders.

Beard, Charles A. *An Economic Interpretation of the Constitution of the United States*. New York: Macmillan, 1913. The influential, classic thesis that the Founding Fathers were motivated chiefly by economic considerations in framing the Constitution.

Brown, Robert E. *Charles A. Beard and the Constitution*. Princeton, N. J.: Princeton University Press, 1956. A critical and detailed attack on Beard's thesis.

Corwin, Edward S. *The Constitution and What It Means Today*. Revised by Harold W. Chase and Craig R. Ducat. Princeton, N.J.: Princeton University Press, 1974. A careful explanation of the Constitution by a foremost scholar.

Diamond, Martin. *The Founding of the Democratic Republic*. Itasca, Ill.: Peacock, 1981. Thoughtful essays about the origin and meaning of the Constitution.

Elkins, Stanley, and Eric McKitrick. *The Founding Fathers, Young Men of the Revolution*. Washington, D.C.: Service Center for Teachers of History, 1962. A brief survey of various views on the origin of the Constitution plus a short but brilliant interpretation by the authors.

Farrand, Max. *The Framing of the Constitution of the United States*. New Haven, Conn.: Yale University Press, 1913. A history of the constitutional convention.

Kammen, Michael G. *A Machine That Would Go of Itself*. New York: Knopf, 1986. A look at perceptions of the Constitution throughout history, suggesting that Americans are basically ignorant about their fundamental law.

Levy, Leonard W., ed. *Encyclopedia of the American Constitution*. New York: Macmillan, 1987. Multivolume collection of essays by scholars on virtually all issues of constitutional law and practice.

McDonald, Forrest. *Novus Ordo Seclorum: The Intellectual Origins of the Constitution*. Lawrence: University of Kansas Press, 1985. The latest major work on the Constitution by this important scholar.

McDonald, Forrest. *We the People: The Economic Origins of the Constitution*. Chicago: University of Chicago Press, 1976. Another skillful challenge to Beard's thesis.

Moore, John Allphin, Jr., and John E. Murphy, eds. *A Grand Experiment: The Constitution at 200*. Wilmington: Scholarly Resources, 1987. Essays by scholars, lawyers, journalists, and civic activists on the meaning and relevance of the Constitution.

Rossiter, Clinton. *1787: The Grand Convention*. New York: Macmillan, 1966. Classical study of the convention.

Vidal, Gore. *Burr*. A novel. New York: Bantam, 1973. An iconoclastic and satiric view of some of the Founding Fathers.

Wills, Garry. *Explaining America: The Federalists*. Garden City, N.Y.: Doubleday, 1981. Stimulating analysis of the *Federalist* papers.

Chapter 4: The President: Shadow and Substance

Barber, James David. *The Presidential Character*. 2nd ed. Englewood Cliffs, N.J.: Prentice-Hall, 1977. Analysis of why presidents act as they do. Based on biographical study of presidents from Taft to Carter.

Burns, James MacGregor. *Leadership*. New York: Harper & Row, 1978. Discussion of an important political topic by a foremost scholar.

Burns, James MacGregor, *The Power to Lead: The Crisis of the American Presidency*. New York: Simon & Schuster, 1984. The latest book by this prolific scholar updating his thesis that institutions frustrate leadership.

Corwin, Edward S. *The President: Office and Powers*. New York: New York University Press, 1957. A traditional and classic exposition of the presidency.

Cronin, Thomas E. *The State of the Presidency*. 2nd ed. Boston: Little, Brown, 1980. An assessment of the roles Americans expect the president to play and why Americans are frequently disappointed.

Dean, John. *Blind Ambition*. New York: Simon & Schuster, 1976. A personal and revealing account of events surrounding the Watergate scandal.

Deaver, Michael. *Behind the Scenes*. New York: William Morrow, 1988. Inside view of the Reagan presidency by a close former adviser.

Haig, Alexander M. *Caveat: Realism, Reagan and Foreign Policy*. New York: Macmillan, 1984. The former Secretary of State's account of foreign policy in the early Reagan years.

Hughes, Emmet John. *The Living Presidency*. New York: Coward, McCann & Geoghegan, 1972. A readable essay on the nature of the modern presidency by a journalist and sometime presidential adviser.

Jordan, Hamilton. *Crisis*. New York: Putnam, 1982. The last year of the Carter administration as viewed by one of its top officials, focusing on efforts to free the hostages in Iran.

Koenig, Louis W. *The Chief Executive*. 3rd ed. New York: Harcourt Brace Jovanovich, 1975. Scholarly study of the various aspects of the presidency.

Lash, Joseph P. *Eleanor and Franklin*. New York: Signet Books, 1971. An intimate but scholarly account of the lives and careers of the Roosevelts.

Neustadt, Richard E. *Presidential Power*. New York: Wiley, 1980. Updated edition of an influential study.

Pious, Richard M. *The American Presidency*. New York: Basic Books, 1979. A comprehensive, well-documented study.

Regan, Donald. *For the Record*. New York: Harcourt Brace Jovanovich, 1988. Caustic memoir of Reagan's dismissed chief of staff.

Rossiter, Clinton. *The American Presidency*. Rev. ed. New York: Harcourt Brace Jovanovich, 1960. A slightly dated but valuable look at the many roles of the president.

Schlesinger, Arthur M., Jr. *A Thousand Days*. New York: Dell Pub. Co. Inc., 1965. A sympathetic but scholarly and insightful account of the Kennedy era, by a prize-winning historian who served in the administration.

Schlesinger, Arthur M., Jr. *The Imperial Presidency*. Boston: Houghton Mifflin, 1973. An assessment of the growing power of the modern president by the historian of Presidents Jackson, F.D. Roosevelt, and Kennedy.

Stockman, David A. *The Triumph of Politics: Why the Reagan Revolution Failed*. New York: Harper & Row, 1986. Critical assessment of Reagan administration by its former budget director.

The Tower Commission. New York: Bantam Books and Times Books, 1987. Full text of the president's special review board investigating the Iran-Contra affair, highlighting flaws in management of the presidential office.

Wayne, Stephen J. *The Legislative Presidency*. New York: Harper & Row, 1978. A study focusing on the development of the legislative role of the president since World War II.

Chapter 5: Congress and Its Critics

Berman, Daniel M. *A Bill Becomes a Law*. New York: Macmillan, 1966. Comparison of passage of two civil rights bills, one in 1960 and another in 1964.

Burns, James MacGregor. *The Deadlock of Democracy*. Rev. ed. Englewood Cliffs, N.J.: Prentice-Hall, 1972. Includes criticisms of the slowness and inadequacy with which Congress responds to national needs.

Congressional Quarterly, Inc. *Powers of Congress* and *Origins and Development of Congress*, 1976. Comprehensive studies of the legislative branch.

Davidson, Roger H., and Walter J. Oleszek. *Congress Against Itself*. Bloomington: Indiana University Press, 1977. A careful study of congressional reform.

Ehrenhalt, Alan, ed. *Politics in America: Members of Congress in Washington and at Home*. Washington, D.C.: Congressional Quarterly, 1983. Compendium of useful information on the Congress.

Green, Mark J., James M. Fallows, and David R. Zwick. *Who Runs Congress?* Rev. ed. New York: Bantam, 1975. A Ralph Nader project study emphasizing congressional weaknesses and lack of responsiveness to the American people.

Keefe, William J. *Congress and the American People.* Englewood Cliffs, N.J.: Prentice-Hall, 1980. A brief, excellent up-to-date analysis of the Congress.

Mann, Thomas E., and Norman J. Ornstein, eds., *The New Congress.* Washington, D.C.: American Enterprise Institute, 1981. Essays on recent changes in the Congress.

Matthews, Donald R. *U.S. Senators and Their World.* New York: Random House, 1960. Description of life in the Senate.

Mayhew, David R. *Congress: The Electoral Connection.* New Haven, Conn.: Yale University Press, 1974. Brief survey of Congress emphasizing that a congressperson's chief motivation is to be reelected.

O'Neill, Thomas P. *Man of the House.* New York: Random House, 1987. Rollicking memoir of the longtime speaker of the House of Representatives.

Polsby, Nelson W. *Congress and the Presidency.* 2nd ed. Englewood Cliffs, N.J.: Prentice-Hall, 1971. Useful analysis of both branches of government.

Riegle, Donald W., and Trevor Ambrister. *O Congress.* Garden City, N.Y.: Doubleday, 1972. A firsthand account of serving in the House of Representatives.

Schwab, Larry M. *Changing Patterns of Congressional Politics.* New York: D. Van Nostrand, 1980. A study emphasizing the many changes in Congress during the 1970s.

Sundquist, James. *The Decline and Resurgence of Congress.* Washington, D.C.: Brookings Institution, 1981. A major study of recent changes in the Congress.

Truman, David B., ed. *The Congress and America's Future.* 2nd ed. Englewood Cliffs, N.J.: Prentice-Hall, 1973. Essays on various aspects of Congress by acknowledged specialists.

Chapter 6: The Courts: The Search for the Just Society

Abraham, Henry J. *The Judicial Process.* 3rd ed. New York: Oxford University Press, 1975. Basic survey of state and federal systems of justice and comparison with other countries.

Bickel, Alexander. *The Supreme Court and the Idea of Progress.* New York: Harper & Row, 1970. A critical assessment of the Warren Court.

Blasi, Vincent. *The Burger Court; The Counter Revolution That Wasn't.* New Haven, Conn.: Yale University Press, 1983. A reassessment of the Court that argues that it has been less conservative than expected.

Congressional Quarterly, Inc. *The Supreme Court and Individual Rights.*

Washington, D.C.: Congressional Quarterly, 1980. Comprehensive view of a major area of the Court's concern.

Garraty, John A., ed. *Quarrels That Have Shaped the Constitution*. New York: Harper & Row, 1964. A series of lively essays explaining the major Court decisions in America from *Marbury v. Madison to Brown v. Board of Education*.

Kelly, Alfred H., et al., *The American Constitution: Its Origins and Development*. New York: Norton, 1983. A history of the Constitution up to the present time.

Kutler, Stanley I., ed. *The Supreme Court and the Constitution*. New York: Norton, 1977. Readings in major cases in American constitutional history.

Lewis, Anthony. *Gideon's Trumpet*. New York: Vintage Books, 1966. A readable chronology of a case from a local jail to the Supreme Court.

McCloskey, Robert G. *The American Supreme Court*. Chicago: University of Chicago Press, 1960. Brief history of the Supreme Court and developing legal ideas.

McLaughlin, Andrew C. *A Constitutional History of the United States*. New York: Appleton-Century, 1935. A classic history, from the origins of the Constitution through the early twentieth century.

Rawles, John. *A Theory of Justice*. Cambridge, Mass.: Harvard University Press, 1971. A lengthy and controversial study. Several useful reviews may be found in the *American Political Science Review* 69 (June 1975): 588–675.

Sindler, Allan P. *Bakke, DeFunis, and Minority Admissions*. New York: Longman, 1979. A detailed review of two important affirmative action cases.

Woodward, Bob, and Scott Armstrong. *The Brethren: Inside the Supreme Court*. New York: Simon & Schuster, 1980. A widely criticized but popular look at the Burger Court.

Chapter 7: Free at Last: Civil and Uncivil Liberty

Baer, Judith A. *Equality under the Constitution: Reclaiming the Fourteenth Amendment*. Ithaca: Cornell University Press, 1983. Excellent study of the Fourteenth Amendment's growing use in civil rights issues.

Berns, Walter. *The First Amendment and the Future of American Democracy*. New York: Basic Books, 1976. Thoughtful assessment of First Amendment freedoms.

Casper, Jonathan D. *The Politics of Civil Liberties*. New York: Harper & Row, 1973. Basic account of the connection between politics and civil liberties.

Congressional Quarterly, Inc. *The Supreme Court and Individual Rights*.

Washington, D.C.: Congressional Quarterly, 1980. Useful study of the issue of individual rights in the United States.

Harrison, Cynthia. *On Account of Sex: The Politics of Women's Issues, 1945–1968*. Berkeley: University of California Press, 1988. Recent study of post-World War II women's movement.

Kluger, Richard. *Simple Justice: The History of Brown v. Board of Education and Black America's Struggle for Equality*. New York: Knopf, 1976. Account of recent history of blacks' struggle for civil rights.

Lewis, Anthony. *Gideon's Trumpet*. New York: Vintage Books, 1966. Story of an accused's encounter with the processes of rights before the law.

Peltason, J. W. *Fifty-eight Lonely Men: Southern Federal Judges and School Desegregation*. New York: Harcourt Brace, 1961. Story of early efforts to achieve desegregation in the South.

Sindler, Allan P. *Bakke, DeFunis, and Minority Admissions*. New York: Longman, 1979. Study of controversial affirmative action cases.

Sorauf, Frank J. *The Wall of Separation: The Constitutional Politics of Church and State*. Princeton: Princeton University Press, 1976. Study of the various groups involved in church-state litigation.

Chapter 8: The Art of Politics: Parties and Elections

Barber, James David, ed. *Race for the Presidency: The Media and the Nominating Process*. Englewood Cliffs, N. J.: Prentice-Hall, 1979. The authors stress the overriding influence of the media in presidential elections.

Burnham, Walter Dean. *Critical Elections and the Mainsprings of American Politics*. New York: Norton, 1970. A major study of the theory of critical elections.

Chambers, William Nisbet, and Walter Dean Burnham, eds. *The American Party System: Stages of Political Development*. 2nd ed. New York: Oxford University Press, 1975. Essays presenting an analytical and historical survey of political parties.

Congressional Quarterly, Inc. *Elections 1988*. Washington, D.C.: Congressional Quarterly, 1987. Updated study of elections in America.

Crotty, William J. *Decision for the Democrats: Reforming the Party Structure*. Baltimore: Johns Hopkins University Press, 1978. A study of the democratization of the Democratic party since 1968.

Drew, Elizabeth. *Politics and Money*. New York: Macmillan, 1983. The new rules of campaign finance, according to this *New Yorker* correspondent, may have removed machine politicians from undue influence, but in their place are more powerful and potentially more sinister special business interests.

Hess, Stephen. *The Presidential Campaign*. Washington, D.C.: Brookings

Institution, 1978. Discusses campaigning for the presidency as compared with being president.

Key, V. O., Jr. *Politics, Parties and Pressure Groups*. 5th ed. New York: Thomas Y. Crowell, 1964. A classic and comprehensive study; indispensable for the serious student.

Ladd, Everett Carll, Jr., with Charles D. Hadley. *Transformation of the American Party System*. 2nd ed. New York: Norton, 1978. Careful analysis of the current situation of the party system.

Mazmanian, Daniel A. *Third Parties in Presidential Elections*. Washington, D.C.: Brookings Institution, 1974. Excellent study of the role of third parties in America.

Mencken, H. L. *The Art of Politics*. New York: Vintage Books, 1960. A collection of the articles by one of America's wittiest observers of the political scene between the two World Wars.

Miller, Arthur H., et al. *American National Election Studies*. Cambridge: Harvard University Press, 1980. Useful data for studying elections.

Polsby, Nelson. *Consequences of Party Reform*. Oxford, England: Oxford University Press, 1983. Examination of changes in presidential nominating procedures from 1968 into the 1980s.

Polsby, Nelson W., and Aaron B. Wildavsky. *Presidential Elections*. 5th ed. New York: Scribner's, 1980. Analysis of how presidential campaigns are conducted.

Pomper, Gerald M., and Susan Lederman. *Elections in America*. New York: Longman, 1980. Study of election procedures at the state and federal levels.

Sorauf, Frank J. *Party Politics in America*. 2nd ed. Boston: Little, Brown, 1972. Examination of the roles of parties, their influence on government, party organizations, and the nature of party supporters.

Chapter 9: Who Rules America? The Elite, the Interests, and the Voter

Almond, Gabriel, and Sidney Verba. *The Civic Culture*. Princeton, N.J.: Princeton University Press, 1963. An important work, containing analyses of participation in politics.

Campbell, Angus, Philip E. Converse, and Warren E. Miller, *The American Voter*. New York: Wiley, 1960. Comprehensive, landmark study of voting behavior compiled by the Survey Research Center of the University of Michigan.

Dahl, Robert A. *Who Governs*? New Haven, Conn.: Yale University Press, 1961. Contains theory of "pluralism" by its chief proponent.

Domhoff, G. William. *Who Rules America Now*? Englewood Cliffs, N.J.: Prentice-Hall, 1983. The latest edition of the classic *Who Rules America*?

Dye, Thomas R. *Who's Running America? The Reagan Years*. Englewood Cliffs, N.J.: Prentice-Hall, 1983. Updated version of power-elite thesis.

Halberstam, David. *The Best and the Brightest*. New York: Fawcett Books, 1973. A critical review of the Kennedy-Johnson administrations and the presumptions that led to disaster in Vietnam.

Lowi, Theodore J. *The End of Liberalism*. Rev. ed. New York: Norton, 1979. Critical analysis of theory and practice of interest groups.

Mills, C. Wright. *The Power Elite*. New York: Oxford University Press, 1956. Classic statement of power-elite thesis.

Nie, Norman H., Sidney Verba, and John R. Petrocik. *The Changing American Voter*. Cambridge, Mass.: Harvard University Press, 1976. Important comprehensive study, challenging some prevalent theories about voting behavior.

Ornstein, Norman J., and Shirley Elder. *Interest Groups, Lobbying, and Policymaking*. Washington, D.C.: Congressional Quarterly Press, 1978. An explanation of recent examples illustrating increased grass roots lobbying.

Polsby, Nelson. *Political Innovation in America: The Politics of Policy Initiation*. New Haven, Conn.: Yale University Press, 1984. Case studies of eight major new policies implemented in the post–World War II era.

Verba, Sidney, and Norman Nie. *Participation in America*. New York: Harper & Row, 1972; and the same authors with Jue-On Kim, *Participation and Political Equality*. London: Cambridge University Press, 1978. Careful studies of the types of political participants and their influence.

Chapter 10: The Bureaucrats: Attendant Lords

Drucker, Peter. *The Age of Discontinuity*. New York: Harper & Row, 1969. One of many works by an important student of bureaucracy.

Galambos, Louis, ed. *The New American State: Bureaucracies and Policies Since World War II*. Baltimore: Johns Hopkins University Press, 1987. Scholarly essays on the growth and functioning of the federal bureaucracy.

Gawthrop, Louis C. *Administrative Politics and Social Change*. New York: St. Martin's, 1977. An investigation of the nature and effectiveness of administrative procedures at the federal level.

Gordon, George J. *Public Administration in America*. New York: St. Martin's, 1978. Basic guide to the subject.

Kaufman, Herbert. *Are Government Organizations Immortal?* Washington, D.C.: Brookings Institution, 1976. A look at the permanence of government agencies.

Marini, Frank, ed. *Toward a New Public Administration*. Scranton, Pa.: Chandler, 1971. Essays on the study of public administration.

Mazmanian, Daniel A., and Paul A. Sabatier. *Implementation and Public Policy*. Glenview, Ill.: Scott, Foresman, 1983. Analysis of how well the government delivers on specific objectives of public policies.

Van Riper, Paul P. *History of the United States Civil Service*. Westport, Conn.: Greenwood, 1976. Details the history of the national civil service.

Wildavsky, Aaron. *The Politics of the Budgetary Process*. Boston: Little, Brown, 1974. Study of the politics of budgeting.

Woll, Peter. *American Bureaucracy*. New York: Norton, 1977. A study of the nature and influence of the bureaucracy.

Chapter 11: Media, the Shadow Government: Power and the Press

Kendrick, Alexander. *Prime Time: The Life of Edward R. Murrow*. Boston: Little, Brown, 1969. A probing and critical look at television news.

Leonard, Thomas C. *The Birth of American Political Reporting*. New York: Oxford University Press, 1986. New, critical approach to the subject, emphasizing that the history of American political coverage too often involves character defamation, is often a story of collaboration between press and politicians, and that the press is at least partly responsible for a decline in voting in the United States.

Liebling, A. J. *The Press*. New York: Ballantine, 1960. An anecdotal but classic work on the role of the press in America before John Kennedy.

McGinniss, Joe. *The Selling of the President, 1968*. New York: Trident, 1969. Eye-opening account of the Nixon media campaign.

McLuhan, Marshall. *Understanding Media*. New York: McGraw-Hill, 1964. Essays by the stimulating and controversial Canadian critic.

Ranney, Austin. *Channels of Power*. Washington, D.C.: American Enterprise Institute, 1983. A distinguished political scientist analyzes the impact of television on American politics and leaves the reader more than a little concerned.

Reston, James. *The Artillery of the Press*. New York: Harper & Row, 1967. A newspaper journalist's view of the press and its relationship to government.

Small, William. *To Kill a Messenger: Television News and the Real World*. New York: Hastings House, 1970. History of TV reportage of major social and political events.

Sperber, A. M. *Murrow: His Life and Times*. New York: Freundlich, 1986. Massive new biography of the radio and television journalist.

Swanberg, W. A. *Luce and His Empire*. New York: Scribner's, 1972. Study of the influential *Time-Life* publisher.

Woodward, Bob, and Carl Bernstein. *All the President's Men*. New York:

Simon & Schuster, 1974. Story of the unraveling of the Watergate scandal by the two Washington *Post* reporters.

Chapter 12: Economics: The Prevailing Smell of Money

Browne, Harry. *How You Can Profit from the Coming Devaluation*. New York: Arlington House, 1970. The first and perhaps most influential of the books prophesying the collapse of the American monetary system.

Ehrlich, Paul R., and Anne H. Ehrlich. *Population, Resources, Environment: Issues in Human Ecology*. 2nd ed. San Francisco: W. H. Freeman, 1972. An alarming analysis of problems of pollution, overpopulation, and hunger.

Energy Policy. Washington, D.C.: Congressional Quarterly, April 1979. A comprehensive review of the energy problem, prospects, and analyses of energy legislation through 1978.

Friedman, Milton. *Capitalism and Freedom*. Chicago: University of Chicago Press, 1962. An important explanation of conservative attitudes.

Friedman, Milton and Rose Friedman. *Free to Choose*. New York: Harcourt Brace Jovanovich, 1980. A popular explanation of the views of the prize-winning economist.

Galbraith, John Kenneth. *American Capitalism*. Boston: Houghton Mifflin, 1956. Influential study containing theory of countervailing power.

Galbraith, John Kenneth. *The New Industrial State*. Boston: Houghton Mifflin, 1969. The popular liberal economist's assessment of the contemporary economic situation.

Gilder, George. *Wealth and Poverty*. New York: Basic Books, 1981. The best seller that promoted supply-side economics.

Harrington, Michael. *The Other America*. Baltimore: Penguin Books, 1962. Well-known survey of poverty in America.

Heilbroner, Robert L. *The Worldly Philosophers*. Rev. ed. New York: Simon & Schuster, 1961. Readable explanations of the ideas of major economic thinkers throughout history.

Novak, Michael. *The Spirit of Democratic Capitalism*. New York: Simon & Schuster, 1982. A panegyric to the political economy developed by the founders of the United States.

Pechman, Joseph A., ed. *Setting National Priorities*. Washington, D.C.: Brookings Institution, 1983. This annual report contains several essays analyzing the budget, the state of the economy, and social issues.

Schumacher, E. F. *Small Is Beautiful*. New York: Harper & Row, 1973. A popular critique of materialism and economic growth.

Thurow, Lester. *The Zero Sum Society*. New York: Basic Books, 1980. Clear discussion of economic issues by an influential economist.

Chapter 13: Trumpets and Flourishes: America in the World

Barnet, Richard J. *Real Security*. New York: Simon & Schuster, 1981. Liberal recommendations for restoring American influence in the world.

Brzezinski, Zbigniew. *Power and Principle*. New York: Farrar, Straus & Giroux, 1983. This Columbia University professor explains America's role in the world during the time he served President Carter as national security adviser.

Carter, Jimmy. *The Blood of Abraham*. Boston: Houghton Mifflin, 1985. Careful, informative study of the Middle East by the former president who negotiated the Camp David Accords.

Combs, Jerald A., ed. *Nationalist, Realist, and Radical: Three Views of American Diplomacy*. New York: Harper & Row, 1972. Conflicting essays on major historical events in American diplomacy.

Eban, Abba. *An Autobiography*. New York: Random House, 1977. A personal history of Israel, with emphasis on its special relationship with America, by that country's former chief delegate to the United Nations.

Fallows, James. *National Defense*. New York: Vintage Books, 1981. Analysis of current defense posture of the United States with suggestions as to how to streamline our defense, make it more effective and yet save money.

Foreign Affairs. Published by the Council on Foreign Relations. A quarterly journal devoted to major issues of international affairs and American foreign policy.

Great Decisions. An annual collection of essays on major foreign policy issues published by the Foreign Policy Association.

Jones, Alan M., Jr. *U.S. Foreign Policy in a Changing World*. New York: D. McKay, 1973. Collection of studies by specialists in particular geographic areas.

Kissinger, Henry. *The White House Years*. Boston: Little, Brown, 1979. Memoirs of Kissinger's service as national security adviser.

Kissinger, Henry. *Years of Upheaval*. Boston: Little, Brown, 1982. Memoirs of the author's service as secretary of state.

LaFeber, Walter. *America, Russia, and the Cold War*. 3rd ed. New York: Wiley, 1976. A scholarly, revisionist study.

Manchester, William. *American Caesar: Douglas MacArthur*. New York: Dell Pub. Co. Inc., 1982. An account of the career of America's most celebrated and controversial soldier, which is also the story of American policy in the Pacific in the twentieth century.

Nathan, James A., and James K. Oliver. *Foreign Policy Making and the American Political System*. Boston: Little, Brown, 1983. Study of foreign policy formulation.

Nixon, Richard. *1999: Victory Without War*. New York: Simon & Schuster, 1988. Thoughtful assessment by the former president of the U.S. role in the world at the end of the twentieth century.

Oye, Kenneth, et al, eds. *Eagle Defiant: United States Foreign Policy in the 1980's*. Boston: Little, Brown, 1983. Essays by experts covering various topics and areas.

Sheehan, Neil, et al. *The Pentagon Papers*. New York: Bantam, 1971. Important collection of articles and documents on America's involvement in Vietnam from the Truman presidency through 1968.

Spanier, John. *American Foreign Policy Since World War II*. 8th ed. New York: Holt, Rinehart & Winston, 1980. Popular, traditional treatment of America in the world since 1945.

Spanier, John, and Eric Uslaner. *How American Foreign Policy Is Made*. 2nd ed. New York: Holt, Rinehart & Winston, 1978. Discussion of the complex ways in which foreign policies are created and carried out.

Taubman, William, ed. *Globalism and Its Critics*. Lexington, Mass.: Heath, 1973. Essays and speeches on American foreign policy from the perspective of the political right, "globalists," "realists," "liberals," and "radicals."

Twain, Mark. *A Pen Warmed Up in Hell*. New York: Harper & Row, 1972. Twain's acid comments on imperialism, war, psuedopatriotism, and hypocrisy.

Vance, Cyrus. *Hard Choices*. New York: Simon & Schuster, 1982. Explanation of U.S. diplomacy during the Carter administration from the perspective of the secretary of state.

Chapter 14: Politics and the Pursuit of Happiness

Banfield, Edward C. *The Unheavenly City Revisited*. Boston: Little, Brown, 1974. An unorthodox and controversial analysis of the American city.

Cox, Harvey. *The Secular City*. New York: Macmillan, 1965. A fascinating and upbeat analysis of the city and its meaning for contemporary society by a popular theologian.

Galbraith, John Kenneth. *A Life in Our Times*. New York: Ballantine, 1981. Memoirs and reflections of one of America's most distinguished liberal thinkers and economists.

Kennedy, Paul. "The (Relative) Decline of America," *The Atlantic*. August, 1987. Taken from the best-selling book *The Rise and Fall of the Great Powers* (New York: Random House, 1988), this essay suggests that the United States's increased military commitments since World War II along with its relative economic slippage conforms to an ominous pattern of decline.

Putney, Snell. *The Conquest of Society*. Belmont, Calif.: Wadsworth, 1972.

An analysis of contemporary American problems with recommendations for action on the part of "autonomous" individuals.

Rosenau, James N. *The Dramas of Politics*. Boston: Little, Brown, 1973. Emphasizes the parallels between the dramas of politics and those of personal life.

Schwarz, John E. *America's Hidden Success: A Reassessment of Twenty Years of Public Policy*. New York: Norton, 1983. A fascinating argument that liberals have nothing to be ashamed of in the policies they promoted and passed in the years since John F. Kennedy.

Smith, Hedrick. *The Power Game*. New York: Random House, 1988. Story of political developments at the federal level during the 1970s and 1980s.

Toffler, Alvin. *Future Shock*. New York: Random House, 1970. Influential study on the rapidity with which our world is changing.

Will, George. *The Pursuit of Happiness and Other Sobering Thoughts*. New York: Harper & Row, 1979. A collection of newspaper columns by one of America's leading conservatives.

Will, George. *Statecraft as Soulcraft: What Government Does*. New York: Simon & Schuster, 1983. A thoughtful essay on the problems and promise of politics.

The Declaration of Independence

In Congress, July 4, 1776: The Unanimous Declaration of the Thirteen United States of America

When in the Course of human events, it becomes necessary for one people to dissolve the political bands which have connected them with another, and to assume among the Powers of the earth, the separate and equal station to which the Laws of Nature and Nature's God entitle them, a decent respect to the opinions of mankind requires that they should declare the causes which impel them to the separation.

We hold these truths to be self-evident, that all men are created equal, that they are endowed by their Creator with certain unalienable Rights, that among these are Life, Liberty and the pursuit of Happiness. That to secure these rights, Governments are instituted among Men, deriving their just powers from the consent of the governed, That whenever any Form of Government becomes destructive of these ends, it is the Right of the People to alter or to abolish it, and to institute new Government, laying its foundation on such principles and organizing its powers in such form, as to them shall seem most likely to effect their Safety and Happiness. Prudence, indeed, will dictate that Governments long established should not be changed for light and transient causes; and accordingly all experience hath shown, that mankind are more disposed to suffer, while evils are sufferable, than to right themselves by abolishing the forms to which they are accustomed. But when a long train of abuses and usurpations, pursuing invariably the same Object evinces a design to reduce them under absolute Despotism, it is their right, it is their duty, to throw off such Government, and to provide new Guards for their future security—Such has been the patient sufferance of the Colonies; and such is now the necessity which constrains them to alter their former Systems of Government. The history of the present King of Great Britain is a history of repeated injuries and usurpations, all having in direct object the establishment of an absolute Tyranny over these States. To prove this, let Facts be submitted to a candid world.

He has refused his Assent to Laws, the most wholesome and necessary for the public good.

He has forbidden his Governors to pass Laws of immediate and pressing importance, unless suspended in their operation till his Assent should be obtained; and when so suspended, he has utterly neglected to attend to them.

He has refused to pass other Laws for the accommodation of large districts of people, unless those people would relinquish the right of representation in the Legislature, a right inestimable to them and formidable to tyrants only.

He has called together legislative bodies at places unusual, uncomfortable, and distant from the depository of their Public Records, for the sole purpose of fatiguing them into compliance with his measures.

He has dissolved Representative Houses repeatedly, for opposing with manly firmness his invasions on the rights of the people.

He has refused for a long time, after such dissolutions, to cause others to be elected; whereby the Legislative Powers, incapable of Annihilation, have returned to the People at large for their exercise; the State remaining in the mean time exposed to all the dangers of invasion from without, and convulsions within.

He has endeavoured to prevent the population of these States; for that purpose obstructing the Laws of Naturalization of Foreigners; refusing to pass others to encourage their migration hither, and raising the conditions of new Appropriations of Lands.

He has obstructed the Administration of Justice, by refusing his Assent to Laws for establishing Judiciary Powers.

He has made Judges dependent on his Will alone, for the tenure of their offices, and the amount and payment of their salaries.

He has erected a multitude of New Offices, and sent hither swarms of Officers to harass our People, and eat out their substance.

He has kept among us, in times of peace, Standing Armies without the Consent of our legislature.

He has affected to render the Military independent of and superior to the Civil Power.

He has combined with others to subject us to a jurisdiction foreign to our constitution, and unacknowledged by our laws giving his Assent to their acts of pretended legislation:

For quartering large bodies of armed troops among us:

For protecting them, by a mock Trial, from Punishment for any Murders which they should commit on the Inhabitants of these States:

For cutting off our Trade with all parts of the world:

For imposing taxes on us without our Consent:

For depriving us in many cases, of the benefits of Trial by jury:

For transporting us beyond Seas to be tried for pretended offences:

For abolishing the free System of English Laws in a neighboring Province, establishing therein an Arbitrary government, and enlarging its Boundaries so as to render it at once an example and fit instrument for introducing the same absolute rule into these Colonies:

For taking away our Charters, abolishing our most valuable Laws, and altering fundamentally the Forms of our Governments:

For suspending our own legislature, and declaring themselves invested with Power to legislate for us in all cases whatsoever.

He has abdicated Government here, by declaring us out of his Protection and waging War against us.

He has plundered our seas, ravaged our Coasts, burnt our towns, and destroyed the lives of our people.

He is at this time transporting large armies of foreign mercenaries to compleat the works of death, desolation and tyranny, already begun with circumstances of Cruelty & perfidy scarcely paralleled in the most barbarous ages, and totally unworthy the Head of a civilized nation.

He has constrained our fellow Citizens taken Captive on the high Seas to bear Arms against their Country, to become the executioners of their friends and Brethren, or to fall themselves by their Hands.

He has excited domestic insurrections amongst us, and has endeavoured to bring on the inhabitants of our frontiers, the merciless Indian Savages, whose known rule of warfare, is an undistinguished destruction of all ages, sexes and conditions.

In every stage of these Oppressions We have Petitioned for Redress in the most humble terms: Our repeated Petitions have been answered only by repeated injury. A Prince, whose character is thus marked by every act which may define a Tyrant, is unfit to be the ruler of a free People.

Nor have We been wanting in attention to our British brethren. We have warned them from time to time of attempts by their legislature to extend an unwarrantable jurisdiction over us. We have reminded them of the circumstances of our emigration and settlement here. We have appealed to their native justice and magnanimity, and we have conjured them by the ties of our common kindred to disavow these usurpations, which would inevitably interrupt our connections and correspondence. They too have been deaf to the voice of justice and of consanguinity. We must, therefore, acquiesce in the necessity, which denounces our Separation, and hold them, as we hold the rest of mankind, Enemies in War, in Peace Friends.

We, therefore, the Representatives of the United States of America, in General Congress, Assembled, appealing to the Supreme Judge of the world for the rectitude of our intentions, do, in the Name, and by Authority of the good People of these Colonies, solemnly publish and declare, That these United Colonies are, and of Right ought to be Free and Independent States; that they are Absolved from all Allegiance to the British Crown and that all political connection between them and the State of Great Britain, is and ought to be totally dissolved; and that as Free and Independent states, they have full Power to levy War, conclude Peace, contract Alliances, establish Commerce, and to do all other Acts and Things which Independent States may of right do. And for the support of this Declaration, with a firm reliance on the Protection of Divine Providence, we mutually pledge to each other our Lives, our Fortunes and our sacred Honor.

JOHN HANCOCK*

The Constitution of the United States

We the people of the United States, in order to form a more perfect union, establish justice, insure domestic tranquility, provide for the common defense, promote the general welfare, and secure the blessings of liberty to ourselves and our posterity, do ordain and establish this Constitution for the United States of America.

Article 1

Section 1

All legislative powers herein granted shall be vested in a Congress of the United States, which shall consist of a Senate and House of Representatives.

Section 2

1. The House of Representatives shall be composed of members chosen every second year by the people of the several States, and the electors in each

* The remaining signatures are omitted.

State shall have the qualifications requisite for electors of the most numerous branch of the State legislature.

2. No person shall be a representative who shall not have attained to the age of twenty-five years, and been seven years a citizen of the United States, and who shall not, when elected, be an inhabitant of that State in which he shall be chosen.

3. Representatives and direct taxes[1] shall be apportioned among the several States which may be included within this Union, according to their respective numbers, which shall be determined by adding to the whole number of free persons, including those bound to service for a term of years, and excluding Indians not taxed, three-fifths of all other persons.[2] The actual enumeration shall be made within three years after the first meeting of the Congress of the United States, and within every subsequent term of ten years, in such manner as they shall be law direct. The number of representatives shall not exceed one for every thirty thousand, but each State shall have at least one representative; and until such enumeration shall be made, the State of New Hampshire shall be entitled to choose three, Massachusetts eight, Rhode Island and Providence Plantations one, Connecticut five, New York six, New Jersey four, Pennsylvania eight, Delaware one, Maryland six, Virginia ten, North Carolina five, South Carolina five, and Georgia three.

4. When vacancies happen in the representation from any State, the executive authority thereof shall issue writs of election to fill such vacancies.

5. The House of Representatives shall choose their speaker and other officers; and shall have the sole power of impeachment.

Section 3

1. The Senate of the United States shall be composed of two senators from each State, chosen by the legislature thereof,[3] for six years; and each senator shall have one vote.

2. Immediately after they shall be assembled in consequence of the first election, they shall be divided as equally as may be into three classes. The seats of the senators of the first class shall be vacated at the expiration of the second year, of the second class at the expiration of the fourth year, and of the third class at the expiration of the sixth year, so that one-third may be chosen every second year; and if vacancies happen by resignation, or otherwise, during the recess of the legislature of any State, the executive thereof may make temporary appointments until the next meeting of the legislature, which shall then fill such vacancies.[4]

[1]See the Sixteenth Amendment.
[2]Partly superseded by the Fourteenth Amendment.
[3]See the Seventeenth Amendment.
[4]See the Seventeenth Amendment.

3. No person shall be a senator who shall not have attained to the age of thirty years, and been nine years a citizen of the United States, and who shall not, when elected, be an inhabitant of that State for which he shall be chosen.

4. The Vice President of the United States shall be President of the Senate, but shall have no vote, unless they be equally divided.

5. The Senate shall choose their other officers, and also a president *pro tempore*, in the absence of the Vice President, or when he shall exercise the office of President of the United States.

6. The Senate shall have the sole power to try all impeachments. When sitting for that purpose, they shall be on oath or affirmation. When the President of the United States is tried, the chief justice shall preside: and no person shall be convicted without the concurrence of two-thirds of the members present.

7. Judgment in cases of impeachment shall not extend further than to removal from office, and disqualification to hold and enjoy any office of honor, trust or profit under the United States: but the party convicted shall nevertheless be liable and subject to indictment, trial, judgment and punishment, according to law.

Section 4

1. The times, places, and manner of holding elections for senators and representatives, shall be prescribed in each State by the legislature thereof; but the Congress may at any time by law make or alter such regulations, except as to the places of choosing senators.

2. The Congress shall assemble at least once in every year, and such meeting shall be on the first Monday in December, unless they shall by law appoint a different day.

Section 5

1. Each House shall be the judge of the elections, returns and qualifications of its own members and a majority of each shall constitute a quorum to do business; but a smaller number may adjourn from day to day, and may be authorized to compel the attendance of absent members, in such manner and under such penalties as each House may provide.

2. Each House may determine the rules of its proceedings, punish its members for disorderly behavior, and, with the concurrence of two-thirds, expel a member.

3. Each House shall keep a journal of its proceedings, and from time to time publish the same, excepting such parts as may in their judgment require secrecy; and the yeas and nays of the members of either House on any question shall, at the desire of one-fifth of those present, be entered on the journal.

4. Neither House, during the session of Congress, shall, without the consent of the other, adjourn for more than three days, nor to any other place than that in which the two Houses shall be sitting.

Section 6

1. The senators and representatives shall receive a compensation for their services, to be ascertained by law, and paid out of the Treasury of the United States. They shall in all cases, except treason, felony and breach of the peace, be privileged from arrest during their attendance at the session of their respective Houses, and in going to and returning from the same; and for any speech or debate in either House, they shall not be questioned in any other place.

2. No senator or representative shall, during the time for which he was elected, be appointed to any civil office under the authority of the United States, which shall have been created, or the emoluments whereof shall have been increased during such time, and no person holding any office under the United States shall be a member of either House during his continuance in office.

Section 7

1. All bills for raising revenue shall originate in the House of Representatives; but the Senate may propose or concur with amendments as on other bills.

2. Every bill which shall have passed the House of Representatives and the Senate, shall, before it become a law, be presented to the President of the United States; if he approve he shall sign it, but if not he shall return it, with his objections to the House in which it shall have originated, who shall enter the objections at large on their journal, and proceed to reconsider it. If after such reconsideration two thirds of that House shall agree to pass the bill, it shall be sent, together with the objections, to the other House, by which it shall likewise be reconsidered, and if approved by two thirds of that House, it shall become a law. But in all such cases the votes of both Houses shall be determined by yeas and nays, and the names of the persons voting for and against the bill shall be entered on the journal of each House respectively. If any bill shall not be returned by the President within ten days (Sundays excepted) after it shall have been presented to him, the same shall be a law, in like manner as if he had signed it, unless the Congress by their adjournment prevent its return, in which case it shall not be law.

3. Every order, resolution, or vote to which the concurrence of the Senate and House of Representatives may be necessary (except on a question of adjournment) shall be presented to the President of the United States; and before the same shall take effect, shall be approved by him, or being disapproved by him, shall be repassed by two thirds of the Senate and

House of Representatives, according to the rules and limitations prescribed in the case of a bill.

Section 8

1. The Congress shall have the power to lay and collect taxes, duties, imposts, and excises, to pay the debts and provide for the common defense and general welfare of the United States; but all duties, imposts, and excises shall be uniform throughout the United States;

2. To borrow money on the credit of the United States;

3. To regulate commerce with foreign nations, and among the several States, and with the Indian tribes;

4. To establish an uniform rule of naturalization, and uniform laws on the subject of bankruptcies throughout the United States;

5. To coin money, regulate the value thereof, and of foreign coin, and fix the standard of weights and measures;

6. To provide for the punishment of counterfeiting the securities and current coin of the United States;

7. To establish post offices and post roads;

8. To promote the progress of science and useful arts, by securing for limited times to authors and inventors the exclusive right to their respective writings and discoveries;

9. To constitute tribunals inferior to the Supreme Court;

10. To define and punish piracies and felonies committed on the high seas, and offenses against the laws of nations;

11. To declare war, grant letters of marque and reprisal, and make rules concerning captures on land and water;

12. To raise and support armies, but no appropriation of money to that use shall be for a longer term than two years;

13. To provide and maintain a navy;

14. To make rules for the government and regulation of the land and naval forces;

15. To provide for calling forth the militia to execute the laws of the Union, suppress insurrections and repel invasions;

16. To provide for organizing, arming, and disciplining the militia, and for governing such part of them as may be employed in the service of the United States, reserving to the States respectively the appointment of the officers, and the authority of training the militia according to the discipline prescribed by Congress;

17. To exercise exclusive legislation in all cases whatsoever, over such district (not exceeding ten miles square) as may, be cession of particular States, and the acceptance of Congress, become the seat of the government of the United States, and to exercise like authority over all places purchased by the consent of the legislature of the State in which the same shall be, for

the erection of forts, magazines, dockyards, and other needful buildings; and

18. To make all laws which shall be necessary and proper for carrying into execution the foregoing powers, and all other powers vested by this Constitution in the government of the United States, or in any department or officer thereof.

Section 9

1. The migration or importation of such persons as any of the States now existing shall think proper to admit, shall not be prohibited by the Congress prior to the year one thousand eight hundred and eight, but a tax or duty may be imposed on such importation, not exceeding ten dollars for each person.

2. The privilege of the writ of *habeas corpus* shall not be suspended, unless when in cases of rebellion or invasion the public safety may require it.

3. No bill of attainder or *ex post facto* law shall be passed.

4. No capitation, or other direct, tax shall be laid, unless in proportion to the census or enumeration herein before directed to be taken.[5]

5. No tax or duty shall be laid on articles exported from any State.

6. No preference shall be given by any regulation of commerce or revenue to the ports of one State over those of another: nor shall vessels bound to, or from, one State be obliged to enter, clear, or pay duties in another.

7. No money shall be drawn from the treasury, but in consequence of appropriations, made by law; and a regular statement and account of the receipts and expenditures of all public money shall be published from time to time.

8. No title of nobility shall be granted by the United States: and no person holding any office or profit or trust under them, shall, without the consent of the Congress, accept of any present, emolument, office, or title, of any kind whatever, from any king, prince, or foreign State.

Section 10

1. No State shall enter into any treaty, alliance, or confederation; grant letters of marque and reprisal; coin money; emit bills of credit; make anything but gold and silver coin a tender in payment of debts; pass any bill of attainder, *ex post facto* law, or law impairing the obligation of contracts, or grant any title of nobility.

2. No state shall, without the consent of the Congress, lay any impost or duties on imports or exports, except what may be absolutely necessary for

---

[5]See the Sixteenth Amendment.

executing its inspection laws; and the net produce of all duties and imposts laid by any State on imports or exports, shall be of the use of the treasury of the United States; and all such laws shall be subject to the revision and control of the Congress.

3. No State shall, without the consent of Congress, lay any duty of tonnage, keep troops, or ships of war in time of peace, enter into any agreement or compact with another State, or with a foreign power, or engage in war, unless actually invaded, or in such imminent danger as will not admit of delay.

Article 2

Section 1

1. The executive power shall be vested in a President of the United States of America. He shall hold his office during the term of four years, and, together with the Vice President, chosen for the same term, be elected, as follows[6]:

2. Each State shall appoint, in such manner as the legislature thereof may direct, a number of electors, equal to the whole number of senators and representatives to which the State may be entitled in the Congress: but no senator or representative, or person holding an office of trust or profit under the United States, shall be appointed an elector.

The electors shall meet in their respective States, and vote by ballot for two persons, of whom one at least shall not be an inhabitant of the same State with themselves. And they shall make a list of all the persons voted for, and of the number of votes for each; which list they shall sign and certify, and transmit sealed to the seat of the government of the United States, directed to the president of the Senate. The president of the Senate shall, in the presence of the Senate and House of Representatives, open all certificates, and votes shall then be counted. The person having the greatest number of votes shall be the President, if such number be a majority of the whole number of electors appointed; and if there be more than one who have such majority, and have an equal number of votes, then the House of Representatives shall immediately choose by ballot one of them for President; and if no person have a majority, then from the five highest on the list said House shall in like manner choose the President. But in choosing the President, the votes shall be taken by States, the representation from each State having one vote; a quorum for this purpose shall consist of a member or members from two thirds of the States, and a majority of all the States shall be necessary to a choice. In every case, after the choice of the President, the person having the greatest number of votes of the electors shall be

---

[6]See the Twenty-second Amendment.

the Vice President. But if there should remain two or more who have equal votes, the Senate shall choose from them by ballot the Vice President.[7]

3. The Congress may determine the time of choosing the electors, and the day on which they shall give their votes; which day shall be the same throughout the United States.

4. No person except a natural born citizen, or a citizen of the United States, at the time of the adoption of this Constitution, shall be eligible to the office of President; neither shall any person be eligible to that office who shall not have attained to the age of thirty-five years, and been fourteen years a resident within the United States.

5. In case of the removal of the President from office, or of his death, resignation, or inability to discharge the powers and duties of the said office, the same shall devolve on the Vice President, and the Congress may by law provide for the case of removal, death, resignation, or inability, both of the President and Vice President, declaring what officer shall then act as President, and such officer shall act accordingly, until the disability be removed, or a President shall be elected.[8]

6. The President shall, at stated times, receive for his services a compensation, which shall neither be increased nor diminished during the period for which he shall have been elected, and he shall not receive within that period any other emolument from the United States, or any of them.

7. Before he enter on the execution of his office, he shall take the following oath or affirmation:—"I do solemnly swear (or affirm) that I will faithfully execute the office of President of the United States, and will to the best of my ability, preserve, protect and defend the Constitution of the United States."

Section 2

1. The President shall be commander in chief of the army and navy of the United States, and of the militia of the several States, when called into the actual service of the United States; he may require the opinion, in writing, of the principal officer in each of the executive departments, upon any subject relating to the duties of their respective offices, and he shall have power to grant reprieves and pardons for offenses against the United States, except in cases of impeachment.

2. He shall have power, by and with the advice and consent of the Senate, to make treaties, provided two-thirds of the senators present concur; and he shall nominate, and by and with the advice and consent of the Senate, shall appoint ambassadors, other public ministers and consuls, judges of the Supreme Court, and all other officers of the United States, whose appointments are not herein otherwise provided for, and which shall

[7]Superseded by the Twelfth Amendment.
[8]See the Twentieth Amendment and the Twenty-fifth Amendment.

be established by law; but the Congress may by law vest the appointment of such inferior officers, as they think proper, in the President alone, in the courts of law, or in the heads of departments.

3. The President shall have power to fill up all vacancies that may happen during the recess of the Senate, by granting commissions which shall expire at the end of the next session.

Section 3

1. He shall from time to time give to the Congress information of the state of the Union, and recommend to their consideration such measures as he shall judge necessary and expedient; he may, on extraordinary occasions, convene both Houses, or either of them, and in case of disagreement between them with respect to the time of adjournment, he may adjourn them to such time as he shall think proper; he shall receive ambassadors and other public ministers; he shall take care that the laws be faithfully executed, and shall commission all the officers of the United States.

Section 4

The President, Vice President, and all civil officers of the United States, shall be removed from office on impeachment for, and conviction of, treason, bribery, or other high crimes and misdemeanors.

Article 3

Section 1

The Judicial power of the United States shall be vested in one Supreme court, and in such inferior courts as the Congress may from time to time ordain and establish. The judges, both of the Supreme and inferior courts, shall hold their offices during good behavior, and shall, at stated times, receive for their services, a compensation, which shall not be diminished during their continuance in office.

Section 2

1. The Judicial power shall extend to all cases, in law and equity, arising under this Constitution, the laws of the United States, and treaties made, or which shall be made, under their authority;—to all cases affecting ambassadors, other public ministers and consuls;—to all cases of admiralty and maritime jurisdiction;—to controversies to which the United States shall be a party;—to controversies between two or more States;—between a state

and citizens of another State[9]—between citizens of the same State claiming lands under grants of different States, and between a State, or the citizens thereof, and foreign States, citizens or subjects.

2. In all cases affecting ambassadors, other public ministers and consuls, and those in which a State shall be party, the Supreme Court shall have original jurisdiction. In all the other cases before mentioned, the Supreme Court shall have original jurisdiction. In all the other cases before mentioned, the Supreme Court shall have appellate jurisdiction, both as to law and to fact, with such exceptions, and under such regulations as the Congress shall make.

3. The trial of all crimes, except in cases of impeachment, shall be by jury; and such trial shall be held in the State where the said crimes shall have been committed; but when not committed within any State, the trial shall be at such place or places as the Congress may by law have directed.

Section 3

1. Treason against the United States shall consist only in levying war against them, or in adhering to their enemies, giving them aid and comfort. No person shall be convicted of treason unless on the testimony of two witnesses to the same overt act, or on confession in open court.

2. The Congress shall have power to declare the punishment of treason, but no attainder of treason shall work corruption of blood, or forfeiture except during the life of the person attained.

Article 4

Section 1

Full faith and credit shall be given in each State to the public acts, records, and judicial proceedings of every other State. And the Congress may by general laws prescribe the manner in which acts, records and proceedings shall be proved, and the effect thereof.

Section 2

1. The citizens of each State shall be entitled to all privileges and immunities of citizens in the several States.

2. A person charged in any State with treason, felony, or other crime, who shall flee from justice, and be found in another State, shall on demand of the executive authority of the State from which he fled, be delivered up to be removed to the State having jurisdiction of the crime.

[9]See the Eleventh Amendment.

3. No person held to service or labor in one State under the laws thereof, escaping into another, shall, in consequence of any law or regulation therein, be discharged from such service or labor, but shall be delivered up on claim of the party to whom such service or labor may be due.

Section 3

1. New States may be admitted by the Congress into this Union; but no new State shall be formed or erected within the jurisdiction of any other State; nor any State be formed by the junction of two or more States, or parts of States, without the consent of the legislatures of the States concerned as well as of the Congress.

2. The Congress shall have power to dispose of and make all needful rules and regulations respecting the territory or other property belonging to the United States; and nothing in this Constitution shall be so construed as to prejudice any claims of the United States, or of any particular State.

Section 4

The United States shall guarantee to every State in this Union a republican form of government, and shall protect each of them against invasion; and on application of the legislature, or of the executive (when the legislature cannot be convened) against domestic violence.

Article 5

The Congress, whenever two-thirds of both Houses shall deem it necessary, shall propose amendments to this Constitution, or, on the application of the legislatures of two-thirds of the several States, shall call a convention for proposing amendments, which, in either case, shall be valid to all intents and purposes, as part of this Constitution when ratified by the legislatures of three-fourths of the several States, or by conventions in three-fourths thereof, as the one or the other mode of ratification may be proposed by the Congress; Provided that no amendment which may be made prior to the year one thousand eight hundred and eight shall in any manner affect the first and fourth clauses in the ninth section of the first article; and that no State, without its consent, shall be deprived of its equal suffrage in the Senate.

Article 6

1. All debts contracted, and engagements entered into, before the adoption of this Constitution, shall be as valid against the United States under this Constitution, as under the Confederation.

2. This Constitution, and the laws of the United States which shall be made in pursuance thereof; and all treaties made, or which shall be made, under the authority of the United States, shall be the supreme law of the land; and the Judges in every State shall be bound thereby, anything in the Constitution or laws of any State to the contrary notwithstanding.

3. The senators and representatives before mentioned, and the members of the several State legislatures, and all executive and judicial officers, both of the United States and of the several States, shall be bound by oath or affirmation to support this Constitution; but no religious test shall ever be required as a qualification to any office or public trust under the United States.

Article 7

The ratification of the conventions of nine States shall be sufficient for the establishment of this Constitution between the States so ratifying the same.

Done in Convention by the unanimous consent of the States present the seventeenth day of September in the year of our Lord one thousand seven hundred and eighty-seven, and of the independence of the United States of America the twelfth. In witness whereof we have hereunto subscribed our names.

[Names omitted]

Articles in Addition To, and Amendment Of, the Constitution of the United States of America, Proposed by Congress, and Ratified by the Legislatures of the Several States, Pursuant to the Fifth Article of the Original Constitution.[10] (The first ten amendments were ratified December 15, 1791, and form what is known as the "Bill of Rights.")

Amendment 1

Congress shall make no law respecting an establishment of religion, or prohibiting the free exercise thereof; or abridging the freedom of speech, or of the press; or the right of the people peaceably to assemble, and to petition the Government for a redress of grievances.

Amendment 2

A well regulated Militia, being necessary to the security of a free State, the right of the people to keep and bear Arms, shall not be infringed.

---

[10]The Twenty-first Amendment was not ratified by state legislatures but by state conventions summoned by Congress.

Amendment 3

No Soldier shall, in time of peace be quartered in any house, without the consent of the Owner, nor in time of war, but in a manner to be prescribed by law.

Amendment 4

The right of the people to be secure in their persons, houses, papers, and effects, against unreasonable searches and seizures, shall not be violated, and no Warrants shall issue, but upon probable cause, supported by Oath or affirmation, and particularly describing the place to be searched, and the persons or things to be seized.

Amendment 5

No person shall be held to answer for a capital, or otherwise infamous crime, unless on a presentment or indictment of a Grand Jury, except in cases arising in the land or naval forces, or in the Militia, when in actual service in time of War or public danger; nor shall any person be subject for the same offence to be twice put in jeopardy of life or limb; nor shall be compelled in any criminal case to be witness against himself, nor be deprived of life, liberty, or property, without due process of law; nor shall private property be taken for public use, without just compensation.

Amendment 6

In all criminal prosecutions, the accused shall enjoy the right to a speedy and public trial, by an impartial jury of the State and district wherein the crime shall have been committed, which district shall have been previously ascertained by law, and to be informed of the nature and cause of the accusation; to be confronted with the witnesses against him; to have compulsory process for obtaining witnesses in his favor, and to have the Assistance of Counsel for his defense.

Amendment 7

In suits at common law, where the value in controversy shall exceed twenty dollars, the right of trial by jury shall be preserved, and no fact tried by a jury, shall be otherwise reexamined in any Court of the United States, than according to the rules of the common law.

Amendment 8

Excessive bail shall not be required, nor excessive fines imposed, nor cruel and unusual punishments inflicted.

Amendment 9

The enumeration in the Constitution, of certain rights, shall not be construed to deny or disparage others retained by the people.

Amendment 10

The powers not delegated to the United States by the Constitution, nor prohibited by it to the States, are reserved to the States respectively, or to the people.

Amendment 11
(Ratified February 7, 1795)

The Judicial power of the United States shall not be construed to extend to any suit in law or equity, commenced or prosecuted against one of the United States by Citizens of another State, or by Citizens or Subjects of any Foreign State.

Amendment 12
(Ratified July 27, 1804)

The Electors shall meet in their respective states and vote by ballot for President and Vice President, one of whom, at least, shall not be an inhabitant of the same state with themselves; they shall name in their ballots the person voted for as President, and in distinct ballots the person voted for as Vice President, and they shall make distinct lists of all persons voted for as President, and of all persons voted for as Vice President, and of the number of votes for each, which lists they shall sign and certify, and transmit sealed to the seat of the government of the United States, directed to the President of the Senate;—the President of the Senate shall, in presence of the Senate and House of Representatives, open all the certificates and the votes shall then be counted;—The person having the greatest number of votes for President, shall be the President, if such number be a majority of the whole number of Electors appointed; and if no person have such majority, then from the persons having the highest numbers not exceeding three on the list of those voted for as President, the House of Representatives shall choose immediately, by ballot, the President. But in choosing the President, the votes shall be taken by states, the representation from each state having one vote; a quorum for this purpose shall consist of a member or members from two-thirds of the states, and a majority of all the states shall be necessary to a choice. [And if the House of Representatives shall not choose a President whenever the right of choice shall devolve upon them, before the fourth day of March next following, then the Vice President shall act as President, as in the case of the death or other constitutional disability of the President.—][11] The person having the greatest number of votes as Vice President, shall be the Vice President, if such number be a majority of the whole number of Electors appointed, and if no person have a majority, then from the two highest numbers on the list, the Senate shall choose the Vice President; a quorum for the purpose shall consist of two-thirds of the whole number of Senators, and a majority of the whole number shall be necessary to a choice. But no person constitutionally ineligible to the office of President shall be eligible to that of Vice President of the United States.

Amendment 13
(Ratified December 6, 1865)

Section 1

Neither slavery nor involuntary servitude, except as a punishment for crime whereof the party shall have been duly convicted, shall exist within the United States, or any place subject to their jurisdiction.

Section 2

Congress shall have power to enforce this article by appropriate legislation.

Amendment 14
(Ratified July 9, 1868)

Section 1

All persons born or naturalized in the United States, and subject to the jurisdiction thereof, are citizens of the United States and of the State

[11]Superseded by Section 3 of the Twentieth Amendment.

wherein they reside. No State shall make or enforce any law which shall abridge the privileges or immunities of citizens of the United States; nor shall any State deprive any person of life, liberty, or property, without due process of law; nor deny to any person within its jurisdiction the equal protection of the laws.

Section 2

Representatives shall be apportioned among the several States according to their respective numbers, counting the whole number of persons in each State, excluding Indians not taxed. But when the right to vote at any election for the choice of electors for President and Vice President of the United States, Representatives in Congress, the Executive and Judicial officers of a State, or the members of the Legislature thereof, is denied to any of the male inhabitants of such State, being twenty-one years of age,[12] and citizens of the United States, or in any way abridged, except for participation in rebellion, or other crime, the basis of representation therein shall be reduced in the proportion which the number of such male citizens shall bear to the whole number of male citizens twenty-one years of age in such State.

Section 3

No person shall be a Senator or Representative in Congress, or elector of President and Vice President, or hold any office, civil or military, under the United States, or under any State, who, having previously taken an oath, as a member of Congress, or as an officer of the United States, or as a member of any State legislature, or as an executive or judicial officer of any State, to support the Constitution of the United States, shall have engaged in insurrection or rebellion against the same, or given aid or comfort to the enemies thereof. But Congress may by a vote of two-thirds of each House, remove such disability.

Section 4

The validity of the public debt of the United States, authorized by law, including debts incurred for payment of pensions and bounties for services in suppressing insurrection or rebellion, shall not be questioned. But neither the United States nor any state shall assume or pay any debt or obligation incurred in aid of insurrection or rebellion against the United States, or any claim for the loss or emancipation of any slave; but all such debts, obligations and claims shall be held illegal and void.

[12]Changed by Section 1 of the Twenty-sixth Amendment.

Section 5

The Congress shall have power to enforce, by appropriate legislation, the provisions of this article.

Amendment 15
(Ratified February 3, 1870)

Section 1

The right of citizens of the United States to vote shall not be denied or abridged by the United States or by any State on account of race, color, or previous condition of servitude.

Section 2

The Congress shall have power to enforce this article by Appropriate legislation.

Amendment 16
(Ratified February 3, 1913)

The Congress shall have power to lay and collect taxes on incomes, from whatever source derived, without apportionment among the several States, and without regard to any census or enumeration.

Amendment 17
(Ratified April 8, 1913)

The Senate of the United States shall be composed of two Senators from each State, elected by the people thereof, for six years; and each Senator shall have one vote. The electors in each State shall have the qualifications requisite for electors of the most numerous branch of the State legislatures.

When vacancies happen in the representation of any State in the Senate, the executive authority of such State shall issue writs of election to fill such vacancies; *Provided*, That the legislature of any State may empower the executive thereof to make temporary appointments until the people fill the vacancies by election as the legislature may direct.

This amendment shall not be so construed as to affect the election or term of any Senator chosen before it becomes valid as part of the Constitution.

Amendment 18
(Ratified January 16, 1919)

Section 1

After one year from the ratification of this article the manufacture, sale, or transportation of intoxicating liquors within, the importation thereof into, or the exportation thereof from the United States and all territory subject to the jurisdiction thereof for beverage purposes is hereby prohibited.

Section 2

The Congress and the several States shall have concurrent power to enforce this article by appropriate legislation.

Section 3

This article shall be inoperative unless it shall have been ratified as an amendment to the Constitution by the legislatures of the several States as provided in the Constitution, within seven years from the date of the submission hereof to the States by the Congress.[13]

Amendment 19
(Ratified August 18, 1920)

The right of citizens of the United States to vote shall not be denied or abridged by the United States or by any State on account of sex.

Congress shall have power to enforce this article by appropriate legislation.

Amendment 20
(Ratified January 23, 1933)

Section 1

The terms of the President and Vice President shall end at noon on the 20th day of January, and the terms of Senators and Representatives at noon on the 3d day of January, of the years in which such terms would have ended if this article had not been ratified; and the terms of their successors shall then begin.

---

[13]Repealed by Section 1 of the Twenty-first Amendment.

Section 2

The Congress shall assemble at least once in every year, and such meeting shall begin at noon on the 3d day of January, unless they shall by law appoint a different day.

Section 3

If, at the time fixed for the beginning of the term of the President, the President elect shall have died, the Vice President elect shall become President. If a President shall not have been chosen before the time fixed for the beginning of his term, or if the President elect shall have failed to qualify, then the Vice President elect shall act as President until a President shall have qualified; and the Congress may by law provide for the case wherein neither a President elect nor a Vice President elect shall have qualified, declaring who shall then act as President, or the manner in which one who is to act shall be selected, and such person shall act accordingly until a President or Vice President shall have qualified.

Section 4

The Congress may by law provide for the case of the death of any of the persons from whom the House of Representatives may choose a President whenever the right of choice shall have devolved upon them, and for the case of the death of any of the persons from whom the Senate may choose a Vice President whenever the right of choice shall have devolved upon them.

Section 5

Sections 1 and 2 shall take effect on the 15th day of October following the ratification of this article.

Section 6

This article shall be inoperative unless it shall have been ratified as an amendment to the Constitution by the legislatures of three-fourths of the several States within seven years from the date of its submission.

Amendment 21
(Ratified December 5, 1933)

Section 1

The eighteenth article of amendment to the Constitution of the United States is hereby repealed.

Section 2

The transportation or importation into any State, Territory, or possession of the United States for delivery or use therein of intoxicating liquors, in violation of the laws thereof, is hereby prohibited.

Section 3

This article shall be inoperative unless it shall have been ratified as an amendment to the Constitution by conventions in the several States, as provided in the Constitution, within seven years from the date of the submission hereof to the States by the Congress.

Amendment 22
(Ratified February 27, 1951)

Section 1

No person shall be elected to the office of the President more than twice, and no person who has held the office of President, or acted as President, for more than two years of a term to which some other person was elected President shall be elected to the office of the President more than once. But this Article shall not apply to any person holding the office of President when this Article was proposed by the Congress, and shall not prevent any person who may be holding the office of President, or acting as President, during the term within which this Article becomes operative from holding the office of President or acting as President during the remainder of such term.

Section 2

This article shall be inoperative unless it shall have been ratified as an amendment to the Constitution by the legislatures of three-fourths of the several States within seven years from the date of its submission to the States by the Congress.

Amendment 23
(Ratified March 29, 1961)

Section 1

The District constituting the seat of Government of the United States shall appoint in such manner as the Congress may direct:

A number of electors of President and Vice President equal to the whole number of Senators and Representatives in Congress to which the District would be entitled if it were a State, but in no event more than the least populous State; they shall be in addition to those appointed by the States, but they shall be considered, for the purposes of the election of President and Vice President, to be electors appointed by a State; and they shall meet in the District and perform such duties as provided by the twelfth article of amendment.

Section 2

The Congress shall have power to enforce this article by appropriate legislation.

Amendment 24
(Ratified January 23, 1964)

Section 1

The right of citizens of the United States to vote in any primary or other election for President or Vice President, for electors for President or Vice President, or for Senator or Representative in Congress, shall not be denied or abridged by the United States or any State by reason of failure to pay any poll tax or other tax.

Section 2

The Congress shall have power to enforce this article by appropriate legislation.

Amendment 25
(Ratified February 10, 1967)

Section 1

In case of the removal of the President from office or of his death or resignation, the Vice President shall become President.

Section 2

Whenever there is a vacancy in the office of the Vice President, the President shall nominate a Vice President who shall take office upon confirmation by a majority vote of both Houses of Congress.

Section 3

Whenever the President transmits to the President pro tempore of the Senate and the Speaker of the House of Representatives his written declaration that he is unable to discharge the powers and duties of his office, and until he transmits to them a written declaration to the contrary, such powers and duties shall be discharged by the Vice President as Acting President.

Section 4

Whenever the Vice President and a majority of either the principal officers of the executive departments or of such other body as Congress may by law provide, transmit to the President pro tempore of the Senate and the Speaker of the House of Representatives their written declaration that the President is unable to discharge the powers and duties of his office, the Vice President shall immediately assume the powers and duties of the office as Acting President.

Thereafter, when the President transmits to the President pro tempore of the Senate and the Speaker of the House of Representatives his written declaration that no inability exists, he shall resume the powers and duties of his office unless the Vice President and a majority of either the principal officers of the executive department or of such other body as Congress may by law provide, transmit within four days to the President pro tempore of the Senate and the Speaker of the House of Representatives their written declaration that the President is unable to discharge the powers and duties of his office. Thereupon Congress shall decide the issue, assembling within forty-eight hours for that purpose if not in session. If the Congress, within twenty-one days after receipt of the latter written declaration, or, if Congress is not in session, within twenty-one days after Congress is required to assemble, determines by two-thirds vote of both Houses that the President is unable to discharge the powers and duties of his office, the Vice President shall continue to discharge the same as Acting President; otherwise, the President shall resume the powers and duties of his office.

Amendment 26
(Ratified July 1, 1971)

Section 1

The right of citizens of the United States, who are eighteen years of age or older, to vote shall not be denied or abridged by the United States or by any State on account of age.

Section 2

The Congress shall have the power to enforce this article by appropriate legislation.

Index

government regulation of, 181
and historical events, 268–269
investigative reporting, 269–270
Kennedy and, 277–278
media events, 295–296
Nixon and, 277–278
as political socializing agent, 241
President and, 101, 102, 104, 269, 271,
276–277
and primary campaigns, 242–243
Reagan and, 270–271, 282–285
types of, 266
See also News; Television.
Meese, Edwin, III, 104, 156
Melting-pot thesis, and American character,
26–28
Mencken, H. L., 29–30, 238, 245, 246
Merrill, John C., 274
Mikulski, Barbara, 118
Military
civilian authority, 63–64
Reagan's policy, 90
Military-industrial complex (MIC), 232–234
Mill, John Stuart, 180
Mills, C. Wright, 9, 226, 234, 237, 376
Mills, Wilbur, 133–134, 281
Minorities
quota system, 165
See also specific groups.
Miranda formula, 162
Miranda v. Arizona, 162, 186
Mirror theory of representation, 125
Mishan, Ezra, 326
Mitchell, John, 156
Mobility, and American character, 39–41
Mondale, Walter, 90, 194
Monetarism, 319–320
Monetary policy, 321
Monroe Doctrine of 1823, 361
Montesquieu, Charles, 57, 61, 67
Moral Majority, 23, 167, 182, 184
Morgenthau, Hans J., 349
Morrison v. Olson, 156
Morse, Wayne, 130
Mountbatten, Lord Louis, 295
Moynihan, Daniel Patrick, 46, 323
Mugabe, Robert, 353
Murder, in American society, 32–33
Murrow, Edward R., 294
Mutual Balanced Force Reduction (MBFR),
358

National Bipartisan Commission on Central
America, 356
National Committee for an Effective Con-
gress, 117, 143
National government, sovereignty of, 66–69
Nationalism, 335–339
foreign policy and, 349, 350, 363
militant nationalism, 336–337

National Security Council (NSC), 343–344
Native Americans, discrimination against, 36
New Deal, 63, 198–199, 220, 229, 232, 313,
371
New Jersey plan, 57
News, 267–268
as business, 272–276
news management, 277–278
scandals and, 269–270
yellow journalism, 273
New York v. Quarles, 165
Nineteenth Amendment, 38, 69, 71, 239
Ninth Amendment, 186
Nixon, Richard, 11, 13, 42, 45, 62, 77, 80,
102, 149, 194, 200
and Congress, 81, 82
"executive privilege" actions, 81
and media, 276, 279–280
popularity of, 81
resignation of, 81
Watergate, 81–82
Nix v. Williams, 164
Nofziger, Lyn, 156
No-growth economy, 326–327
Nonpartisan, 213
North Atlantic Treaty Organization (NATO),
340, 347, 357
North, Oliver, 90, 156, 253, 254, 288, 344,
356
NOW (National Organization for Women),
213
Nuclear war, 339–340
arms limitations treaty, 91, 340–341
deterrence policy, 340–341

Obscenity, 164, 180
O'Connor, Sandra Day, 38, 154
One-person, one-vote rule, 118, 162
Organization for Economic Cooperation and
Development (OECD), 300
Organization of Petroleum Exporting Coun-
tries (OPEC), 351
Organized crime, influence in America, 30–32
Ortega, Katherine, 38

Paine, Thomas, 175
Panama Canal treaties, 352
Parliament, 141
Parrington, Vernon Louis, 24
Partisans, 123, 213
Passell, Peter, 327
Paterson, William, 57
Patterson, Joseph, 29, 273
Peace and Freedom party, 206
Peace Treaty of 1783, 361
Pearl Harbor, 233, 345
Pendleton Civil Service Act of 1883, 258, 259
Pentagon Papers, 46, 168, 181, 279, 280
Petit juries, 155
Phillips, Kevin, 221